THE HEBREW BIBLE
IN SOCIAL PERSPECTIVE

Series Editor

Francesca Stavrakopoulou
University of Exeter, UK

LIFE AND DEATH

SOCIAL PERSPECTIVES ON BIBLICAL BODIES

Edited by
Francesca Stavrakopoulou

t&tclark
LONDON • NEW YORK • OXFORD • NEW DELHI • SYDNEY

T&T CLARK
Bloomsbury Publishing Plc
50 Bedford Square, London, WC1B 3DP, UK
1385 Broadway, New York, NY 10018, USA
29 Earlsfort Terrace, Dublin 2, Ireland

BLOOMSBURY, T&T CLARK and the T&T Clark logo are trademarks of Bloomsbury Publishing Plc

First published in Great Britain 2021
This paperback edition published in 2023

Copyright © Francesca Stavrakopoulou and Contributors, 2021

Francesca Stavrakopoulou has asserted her right under the Copyright, Designs and Patents Act, 1988, to be identified as Editor of this work.

Cover design: Charlotte James
Cover image © A.D. Riddle/BiblePlaces.com, courtesy of the Oriental Institute Museum.

All rights reserved. No part of this publication may be reproduced or transmitted in any form or by any means, electronic or mechanical, including photocopying, recording, or any information storage or retrieval system, without prior permission in writing from the publishers.

Bloomsbury Publishing Plc does not have any control over, or responsibility for, any third-party websites referred to or in this book. All internet addresses given in this book were correct at the time of going to press. The author and publisher regret any inconvenience caused if addresses have changed or sites have ceased to exist, but can accept no responsibility for any such changes.

A catalogue record for this book is available from the British Library.

Library of Congress Cataloging-in-Publication Data
Names: Stavrakopoulou, Francesca, editor.
Title: Life and death : social perspectives on biblical bodies /
edited by Francesca Stavrakopoulou.
Description: London ; New York, NY : T&T Clark, 2021. |
Series: The Hebrew Bible in social perspective; 2 |
Includes bibliographical references and index. |
Summary: "This book explores some of the social, material, and ideological dynamics shaping life and death in both the Hebrew Bible and ancient Israel and Judah"– Provided by publisher.
Identifiers: LCCN 2020044079 (print) | LCCN 2020044080 (ebook) |
ISBN 9780567656728 (hardback) | ISBN 9780567699336 (epdf) |
ISBN 9780567699312 (epub)
Subjects: LCSH: Death–Biblical teaching. | Life–Biblical teaching. |
Bible. Old Testament–Criticism, interpretation, etc.
Classification: LCC BS1199.D34 L54 2021 (print) |
LCC BS1199.D34 (ebook) | DDC 296.3/3–dc23
LC record available at https://lccn.loc.gov/2020044079
LC ebook record available at https://lccn.loc.gov/2020044080

ISBN: HB: 978-0-5676-5672-8
PB: 978-0-5676-9932-9
ePDF: 978-0-5676-9933-6
ePUB: 978-0-5676-9931-2

Series: The Hebrew Bible in Social Perspective

Typeset by Newgen KnowledgeWorks Pvt. Ltd., Chennai, India

To find out more about our authors and books visit www.bloomsbury.com and sign up for our newsletters.

CONTENTS

LIST OF FIGURES	vii
NOTES ON CONTRIBUTORS	viii
EDITOR'S NOTE	x
LIST OF ABBREVIATIONS	xi

1 The materiality of life and the sociality of death: An introduction 1
   Francesca Stavrakopoulou

PART ONE Praxis and materiality 25

2 Blood and hair: Body management and practice 27
   Susan Niditch

3 Wherever the corpse is, there the vultures will gather 43
   Matthew J. Suriano

4 'Know well the faces of your sheep': Animal bodies and human bodies 61
   Rebekah Welton

PART TWO Value, status and power 73

5 Birthing new life: Israelite and Mesopotamian values and visions of the preborn child 75
   Shawn W. Flynn

6 Persons with disabilities, unprotected parties and Israelite household structures 93
   Jeremy Schipper

7 Modifying manly bodies: Mourning and masculinities in Ezra 9–10 105
   Elisabeth Cook

8 The wisdom of ageing 123
   Hugh S. Pyper

PART THREE Extended sociality 139

9 Immortality and the rise of resurrection 141
   Nicolas Wyatt

10 Forming divine bodies in the Hebrew Bible   171
    Daniel O. McClellan

INDEX OF ANCIENT SOURCES   195
INDEX OF AUTHORS   204
INDEX OF SUBJECTS   210

FIGURES

1.1 Citizens leaving Lachish, among them young girls and small boys. BM 124908 (detail)   3
1.2 Women and children in an ox-drawn cart. Scene from the Lachish reliefs. BM 124908 (detail)   3
1.3 An infant in the arms of a female carer. Scene from the Lachish reliefs. BM 124908 (detail)   5
1.4 Men at the head of the line of deportees from Lachish, humbling themselves as they approach Sennacherib's royal encampment. BM 124911 (detail)   7
1.5 Sennacherib enthroned in the royal encampment outside Lachish, surrounded by officials and attendants. BM 124911 (detail)   8
1.6 Naked corpses stretched out for flaying. Scene from the Lachish reliefs. BM 124909 (detail)   10
1.7 Naked bodies impaled before the walls of Lachish. BM 124906 (detail)   11
3.1 Depiction of vultures and corpses in Shrine VII, 8, Çatalhöyük (from Mellaart 1964: 65, Figure 20)   44
3.2 Vultures carrying away the remains of the dead. Top left of the Stele of Vultures, reverse, Register 4 (picture from Heuzey 1884: Plate 24 A)   48
3.3 Workers climbing a mound of naked corpses, carrying materials to build a burial mound. Stele of Vultures, reverse, Register 2 (picture from Heuzey 1884: Plate 24 C)   49
3.4 Reconstruction of the reverse side of the Stele of Vultures (from Winter 1985: 16, Fig. 8; drawing by Elizabeth Simpson)   50

CONTRIBUTORS

Elisabeth Cook is a Professor of Hebrew Bible and Biblical Interpretation in the School of Biblical Studies at the Universidad Bíblica Latinoamericana in San José, Costa Rica, where she is also Rector of the University. Her research focuses on religion, social constructs and gender in the Hebrew Bible and Latin American biblical interpretation. She is particularly interested in the ways ritual performance, embodiment and materiality participate in the construction of gendered identities in biblical texts, and their impact on modern gender imaginaries. She has published a number of articles on these themes in Spanish-language books and journals. Her first English-language monograph, on men and masculinities in Ezra 9–10, is forthcoming.

Shawn W. Flynn is an Associate Professor of Hebrew Bible at St. Joseph's College, University of Alberta, Canada, and Vice-President (academic) and Dean of the College. His research focuses on divinity in ancient Israel and the role of children in the ancient Near East. His publications include *YHWH Is King* (2014), *Children in Ancient Israel: The Hebrew Bible and Mesopotamia in Comparative Perspective* (2018) and *A Story of YHWH: Cultural Translation and Subversive Reception in Israelite History* (2020). He is also the editor of *Children in the Bible and the Ancient World: Comparative and Historical Methods in Reading Ancient Children* (2019).

Daniel O. McClellan is an adjunct instructor at Brigham Young University in Utah and a Scripture translation supervisor for The Church of Jesus Christ of Latter-Day Saints. He received his PhD in Theology and Religion from the University of Exeter in 2020. His research interests include the conceptualization of deity, the cognitive science of religion, cognitive linguistics and textual criticism of the Hebrew Bible. His publications include journal articles in *Biblical Interpretation* and the *Journal of Biblical Literature*, and a chapter on 'religion' in *Method Today: Redescribing Approaches to the Study of Religion* (edited by Brad Stoddard, 2018). He is currently preparing for publication of his first monograph, which explores the concept of deity in the Hebrew Bible.

Susan Niditch is the Samuel Green Professor of Religion at Amherst College in Massachusetts. Her research on the cultures of ancient Israel draws upon the fields of folklore studies, oral studies and religious studies and reflects particular interests in gender, the body and lived religion. Her publications include *Judges: A Commentary* (2008), *'My Brother Esau Is a Hairy Man': Hair and Identity in Ancient Israel* (2008) and *The Responsive Self: Personal Religion in Biblical Literature of the Neo-Babylonian and Persian Periods* (2015). She is also the editor of *The Wiley Blackwell Companion to Ancient Israel* (2016).

Hugh S. Pyper is Emeritus Professor of Biblical Interpretation at the University of Sheffield, UK. His research focuses particularly on the literary, sociocultural and gendered dynamics of the Hebrew Bible, both in its ancient and modern contexts, and many of his publications explore the implications of reading biblical texts 'against the grain' of conventional assumptions. His books include *An Unsuitable Book: The Bible as Scandalous Text* (2005) and *The Unchained Bible: Cultural Appropriations of Biblical Texts* (2012). He is also the co-editor (with Caroline Vander Stichele) of *Text, Image, and Otherness in Children's Bibles: What Is in the Picture?* (2012).

Jeremy Schipper is Professor of Religion at Temple University in Philadelphia. His research focuses on issues of identity, especially representations of disability in the Hebrew Bible, and the Bible and race in the United States. His books include *Disability Studies and the Hebrew Bible* (2006), *Disability and Isaiah's Suffering Servant* (2011), and a commentary on Ruth in the Anchor Yale Bible series (2016). Most recently, he co-authored *Black Samson: The Untold Story of an American Icon*, with Nyasha Junior (2020). Currently, he is working on a book titled *Denmark Vesey's Bible*, for which he received a Guggenheim Fellowship.

Francesca Stavrakopoulou is Professor of Hebrew Bible and Ancient Religion at the University of Exeter, UK. She specializes in the social, material and religious realities of ancient Israel and Judah, and the portrayal of the past in the Hebrew Bible. Her books include *King Manasseh and Child Sacrifice: Biblical Distortions of Historical Realities* (2004), *Land of Our Fathers: The Roles of Ancestor Veneration in Biblical Land Claims* (2010) and *Religious Diversity in Ancient Israel and Judah* (co-edited with John Barton, 2010). Her latest book, *God: An Anatomy*, is currently in press. She is the editor of the Hebrew Bible in Social Perspective series and co-editor of the Biblical Refigurations monograph series.

Matthew J. Suriano is an Associate Professor in the Joseph and Rebecca Meyerhoff Center for Jewish Studies at the University of Maryland. His research focuses on the history and culture of ancient Israel through the integration of biblical literature, epigraphy and the archaeology of the Levant. He received his PhD from the University of California, Los Angeles, in Near Eastern Languages and Cultures. His award-winning book, *A History of Death in the Hebrew Bible*, was published in 2018.

Rebekah Welton is a lecturer in Hebrew Bible at the University of Exeter, UK, and has recently published her first monograph, *'He is a Glutton and a Drunkard': Deviant Consumption in the Hebrew Bible* (2020). Her research focuses on the socio-religious roles of food and drink in the Hebrew Bible, archaeological and anthropological approaches to biblical interpretation and the reception of the Bible in popular visual media, especially video games and television programmes. She has published journal articles on these themes in *Biblical Interpretation* and the *Journal for the Study of the Old Testament*.

Nicolas Wyatt is Emeritus Professor of Ancient Near Eastern Religions in the University of Edinburgh, UK. His research is particularly focused on cosmology, royal ideology and myth in Ugaritic and biblical texts. His books include *The Mythic Mind: Essays on Cosmology in Ugaritic and Old Testament Literature* (2005), *'There's Such Divinity Doth Hedge a King': Selected Essays of Nicolas Wyatt on Royal Ideology in Ugaritic and Old Testament Literature* (2005), *Word of Tree and Whisper of Stone, and Other Papers on Ugaritian Thought* (2007) and *The Archaeology of Myth: Papers on Old Testament Tradition* (2010).

EDITOR'S NOTE

The Hebrew Bible in Social Perspective is a new series of multi-authored volumes addressing major themes integral to the academic study of the Hebrew Bible. Despite the divine origins and influences they have often been ascribed, religious texts do not simply descend from the heavens, nor are they set in stone. They are human creations, variously reflecting and transforming those who once made, read, heard and curated them and those who continue to engage them today. As such, the texts and traditions of the Hebrew Bible are both social products and social agents, and it is this sociality this series aims to take seriously. Comprising specially commissioned pieces from some of the most innovative scholars in the field, each volume offers stimulating, cutting-edge insights into the social worlds of the Hebrew Bible, whether past or present. These exciting volumes will both refresh and revitalize key debates and tricky issues clustering within and around the Hebrew Bible – and, in doing so, tell us something new about the people caught up in its social worlds.

Taking full advantage of my role as series editor, I have been lucky enough to assemble an outstanding group of scholars to write for this particular book. *Life and Death: Social Perspectives on Biblical Bodies* explores some of the social, material and ideological dynamics shaping life and death in both the Hebrew Bible and ancient Israel and Judah. Analysing topics ranging from the bodily realities of gestation, subsistence and death, and embodied performances of gender, power and status, to the imagined realities of post-mortem and divine existence, the chapters in this volume offer new trajectories in our understanding of the ways in which embodiment played out in the societies in which the texts of the Hebrew Bible emerged.

On a more personal note, it is important (if boldly unconventional) to acknowledge the circumstances in which this book has finally come into being. The idea for this volume – and the series in which it appears – was conceived several years ago, when my research into the material realities of the past turned towards human bodies. But the process of bringing this book to birth has proved difficult for various personal reasons, not least because my own repeated experience of the bodily realities of life and loss has stalled its delivery several times. Now, as I prepare to send the finished manuscript to press, we are all living with the threat of another distressing bodily reality: COVID-19. The precarious, delicate balance between life and death has come into sharp relief once more, and as the near-global lockdown poses a further delay to this book's appearance, I find myself wondering again quite when this edited collection will be born. It is for these reasons that I would like to express my heartfelt gratitude to the contributors to this volume, whose generosity, patience and kindness have proved boundless. It is to them, and their loved ones, that I dedicate this book.

April 2020

ABBREVIATIONS

ABL	*Assyrian and Babylonian Letters Belonging to the Kouyunjik Collections of the British Museum,* 14 vols. Edited by R. F. Harper. Chicago, IL: University of Chicago Press, 1892–1914.
AMT	*Assyrian Medical Texts from the Originals in the British Museum.* R. Campbell Thompson. Oxford: Milford/Oxford University Press, 1923.
ANET	*Ancient Near Eastern Texts Relating to the Old Testament,* 3rd edn. Edited by J. B. Pritchard. Princeton, NJ: Princeton University Press, 1969.
BHS	*Biblia Hebraica Stuttgartensia.* Edited by K. Elliger and W. Rudolph. Stuttgart: Deutsche Bibelgesellschaft, 1983.
BM	The British Museum (inventory number).
CAD	*The Assyrian Dictionary of the Oriental Institute of the University of Chicago.* Edited by A. L. Oppenheim, E. Rainer et al. Chicago, IL: Oriental Institute, 1956–2010.
COS	*The Context of Scripture,* 4 vols. Edited by W. W. Hallo and K. Lawson Younger, Jr. Leiden: Brill, 1997–2017.
GKC	*Gesenius' Hebrew Grammar,* 2nd edn. Edited by E. Kautzsch. Translated by A. E. Cowley. Oxford: Clarendon, 1910.
HALOT	*The Hebrew and Aramaic Lexicon of the Old Testament,* 5 vols. L. Koehler, W. Baumgartner and J. J. Stamm. Translated and edited under the supervision of M. E. J. Richardson. Leiden: Brill 1994–2000.
KAI	*Kanaanäische und aramäische Inschriften,* 2nd edn. H. Donner and W. Röllig. Wiesbaden: Harrassowitz, 1966–1969.
KTU	*Die keilalphabetischen Texte aus Ugarit,* 3rd enlarged edn. Edited by M. Dietrich, O. Loretz and J. Sanmartín. Münster: Ugarit-Verlag, 2013.
LXX	Septuagint.
MT	Masoretic Text.
RIMA	The Royal Inscriptions of Mesopotamia, Assyrian Periods.
TIM	Texts in the Iraq Museum.
VAT	Vorderasiatische Abteilung Tontafel. Vorderasiatisches Museum, Berlin.
YOS	Yale Oriental Series.

CHAPTER ONE

The materiality of life and the sociality of death: An introduction

FRANCESCA STAVRAKOPOULOU

Families file out of the city, their belongings bundled into bags on their backs or stacked high on ox-drawn carts. Small children toddle alongside their parents, some hanging onto their mother's skirts, others clutching their father's legs. Those too young or too tired to walk are carried on adults' shoulders. The women and children of one household are squeezed into a cart, balanced on their baggage; one woman cradles an infant on her lap, while the arms of an older child sitting behind her are clasped around her waist. Ahead of them is a man, perhaps a member of the same household, walking alongside the oxen, using a slender stick to keep the animals on course; behind the wagon is another male figure, carrying a heavy load on his back. Just one group among many, the motley procession makes its way across the mountainous landscape, past trees and vines heavy with fruit. But this is no liberating exodus. Soldiers flank the families deserting the battered city, marching the long line of men, women, children and animals past impaled bodies and corpses stretched out for flaying. On they go across the rugged landscape, towards their own particular fate: incorporation into Assyria. The supreme power of the empire is embodied by King Sennacherib himself, who sits upon a lofty throne, upheld by divine beings, overseeing the sack of the city and the parade of the spoils of war (see Figures 1.1–1.6).[1]

It is fitting to begin a book about bodies in the Hebrew Bible with an iconographic portrayal of some of those who lived and died in the world in which the biblical texts emerged. The Lachish reliefs of Nineveh's Southwest Palace are frequently held to be the closest we can come to a snapshot of the people of ancient Judah. Commissioned by Sennacherib as part of a series celebrating his subjugation of far-flung territories (Russell 1991, 1994; Barnett, Bleibtreu and Turner 1998; Lippolis 2011), the vast gypsum wall panels excavated from room XXXVI of the palace (Layard 1853) depict the Assyrian attack on Judah's second city in 701 BCE (Ussishkin 1982, 2003, 2014a, 2014b). Although the beleaguered citizens of Lachish feature only as bit-players in this visual drama, the reliefs have become a prominent touchstone in wider analyses of the social and material realities

---

1 High-resolution colour photographs of the images discussed here are easily accessed via https://www.britishmuseum.org/collection. The opening paragraph of this chapter draws on another in Stavrakopoulou (forthcoming).

of Iron II Judahite culture. Encouraged by archaeological and topographical studies of the site of ancient Lachish (Tell ed-Duweir), which are argued to corroborate the iconographic portrayal of the city's siege, there is a scholarly tendency to cast the reliefs as realistic rather than schematic reflections of the battle and its aftermath, based, perhaps, on sketches produced by on-site Assyrian artists (Ussishkin 1982: 119, 126; Dever 2012: 356) or the eyewitness testimonies of those who experienced the campaign (Russell 1991: 208–9; cf. Barnett 1958).[2] Dazzling in their detail, these stone artworks thus appear to offer us images of the 'real' people of the 'biblical' past, inviting us to scrutinize their physical appearance, their belongings, their animals and their city for evidence of the social, material and ideological dynamics shaping Judahite and (by extension) Israelite life.[3]

These are the social and cultural dynamics with which this book is concerned. Scholars have long understood that human bodies are far from 'neutral' sites of sociocultural significance. Rather, our bodies are the material places at which various identities and differences (such as gender, status, sexuality or ethnicity) are constructed, communicated and negotiated (Shilling 2003; Mascia-Lees 2011; Turner 2012; Robb and Harris 2013). From the foods we eat and the ways we dress, to the activities we undertake to deal with the dead or imagine other-worldly beings, our bodies manifest the ways in which we relate to those within and beyond the various social groups into which we are incorporated. Just as bodilyness is inherently social, so sociality is inextricably bodily and material (Lambert and McDonald 2009; Attala and Steel 2019), encoding our bodies as the very sites at and by which personhood – what it is to be socially recognized as a 'person' – is constituted (Fowler 2004, 2010; Appell-Warren 2014; McIntosh 2018). But the body is more than a static symbol or passive marker of sociality and personhood. The very materiality and malleability of our bodies render them unfixed and unstable sites of identity and difference, for our bodies are continuously and recursively brought into 'being' by means of social relations, material practices and cultural performances (see Stavrakopoulou 2013, and the literature cited there). The chapters in this book – detailed further below – explore some of the ways in which bodily sociality operated in the world giving rise to the Hebrew Bible. By way of introduction, closer consideration of selected scenes from the Lachish reliefs can help to contextualize some of the issues explored in subsequent chapters.

Among the displaced citizens on the reliefs, for example, different social groups are distinguished in terms of gender and age by their clothing and hair: men are bearded, and wear soft caps with prominent ear flaps, and short tunics accessorized with thick belts and dangling sashes. By contrast, women wear plain, loose-fitting, ankle-length tunics and long hooded cloaks, covering their hair. Children, too, are gendered by their dress. The girls wear mini-versions of adult female clothing, including long head coverings, while the boys are dressed in short belted tunics (Figures 1.1 and 1.2). Unlike the girls, who are imaged simply as smaller versions of grown women, the boys' younger age in relation to men seems to be signalled by their thinner belts, close-cropped hair or skull caps, and an absence of sashes (Albenda 1983; Garroway 2020; Riley 2020).

As is now widely understood, the material manifestation of gender by means of dress and hair management (whether grooming, shaving or covering) is neither culturally incidental nor reductively reflexive of physiology. Rather, the use of clothing and hair

---

2 For persuasive critiques of the view that the reliefs are eyewitness reflections of the fall of the city, see Jacoby (1991); Uehlinger (2003).
3 Notice, for example, that King and Stager (2001) draw heavily on details from the Lachish reliefs to illustrate 'life in biblical Israel'.

FIGURE 1.1: Citizens leaving Lachish, among them young girls (left) and small boys (right). BM 124908 (detail). Image courtesy of the British Museum.

FIGURE 1.2: Women and children in an ox-drawn cart. Scene from the Lachish reliefs. BM 124908 (detail). Image courtesy of the British Museum.

practices to gender the body reflects and projects social processes of enculturation, which are themselves bound up with wider sociocultural preferences about the ways in which people's bodies variously mediate and negotiate identity and difference, status and role, and notions of personhood. In this way, the 'dressed' body is a body modified, so that differences in clothing and hairstyle, including the covering or uncovering of certain body parts by means of textiles or hair, might serve to 'make' and 'remake' bodies and mark their social differences, both in everyday life and in more specialized or temporary circumstances (Cifarelli and Gawlinksi 2017; Han and Antrosio 2018; Cifarelli 2019).

Something of the enculturation of gender can be seen on the Lachish reliefs. Here, the infancy of a cradled child (Figures 1.2 and 1.3) is signalled not only by its long sidelock – a relatively common motif in the iconography of young children in ancient Southwest Asia – but also by its nakedness, rendering its gendered identity as a 'boy' or a 'girl' seemingly unmarked (Schwyn 2000, 2006; Garroway 2020; Riley 2020; cf. Garroway 2012).[4] This is not to suggest, however, that the child is ungendered. Rather, the infant's nudity is suggestive of a form of 'non-binary' gender – a designation which is not without its problems, but serves here as an umbrella term for a range of ancient-world gender constructs which might also encompass intersex persons (both mortal and divine) and those of composite, intersectional, transitional, multiple, fluid, ambiguous or modified genders, including those persons conventionally termed 'eunuchs' (Peled 2016; Asher-Greve 2018; Green 2018; Helle 2018). While a number of non-binary genders appear to have indexed powerful modes of personhood (some more so than others), a close association with liminality underscores many. And it is the liminality of infancy that appears to be signalled by child nakedness on the Lachish reliefs: unlike the older, clothed children among the deportees, the cradled infant is neither a 'boy' nor a 'girl' (Pyschny 2019: 131–2; Garroway 2020: 50–1; cf. Helle 2018, 2019).

It may be that the child's close face-to-face positioning with their female caregiver, expressing an intensely dependent bodily relationship, further expresses this socialized ambiguity (Figure 1.3). The extent to which very young children were considered 'sufficiently' distinct from their mothers or other breastfeeders and carers to render them appropriately socialized persons is uncertain. But in common with other traditional societies (Lancy 2014), there are indications across ancient Southwest Asian sources that weaning – at about 3 years of age – played an important role in reconstituting the relational personhood of young children, transforming their social identities (Stavrakopoulou 2016: 358–9; cf. Gruber 1989; Maher 1992; Stol 2000; Garroway 2019). Perhaps this was the point at which the liminality of infancy began to be re-gendered and re-'dressed'.[5]

The Lachish reliefs offer us further illustrations of the ways in which forms of relational sociality might have been configured, for bodily manifestations of socialized difference

---

4 The extent to which 'nakedness' (the state of having no clothes on) might be distinguished from 'nudity' (as the display of the undressed body) in ancient Southwest Asian art is uncertain, hence the neutral use of these terms here (on their loaded use, see Barcan 2004). But as argued in Asher-Greve and Sweeney (2006), ancient Southwest Asian iconographic motifs of the unclothed body appear to be both situational and relational, so that (for example) the absence of clothing in agricultural or domestic scenes differs in function from the absence of clothing in ritual, mythological or 'erotic' scenes. See further Garcia-Ventura (2019).

5 Analyses of the representation of children across neo-Assyrian palace reliefs reveal a tendency to cast men only as caregivers to boys, in contrast to the more frequent portrayal of women and girls as caregivers to children of any gender. Schwyn (2000) suggests this might indicate (from a neo-Assyrian perspective, at least) that the gendering of boys included a shift away from the 'female world' of their primary caregivers, granting them access to the 'male world' from which girls and women were relatively excluded; cf. Albenda (1983); Garroway (2020).

FIGURE 1.3: An infant in the arms of a female carer. Scene from the Lachish reliefs. BM 124908 (detail). Author's photograph, used by permission of the British Museum.

also play out in a hierarchy of sociopolitical power among the captives. At the front of the procession of prisoners are those men nearing the royal Assyrian encampment. Holding up their arms in supplication (some appealing to stylus-wielding Assyrian officials, others prostrate before Sennacherib himself), they too are bearded, but unlike their short-skirted, muscular compatriots, who carry heavy loads or manage their oxen, they are wearing long tunics suggestive of a more sedentary and authoritative lifestyle (Figure 1.4). These citizens appear to be the sociopolitical elites of Lachish (Wäfler 1975: 57–60; King and Stager 2001: 266–9; Uehlinger 2003: 282; 2007: 179; cf. Barnett 1958).[6] But while their social status eclipses that of their fellow captives, it is also constructed in relation to a more dominant and distinctly Assyrian power. This is explicitly illustrated, of course, by those among them who crouch or kneel as they approach Sennacherib, whose social supremacy is manifest in the elevated height of his towering throne and tall footstool (Prinsloo 2000: 351; see Figure 1.5). But it is also evident in the display of lavish Assyrian bodies: from the uniforms and weaponry of soldiers, and the scribal and ceremonial equipment of officials, to Sennacherib's highly ornamented dress and furniture, which is embellished with amulets and emblems demonstrating his divine protection and endorsement, every Assyrian is layered with material manifestations of power.[7] By contrast, the submissive elites of Lachish appear to be stripped back to plain tunics, their feet and heads bare.[8]

Now housed in the British Museum in a space arranged to echo their display in the Southwest Palace, the reliefs' staggering details encourage us, quite deliberately, to step closer and wonder at the minutiae and drama of every scene.[9] It is no surprise they have come to be used as a vital resource for better understanding the social and cultural dynamics of the world in which the texts and traditions of the Hebrew Bible emerged. But we must also step back and consider what is not there. Despite their differences in age, gender and status, there is relatively little social diversity among the citizens processing away from Lachish. There are no observably pregnant women, for example, and no obviously elderly citizens; there are no people with visually discernible disabilities,

---

6 Some assume these particular citizens are better identified not as Judahites but as Kushite Nubians, given what Dalley (2004: 391) describes as their 'curly hair and bulbous noses'; cf. Collon (1995: 144–5); Barnett, Bleibtreu and Turner (1998: vol. 2, 322–52). The white, Western projection of racializing tropes onto the iconography of the Lachish reliefs is not new: the physical features of the same group prompted Layard (1853: 153) to insist that the prostrating captives were 'undoubtedly Jews' for 'their physiognomy was strikingly indicated'. On 'racial seeing' in the interpretation of these reliefs as colonial museum exhibits, see Cuéllar (2019: 164–70). For the extent to which different facial motifs and body postures might be used to index qualities of personhood in neo-Assyrian art, see Cifarelli (1998); Bahrani (2006); Foster (2011). On the possibility of Kushites at Lachish (and on the reliefs), see Franklin (2018); Burrell (2020: 179–99). On the representation of 'ethnic' groups as 'expressions of difference' in neo-Assyrian visual culture, see Brown (2014); cf. DeGrado (2019), who explores the ways in which an emphasis on cultural diversity served as imperial strategy.
7 On the divine status of Sennacherib's *nēmedu* throne (referenced in the scene's accompanying epigraph, Figure 1.5), see Uehlinger (2003: 287–8); Ornan (2014: 588–9).
8 For the possibility that the plainness of the elite captives' dress reflects the deliberate deployment of less-skilled, junior artisans, see Wagstaff (2017: 188–90), drawing on Aker (2007).
9 My thanks to Jonathan Taylor (British Museum) and Paul Collins (formerly of the British Museum, now at the Ashmolean), who confirmed in personal communications that the current layout of gallery room 10 remains much as it did when its exhibits were rearranged in the 1960s to better reflect the suite of rooms in which Sennacherib's reliefs were found; cf. Barnett (1970). On the performativity of the Lachish reliefs within their ancient spatial setting, see McCormick (2002: 74–86); Battini (2019a, 2019b). On the sociality and affective agency of neo-Assyrian art and ceremonial architecture, see especially Bahrani (2003, 2006); McMahon (2013); Morello (2016); Portuese (2019); cf. Feldman (2010). For a discussion of the modern-day sociality of exhibited visual art as both performance and participation, see DeMarris and Robb (2013).

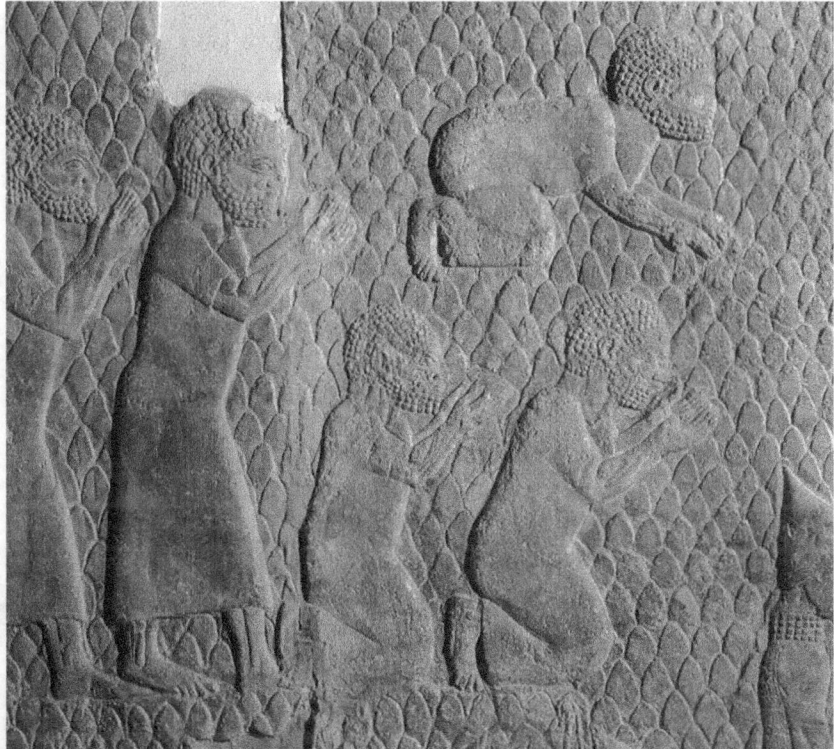

FIGURE 1.4: Men at the head of the line of deportees from Lachish, humbling themselves as they approach Sennacherib's royal encampment. BM 124911 (detail). Image courtesy of the British Museum.

nor women among the prostrating elites. The extent to which these absences should be taken to reflect socio-historical realities, artistic conventions or imperial ideologies is uncertain (and dependent on the degree to which the reliefs are to be considered 'firsthand' witnesses to the event). But more telling is the absence of material markers of socio-economic diversity among the deportees. Beyond the short tunics and thick belts of some of the men, which are often – but perhaps mistakenly – assumed to mark their 'warrior' status,[10] there are few clear indicators among the exiles and their luggage of the other trades and professions we might expect to find in an ancient city, and upon which the economic mechanics and conspicuous consumption of ancient empires explicitly relied (cf. Thomason 2005; Nadali and Vidal 2014).[11] It is an absence heightened by the

---

10 Offering freedom of movement, the men's short tunics are suggestive of a vigorous masculinity associated with physical labour as much as warfare; cf. Zwickel (2019: 190). By contrast, the Assyrians' tunics are 'armoured' with scales (whether leather, iron or bronze); cf. Barron (2010: 147–78). Across ancient Southwest Asian cultures, belts were similarly associated with a vigorous masculinity, but it was their staining (both conceptually and with a red pigment or blood) that appears to have re-coded or empowered them as items of 'warrior' dress; cf. Ames (2014).
11 Contrary to some interpretations, the drinking vessels that the captives carry appear to be for their personal use on the journey (as on other neo-Assyrian palace reliefs), rather than explicit markers of olive oil and wine production, the imperial benefits of which are signalled instead by the fruiting vines and trees in the landscape. Nor is there any compelling reason to identify the lyre players on a relief from another room in the Southwest Palace (XLVII) as captives from Lachish (BM 124947). This common assumption appears to be based on

FIGURE 1.5: Sennacherib enthroned in the royal encampment outside Lachish, surrounded by officials and attendants. BM 124911 (detail). Image courtesy of the British Museum.

variety of occupational paraphernalia accessorizing and empowering the reliefs' Assyrian characters. In essence, the reliefs offer us only caricatures of the disempowered, defeated and displaced.

To a certain extent, the caricaturing of the citizens of Lachish likely reflects a degree of expediency. Sennacherib's teams of artisans were not simply working to order but working efficiently, for the reliefs were among a number to be produced en masse for the Southwest Palace (Barnett 1970: 26; Collins 2008: 76; cf. Lippolis 2011). In order to fill the huge stone panels lining the palace's interior rooms, teams of artists probably employed certain stock motifs to indicate the general characteristics of military action, annexed landscapes and the people populating them (Wäfler 1975; cf. Uehlinger 2003: 274–7; 2007: 215–18). Then as now, however, stock images could also operate as a visual shorthand to both distinguish and signal more complex sociocultural conventions and ideologies.

---

references to singers or musicians in the neo-Assyrian catalogue of tribute Hezekiah paid to Sennacherib (*COS* 2: 302–3; cf. 2 Kgs 18.13-16) and is perhaps encouraged by Ps. 137.1-4, in which exiled Judahite musicians refuse to play for their Babylonian captors.

It is for this reason, for example, that all the subjugated citizens of Lachish are depicted barefooted, in contrast to their Assyrian overlords. In a wider Southwest Asian world in which gods trampled their humiliated enemies and kings set a proprietorial foot on conquered lands and submissive vassals, shoes were not simply practical footwear, but power objects bound up with predominantly elitist ideologies of cosmic and earthly dominance, authority and status (Thomas 2008; Palmer 2013; cf. Krause 2019). But this is not to reduce the shoe or sandal to a 'mere' symbol. In contrast to present-day Western cultures of dress, which revolve around the individual's wardrobe of multiple, interchangeable pieces, most people in the ancient world tended to have very few (if any) substitutes for the items they wore all day, every day. Accordingly, a habitually worn garment was not as conceptually distinct or separable from the body as we might imagine. Instead, it played a crucial role in the constitution of the individual's socio-physical form and visual shape, and was so thoroughly entangled in the identity and agency of the wearer that the garment could function performatively as a material extension of the body and personhood (McFerrin 2017: 154–5, citing Jones and Stallybrass 2000: 2; cf. Wagstaff 2017; Cifarelli 2019). Set within this interpretative frame, footwear and other highly charged items worn on the body (such as a weapon, amulet, jewellery or head covering) might be described as forms of 'somato-prosthesis' which not only redefined 'the end-limits of the body' (N'Shea 2019: 178) but could also serve as 'partible' aspects of personhood (see especially Meskell and Joyce 2003; Meskell 2004; Fowler 2004, 2016; Assante 2010; Porter 2014; Wagstaff 2017).[12] In this context, the stark contrast between bare feet and shod feet on the Lachish reliefs signals a bodily dynamic of power that goes beyond the symbolic: the captives' bare feet not only mark their territorial disempowering and displacement by their surefooted, shoe-wearing oppressors but also point to a reduction of their bodily agency and personhood.

Against this broader socio-material backdrop, the elites who grovel before Sennacherib look similarly minimized in bodily agency. Seemingly reduced to their plain tunics, devoid of headwear, footwear and the luggage of exile, they look strikingly stripped back. But the reliefs also illustrate one of the ways in which the imperial might of Assyria could further diminish the material personhood of their enemies. Stretched out on the ground, in full sight of the deportees, are the corpses of two men, grasped at the ankles by Assyrian soldiers (Figure 1.6).[13] Naked, the bodies have already lost one form of social skin; now, they are about to lose another, for the soldiers appear to be flaying the dead.

While neo-Assyrian texts indicate that this form of corpse abuse functioned as much as a visual act of terror as a punishment for insurrection (Bagg 2016), they also recognize that the efficacy of corpse abuse was bound up with the sociality of the dead (Richardson 2007). In ancient Southwest Asian cultures – including those of Israel and

---

12 As I explain in Stavrakopoulou (2019: 23–5), notions of the 'partible' person, attested across a number of ancient and traditional societies, operate on the premise that persons (often including deities and animals) are not bounded or indivisible entities, but tend towards the fluid, fragmentable or 'dividual', so that the social relationships forming a person might be extended, 'externalized' or distributed in both associated objects and body parts (including hair, blood and remains). In Pss. 60.10; 108.10 (MT 60.8; 108.9), the image of Yahweh hurling his shoe on Edom is a vivid biblical illustration of the role of footwear as both an extension of the body and a manifestation of partible personhood. Compare too the role of Elijah's mantle in 1 Kings 19 and 2 Kings 2, explored in Wagstaff (2017).
13 Given the splayed posture of these naked bodies and the absence of restraining cuffs (attested on other reliefs), they are best understood as corpses, rather than living victims.

FIGURE 1.6: Naked corpses stretched out for flaying. Scene from the Lachish reliefs. BM 124909 (detail). Image courtesy of the British Museum.

Judah – death did not break the active social bonds between people but changed the nature and dynamics of those relationships. Mortuary practices and ongoing ritual activities served not only to manage and 'process' dead bodies but also to re-socialize the dead, transforming them from once-living persons into post-mortem persons who continued to engage with the living (cf. Bloch-Smith 1992; Olyan 2005; Laneri 2007; Stavrakopoulou 2010; Porter and Boutin 2014; Suriano 2018). The continued existence and well-being of the dead was inextricably bound to the state and fate of their material remains, which were ordinarily curated by their descendants and extended kin, who tended their bones (or ashes) and graves. As such, the corpse (and later, its bony or ashy reduction) was not simply a material entity but a social presence within the community, indexing the ongoing agency and personhood of the deceased (Stavrakopoulou 2019). Consequently, in Southwest Asian deathways of the Iron Age, the manual defleshing of fresh corpses was inherently antisocial, so that flaying (as well as corpse decapitation and dismemberment, disinterment, bone-crushing and the exposure or exhibition of bodies or their parts) served as a targeted attack on the well-being and agency of the dead, damaging their relationship with the living community. Within the constellation of imagery on the Lachish reliefs, corpse-flaying is an intensification of the strategic means of diminishing the materiality of personhood and the sociality of the defeated (cf. Olyan 2015; Lemos 2017).

The sociality of the dead is seen to be further exploited by Assyrian soldiers at Lachish, two of whom are shown on the reliefs manoeuvring a group of naked corpses, impaled on tall stakes, into position against the city walls (Figure 1.7). As neo-Assyrian texts indicate,

FIGURE 1.7: Naked bodies impaled before the walls of Lachish. BM 124906 (detail). Author's photograph, used by permission of the British Museum.

impalement functioned as a high-visibility form of terror, for the corpses remained fixed in place as a public exhibit (Radner 2015). Elevated against the walls of Lachish, the impaled bodies serve as a grotesque installation, marking the Assyrians' remaking of the material world – human and urban – by means of military domination (cf. Richardson 2007: 196–200; Bahrani 2008: 154–8; De Backer 2010). As an installation, the impaled dead also manifest the imperial re-ordering of the post-mortem world, too. The vertical positioning and posture of the corpses deliberately inverts the wider cultural preference for the horizontal, restful repose of the dead and evokes the upright position of the living, imbuing them with a startlingly active somatic sociality. At the same time, the incorporation of stakes into the bodies transforms them from 'ordinary' corpses into 'curated' corpses – a new type of body that is neither 'natural' flesh, blood and bone nor a 'prosthetic' body akin to a statue but a composite creation, made by Assyria (cf. Stavrakopoulou 2019: 23–30; drawing on Meskell 2008).

Rather than denying the sociality of the dead, the depiction of corpse abuse on the Lachish reliefs illustrates some of the ways in which the agency of corpses might be harnessed and transformed into both a weapon of war and a triumphalist memorial. But in doing so, the visuality of their somatic power is as carefully controlled and constrained as that of their living compatriots. Whether living or dead, enemy bodies are denied the ornamented power of Assyrian bodies. From barefootedness to skin flaying, the defeated are not 'wholly' persons. Even the vertically animated agency of impaled corpses is undercut by their floppy, folded forms, contrasting with the erect, muscular postures of every Assyrian on the reliefs. It is this superior form of bodily masculinity that pervades the iconographic story of the fall of Lachish. While neo-Assyrian artisans tended to portray the enemy as vigorously muscular and conspicuously bearded men in order to heighten the glory of conquest (even the wrists and ankles of the long-robed, prostrating captives of Lachish are contoured with hard muscle), the motif of vigorous muscularity operated within a spectrum of masculinities, rendering the 'manliness' of the defeated necessarily inferior to that of Assyrians (Cifarelli 1998; Chapman 2004; Assante 2017; N'Shea 2018). On the Lachish reliefs, this spectrum is evident in the contrast between the stripped-back bodies of captives and the ornamented, hyper-masculinity of Assyrian bodies, be it a foot soldier or Sennacherib himself. Even the beardless, soft-faced masculinity of the 'eunuchs' standing behind Sennacherib's throne (Figure 1.5) eclipses that of the men of Lachish (cf. N'Shea 2016, 2018: 327–31). Ultimately, it is a visual rhetoric of somatic power that contours the portrayal of life and death on these reliefs.

This brisk analysis of selected motifs in the iconography of the Lachish reliefs has both introduced and illustrated some of the ways in which the materiality of life and the sociality of death played out in the broader Southwest Asian world of which ancient Israel and Judah were a part. From the construction of gender, status and power to the constitution and negotiation of agency and personhood, sociality was (and is) intrinsically bodily and material. This is not to say, however, that the visual portrayal of somatic sociality on the reliefs is a wholly reliable witness to the realities of life and death in either Assyria or Judah at this particular point in their histories. Much like the texts of the Hebrew Bible, the Lachish reliefs are far from 'neutral' representations of the past (Uehlinger 2003, 2007) but carefully crafted configurations, designed and exhibited for the benefit of Sennacherib's more intimate circles – including the 'timeless' audiences of his gods and his royal successors (Shafer 2014; Nadali 2020: 223–5). Whether iconographical or textual, any material created or curated by and for specific social groups is inherently skewed or limited in the ways it might serve as an 'objective', reliable or broadly representative witness to certain historical events and social realities: it arguably reveals more about its creators, curators and target audiences than it does about any 'others' caught up in their literary or visual worlds.

As biblical scholars, we are accustomed to negotiating the tensions and uncertainties arising from the literary and artefactual sources on which we draw to better understand the societies in which the traditions of the Hebrew Bible emerged. In this volume, those negotiating skills are carefully deployed in a collection of chapters exploring some of the ways in which the dynamics of life and death were embodied in ancient Israelite, Judahite and early Jewish societies. And it is to these chapters that we now turn.

The chapters

The present volume is divided into three parts. The first, 'Praxis and materiality', brings the fleshy realities of bodies to the fore. It begins with Susan Niditch's chapter on human body management and practice, in which she dissects selected biblical texts to illustrate the ways in which blood and hair functioned as socially performative substances in the construction of religious and social identities (Chapter 2). Drawing on ritual theory and socio-anthropological approaches to the body, she argues that blood and hair were multivalent symbols ('expressive, malleable, visual and tactile') which could configure social relationships between individuals and the group in ancient Israel and Judah. As the 'life force' of living beings, blood was a powerfully transformative ritual material, charging humans and cultic objects with a quality altering their identity, status and function, and their relationship to the deity. But its power could also play out in the enculturation of gender. Niditch analyses the ways in which men's responses to the blood of menstruation and childbirth sought to manage women's bodies and suggests that this masculinist strategy expressed a need to respond to and control the mysterious, 'dangerous' power of women's bodies. Hair practices, too, were bound up with constructs of gender and power. As a body part both living and dead, hair could not only signal more complex cultural ideas about the individual, their status and their relationships with others, but also functioned as a site of material transformation in life-altering moments, as the biblical examples of Esau and Absalom suggest. From the heroic performance of manhood, as in the story of Samson, to the cultural and ritual manipulation of women's hair (whether voluntary, as with female Nazirites, or imposed, as in the case of the accused wife in Num. 5.11-21), hair practices could manifest both socially sanctioned and subversive or disruptive ways of (re)constituting personhood.

The interplay between socially sanctioned and disruptive modes of body management is also explored by Matthew Suriano, whose chapter emphasizes the complexities of sociocultural responses to human corpses (Chapter 3). As he reminds us, in any human society, the corpse is not only a biological reality but also a cultural construct, reflecting its social role as a prime site of meaning-making. Suriano's analysis of the cultural corpse in ancient Southwest Asian societies focuses on the long-lived association of scavenging vultures with dead bodies, as attested in three independent sources: the iconography of Çatalhöyük, a Neolithic site in Anatolia; the Stele of Vultures from Sumer, dated to the Early Dynastic III period; and the prophetic vision of Gog's defeat and burial in Ezekiel 39. Close examination of these media reveals that the vulture's status as a scavenger did not necessarily render it a malevolent presence in ancient deathscapes. Rather, Suriano argues, the vulture functioned as a cipher for cultural responses to different sorts of human corpses – enemy and kin – and that these responses were themselves enmeshed within wider social, political and cosmic constructs of the human experience. Tracking the image of the vulture across his three chosen sources, Suriano argues that it was the bird's close association with the timelessness of the natural world, and the uncontrollable but inevitable nature of death, that rendered it a prominent and malleable symbol in the socio-religious imagination. Playing variously benign or hostile roles in ancient Southwest Asian discourses about life and death, order and chaos, myth and history, and divine and human relationships, the vulture marks 'the ideological horizon of life and death'.

A different approach to the visceral interrelation of human bodies and animal bodies is offered by Rebekah Welton, whose contribution to this volume examines the social roles of sheep, cows and goats in Israelite and Judahite households (Chapter 4). Pointing to archaeological evidence and ethnographic analyses of traditional agropastoral societies, Welton explains that these species were primarily raised not for their meat but for their lifetime products – milk, dung, hide, fleece and traction power. Sheltered in the homestead – and in some seasons within the buildings in which families lived – these animals' lives were spent in close proximity to their human keepers. Exploring the social dimensions of this interdependent relationship, Welton argues that these animals were considered non-human members of the household, valued in the everyday lives of ordinary people as collaborators in the material maintenance and perpetuation of the extended family. Her analysis of biblical texts including Prov. 27.23-27 and 2 Samuel 12 illustrates the close social bonds between humans and domesticated animals – bonds which were underscored, rather than broken, in the sacrificial cult. As a ritual form of slaughter, Welton argues, animal sacrifice was not only a grateful response to life-giving gods for the sustenance and well-being of both humans and the animals on which they relied, but also a ritual means of socializing the strategic culling of lambs, kids and calves. Despite their differences, ritual regulations in Leviticus and Deuteronomy concerning 'legitimate' and 'illegitimate' animal sacrifice attest to the sociality of household animals as non-human members of the community.

The second part of this book, 'Value, status and power', focuses on the ways in which constructs of embodiment played out for particular social groups and intersected with the wider social and cultural dynamics structuring communities in ancient Israel and Judah. In his chapter, Shawn Flynn brings the social analysis of childhood to the fore (Chapter 5). Scholarly interest in this topic has been characterized by a focus on the period from birth to puberty or marriage, but Flynn demonstrates that in ancient Southwest Asian cultures, the growing foetus was already a valued social member of the household – so much so, that motherhood often appears to be marginalized in ancient ritual and literary discourse. Engaging a wealth of Mesopotamian material, including personal prayers and magico-medical texts, he argues that the unborn child was not only the focus of key rituals in the domestic cult but also the agent around which the social relationship between the family and its deities turned. Biblical texts suggest that in ancient Israelite and Judahite households, the preborn child played a similar role, so that in Jer. 1.4-5; Ps. 139.13-15 and Job 10.8-11, it is the language of the domestic cult that is used to describe Yahweh's role in creating, materially shaping and sustaining the child from the womb to delivery. In these texts, Flynn argues, the social bond between Yahweh and the preborn child is not only assumed and celebrated but also presented as the foundation on which adults might continue to build and reconfigure their relationship with the deity, particularly in times of personal distress. Flynn sets the biblical interest in the preborn child within the context of the 'monotheistic' ideologies of a centralized temple cult: Yahweh not only assumes the baby-shaping and midwifery roles traditionally performed by goddesses, but his high-status temple cult offers itself as a powerful replacement for the household cult.

The social dynamics of the household also shape the focus of Jeremy Schipper's chapter dealing with those groups typically cast in the Hebrew Bible as socially vulnerable (Chapter 6). In a number of biblical texts, people characterized as blind, deaf or lame often feature alongside the poor, the orphaned, the widowed and the landless as socially vulnerable parties. Given this broader biblical backdrop, however, it is curious that persons with disabilities are not included in the Torah's formulaic lists of those socially vulnerable groups to whom the wider community is to offer protection. Schipper argues that the biblical portrayal of the household is the key to understanding this apparent absence. Idealized in the Hebrew Bible as the 'house of the father', the household is portrayed as a socio-economic unit living on its own inheritable and inalienable plot of land and headed by a senior male who is directly responsible for the household's other members: his wives and unmarried daughters, plus his sons and their wives and children. It is in relation to this idealized structure, Schipper argues, that the Torah's formulaic references to the socially vulnerable are best understood. Widows (or better, 'unprotected women'), orphans, the landless and even Levites are all those who necessarily fall beyond the bounds of the 'house of the father' and are consequently rendered vulnerable and in need of community care. His discussion makes the important point that while persons with disabilities might have been perceived as potentially vulnerable in other social contexts, 'disabilities in and of themselves did not usually affect a person's status within the household'.

It is the embodiment and performance of masculinities that is the subject of Elisabeth Cook's analysis of Ezra's behaviour in Ezra 9–10, a narrative depicting the crisis triggered by 'intermarriage' in Yehud's *golah* community (Chapter 7). While most scholars tend to focus on the 'foreignness' of the wives in this story, Cook argues that it is the social construction and negotiation of manhood and masculinities that is at issue in the text. Her discussion explores the ways in which masculinities are constituted in relation to other men and masculine performances. Engaging socio-anthropological perspectives on body modification and ritual, Cook analyses the penitential mourning practices undertaken by Ezra in response to the marriage crisis: tearing his hair, beard and clothing; adopting submissive postures; and fasting in the Jerusalem temple. She argues that these actions are carefully calibrated to 'remake' Ezra's manliness in relation to the superior masculinity of Yahweh. It is a performance of relational masculinity, she contends, for as a community leader, Ezra is not simply appeasing the deity who might be offended – and emasculated – by the marriages but modelling a masculinity that is quickly embodied by his supporters. The result is a reconstitution of the manliness of the men of Yehud, countering the over-assertive masculinity of the 'guilty' men among them who have 'taken', 'lifted' and 'settled' 'foreign' women. Cook's discussion reminds us that the gendering of bodies is neither a fixed nor a linear process of enculturation but a shifting, socially recursive and contextual process, in which bodies, actions and individual and communal performance can combine to reconfigure social identities.

The closing chapter in this section of the book explores a social category of bodily experience that is more usually overlooked in biblical scholarship: old age. In this piece, Hugh Pyper explores the biblical association of aging with wisdom and asks what we might learn from the 'very old' in the Hebrew Bible (Chapter 8). The lessons are not always easy. While old age is frequently cast as a sign of divine favour, it is a blessing held in tension with the bodily realities of aging and dying: the clay of all new life eventually dries, cracks and crumbles to dust. But as Pyper observes, there are distinctions to be drawn between chronological age and functional or social age, so that the specifics of health, gender, status and socio-economic positioning could 'age' people in different ways. And yet the wisdom of the very old suggests that neither wealth nor status can protect those 'blessed' with a long life from degeneration. Drawing on Qoheleth 12, in which the frailty of an elderly householder and the decay of his comfortable home are virtually indistinguishable, Pyper not only reminds us that bodies are almost inseparable from their socio-material contexts but also highlights the social and physical vulnerability that comes with old age, when we inevitably become more dependent on others. Pyper suggests this was a vulnerability likely felt or anticipated by the biblical writers themselves, for their traditions are so often inflected with the voice of a learned elder. Those who committed the traditions of the past to writing had a vested interest in the ongoing remembrance of a past in which ancestors and elders are powerfully promoted, and the young are urged to respect and care for their elders. In the Hebrew Bible, the most valuable form of wisdom that aging can bring is the art of remembering.

The third and final part of this book, 'Extended sociality', comprises two chapters dealing with those bodies that were so extraordinary in the ways in which they indexed life and/or death that their material sociality reached across cosmic boundaries. In the first of these discussions, Nicolas Wyatt traces the rise of resurrection in biblical and early Jewish traditions (Chapter 9). While the dead had long been understood to enjoy (or endure) a form of post-mortem existence in the underworld, the notion that individuals might physically resurrect appears to have been a relatively specialized elaboration on human (im)mortality. The idea that the righteous and the wicked might rise up from death to face divine judgement emerged during the Maccabaean period, when the lived experience of injustices of cultural oppression and intra-community conflict made theological space for an embodied reckoning in the afterlife (cf. Dan. 12.2-3). But as Wyatt argues, these ideas were shaped by a constellation of older socio-religious and mythic motifs. Traditions about various deities' escape from death or the underworld likely rendered a return from the socio-material space of death conceptually plausible. But among Yahweh's worshippers, it was the interrelation of high-status groups with the divine, and the dislodging of the traditional cult of 'gathered' ancestors, which helped lay the foundations for the possibility of human immortality. Calling on evidence from Persia, Mesopotamia, Egypt, Ugarit and the Hebrew Bible (particularly Isa. 14.9-20; Ezek. 37.1-14 and the 'Levitical' traditions reflected in Ps. 16; 49.15-16; 73.24-26), Wyatt reveals that the socio-religious and cultural roots of resurrection were diverse, fluid and very tangled. It is often assumed that the notion of bodily resurrection was a prominent if contentious feature of early Jewish beliefs. But this was not the case. As Wyatt reminds us, the idea of resurrection had always been 'rather woolly', but his analysis pulls at its central threads to guide us through the complexities of its backstory.

The volume closes with a discussion of the most powerful and fluid form of bodily sociality in the ancient world: divine embodiment. Here, Daniel McClellan examines the socio-material manifestation of Yahweh in the cult practices and traditions of ancient Israel and Judah (Chapter 10). Harnessing insights drawn from the cognitive science of religion and socio-anthropological approaches to materiality, he explores ancient Southwest Asian conceptions of the divine to argue that deities had partible and permeable bodies which might be materialized or 'presenced' in images, stelae and other cultic objects. In this, deities were not unlike the dead, whose social agency and personhood might be 'hosted' in mortuary objects, much as the inscription on the famous Katumuwa stele demonstrates. Turning to the Hebrew Bible, McClellan further explores this material form of divine embodiment. While the story of Jacob anointing a standing stone at Bethel indicates that traditional constructs of divine socio-materiality remained potent, biblical anxieties about cult images point to an increasing tendency to centralize the deity's primary location elsewhere and out of sight. But McClellan suggests that some material forms of divine embodiment continued to 'presence' Yahweh. One was the ark of the covenant, which McClellan argues was a manifestation of Yahweh's partible body, much as its direct cultic address as 'Yahweh' suggests. The other material form of divine embodiment was the Torah, which not only filled the cultic gap created by the loss of the ark but was underwritten by older conventions identifying inscribed standing stones as 'presencing media' for divine bodies, as Deut. 27.1-10 suggests. More than symbolic markers of the deity, the ark and the Torah were the 'body' of Yahweh.

Diverse in focus and richly textured in analysis, the chapters in this volume offer invigorating new insights into the materiality of life and the sociality of death in the ancient cultures in which the biblical traditions emerged, helping us to better understand how notions of embodiment play out in the Hebrew Bible. Taken together, these discussions remind us that the fleshy realities of being human are at the very heart of any culture, indexing the sociocultural complexities shaping life and death and contouring people's constructs of the wider world – in all its variously tangible and imagined forms.

References

Aker, J. (2007), 'Workmanship as Ideological Tool in the Monumental Hunt Reliefs of Assurbanipal', in J. Cheng and M. H. Feldman (eds), *Ancient Near Eastern Art in Context: Studies in Honor of Irene J. Winter by her Students*, 229–63, Leiden: Brill.

Albenda, P. (1983), 'Western Asiatic Women in the Iron Age: Their Image Revealed', *Biblical Archaeologist* 46 (2): 82–8.

Ames, F. R. (2014), 'The Red-Stained Warrior in Ancient Israel', in B. E. Kelle, F. R. Ames and J. L. Wright (eds), *Warfare, Ritual, and Symbol in Biblical and Modern Contexts*, 83–109, Atlanta, GA: Society of Biblical Literature.

Appell-Warren, L. (2014), *Personhood: An Examination of the History and Use of an Anthropological Concept*, Lewiston, NY: Edwin Mellen Press.

Asher-Greve, J. M. (2018), 'From La Femme to Multiple Sex/Gender', in S. Svärd and A. Garcia-Ventura (eds), *Studying Gender in the Ancient Near East*, 15–50, University Parks, PA: Eisenbrauns.

Asher-Greve, J. M., and D. Sweeney (2006), 'On Nakedness, Nudity, and Gender in Egyptian and Mesopotamian Art', in S. Schroer (ed.), *Images and Gender: Contributions to the Hermeneutics of Reading Ancient Art*, 111–62, Orbis Biblicus et Orientalis 220, Fribourg/Göttingen: Academic Press/Vandenhoeck & Ruprecht.

Assante, J. (2010), 'Inside and Outside: Extra-Dimensional Aspects of the Mesopotamian Body, with Egyptian Parallels', in M. Dietrich, W. Dipre, A. Häußling, A. Mertens and R. Schmitt (eds), *Religion und Menschenbild*, 3–18, Mitteilungen für Anthropologie und Religionsgeschichte 20, Münster: Ugarit-Verlag.

Assante, J. (2017), 'Men Looking at Men: The Homoerotics of Power in the State Arts of Assyria', in I. Zsolnay (ed.), *Being a Man: Negotiating Constructs of Masculinity*, 42–82, London: Routledge.

Attala, L., and L. Steel, eds (2019), *Body Matters: Exploring the Materiality of the Human Body*, Cardiff: University of Wales.

Bagg, A. (2016), 'Where Is the Public? A New Look at the Brutality Scenes in Neo-Assyrian Royal Inscriptions and Art', in L. Battini (ed.), *Making Pictures of War: Realia et Imaginaria in the Iconology of the Ancient Near East*, 57–82, Oxford: Archaeopress.

Bahrani, Z. (2003), *The Graven Image: Representation in Babylonia and Assyria*, Philadelphia: University of Pennsylvania Press.

Bahrani, Z. (2006), 'Race and Ethnicity in Mesopotamian Antiquity', *World Archaeology* 38: 48–59.

Bahrani, Z. (2008), *Rituals of War: The Body and Violence in Mesopotamia*, Brooklyn, NY: Zone Books.

Barcan, R. (2004), *Nudity: A Cultural Anatomy*, Oxford: Berg.

Barnett, R. D. (1958), 'The Siege of Lachish', *Israel Exploration Journal* 8: 161–4.

Barnett, R. D. (1970), 'Rebuilding of the Assyrian Galleries', *British Museum Society Bulletin* 3: 2–3.

Barnett, R. D., E. Bleibtreu and G. Turner (1998), *Sculptures from the Southwest Palace of Sennacherib at Nineveh*, 2 vols, London: British Museum.

Barron, A. E. (2010), 'Late Assyrian Arms and Armour: Art versus Artifact', PhD thesis, University of Toronto.

Battini, L. (2019a), 'Consented Violence in the Collective Memory: The Lachish Case from Epigraphic and Iconographic Data', *Semitica* 61: 337–71.

Battini, L. (2019b), 'Light as Experience: Rethinking Neo-Assyrian Reliefs in Their Architectural Context', *Ash-sharq* 3 (2): 69–104.

Bloch-Smith, E. (1992), *Judahite Burial Practices and Beliefs about the Dead*, Journal for the Study of the Old Testament Supplement 123, Sheffield: JSOT Press.

Brown, B. A. (2014), 'Culture on Display: Representations of Ethnicity in the Art of the Late Assyria State', in B. A. Brown and M. H. Feldman (eds), *Critical Approaches to Ancient Near Eastern Art*, 515–42, Berlin: Walter de Gruyter.

Burrell, K. (2020), *Cushites in the Hebrew Bible: Negotiating Ethnic Identity in the Past and Present*, Leiden: Brill.

Chapman, C. R. (2004), *The Gendered Language of Warfare in the Israelite-Assyrian Encounter*, Winona Lake, IN: Eisenbrauns.

Cifarelli, M. (1998), 'Gesture and Alterity in the Art of Ashurnasirpal II of Assyria', *Art Bulletin* 80 (2): 210–28.

Cifarelli, M., ed. (2019), *Fashioned Selves: Dress and Identity in Antiquity*, Oxford: Oxbow.

Cifarelli, M., and L. Gawlinski, eds (2017), *What Shall I Say of Clothes? Theoretical and Methodological Approaches to the Study of Dress in Antiquity*, Boston, MA: Archaeological Institute of America.

Collins, P. (2008), *Assyrian Palace Sculptures*, London: British Museum Press.

Collon, D. (1995), *Ancient Near Eastern Art*, London: British Museum Press.

Cuéllar, G. L. (2019), *Empire, the British Museum, and the Making of the Biblical Scholar in the Nineteenth Century: Archival Criticism*, Cham: Springer/Palgrave Macmillan.

Dalley, S. (2004), 'Recent Evidence from Assyrian Sources for Judaean History from Uzziah to Manasseh', *Journal for the Study of the Old Testament* 28 (4): 387–401.

De Backer, F. (2010), 'Fragmentation of the Enemy in the Ancient Near East during the Neo-Assyrian Period', in M. Kitts (ed.), *State, Power, and Violence*, 393–412, Wiesbaden: Harrassowitz.

DeGrado, J. (2019), 'King of the Four Quarters: Diversity as a Rhetorical Strategy of the Neo-Assyrian Empire', *Iraq* 81: 107–125.

DeMarris, E., and J. Robb (2013), 'Art Makes Society: An Introductory Visual Essay', *World Art* 3 (1): 3–22.

Dever, W. G. (2012), *The Lives of Ordinary People in Ancient Israel: Where Archaeology and the Bible Intersect*, Grand Rapids, MI: Eerdmans.

Feldman, M. H. (2010), 'Object Agency? Spatial Perspective, Social Relations, and the Stele of Hammurabi', in S. R. Steadman and J. C. Ross (eds), *Agency and Identity in the Ancient Near East: New Paths Forward*, 148–65, London: Equinox.

Foster, B. (2011), 'The Person in Mesopotamian Thought', in K. Radner and E. Robson (eds), *The Oxford Handbook to Cuneiform Culture*, 117–39, Oxford: Oxford University Press.

Fowler, C. (2004), *The Archaeology of Personhood: An Anthropological Perspective*, London: Routledge.

Fowler, C. (2010), 'From Identity and Material Culture to Personhood and Materiality', in D. Hicks and M. C. Beaudry (eds), *The Oxford Handbook of Material Culture Studies*, 352–85, Oxford: Oxford University Press.

Fowler, C. (2016), 'Relational Personhood Revisited', *Cambridge Archaeological Journal* 26 (3): 397–412.

Franklin, N. (2018), 'The Kushite Connection: The Destruction of Lachish and the Salvation of Jerusalem', in I. Shai, J. R. Chadwick, L. Hitchcock, A. Dagan, C. McKinny and J. Uziel (eds), *Tell It in Gath: Studies in the History and Archaeology of Israel. Essays in Honor of Aren M. Maeir on the Occasion of his Sixtieth Birthday*, 680–95, Münster: Zaphon.

Garcia-Ventura, A. (2019), 'Clothing and Nudity in the Ancient Near East from the Perspective of Gender Studies', in C. Berner, M. Schäfer, M. Schott, S. Schulz and M. Weingärtner (eds), *Clothing and Nudity in the Hebrew Bible*, 19–32, London: T&T Clark.

Garroway, K. H. (2012), 'Gendered or Ungendered? The Perception of Children in Ancient Israel', *Journal of Near Eastern Studies* 71 (1): 95–114.

Garroway, K. H. (2019), 'Methodology: Who Is a Child and Where Do We Find Children in the Ancient Near East?', in S. Betsworth and J. F. Parker (eds), *T&T Clark Handbook of Children in the Bible and Biblical World*, 67–90, London: T&T Clark.

Garroway, K. H. (2020), '(Un)Dressing Children in the Lachish Reliefs: Questions of Gender, Status, and Ethnicity', *Near Eastern Archaeology* 83: 46–55.

Green, J. D. M. (2018), 'Gender and Sexuality', in A. C. Gunter (ed.), *A Companion to Ancient Near Eastern Art*, 179–207, Hoboken: Wiley-Blackwell.

Gruber, M. (1989), 'Breast-Feeding Practices in Biblical Israel', *Journal of Ancient Near Eastern Studies* 19: 61–83.

Han, S., and J. Antrosio (2018), 'Hair Everywhere: Anthropological Notes on the Long and Short of It', *Open Anthropology* 6, no. 2. Available online at https://www.americananthro.org/StayInformed/OAArticleDetail.aspx?ItemNumber=22949 (accessed 7 March 2020).

Helle, S. (2018), '"Only in Dress?" Methodological Concerns Regarding Non-Binary Gender', in S. L. Budin, M. Cifarelli, A. Garcia-Ventura and A. Millet-Albà (eds), *Gender and Methodology in the Ancient Near East: Approaches from Assyriology and Beyond*, 41–53, Barcino Monographica Orientalia 10, Barcelona: Universitat de Barcelona.

Helle, S. (2019), 'Weapons and Weaving Instruments as Symbols of Gender in the Ancient Near East', in M. Cifarelli (ed.), *Fashioned Selves: Dress and Identity in Antiquity*, 105–15, Oxford: Oxbow.

Jacoby, R. (1991), 'The Representation and Identification of Cities on Assyrian Reliefs', *Israel Exploration Journal* 41: 112–31.

Jones, A. R., and P. Stallybrass (2000), *Renaissance Clothing and the Materials of Memory*, Cambridge Studies Renaissance Literature and Culture 38, Cambridge: Cambridge University Press.

King, P. J., and L. E. Stager (2001), *Life in Biblical Israel*, Library of Ancient Israel, Louisville, KY: Westminster John Knox.

Krause, J. J. (2019), 'Barefoot before God: Shoes and Sacred Space in the Hebrew Bible and Ancient Near East', in C. Berner, M. Schäfer, M. Schott, S. Schulz and M. Weingärtner (eds), *Clothing and Nudity in the Hebrew Bible*, 315–22, London: T&T Clark.

Lambert, H., and M. McDonald (2009), *Social Bodies*, Oxford: Berghahn.

Lancy, D. F. (2014), '"Babies Aren't Persons": A Survey of Delayed Personhood', in H. Otto and H. Keller (eds), *Different Faces of Attachment: Cultural Variations on Universal Human Need*, 66–109, Cambridge: Cambridge University Press.

Laneri, N., ed. (2007), *Performing Death: Social Analyses of Funerary Traditions in the Ancient Near East and Mediterranean*, Oriental Institute Seminars 3, Chicago, IL: University of Chicago Press.

Layard, A. H. (1853), *Discoveries in the Ruins of Nineveh and Babylon; with Travels in Armenia, Kurdistan and the Desert: Being the Result of a Second Expedition Undertaken for the Trustees of the British Museum*, London: John Murray.

Lemos, T. M. (2017), *Violence and Personhood in Ancient Israel and Comparative Contexts*, Oxford: Oxford University Press.

Lippolis, C., ed. (2011), *The Sennacherib Wall Reliefs at Nineveh*, Monografie di Mesopotamia 15/Missione in Iraq 5, Florence: Le Lettere.

Maher, V., ed. (1992), *The Anthropology of Breast-Feeding: Natural Law or Social Construct*, Oxford: Berg.

Mascia-Lees, F. E., ed. (2011), *A Companion to the Anthropology of the Body and Embodiment*, Chichester: Wiley-Blackwell.

McCormick, C. M. (2002), *Palace and Temple: A Study of Architectural and Verbal Icons*, Beihefte zur Zeitschrift für die alttestamentliche Wissenschaft 313, Berlin: Walter de Gruyter.

McFerrin, N. (2017), 'Fabrics of Inclusion: Deep Wearing and the Potentials of Materiality on the Apadana Reliefs', in M. Cifarelli and L. Gawlinski (eds), *What Shall I Say of Clothes? Theoretical and Methodological Approaches to the Study of Dress in Antiquity*, 143–59, Boston, MA: Archaeological Institute of America.

McIntosh, J. (2018), 'Personhood, Self, and Individual', in H. Callan (ed.), *The International Encyclopedia of Anthropology*, Hoboken, NJ: Wiley. Available online at https://onlinelibrary.wiley.com/doi/abs/10.1002/9781118924396.wbiea1576 (accessed 6 March 2020).

McMahon, A. (2013), 'Space, Sound, and Light: Toward a Sensory Experience of Ancient Monumental Architecture', *American Journal of Archaeology* 117: 163–79.

Meskell, L. M. (2004), *Object Worlds in Ancient Egypt: Material Biographies Past and Present*, Oxford: Berg.

Meskell, L. M. (2008), 'The Nature of the Beast: Curating Animals and Ancestors at Çatalhöyük', *World Archaeology* 40: 373–89.

Meskell, L. M., and R. R. Joyce (2003), *Embodied Lives: Figuring Ancient Maya and Egyptian Experience*, London: Routledge.

Morello, N. (2016), 'A GIŠ on a Tree: Interactions between Images and Inscriptions on Neo-Assyrian Monuments', in M. Hilgert (ed.), *Understanding Material Text Cultures: A Multidisciplinary View*, 31–68, Berlin: Walter de Gruyter.

Nadali, D. (2020), 'How Ancient and Modern Memory Shapes the Past: A Canon of Assyrian Memory', in A. R. Gansell and A. Shafer (eds), *Testing the Canon of Ancient Near Eastern Art and Archaeology*, 217–31, Oxford: Oxford University Press.

Nadali, D., and J. Vidal, eds (2014), *The Other Face of the Battle: The Impact of War on Civilians in the Ancient Near East*, Alter Orient und Altes Testament 413, Münster: Ugarit-Verlag.

N'Shea, O. (2016), 'Royal Eunuchs and Elite Masculinity in the Neo-Assyrian Empire', *Near Eastern Archaeology* 79 (3): 214–21.

N'Shea, O. (2018), 'Empire of the Surveilling Gaze: The Masculinity of King Sennacherib', in in S. Svärd and A. Garcia-Ventura (eds), *Studying Gender in the Ancient Near East*, 315–35, University Parks, PA: Eisenbrauns.

N'Shea, O. (2019), 'Dressed to Dazzle, Dressed to Kill: Staging Assurbanipal in the Royal Lion Hunt Reliefs from Nineveh', in M. Cifarelli (ed.), *Fashioned Selves: Dress and Identity in Antiquity*, 175–84, Oxford: Oxbow.

Olyan, S. M. (2005), 'Some Neglected Aspects of Israelite Interment Ideology', *Journal of Biblical Literature* 124: 601–16.

Olyan, S. M. (2015), 'The Instrumental Dimensions of Ritual Violence against Corpses in Biblical Texts', in S. M. Olyan (ed.), *Ritual Violence in the Hebrew Bible: New Perspectives*, 125–36, Oxford: Oxford University Press.

Ornan, T. (2014), 'A Silent Message: Godlike Kings in Mesopotamian Art', in B. A. Brown and M. H. Feldman (eds), *Critical Approaches to Ancient Near Eastern Art*, 569–95, Berlin: Walter de Gruyter.

Palmer, C. (2013), 'Unshod on Holy Ground: Ancient Israel's "Disinherited" Priesthood', in L. J. Greenspoon (ed.), *Fashioning Jews: Clothing, Culture and Commerce*, 1–17, Studies in Jewish Civilization 24, West Lafayette, IN: Purdue University Press.

Peled, I. (2016), *Masculinities and Third Gender: The Origins and Nature of an Institutionalised Gender Otherness in the Ancient Near East*, Alter Orient und Altes Testament 435, Münster: Ugarit-Verlag.

Porter, A. (2014), 'When the Subject *Is* the Object: Relational Ontologies, the Partible Person and Images of Naram-Sin', in B. A. Brown and M. H. Feldman (eds), *Critical Approaches to Ancient Near Eastern Art*, 597–617, Berlin: Walter de Gruyter.

Porter, B. W., and A. T. Boutin, eds (2014), *Remembering the Dead in the Ancient Near East: Recent Contributions from Bioarchaeology and Mortuary Archaeology*, Boulder: University Press of Colorado.

Portuese, L. (2019), 'The Throne Room of Aššurnasirpal II: A Multisensory Experience', in A. Hawthorn and A.-C. Rendu Loisel (eds), *Distant Impressions: The Senses in the Ancient Near East*, 63–92, Recontre Assyriologique Internationale 61, University Park, PA: Eisenbrauns.

Prinsloo, G. T. M. (2000), 'Sennacherib, Lachish and Jerusalem: Honour and Shame', *Old Testament Essays* 13 (3): 348–63.

Pyschny, K. (2019), 'Concepts and Contexts of Male and Female Nudity in the Iconography of the Southern Levant', in C. Berner, M. Schäfer, M. Schott, S. Schulz and M. Weingärtner (eds), *Clothing and Nudity in the Hebrew Bible*, 127–62, London: T&T Clark.

Radner, K. (2015), 'High Visibility Punishment and Deterrent: Impalement in Assyrian Warfare and Legal Practice', *Zeitschrift für altorientalische und biblische Rechtsgeschichte* 21: 103–28.

Richardson, S. (2007), 'Death and Dismemberment in Mesopotamia: Discorporation between the Body and Body Politic', in N. Laneri (ed.), *Performing Death: Social Analyses of Funerary Traditions in the Ancient Near East and Mediterranean*, 189–208, Oriental Institute Seminars 3, Chicago, IL: University of Chicago Press.

Riley, J. A. (2020), 'Children Should Be Seen: Studying Children in Assyrian Iconography', in K. H. Garroway and J. W. Martens (eds), *Children and Methods: Listening to and Learning from Children in the Biblical World*, 76–103, Leiden: Brill.

Robb, J., and O. J. T. Harris (2013), *The Body in History: Europe from the Palaeolithic to the Future*, Cambridge: Cambridge University Press.

Russell, J. M. (1991), *Sennacherib's 'Palace without Rival' at Nineveh*, Chicago, IL: University of Chicago Press.

Russell, J. M. (1994), 'Sennacherib's Lachish Narratives', in P. J. Holliday (ed.), *Narrative and Event in Ancient Art*, 53–73, Cambridge: Cambridge University Press.

Schwyn, I. (2000), 'Kinderbetreuung im 9.-7. Jahrhundert: Eine Untersuchung anhand der Darstellingen auf neuassyrischen Reliefs', *Lectio Difficilor* 1: 1–14.

Schwyn, I. (2006), 'Kinder und ihre Betreuungspersonen auf den neuassyrischen Palastreliefs', in S. Schroer (ed.), *Images and Gender: Contributions to the Hermeneutics of Reading Ancient Art*, 323–30, Fribourg/Göttingen: Academic Press/Vandenhoeck & Ruprecht.

Shafer, A. (2014), 'The Assyrian Landscape as Ritual', in B. A. Brown and M. H. Feldman (eds), *Critical Approaches to Ancient Near Eastern Art*, 713–39, Berlin: Walter de Gruyter.

Shilling, C. (2003), *The Body and Social Theory*, 2nd edn, London: Sage.

Stavrakopoulou, F. (2010), 'Gog's Grave and the Use and Abuse of Corpses in Ezekiel 39:11–20', *Journal of Biblical Literature* 129: 67–84.

Stavrakopoulou, F. (2013), 'Making Bodies: On Body Modification and Religious Materiality in the Hebrew Bible', *Hebrew Bible and Ancient Israel* 2: 532–53.

Stavrakopoulou, F. (2016), 'Religion at Home: The Materiality of Practice', in S. Niditch (ed.), *The Wiley Blackwell Companion to Ancient Israel*, 345–63, Chichester: Wiley-Blackwell.

Stavrakopoulou, F. (2019), 'Curating King Saul: The Transformation of a Troublesome Corpse', in L. Quick, E. E. Kozlova, S. Noll and P. Y. Yoo (eds), *To Gaul, to Greece and into Noah's Ark: Essays in Honour of Kevin J. Cathcart on the Occasion of his Eightieth Birthday*, 19–35, Journal of Semitic Studies Supplement 44, Oxford: Oxford University Press.

Stavrakopoulou, F. (forthcoming), *God: An Anatomy*, London: Picador.

Stol, M. (2000), *Birth in Babylonia and the Bible: Its Mediterranean Setting*, Groningen: Styx.

Suriano, M. J. (2018), *A History of Death in the Hebrew Bible*, Oxford: Oxford University Press.

Thomas, P. B. (2008), 'The Riddle of Ishtar's Shoes: The Religious Significance of the Footprints at 'Ain Dara from a Comparative Perspective', *Journal of Religious History* 32 (3): 303–19.

Thomason, A. K. (2005), *Luxury and Legitimation: Royal Collecting in Ancient Mesopotamia*, Aldershot: Ashgate.

Turner, B. S., ed. (2012), *Routledge Handbook of Body Studies*, London: Routledge.

Uehlinger, C. (2003), 'Clio in a World of Pictures – Another Look at the Lachish Reliefs from Sennacheribs's Southwest Palace at Nineveh', in L. L. Grabbe (ed.), *'Like a Bird in a Cage': The Invasion of Sennacherib in 701 BCE*, 221–305, Journal for the Study of the Old Testament Supplement Series 363/European Seminar in Historical Method 4, Sheffield: Sheffield Academic Press.

Uehlinger, C. (2007), 'Neither Eyewitnesses, Nor Windows to the Past, but Valuable Testimony in Its Own Right: Remarks on Iconography, Source Criticism, and Ancient Data-Processing', in H. G. M. Williamson (ed.), *Understanding the History of Ancient Israel*, 173–228, Proceedings of the British Academy 143, Oxford: Oxford University Press.

Ussishkin, D. (1982), *The Conquest of Lachish by Sennacherib*, Tel Aviv Publications of the Institute of Archaeology 6, Tel Aviv: Tel Aviv University.

Ussishkin, D. (2003), 'Symbols of Conquest in Sennacherib's Reliefs of Lachish: Impaled Prisoners and Booty', in T. Potts, M. Roaf and D. Stein (eds), *Culture through Objects: Ancient Near Eastern Studies in Honour of P. R. S. Moorey*, 207–17, Oxford: Griffith Institute.

Ussishkin, D. (2014a), *The Renewed Archaeological Excavations at Lachich (1973–1994), Volume 2: The Iron Age Stratigraphy and Architecture*, Proceedings of the Institute of Archaeology 22, Tel Aviv: Emery and Claire Yass Publications in Archaeology.

Ussishkin, D. (2014b), *Biblical Lachish: A Tale of Construction, Destruction, Excavation, and Restoration*, Jerusalem: Israel Exploration Society.

Wäfler, M. (1975), *Nicht-Assyrer neuassyrischer Darstellungen*, Alter Orient und Altes Testament 26, Kevelaer/Neukirchen-Vluyn: Butzon & Bercker/Neukirchener Verlag.

Wagstaff, B. J. (2017), 'Redressing Clothing in the Hebrew Bible: Material-Cultural Approaches', PhD thesis, University of Exeter.

Zwickel, W. (2019), 'Fabrication, Functions, and Uses of Textiles in the Hebrew Bible', in C. Berner, M. Schäfer, M. Schott, S. Schulz and M. Weingärtner (eds), *Clothing and Nudity in the Hebrew Bible*, 187–216, London: T&T Clark.

PART ONE

Praxis and materiality

CHAPTER TWO

Blood and hair: Body management and practice

SUSAN NIDITCH

The study of biblical bodies contributes to and draws upon important threads in contemporary religious studies. Under the headings of 'material religion' and 'personal religion', scholars seek to assess the personal and public significance of deportment, treatments of the body and objects or substances worn, carried or manipulated. An analysis of 'body management and practice' as portrayed in the Hebrew Bible relates to critical ideas suggested by terms such as 'symbol', 'culture', 'tradition' and 'self', pointing to the relevance of classic theories in the study of religion concerning life passages, mediation, chaos and order, reciprocity, power and the habitual. The theoretical framework is further deepened by contemporary approaches to the body as 'a social project' and 'a site of religious performativity' (Stavrakopoulou 2013: 552). All of these considerations relate in integral ways to matters of life and death.

I have selected case studies, drawn from the Hebrew Bible, dealing with two bodily substances: blood and hair. My interest is twofold: (1) to examine via close work with biblical texts some of the theoretical issues involved in the study of material religion and (2) to uncover specifics about religion as lived, described and manifested in the ancient Hebrew anthology of the Bible, to better understand the richness and variety of religious expression in ancient Israel.[1]

Certain key questions arise in exploring these examples of body management and practice: How does the treatment or framing of the body maintain equilibrium for individuals and the group within particular cultural settings? Who benefits from customs involving blood or hair? How is cultural identity proclaimed by forms of body management or practice? What messages are conveyed about gender? How is change achieved, acknowledged and experienced in such practices?

Blood

Blood is mentioned frequently in the Hebrew Bible, playing an integral role within various ritual processes and serving as a metonymic marker of various states of being: clean and unclean, divine and human, Israelite and Other. Depending upon their own cultural

---

1 In what follows, the designation 'ancient Israel' functions as a blanket term for the ancient societies in which the literature of the Hebrew Bible emerged.

background, readers new to the biblical tradition are often astonished at the emphasis placed on embodied blood: the uncleanness of the menstruating woman and the woman who has just given birth, both of whom bleed under what we would consider normal procreative circumstances; the way in which priests are initiated by the daubing of blood at critical locations on their persons; the enigmatic commandment not to eat meat with the blood in it, a rule affecting consumption; the sheer amount of blood of sacrificial animals that is tossed, poured, drenched or painted in ritual performance, upon persons and places, thereby no doubt also spraying or spotting the priestly adept himself as he engages in ritual actions.

Blood is a multivalent symbol (Turner 1967; Niditch 2011). It can be unclean-rendering, cleansing and purifying or entirely neutral. As a symbol, blood is a fluid means of representing ideas shared by a group – expressive, malleable, visual and tactile, as imagined or actually touched. Given the emphasis of this chapter on body management and practice, certain case studies concerning blood are especially pertinent: those pertaining to customs of meat-eating, that which enters the body and sustains it (Noah in Gen. 9.3-4, Saul in 1 Sam. 14.32 and the related legal passages: Lev. 7.26-27; 17.10-14; Deut. 12.15-16, 23-25); those in which blood is actually set upon bodies as a means of transformation or passage from one status to another, such as the ordination or consecration of priests (Lev. 8.24; Exod. 29.20-21), the 'blood of the covenant' forming a relationship between the deity and Israel (Exod. 24.8), the purification of the leper (Lev. 14.25); passages in which the implicit message is that the blood of humans, or more typically the substituted blood of animals, is a means of satiating the all-powerful deity, source of life (Exod. 4.24-26; 12.21-27); and those in which the body itself exudes blood (Lev. 12.1-8; 15.19-30).

A first important indicator of attitudes to blood appears near the end of the mythic complex surrounding the primordial adventures of Noah, survivor of the great flood. Echoing the language of the food proscription of Gen. 2.16-17 that allows for the consumption of vegetation in the garden but forbids fruit from the tree of knowledge, the deity, in this new post-flood creation, allows for the eating of meat but forbids meat-eating of a certain kind, namely 'with its life-force, its blood'. This proscription is emphasized also at Lev 7.26-27; 17.10-14 and Deut. 12.15-16, 23-25 with the message that 'the life of the flesh is in the blood' (Lev. 17.11) and 'the blood is the life-force' (Deut. 12.23). Does this language, drawing the line between what is acceptable concerning the consumption of meat and what is forbidden, suggest revulsion from a kind of inter-species cannibalism in which one virtually devours a creature's life? Alternatively does the prohibition reflect fear of taking what originates with and properly belongs to the deity alone? In either case, the prohibition involves a way of thinking about food and consumption, about what enters the body to sustain life. The ritual process of pouring the blood onto the absorbent ground makes the consumer think more carefully about what he or she is eating, about the living, throbbing animal who died for people to obtain food protein. It is thus a personal statement and comments on one's relationship with other living beings, as reflected in food habits (see Welton in this volume). On the one hand such framing of meat-eating might be seen to suggest that eating meat is special, always to some extent sacralized, an activity that takes place as part of larger ritual patterns. Ordinary day-to-day food consumption in ancient Israel was largely meat-free (see King and Stager 2001: 12–19, 85–122). Slaughtering a lamb marks preparation for a visitor, a calendrical celebration or special occasion as in the invitation to Saul to partake of Samuel's table (1 Sam. 9.19). Meat sharing is part of sacrificial activities at local shrines. Possibly reflecting a Southern reform movement intent on the centralization of worship in the Jerusalem shrine, Deuteronomy

12 moves in a different direction and makes meat-eating a somewhat desacralized activity, a more ordinary way of obtaining protein that is nevertheless culturally and religiously demarcating. Deuteronomy 12 thus reflects an interesting diachronic development in meat-eating practice or attitudes (see Deut. 12.15). And yet in this case as well, the blood is to be poured on the ground (12.16), and slaughtering continues to suggest a special framing and ritual acknowledgement, even in the absence of sacrifice.

Exploring the connections between sin, the shedding of blood and the avoidance of eating blood, Stephen A. Geller (1992) has suggested that the eating of meat reflects a kind of 'concession' after the flood, an admission that human beings are violent, blood-shedding creatures; the consumption of meat involving the shedding of animal blood has negative connotations. He writes, 'Perhaps there is a hint that by refraining from blood (="life") it is as if no life had been taken, a comforting fiction. Maybe there is an intimation that even through licit slaughter humanity incurs a degree of "blood-guilt"' (Geller 1992: 112–13). Slaughtering in a fashion that involves a particular treatment of the animal's blood allows each person who eats meat to eschew guilt, to avail himself of valuable food protein in a controlled, circumscribed way enjoined by the mythic tradition and reinforced by a particular world view. The implication is that meat-eating itself is a troubling or anxiety-producing activity.

The pouring of the blood and avoidance of its consumption is a culturally self-defining statement, for others do eat meat 'with the blood'. In ancient Israel and Judah, 'eating with the blood' suggests becoming less than a civilized, acculturated human (e.g. Ezek. 33.25). Eating blood is what foreigners do, the custom of the Other as indicated by Lev. 7.26-27; 17.10. The person who eats with the blood is to be cut off from the community. Implicit is the message that 'they' are barbarians, whereas 'we' are civilized. The prohibitions concerning the consumption of blood thus serve as a social index, a concept applied to ritual actions concerning blood by William Gilders (2004: 78–82).

The scene involving Saul's establishment of an impromptu altar at 1 Sam. 14.32-36 underscores the ways in which alimentary customs that involve 'eating meat with (or without) the blood' define cultural identity. Saul has made a war-vow declaring that none of his troops will eat until they are victorious over the enemy, and they do win their battle against the Philistines. The story of the war-vow that frames this scene about ways of eating is complicated by Jonathan's having, in fact, eaten some honey to sustain himself, thereby breaking his father's vow. These complications are not revealed immediately, however, and the narrator pauses to describe the actions of the ravenous and exhausted troops returning from battle. They fall upon the spoil of sheep and cattle, slaughtering them on the ground, and are said to eat 'upon/with the blood'. In heroic fashion, Saul intervenes, urging his men not to sin against Yahweh in this way. He orders that a big stone be brought to him and there they are to slaughter and then eat meat. Establishing an altar like the patriarchs of old, he thus insists on ritually framing the consumption of meat so that no one sins by eating meat with the blood. Implicit in this vignette is a fascinating positive portrayal of Saul in the midst of the larger and more insistent pro-Davidic theme about Saul's loss of divine favour.

This scene, perhaps a residue of epic traditions concerning the last judge and first king, reflects and reinforces attitudes to blood, food and the body in an important and revealing biblical thread. Meat-eating is sacralized, so that the person who consumes the meat is not tainted by uncontrolled violence. Saul turns his horde of beast-like and barbarian soldiers into Yahweh-faithful, civilized men, respectful of life as demonstrated by their mode of meat consumption. A comparison is thus drawn between acting like the people of God and sinning against the deity by eating as the 'Other' eats. Chaotic behaviour contrasts with proper orderly consumption preceded by ritual slaughter that implies not only respect for life but also group identity as God's people subject to alimentary rules. One thinks here of Mary Douglas's emphasis on boundaries and categories imposed on bodily behaviour as revealing of cultural attitudes and concepts of self-definition (Douglas 1966).

The view of blood as quintessential life and the deity's interest in its disposition relate as well to the use of blood in rituals of transformation. William Gilders (2004) has provided a review of scholarly opinions concerning the role of blood manipulation. Some suggest that blood as it figures in a number of ritual contexts is a substitute for the human being's 'self-giving', a form of ransom. Others view the daubing, spattering or sprinkling of blood as a means of restoring life threatened by sin, impurity and death (Gilders 2004: 46, 159–63). In exploring blood as a bodily medium, it is especially important to appreciate blood as a border substance, a quality of blood as cultural symbol examined by Geyer (2007: 2–4), Barmash (2005:188) and myself (Niditch 2011). It is associated with death and life, loss and renewal. It points to the human condition with its mortality and limitations and is at the same time the divine life-force within us. A mediating substance, blood effects embodied passages that point to larger issues in personal and cultural identity.

The ritual ordination of priests described in Lev. 8.24 is a rite of passage mediated in part through the daubing of blood mixed with oil on the right earlobe and the right big toe of the initiate. The blood helps to effect passage from ordinary status to priestly status, common to elite, mundane to sacred. Similarly, at Exod. 24.8 blood obtained from the well-being offering of oxen is dashed on the people as 'the blood of the covenant', a confirmation and creator of the bond of reciprocity between Yahweh and Israel. The blood once again leads to identity, the joining of a group. Finally, the daubing of blood on the lobe of the right ear, the thumb of the right hand and the toe of the right foot, in this case the blood of a guilt or reparation offering, allows the cured leper to return to quotidian life, rejoining the community (Lev. 14.14). The leper, akin to the living dead, marginalized and exiled from the community, transitions back to the world of the living and the healthy. In each case status is emphasized and altered or confirmed. Claude Lévi-Strauss's structuralism (1968) and Victor Turner's description (1969) of the liminal midpoint in rites of passage that lead from one status to another suggest that this medium is especially appropriate to transition and transformation, holding a mediating position. Both theoreticians point to the human need to rebalance when faced with contradiction, social anxiety or nodal life changes. Lévi-Strauss suggests that human beings set in cultures see the world in terms of a series of contradictions, such as those between nature and culture, life and death, human and divine. In the expressive symbolic media of ritual action and myth-telling, third intermediate categories or representations keep these irresolvable contradictions in balance and bridged. The daubing or sprinkling of blood imagined in these biblical contexts is a reminder of the trajectory spanning life and death in the case of the leper, a marker of humanness and sacral responsibilities in the case of the priestly initiate and a confirmation of the special and specific relationship between Israelite human beings and the deity Yahweh in the case of the blood of the covenant. Victor Turner, like Arnold van Gennep ([1908] 1960), points to the way in which changes in status are culturally marked by symbolic representations that evoke the state of being betwixt and between. The life passenger moves through a symbolic doorway. Often such a state of change is marked on the body – by nakedness, for example, or special clothing. In the cases explored above, the passengers wear blood, a symbol that partakes of each side of key culture-defining dichotomies: life and death; earthly and divine. The blood operates as a link between one status and another (e.g. secular versus priestly or mundane versus sacred) and keeps these poles of self-definition in play.

Blood's role as mediator and transformer is important to its function in each ritual process, but the tactile experience of bloodiness cannot be overemphasized. The blood, wet, viscous, perhaps still warm from the animal of its source, is felt on the body. The participant in the ritual feels in a material way his or her transformation from isolated leper to included member of the community, from commoner to priest. Those splashed with blood of the covenant experience becoming God's people, doused with the life-force, the substance of God.

Another case study involving biblical bodies and blood has to do with protection of the human and satiation of the deity. The scene at Exod. 4.24-26 marks a critical transition point in the story of Moses. On his way back to Egypt to serve as his people's leader and liberator, Moses is met by a threatening manifestation of Yahweh, who seeks to kill him. Moses is rescued by Zipporah, his wife. She cuts off their son's foreskin and touches his (Moses'?) feet (his reproductive member?) with the bloody foreskin and declares, 'For you are a bridegroom of blood to me.' The deity lets go of him and she punctuates the scene with the words, 'a bridegroom of blood by the circumcision'. This enigmatic passage, in which meanings of 'his' and 'feet' are ambiguous, may reflect rites of puberty and marriage in which circumcision relates to the male's transition from youth to adulthood as he assumes the bodily form of an adult man, shared with other males of his cultural group, and readiness for marriage and procreation (Eilberg-Schwartz 1990: 141–76). Zipporah's double mention of the *'bridegroom* of blood' seems to point in this direction, and yet in Exodus 4 it is Moses and not his son who is the groom and the son who is circumcised. The frame and focus of the situation moreover seem to be the threat to the hero at a critical passage in his life, comparable perhaps to Jacob's encounter with the divine being at the River Jabbok (Gen. 32.22-32). The bloody foreskin seems to protect the man or to ward off the deity much as the blood on the doorways of Israelite houses causes the Destroyer to spare the firstborn of the Hebrews during the final plague of the exodus events. And finally we note with Stephen Geller that the bloodiness of the foreskin seems critical here, 'even though P prefers not to mention the "drop of blood" aspect' (Geller 1992: 114); the blood is life, the blood ransoms (see Gilders 2004: 92; on Ibn Ezra see Gilders 2004: 46, 228 n.6), the blood perhaps even satiates the deity in his terrifying and aggressive mode. Blood, again a mediating substance, creates a relationship between Yahwist males all of whom undergo circumcision, between men and women of the community who will marry and procreate and between Hebrews and their covenant partner the deity. The mark of these relationships, forged in the blood of the circumcision, is worn on the male body declaring identity, social connection and theological perspective. Concepts of 'social project' and 'religious performativity' apply well. The male's body performs maleness as socially or culturally constructed, and the deity who is assuaged by blood is associated with life and death, is rescuer and destroyer.

With the exception of the mysterious reference to blood in Zipporah's ritual actions, other cases involving blood discussed thus far involve the bodies of sacrificial animals, whether their blood is employed in ritual or avoided as food. The blood is a by-product of eating animal flesh to sustain human life or is a means, in its own right, of cleansing or protecting. What about blood that issues forth from human bodies, other than blood of the circumcision?

Blood is generally presented in biblical ritual accounts as a super purifying substance, a detergent with cleansing capacities, in Milgrom's terms (1998: 711), or as neutral. That is, the blood of a wound does not render the bleeding person unclean nor the one who comes in contact with him. Important exceptions are menstrual blood and blood discharged by the woman who has just given birth (Lev. 15.19-24; 12.1-8). These cases lead us to think again about clean and unclean bodies, as well as about practices pertaining to bodies and gender.

Milgrom suggests that, like semen, menstrual blood is associated with life so that its loss has to do with death and in turn with the condition of ritual impurity (Milgrom 1998: 766–8, 1000–4; see also Geyer 2007: 2). As Jonathan Klawans notes, however, the blood that issues forth from a person with a life-threatening wound is not unclean rendering (Klawans 2006: 57). Moving in another direction, Howard Eilberg-Schwartz equates the degree of pollution from bodily discharges with the degree of controllability. Menstrual blood, non-menstrual vaginal blood and non-seminal discharge are not controllable, whereas tears, milk and urine can be controlled (Eilberg-Schwartz 1990: 187). Thus the former render unclean, the latter substances not, and seminal discharges render a person less unclean than menstruation, as presumably the man can control his ejaculation. Blood that gushes forth from the body because of an accident is, however, not in a person's control and yet, as noted above, uncontrolled, even violent, sudden bleeding that may rob the person of his life is not a source of impurity. Some other kind of culturally constructed response seems to be at play.

The ultimate issue here does seem to be management of the body, but the special focus of the concern with unclean blood is the management of *women's* bodies as noted by Jacob Neusner in relation to Mishnaic elaborations of laws of *niddah* (Neusner 1982: 134). The management of irregular vaginal bleeding would seem to suit Eilberg-Schwartz's conception, rooted perhaps in the work of Mary Douglas (1966), about human concerns with order, regularity and related issues of uncontrollability. The regular rhythm of menstruation and the typical bloody process of childbirth, however, really belong under the heading of the everyday, the predictable and the ordinary experience of women. That this blood is placed in a special category with a capacity to make the person who bleeds ritually unclean and render others unclean by contact, in a category that requires a rite of passage to return to 'normalcy', points not to uncontrollability but to the desire by men to control and frame women's reproductive capacity. Implicit is an admission that something mysterious and denied to men is involved in these cases of bleeding. The fact that birthing girl babies, who themselves will someday become menstruating women, causes the birth mother to be ritually unclean for twice the length of time as does the birthing of male children (Lev. 12.5), seems to emphasize this gendered message.

Building upon the assignment of menstrual blood to the category of the unclean, a material produced by women's bodies that must be safely treated and circumscribed, is the much more extreme imagery of Ezekiel's *mashal* of the boiling pot that associates women's monthly bleeding not merely with the physical condition of impurity but with sin itself, a moral condition. As discussed by Peggy L. Day (see n. 2), this powerful and visceral scene in Ezekiel 24 purposefully draws upon terminology and images associated with menstruation. The term frequently translated 'rust' (e.g. NRSV Ezek. 24.6, 12), rooted in the term for being diseased, is coloured by the coppery-redness of the pot alluded to in v. 11. The copper term is used in parallel with 'nakedness' in Ezek. 16.36 (pouring out your 'copper'/revealing your 'nakedness' or 'genitals'). This sexual imagery together with the emphasis on blood itself and the gender of the city combine with references to her shedding blood and not properly dealing with it and with overt references to conditions of 'clean' and 'unclean'. Altogether the imagery points to menstruation.² The city is an unclean woman immersed in her bloody filth. And thus for Ezekiel, a priest of the Jerusalem establishment, who worries a good deal about the keeping of menstrual taboos, the uncleanness of women becomes a quintessential symbol of sinfulness and alienation from God, a condition tinged with illicit sexuality or lewdness (Ezek. 24.13).

Menstrual blood in its very uncleanness contains a kind of feminine danger but this very danger also betokens a feminine power. The power of this blood is revealed in the scene shared by Laban and his daughter Rachel in Gen. 31.33-35. Fleeing from the patriarch with her husband Jacob, her sister Leah and their families, Rachel has stolen Laban's *teraphim*, statuary that seems to have involved status, identity and divinatory value. Rachel has hidden the *teraphim* under a camel saddle and sits upon them as Laban looks for his possessions (Gen. 31.34). She tells her father that she is menstruating and cannot rise; he searches a bit more, and then he leaves. Could it be that he fears her 'uncleanness', her condition of bloodiness? Menstrual blood might be seen in this way to circumscribe women's access to establishment ritual contexts but to empower them in religion as lived. This aspect of women's bodies may be a subversive source of power that is expressed in round about ways, but it is power nevertheless.

Hair

Hair provides a second medium that underscores ways in which bodily practices relate to personal and cultural identity, life passages and modes of self-creation and self-proclamation. Long, short or absent, covered or exposed, ornately styled or wildly loose, hair sends messages about its wearer in relation to culture. A peculiar bodily substance that is both alive and dead, hair offers people opportunities to express who they are as individuals and members of communities, to adhere to convention or express opposition to the establishment. Hair demarcates status and the altering of status. Three case studies that reveal the power and significance of hair are (1) the association between manliness, warrior status, holiness and long hair (thus Nazirites such as Samson and Samuel, prophets such as Elijah and would-be leaders such as Absalom); (2) the significance of hair-cutting whether self-imposed or imposed by others (the story of Samson and Delilah in Judges 16, the story about David's emissaries in 2 Samuel 10, mourning rites and pictorial evidence); (3) the significance of covered, uncovered or severed hair for women's status and identity (the ritual concerning the woman accused of adultery in Numbers 5; the treatment of the captive bride in Deuteronomy 21).

A thread of visual references in the Hebrew Bible associates men's long hair with charisma, warrior status and virility. The connection is overt in the story of the hero judge Samson (Judges 13–16) whose superhuman strength is integrally related to his hair, never cut since birth – a condition of Nazirite status demanded of his barren mother by a divine messenger even before his conception, a part of an annunciation scene. He is an ancient Israelite version of a common folk tale type in which the hero's strength resides in some aspect of his body, and when that body feature is altered or impaired, he becomes weak like other men. The associations between hair and manly charisma, however, are

---

2 As Peggy Day pointed out in her lecture titled 'Women's Blood in Ancient Israel: Rituals and Metaphors', delivered at Amherst College, Amherst, MA, in November 1993.

not unique to Samson. Samuel, son of Hannah, another woman who cannot conceive, is vowed to divine service by his mother, his hair never to be cut, should the deity answer her plea for a child (1 Samuel 1). Some of the manuscript traditions overtly refer to him as a Nazir. Again, uncut hair is emphasized concerning this man-child who will become a bold leader, priest, prophet and oversee a number of Israelite victories on the battlefield. The prophet Elijah, also associated with battle and victory (see 2 Kgs 2.12), is referred to as 'a man (who is literally an owner or lord of) of hair' (2 Kgs 1.8). Formulaic language in Judg. 5.2 and Deut. 32.42 suggests that the warrior has long locks (see the discussion of translation issues in Niditch 2008: 75–7). It is in part his long thick hair that identifies Absalom, son of King David, as a charismatic leader (2 Sam. 14.25-26) who is able to turn the heads of the people (2 Sam. 15.5-6), an appropriate royal heir, but in the beautifully developed tale of this would-be king, the hair purposefully misdirects and becomes the cause of his death. As Absalom flees from the unsuccessful battle against his own father, his hair becomes entangled in the branch of an oak and he hangs there impotent until he is killed by Joab, David's general (2 Sam. 18.9-15). It is the expected cultural meaning of hair as a marker of manly potency and warrior status that informs the tale's ironic twists and turns. Absalom ultimately was only a 'player', a rebellious son, not selected by God. Absalom's performance of power is ultimately unconvincing.

Esau's hairiness is another purposeful biblical misdirection concerning his future status, for it is the smooth son, his mother's favourite Jacob, who obtains the birthright and the blessing via tricksterism (Gen. 25.21-34). The hairy, red, manly hunter, his father's favourite and the eldest son, Esau, is not the one chosen by the deity to lead. This thread in biblical biographies reflects the traditional pattern of the success of the unlikely son and supports a message about divine autonomy or apparent serendipity. The tale about the success of the smooth man may also point to the presence of a female voice in Genesis, a collection that frequently presents women tricksters who fool the men around them and who have particular knowledge about matters pertaining to their sons (e.g. Rebekah, Rachel and Tamar).

Other biblical writers employ the hair motif to frame tales about status and competition between groups of men; the significance of enforced hair-cutting is at play in these accounts and further points to the role of this aspect of the body in creating and reinforcing cultural messages about gender and power (see Cook in this volume).

The interaction between Samson and Delilah in Judges 16 is probably the best-known scene of hair-cutting in the Western literary tradition. Samson's strength resides in his hair, worn in plaits like those of the hero Hercules. The source of his strength is, however, the hero's secret, and the Philistines hire a woman to seduce Samson into revealing how he can be made weak. The scene has often been treated as proof of the hero's foolishness, but, in fact, the passage preserves a tale of hubris built upon traditional-style repetition. With each response to Delilah's recurring question about the source of his strength, Samson offers a lie. Gut cords will tie him down, or is it rope, or is it weaving his hair in a loom? The final lie, invoking the webs of women, involves the hair but hides the full truth. The narrator thus builds drama before the true revelation. Finally Samson reveals the truth that no razor has ever touched his hair; it has grown free since his birth, for he is a Nazirite, a status demanded by the deity. If the hair is severed, his strength will be cut down. Samson expects to break free from the captors as before, but instead he is felled, bound and imprisoned. He frees himself and wreaks vengeance on the Philistines only once the hair grows back. Various oppositions emerge in this passage: between male and female; between Philistine and Israelite; between being an acculturated human and a free creature of nature; and between human status and divine.

Delilah ultimately controls Samson, and when he loses the deeply symbolic bodily medium of hair, his power is overcome, the heroic power of manhood. The Philistines make him 'play' before them, a term sometimes connected with sexual play (Gen. 26.8; Judg. 16.25). The language metaphorically thus suggests his being turned into a woman, a toy-thing. The long-haired Samson is, moreover, a feral creature, a being who lives apart from family and people, often dwelling in caves; he is unsuccessful in forming marital and affinal bonds and deals with ordinary human beings by means of secrecy and deception (Bynum 1990). He is, however, a favourite of the deity, chosen before birth to be a liberator. God makes water miraculously gush forth for Samson, a sign of his charismatic status, and his body is tamed or constructed only temporarily by Delilah and her allies. The long, never-cut hair thus invokes various complex aspects of Samson's identity, having to do with gender, ethnicity, acculturation and relationship to a personal deity. It is, however, the association between hair and manly power that most dominates imagery of long hair in the ancient literature of the Hebrew Bible, and, like blood, hair is a medium involved in the transformation of status (Olyan 1998). An excellent example is offered by 2 Sam. 10.4-5. Emissaries of David are treated by Ammonites as spies and sent back to the king with their beards shaven and their robes cut to the waist. The loss of hair conveys unmanning and humiliation as David himself acknowledges when he tells the men to return to the privacy of their homes until their beards grow back.

Irene J. Winter (1997) and Cynthia Chapman (2004) have explored visual evidence for absent and present hair in Assyrian iconography, noting that the figure who has the most and best hair has the power. Beards that drag in the dust belong to the vassal or prisoner or supplicant while the king's hair, proud and fulsome, reigns over the scene (Niditch 2008: 48–9; Chapman 2004: 39). Judahites who have been defeated are depicted in the triumphalist Assyrian Lachish reliefs as wearing stubble rather than beards (Niditch 2008: 55–6; for additional examples of hair in battle scenes see also Cifarelli 1998: 56–9; Winter 1997: 371). The loss of hair thus marks the loss of status in biblical worlds and the wider Levant, the diminishing of military or political power, but purposeful alteration of hair also provides a cultural means of observing and experiencing the personal loss of death.

Hair treatment, its cutting or dishevelment, is associated with mourning practices in a number of biblical sources discussed by Saul Olyan (1998) who emphasizes the transformative meanings and effects of such alterations in appearance. A variety of texts mention balding of the head and clipping of the beard (e.g. Job 1.20; Isa. 15.2; Jer. 16.6; 48.37; Ezek. 7.18), pointing to customs of male mourners, but some priestly texts place limits on the cutting of hair by a priest when someone close to him dies (Lev. 21.5, 10, 11). The high priest is not even allowed to dishevel his hair, perhaps a token version of hair-cutting allowed to other priests (see Niditch 2008: 107). The priest who is to avoid the dead and stay in a condition of ritual purity that allows him to enter sacred spaces and approach the deity is thus not permitted, to one degree or another, fully to partake in the custom of cutting hair for the dead. This practice must have been a comforting symbolization of change and loss, helping the mourner to announce his situation to those who would empathize and sympathize. It is also interesting that other texts generalize the prohibitions against the mourner's cutting of hair to all Israelites, implying perhaps that all Israelite men are holy (Deut. 14.1; Lev. 19.2) or clearly demarcating between customs of the body observed by Yahwists, a priestly people, and the customs of foreigners (Lev. 19.27-28).

These mourning customs pertaining to hair probably apply only to men, for some evidence, scant though it is, seems to suggest that women would have covered their hair while in public. The same eighth century BCE Assyrian reliefs that portray male Judahite exiles as wearing stubble rather than beards portray Judahite women who march into exile as wearing head coverings, even in the dire and humiliating circumstances of forced migration (Niditch 2008: 124). On the other hand, Isa. 3.24 does allude to aristocratic women's fancy hairdos, which in settings of divine punishment manifested in war, death and imprisonment will be replaced by balding. Michal Dayagi-Mendels, who studies material culture related to women's toilette in the ancient Levant, reads this passage to suggest a style of 'hair gathered and rolled in a knot at the back of the head, or a rolled up plait held by a pin in the Mesopotamian style' (Dayagi-Mendels 1993: 76–7). Perhaps such hair treatments would be exhibited only within the privacy of family quarters. The Judahite female figurines dating from the ninth to seventh centuries BCE also exhibit a variety of ornate hairstyles, but the issue of covering the hair or not covering might not be relevant to this sort of iconic material. Evidence from material culture that begins to address questions about the everyday appearance of women's hair is good to keep in mind, however, as we explore three biblical passages in legal corpora relating to the management of women's hair, a management controlled by men: Numbers 6 concerning a voluntary Nazirite vow available to women and men; Num. 5.11-31 dealing with the treatment of the woman accused of adultery in the absence of witnesses; and Deut. 21.10-14 discussing the treatment of captive women taken to wife. These examples of body management relate to the construction of gender, forms of cultural identity, ways of dealing with life-altering moments and means of transformation.

The self-assumed Nazirite vow not only parallels the Nazirism of Samson in the growing of hair but also involves a personal vow made by the would-be Nazirite, rather than divine selection (as in the case of Samson and the young men of Amos 2.11) or the vow of one's mother (as in the case of Samuel). Moreover, the vow emphasizes the avoidance of wine, a feature of Samson's mother's obligation while pregnant with her special son, and includes avoidance of the dead, a set period of time and ritual practices. Self-assumed Nazirism involves sacrificial offerings overseen by the priest at the opening and closing of the period of the vow. The vow moreover is available to men and to women. What does the female voluntary Nazirite get out of the vow, how is her status made manifest and how might others respond to her status?

If women did generally cover their hair in public, not cutting the hair might not be a visible sign of Nazirism. On the other hand, wearing the hair uncovered might serve as a public sign and wearing it very simply or down, a private sign, but the passage does not deal directly with these issues of visibility or with the range of meanings implied by the term פרע. To be sure, there is a quantity of hair to be shaved at the end of the vow period. Theoretically, a lengthy Nazirite commitment could lead to the locks becoming extremely long, but again this fullness of hair would make a public statement only if the woman showed her hair. If hair is a private matter, then women's not participating in funeral rites and in the conviviality of wine-drinking at festive occasions might be clearer public markers of this self-imposed status.

For men and women, the assumption of the vow, manifested in matters pertaining to the body such as the avoidance of the dead, the non-consumption of wine and the style of the hair, would be not only an act of devotion but also an assumption of an enviable holiness evocative of priests' sobriety before offering sacrifice and of their avoidance of the dead. Given the cost of sacrifices, the assumption of this status would also be a mark of enviable wealth. Priestly writers of the sixth century BCE, responsible for Numbers 6, might have offered or approved of a domesticated, gender-neutral form of holiness to rein in the significance of long-haired charismatic holy men who laid a claim to divine selection rather than personal piety. Any woman of wealth with the approval of husband or father (Num. 30.3-16), or any widow who makes her own choices concerning vows, can assume this variety of Nazirism as long as she has the means.

Being under the Nazirite vow not only projects wealth and sacred status but is also a strongly embodied and experiential form of religious experience. Untended, uncut hair in the ancient world may well be lice-ridden, as noted by Penina Galpaz-Feller (2004); it is a source of discomfort, a reminder of the vow. This condition, like being splashed with blood, evokes a physical response. She is temporarily transformed, and the holiness infuses her hair, which at the end of the vow is offered up under the well-being sacrifice. Her self-image and status are enhanced, and she is personally empowered by the act of vowing. At the same time, however, she helps the establishment to reframe the meaning and significance of Nazirism from a sign indicating the divine selection of particular men to an indication of personal devotion by any person, male or female.

Ritual actions involving the hair of a woman accused of adultery (Num. 5.11-31) and the hair of the captured bride (Deut. 21.10-14) are also rich in gendered implications and further emphasize the interplay between individual and social, personal and public dimensions that characterize body management and practice. In the former case, a woman is accused of adultery by her husband in the absence of witnesses, and the priest adjudicates by means of a series of ritual actions. In the climax of the ritual scene the woman is made to drink holy water that contains dust from the floor of the tabernacle and the ink of a curse, washed off from the document upon which the curse is written. The curse indicates that if she is guilty she will suffer bodily harm in her reproductive organs, but if she is innocent, no illness or impairment will follow. Her demeanour during this ritual includes a particular treatment of her hair by the priest (Num. 5.18). What does the phrase פרע את ראש האשה in this verse mean? He is doing something to the hair of her head. In noun form the term פרע refers to the long locks of the Nazirite. Clearly he cannot be making her suddenly have long locks. What is meant is probably letting her hair down, undoing a coiffure, dishevelling, having her hair revealed in a natural, naked state. The hair as symbol of her present status and situation relates well to the simple unoiled, un-spiced grain offering of jealousy, prepared by her husband, that the woman is given by the priest to hold as part of the ritual process, and to the uncomplicated water of bitterness that she must drink. Symbolism suggests the elemental and a kind of personal exposure. The grain she holds is unadorned, the watery concoction she consumes is composed of simple substances, and the hair is not covered or arrayed. She is being made at one level to go basic, to come clean, to let the truth be known, but at the same time she is under the control of others, the men around her, the accusing husband and the mediating priest. The ritual is publicly overseen by a figure of the religious establishment. The priest lays bare her hair, which is no longer modestly covered or coiffured to suit her status, age and taste. On the one hand, she becomes a kind of clean slate at the midpoint of a rite of passage, in what anthropologist Victor Turner calls the liminal or betwixt-and-between phase. On the other hand she is being laid bare, humiliated, for all to see. It is no coincidence that the Rabbinic presentation of the law concerning the woman accused of adultery suggests that she be stripped of her clothing as well (*m. Sot.* 1.5-7). Their discussion of how much of her body should be revealed in this ritual performance acknowledges the erotic and titillating nuances of the ritual from their perspective. Hair treatment thus marks status in transition, and a passage from guilty to punished or innocent to vindicated, but it also connotes cultural power, the power of the priest as figure of the male establishment and the vulnerability of the woman.

The treatment of women's hair again arises in questions concerning women captured in war. The point of view, once again, is that of the men who hold power over the women. From a sociocultural perspective, the problem addressed by Deut. 21.10-14 is how to transform 'their' women into 'our' women, how to effect a change in identity. The degree to which the woman's identity is constructed by male victors is very strong. Androcentrism and military triumphalism thus intertwine. If a man sees a woman he finds attractive – again the erotic is at play – he can take her as a wife. She is to go through ritual transformation whereby she is to shave her head, cut her nails and remove her clothing, dwelling in the conquering man's house and mourning her father and mother for a month. She has been separated from kin by means of their literal death or by her forced migration. Symbols of the body (hair, nails and clothing) join ritual crying and physical separation from her former life. She is from the writer's perspective beginning anew, and her demeanour and actions demarcate for him the passage from war to peace, and the resumption of ordinary life whereby the enemy is incorporated into the world of the victors. The male who claims her as spoils of war contextualizes her and she has no choice. For her, the cutting of her hair, like the letting down of the hair of the woman accused of adultery, once again marks humiliation, the altering or removal of identity, the process of transformation and the control of a man. Control of the hair connotes control of the person.

Deuteronomy 21.14, however, admits of some discomfort on the writer's part. Should he decide he does not wish to have the captive as a wife after all, he can divorce her, but he cannot sell her into slavery. He has to let her go because he has 'humiliated her' or 'raped her' or 'afflicted her'. All of these nuances are included in the piel of the root ענה. This verb describes the rape of Dinah (Gen. 34.2), the enslavement of the Israelites in Egypt (Deut. 26.6) and Sarah's harsh treatment of Hagar (Gen. 16.6). The underlying message is perhaps that this way of obtaining a wife is not to be desired.

Closing thoughts

Close work with bodily media of blood and hair points to the continuing relevance of theoretical reflections on the material of religious identity, offered by seminal scholars such as Mary Douglas (1966), Claude Lévi-Strauss (1968), Victor Turner (1967, 1969), Pierre Bourdieu (1990) and Clifford Geertz (1973), whose ideas explicitly or implicitly lie behind my study. Also at play is the work of scholars such as Meredith McGuire (2008), Robert Orsi (2003) and Colleen McDannell (1995), whose attention to lived religion and material religion relates well to the concept of the body as 'social project' employed by Francesca Stavrakopoulou (2013) in her study of body modification.

Body practices are not only embedded in cultural contexts and performatively and publicly expressed but also have to do with the personal, experiential and private dimensions of lived religion. Interplays between the poles of self and society, private and public, operate in each of the case studies presented above. Human beings moreover make sense of their immediate situations with reference both to workaday life settings and the broader cosmic scheme of things. Our case studies thus point to the experiential, visceral aspect of being daubed with blood, of possibly feeling guilty about eating animal flesh or about participating in the rape of foreign women made wives against their will, of feeling lice crawling in long, uncut Nazirite hair and thereby being reminded that one is engaged in an act of devotion. We point to the self in transition being remade or whole via balding or dishevelment after contact with the dead or after recovering from leprosy, of the self being exhibited in an accusation of adultery. We might think of the way in which the captured bride experiences being remade against her will with the loss of her hair, the unmanning experienced by shaved captives. At the same time treatments of blood and hair involve public display and interaction with the religious establishment in the ritual for the woman accused of adultery or the conclusion of the Nazirite vow. Life passages achieved via the manipulation of blood or hair, or daily habits concerning these bodily substances, identify participants as sharing a cultural identity or indicate place in a social index. Being a member of 'our' group versus 'theirs', being male rather than female, or female rather than male, is publicly exhibited, and cultural categories are demarcated and reinforced. Power is negotiated and displayed: the lost power of Samson or the captured woman, the self-imposed status of the Nazirite, the power of the priest to make clean or exonerate or condemn. To adapt the language of Clifford Geertz (1973: 114), body practices provide not only models of what one believes but also a model for believing it. A person's own identity is announced and performed in the relationship to blood or hair, even while reinforcing the sense of identity shared by others who observe or participate in his or her behaviour. The construction of gender, personally experienced and publicly displayed, is a recurring theme in our study: it is evident, for example, in the way in which hair treatment relates to Absalom's manly pretensions or the vulnerability of the captured bride, and it is attested in the power of Rachel's menstrual blood. Finally, the study of body practices involving blood and hair points to the complexity, multivocality and fluidity in material expressions of lived religion, the changes that occur through time and the differences of meaning that exist at the same time: the way in which menstrual blood disempowers and empowers; the way in which meat-eating detached from sacrifice becomes more habitual, even while nuances of blood symbolism remain; the way in which the hair of the Nazirite, closely related to manly power of the divinely chosen, becomes an available identifier of religious orientation for wealthy women; the way in which blood is forbidden for consumption, but is cleansing of the leper and satiating to the deity.

The treatments of blood and hair in biblical literature evidence humans beings' efforts to grapple with essential matters in life and death: ambivalence concerning the process of sustaining life by killing and consuming the flesh of other living beings; men's ambivalences concerning the mysteries of women's procreation; ways of marking the loss of kin; means of satisfying a devouring deity who holds the power of life and death; ways of dealing with the life-altering effects of war.

References

Barmash, P. (2005), *Homicide in the Biblical World*, Cambridge: Cambridge University Press.
Bourdieu, P. (1990), *The Logic of Practice*, trans. Richard Nice, Stanford, CA: Stanford University Press.
Bynum, D. E. (1990), 'Samson as a Biblical φὴρ ὀρεκῷος', in S. Niditch (ed.), *Text and Tradition: The Hebrew Bible and Folklore*, 57–73, Semeia Studies, Atlanta, GA: Scholars Press.

Chapman, C. (2004), *The Gendered Language of Warfare in the Israelite-Assyrian Encounter*, Harvard Semitic Monographs, Winona Lake, IN: Eisenbrauns.

Cifarelli, M. (1998), 'Gesture and Alterity in the Art of Ashurbanipal II of Assyria', *Art Bulletin* 80: 210–28.

Dayagi-Mendels, M. (1993), *Perfumes and Cosmetics in the Ancient World*, Jerusalem: Israel Museum.

Douglas, M. (1966), *Purity and Danger: An Analysis of Concepts of Pollution and Taboo*, New York: Praeger.

Eilberg-Schwartz, H. (1990), *The Savage in Judaism: An Anthropology of Israelite Religion and Ancient Judaism*, Bloomington, IN: Indiana University Press.

Galpaz-Feller, P. (2004), 'Hair in the Hebrew Bible and in Ancient Egyptian Culture: Cultural and Private Connotations', *Biblische Notizen* 125: 75–94.

Geertz, C. (1973), *The Interpretation of Cultures*, New York: Basic Books.

Geller, S. A. (1992), 'Blood Cult: Toward a Literary Theology of the Priestly Work of the Pentateuch', *Prooftexts* 12: 97–124.

Gennep, A. van ([1908] 1960), *The Rites of Passage*, Chicago, IL: University of Chicago Press.

Geyer, J. B. (2007), 'Blood and the Nations in Ritual and Myth', *Vetus Testamentum* 57: 1–20.

Gilders, W. (2004), *Blood Ritual in Hebrew Bible: Meaning and Power*, Baltimore, MD: Johns Hopkins University Press.

King, P. J., and L. E. Stager (2001), *Life in Biblical Israel*, Louisville, KY: Westminster John Knox Press.

Klawans, J. (2006), *Purity, Sacrifice, and the Temple: Symbolism and Supersessionism in the Study of Ancient Judaism*, Oxford: Oxford University Press.

Lévi-Strauss, C. (1968), 'The Structural Study of Myth', in T. A. Sebeok (ed.), *Myth: A Symposium*, 81–106, Bloomington: Indiana University Press.

McDannell, C. (1995), *Material Christianity: Religion and Popular Culture in America*, New Haven, CT: Yale University Press.

McGuire, M. B. (2008), *Lived Religion: Faith and Practice in Everyday Life*, Oxford: Oxford University Press.

Milgrom, J. (1998), *Leviticus 1–16: A New Translation with Introduction and Commentary*, Anchor Yale Bible Commentary, New Haven, CT: Yale University Press.

Neusner, J. (1982), *Formative Judaism. Religious, Historical, and Literary Studies*, Brown Judaic Studies, Chico, CA: Scholars Press.

Niditch, S. (2008), *'My Brother Esau Is a Hairy Man': Hair and Identity in Ancient Israel*, Oxford: Oxford University Press.

Niditch, S. (2011), 'Good Blood, Bad Blood: Multivocality, Metonymy, and Mediation in Zechariah 9', *Vetus Testamentum* 61: 629–45.

Olyan, S. M. (1998), 'What Do Shaving Rites Accomplish and What Do They Signal in Biblical Ritual Contexts?', *Journal of Biblical Literature* 117: 611–22.

Orsi, R. (2003), 'Is the Study of Lived Religion Irrelevant to the World We Live In?' *Journal for the Scientific Study of Religion* 42: 169–74.

Stavrakopoulou, F. (2013), 'Making Bodies: On Body Modification and Religious Materiality in the Hebrew Bible', *Hebrew Bible and Ancient Israel* 2 (4): 532–53.

Turner, V. (1967), 'Themes in the Symbolism of Ndembu Hunting Ritual', in J. Middleton (ed.), *Myth and Cosmos: Readings in Mythology and Symbolism*, 249–69, Garden City, NY: Natural History Press.

Turner, V. (1969), *The Ritual Process: Structure and Anti-Structure*, Ithaca, NY: Cornell University Press.

Winter, I. J. (1997), 'Art in Empire: The Royal Image and the Visual Dimensions of Assyrian Ideology', in S. Parpola and R. M. Whiting (eds), *Assyria 1995: Proceedings of the 10th Anniversary Symposium of the Neo-Assyrian Text Corpus Project, Helsinki, September 7–11, 1995*, 359–81, Winona Lake, IN: Eisenbrauns.

CHAPTER THREE

Wherever the corpse is, there the vultures will gather

MATTHEW J. SURIANO

The natural association of vultures with corpses is one that resonates in cultures past and present, ranging from the New Testament (Mt. 24.28; Lk. 17.37), quoted in the title of this chapter, to images that are found throughout the media (Van Dooren 2011: 12–54). The threatening images of human bodies devoured by vultures are manifold, appearing in epic literature from *Gilgamesh* to Homer, in ancient Near Eastern royal inscriptions and palace reliefs, as well as in biblical literature. These images certainly conjure negative reactions, but the vulture as a symbol in sources both modern and ancient can also be viewed as benign and even benevolent (McMahon 2016: 178–81). The animal has not always been seen as a herald of doom and destruction even in the starkest examples of vultures feeding upon corpses. The diversity of cultural images associated with the carrion-feeding species, particularly the fact that the bird's relation to corpses can evoke different responses, says as much about vultures as it does about dead bodies.

The vulture's role as positive or negative is culturally determined. This is evident in the *dakhma* (or Tower of Silence) in Zoroastrian mortuary practices as well as with Tibetan sky burials, both of which involve vultures defleshing the corpse (Van Dooren 2011: 62–70). In ancient Egypt, where vultures were mummified, their imagery is connected to goddesses such as Mut and Nekhbet (Ikram 2012: 41), and they were associated with protection (Shonkwiler 2012). The prominence of vulture imagery in Late Chalcolithic sealings from northern Mesopotamia may be due to the bird's useful role in reducing accumulated organic waste, including animal remains, which would have been a problem during the region's rapid urban growth during the early fourth millennium BCE (McMahon 2016: 180–1). It has even been suggested that early hominids used hovering vultures to locate carcasses as sources of meat (Morelli et al. 2015: 450–1). It is easy to imagine how the vulture could develop powerful and at times even positive associations in early human cultures, but vulture imagery could also be puzzling. The role of the vulture in scenes of the dead can vary depending on how human cultures respond to death, conjuring associations that are benign, benevolent or negative.

The various responses to vultures and dead bodies reflect, in part, the extent to which corpses are both biological realities and cultural constructs (see Suriano 2018: 19–28, and Stavrakopoulou in this volume). The treatment of the dead body, the body's contextualization, the manners by which the remains of the dead are controlled and

FIGURE 3.1: Depiction of vultures and corpses in Shrine VII, 8, Çatalhöyük (from Mellaart 1964: 65, Fig. 20). Image reproduced by permission of Cambridge University Press.

manipulated, all assign meaning to the corpse.[1] But the meanings assigned to a corpse due to the presence of vultures can vary. This chapter will look at three independent occurrences of Near Eastern scenes that involve live carrion-feeding raptors (vultures) and the remains of dead humans (corpses). The three examples are otherwise unrelated and come from Anatolia during the Neolithic period (Çatalhöyük), Mesopotamia during the Early Dynastic III (the Stele of Vultures from Girsu) and the Hebrew Bible (Ezekiel 39). In each occurrence, the vulture lends different meanings to the corpse. Moreover, the vulture as symbol in relation to the corpse can evoke varying imagery related to either the divine cosmos or the natural world, and this imagery can serve different functions, either mythological or historical.

Vulture and corpse at Çatalhöyük

James Mellaart's 1960s excavations at the Neolithic site of Çatalhöyük in the central Anatolian plateau revealed multiple examples of wall art prominently featuring vultures and corpses. Painted scenes discovered in two so-called 'shrines' from Level VII (8 and 21) and a third from Level VIII (8) depict large birds, griffon vultures (*Gyps fulvus*), together with smaller human bodies that are headless (Mellaart 1964: 64, Plates VII [b], VIII [a], IX; see Figure 3.1). Although one human figure is headed, apparently waving at the vultures, the general absence of heads suggests that the human figures are corpses. This point is further supported by the horizontal position of the bodies beneath the vultures. The carrion birds are bigger than the humans and are rendered in greater detail as they hover above. The association of vulture and corpse is natural, given the bird's role as scavenger and carrion-feeder. Yet despite this natural association, the role of the

---

1 Of course, even the use of the word 'corpse' to distinguish a dead body can be value-laden. In this chapter the word will be used to describe any identifiable human body-part that is still fleshed.

vulture is unclear and open to interpretation. Indeed, vultures have played a prominent role in the interpretation of the complicated and somewhat enigmatic mortuary culture at Çatalhöyük.

To begin, the wall art never depicts the vultures feeding directly upon the dead bodies, nor are they seen carrying body parts. The relationship between corpse and vulture at Çatalhöyük is not as clear as was once thought (see Figure 3.1). Corpses and disarticulated body parts also play a prominent role at the site. Excavations have discovered several intramural burials as well as collections of human remains (specifically skulls). The burials are generally found in what Ian Hodder (2016: 1–2) calls multiple 'burial houses' and 'history houses'. The latter term is the name Hodder gives to Mellaart's 'shrines', structures that were rebuilt over multiple phases above multiple burials (Hodder 2016: 1). Hodder's work on the history houses, in fact, offers insight into the intersecting roles of vultures and the dead.

James Mellaart (1967) first suggested that the people at Çatalhöyük practiced exposure as a means of defleshing the corpse. The portrayal of vultures circling above corpses was seen as a depiction of this process. Once the process of excarnation was complete, the bones would be secondarily interred under the floors of homes. Mellaart theorized further that the ancient inhabitants of Çatalhöyük used a charnel room or platform that facilitated the vultures' feeding while protecting the bones from other scavengers that might destroy the corpse. The practice of excarnation, or defleshing, was also tied to the burial of headless bodies and the preservation of skulls found in some of the homes, at least one of which was plastered. For Mellaart (1964: 64), the vultures symbolically represented 'the Great Goddess in her aspect of death'. According to Mellaart, the animal's importance was reflected in the preservation of vulture skulls on the plastered walls of homes.

Mellaart's theories regarding the burial customs and religious practices at Çatalhöyük have been contested over the years. In particular, his concept of a religion centred around a great goddess has been largely abandoned (Hodder 2006). Mellaart's idea of excarnation gained some adherence largely due to the prominence of vultures in the wall paintings (see Macqueen 1978). Yet subsequent studies have pointed out problems with the theory, beginning with the fact that there is no apparent charnel room among the remains at Çatalhöyük (Düring 2003: 1–15). Hodder's re-excavation of the site has shown that the majority of burials were single inhumations (also called primary burials), which challenged Mellaart's earlier explanations involving vultures and secondary burials (Andrews, Molleson and Boz 2005; Boz and Hager 2013). Furthermore, osteological analysis notes that the human bones display little evidence of defleshing by animals (Andrews, Molleson and Boz 2005: 264–6; Boz and Hager 2013: 415).

Over time, other theories have formed around the unique remains at Çatalhöyük. One recent suggestion is that the scenes of vultures hovering over headless bodies depict a military victory, and the skull collections served as some form of 'head hunting' (see Dolce 2018: 36–37; citing Testart 2008). The theory is unlikely. Skull curation is part of a wider phenomenon of manipulating dead bodies at Çatalhöyük. Moreover, the reuse of space in the history rooms, and the practice of intramural burial in those spaces, seems to relate to a concept of ancestry tied to the house (Hodder 2006: 163–5; 2016: 1–6). Skull curation and bone retrieval were part of a cultural strategy to create memory. The question again, however, is how to explain more clearly the symbolic role of the vultures. In the past few years the theory of defleshing by vultures at Çatalhöyük has come full circle. Recent experimental work on the feeding habits of vultures has shown that the species of bird mainly consumes the body's soft tissue in a manner that does not result in the total disarticulation of the corpse, nor does it leave clear markings on the bones (Pilloud et al. 2016: 735–43; Haddow and Knüsel 2017: 65; see already Andrews, Molleson and Boz 2005: 275). Furthermore, vultures will deflesh a corpse in a relatively short period of time, which would be beneficial for secondary burials.

These observations raise the possibility that secondary burial was practised, involving defleshed skeletal remains that were relatively intact. At Çatalhöyük, skull curation, single inhumations alongside reburials, and the retrieval and collection of skeletal remains present a range of mortuary practices that defy typical definitions of primary and secondary burials (Pilloud et al. 2016; Haddow and Knüsel 2017). These extensive mortuary remains reveal that the interaction between the living and the dead was complex and dynamic. The carrion bird may have been involved in this interaction, though it is no longer necessary to associate vultures with a great goddess. The iconography at Çatalhöyük links vultures with corpses and this association is found at other Neolithic sites (Hodder 2006: 146; Hodder and Meskell 2011).[2] At Çatalhöyük, the headless bodies found in the intramural inhumations and the practice of skull curation, including one that was plastered, speak to particular value placed on the removal of the human head. The phenomenon of plastered skulls appears elsewhere in the Near East during the Neolithic period, notably the Levant (Twiss 2007: 30–1), and although it is often seen as a physical means of constructing ancestors, the exact nature of the practice is unclear (Hodder 2006: 146–7). That the skulls were not exclusively those of mature males (Bonogofsky 2003; 2005) simply means that we must recognize other forms of ancestral identity encompassing various age and gender categories (Meskell 2008: 380).

Lynn Meskell (2008) has suggested that at Çatalhöyük, headless and postcranial bodies, figurine artistry and the preservation of animal remains reveal a common desire for permanence. The plastering of animal skulls and horns, including vulture beaks and talons, is a form of refleshing that blurs the boundaries modern interpreters create separating animals and ancestors (Meskell 2008: 383; Hodder and Meskell 2011: 248–9). The plastering of skulls and the plastered animal heads embedded on the walls of homes are ways of creating objects that exist in the present yet are durable reminders of the past.

Still, the symbolic role of the vulture and the relationship between this species of bird and dead bodies requires further explanation. Elsewhere, Meskell and Hodder (2011) refer to the embedding of vulture beaks and claws on the plaster walls of homes, and Mellaart (1964: 70) described plastered vulture skulls in Shrine VI.B.10, but the analysis of bird bones from the renewed excavations identified only a single vulture bone (Russell and McGowan 2005: 104–5). This relative paucity is telling. According to one study (Pilloud et al. 2016: 741), 'the lack of vulture remains on site is consistent with it being a symbolic/totemic symbol, similar to the lack of other wild animals remains found on site, despite their frequent depiction in the art (e.g., bear and leopard)'. It is equally possible that the situation is due to the vulture's symbolic power as an avatar of death, where the animal becomes specifically related to conceptualizations of mortality. The idea of symbolically refleshing human and animal heads with plaster, inside the settlement, can

---

2 For instance, phallic and headless imagery are combined and displayed alongside (possible) skull and raptor imagery in a monumental T-shaped pillar discovered at the Neolithic site of Göbleki Tepe in eastern Turkey; see Meskell (2008: 376).

be paralleled with the possible defleshing of the dead by means of vulture, outside the settlement. This suggestion coincides with Meskell's observation (2008) that the ritual collection and preservation of bodies served as a means of transcending domains both non-human and human.

If the headless forms represent corpses, and as such stand for death, the hovering vultures could reasonably stand for the chaotic power of death. The vulture's appearance in the cultural practices at Çatalhöyük, most prominently in the wall art, would relate to wider concerns of control that are set within the site but reflect the world surrounding it. Referring to the wall art depicting headless bodies and similar depictions, though not the vultures specifically, Meskell writes (2008: 376): 'these evocations are part of a domesticated social reality, grappling with vagaries of the past, the fear of the unknown and an attempt to control the future'. Hodder has even suggested that historical thought at Çatalhöyük was domestically situated, hence the term 'history houses'. According to Hodder,

> There seem to be two main types of history making that occur at Çatalhöyük. The first involves repetitive practices in which the same activity occurs in the same place in a building over time. The second involves the curation and retrieval of objects from earlier building and their deposition in later buildings. (Hodder 2016: 2)

The repetition not only of architectural forms but also of painted scenes can be read as an early exercise in historical thought. The mythic motif of the vulture, so common elsewhere in the Neolithic Near East, here takes on a specific valence through the repetition of wall art showing the birds flying above headless bodies. This coincides with the second form of history-making: the collection and management of human remains, specifically heads, from the intramural burials. Whereas the collection of human remains probably related to genealogical formations of the past involving ancestors, the vulture's natural association as carrion-feeder here plays a timeless role in relation to the reoccurrence of death in the present world.

The Stele of Vultures from Girsu

The second example, known as the Stele of Vultures, comes from Sumer and dates to the Early Dynastic III period. The artefact's name comes from the scene that adorns the top portion of the stone slab that depicts vultures flying away with the remains of the dead (see Figures 3.2 and 3.4). The fragments of the stele were discovered in the sacred precinct of Girsu (modern Telloh); today it is reconstructed and displayed at the Louvre.[3] The stele is a victory monument, commemorating the defeat of the Sumerian city-state of Umma by its rival Lagash. The stele has artwork and cuneiform writing on both sides. The iconography on either side differs in that the obverse shows the god of Lagash, Ningirsu, seated and holding a net filled with defeated soldiers, whereas the reverse shows the victorious forces of Lagash and corpses of Umma's defeated army. The contrast in the scenes on the obverse and reverse sides has been interpreted as reflecting a duality of the mythic and historical, respectively (Winter 1985: 20 nn. 44–6; see also Moortgat 1969: 42–3). Additionally, the inscription does not easily fit the iconography – they

---

3 See further Cooper (1983; 1986: 33–9); Frayne (2008: 126) [=RIMA E1.9.3.1]; also Winter (1985: 13–16); Bahrani (2008: 147–50).

FIGURE 3.2: Vultures carrying away the remains of the dead. Given the size of the raptors relative to the human body parts they carry, the birds are probably cinereous vultures (*Aegypius monachus*), one of the largest of the Old World vultures. Top left of the Stele of Vultures, reverse, Register 4 (picture from Heuzey 1884: Plate 24 A).

both tell similar stories but with different agendas (Winter 1985: 22). The agenda of the narrative art, to use Irene Winter's term, is what concerns us here. The narrative is organized into four registers, the bottom of which is almost entirely destroyed. At least two of the scenes that follow in the three registers above it, however, feature corpses in different states. The culminating scene shows body parts being consumed by vultures. As such, the narrative art offers valuable insight into the role of vultures in the phenomenology of death in the ancient Near East.

The order of the registers has been a point of discussion. Although most scholars read the scenes from top to bottom, Winter (1985: 18–19 n. 37) argued that the narrative begins at the bottom (see Figure 3.4). Her reading of the narrative art sought to explain how it complements the accompanying Sumerian inscription, which tells a slightly different story. In the inscription the ruler of Lagash, E-annatum, has a dream-vision that promises him victory in his city-state's long-standing territorial dispute with neighbouring Umma (RIMA E1.9.3.1 obv. *vi*, 25–32). The cuneiform text continues and records E-annatum's subsequent victory over Umma. The narrative art depicts E-annatum's victory and portrays his defeated enemy as corpses in the second and fourth registers. These scenes are the fulfilment of the divine word given to E-annatum. The top register featuring the vultures is allusive of the line in the text (RIMA E1.9.3.1 obv. *vii*, 21–22) where the ruler of Lagash is told: 'Their [Umma's] myriad corpses will reach the base of heaven.' The

FIGURE 3.3: Workers climbing a mound of naked corpses, carrying materials to build a burial mound (saḫar-du$_6$-tag$_4$). Stele of Vultures, reverse, Register 2 (picture from Heuzey 1884: Plate 24 C).

second register corresponds with another part of the text (RIMA E1.9.3.1 obv. *xi*, 12–14) that envisions a victorious E-annatum constructing twenty tumuli (saḫar-du$_6$-tag$_4$) for the mass burial of Umma's dead (see Figure 3.3). Thus, according to Winter (1985: 19–23), the scenes progressively tell of the vision's promise of victory and the final realization of this promise. According to this reading, the culmination of the narrative art is the scene in the top register (the fourth) that shows Umma's discarded dead littering the battlefield where vultures feed upon them.

The vultures play a prominent role in the stele's narrative, regardless of which direction one reads, and despite the fact that there is no mention of birds within the text. Vultures are featured in the uppermost area of the top register, filling the sky above the battlefield. The vultures either begin or end this story of victory. But the birds are not shown in isolation from the rest of the action; they are part of the story as they carry off the mortal remains of Lagash's foes. The association of corpse and vulture is key to this scene, and it raises questions regarding the role of dead bodies in the narrative art of the stele's reverse side. In the top register we see vultures carrying off specific body parts: arms and several heads. On the same register's left side, the army of Lagash follows their leader, marching on top of the fallen bodies of their enemies. Thus the corpse is depicted in two

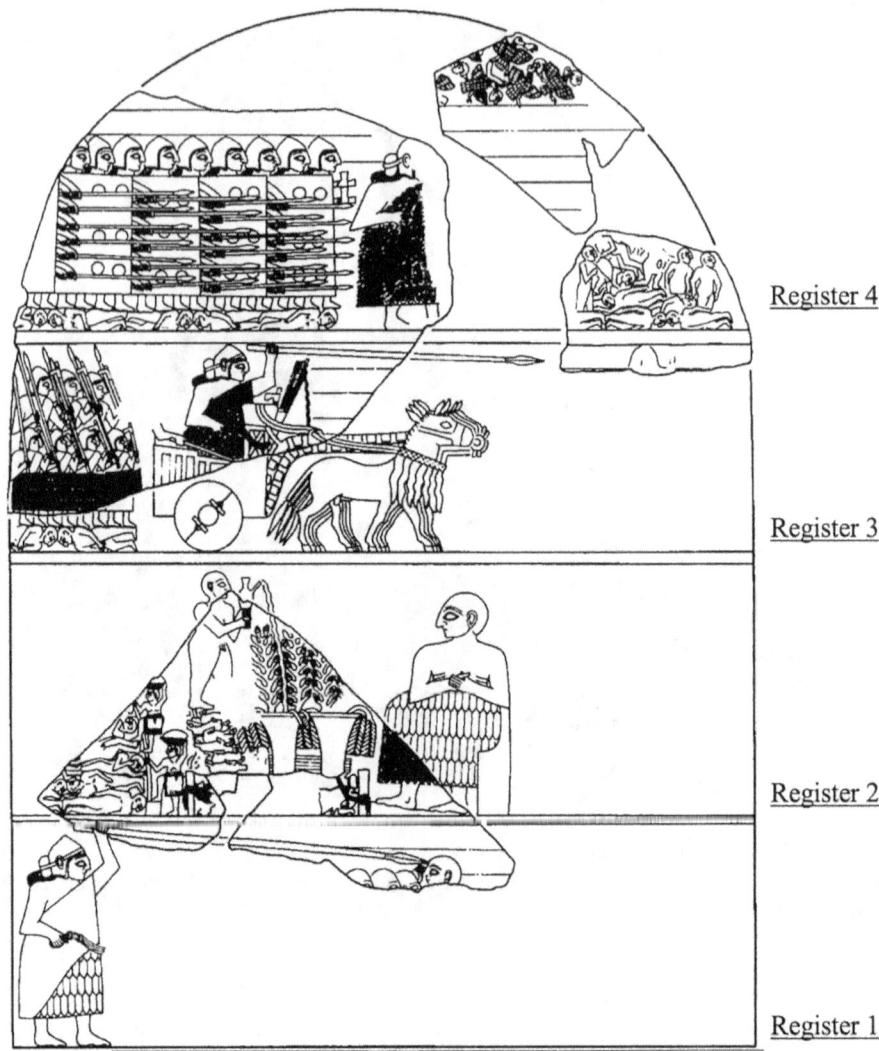

FIGURE 3.4: Reconstruction of the reverse side of the Stele of Vultures. From Winter (1985: 16, Fig. 8; drawing by Elizabeth Simpson). Image courtesy of Irene Winter.

forms: intact and trampled upon by humans, and torn apart by the forces of nature. In the wake of Lagash's victory, the ground below and sky above are both filled with Umma's unburied dead.

The second register also features corpses, but the scene here contrasts with the top (fourth) register. Here dead bodies are amassed and workers are shown climbing atop the mass burial, covering the dead with debris (Figure 3.3). The contrast between this scene of burial and the unburied dead in the top register has led some to suggest that the dead in the second belong to Lagash (Parrot 1961: 136; Frankfort 1996: 71; Selz 2004: 196–7), so that the scene depicts E-annatum burying his own dead, standing in contrast to the depiction of Umma's dead at the top of the stele. The problem with this reading begins with the fact that the bodies are naked. The nakedness of the corpses displays shame, but it also robs the dead of any form of identity. Unlike the army of Lagash depicted in the above registers, Umma's dead in the second register are stripped of weapons, shields and anything else that would identify their status as warriors. Their state is assumed in their mass burial. This point relates to the main contrast in the depiction of corpses in the second and fourth registers. In the second register, Umma's dead are buried by E-annatum's forces. The burial is a final act of victory by Lagash and this display of the dead serves as a type of victory monument (Nadali 2007: 352). Umma is unable to gather its dead from the battlefield because Lagash controls the area. The dire consequences of this situation can be seen at the top of the stele. Left unburied, Umma's dead will be destroyed by both nature and humans. The situation is rectified instead by Lagash, but the form of interment is ignominious.

The mass burial displayed in the second register serves several important functions. Aage Westenholz had suggested two possible reasons for this scene and for similar ones found elsewhere in the ancient Near East:

> The reasons for burying the enemies in mounds may have been either that the wars in Mesopotamia of the third millennium were normally fought between cities close enough to each other, so that the victor as well as the defeated had reason to fear wrathful and restless spirits of the unburied dead ... Or the reason may be that the victorious king wanted the burial mounds to stand as a warning to future adversaries, much like the victory stelas with their reliefs and inscriptions commemorating the defeat of the enemy and usually set up near the battlefield itself. (Westenholz 1970: 30)

While the first reason is speculative,[4] the second is grounded in the realities surrounding the stele. Moreover, E-annatum's appropriation of corpses denies Umma agency over its dead. Umma cannot collect the bodies of its defeated forces; it cannot bury its own dead. The mass burial performed by Lagash serves a critical function in this stele. E-annatum uses Umma's dead to mark the extent and reach of his power. The conflict between Umma and Lagash was territorial, their dispute was over an area known as the Gu'edena (Cooper 1983: 24–8; Levtow 2014: 28–31). The specific type of burial erected by E-annatum is called the saḫar-du$_6$-tag$_4$. The term can be roughly translated as 'burial mound' (Suriano 2012: 218–20), but the compound word includes the Sumerian words for 'dust' (saḫar) and 'mound' or 'ruin-hill' (du$_6$). The term is known from other Sumerian sources and is part of a long tradition in Mesopotamia of burying enemies (Westenholz 1970: 29; Richardson 2007: 193–6). In the second register, a layer of debris is shown covering the mound of corpses. Workers who climb this mound bring debris carried in baskets atop their heads. These mounds were physical markers and here they marked the boundaries of Lagash over and against Umma. Moreover, the references to stelae throughout the cuneiform text (Levtow 2014), together with the references to the burial mound and the depictions of the dead, come together in the Stele of Vultures to form the final statement at the conclusion of Lagash's long-standing border war with Umma (Bahrani 2008: 151). The carrion-feeding vultures are reminders of what is at stake if Umma violates conditions that set this boundary.

---

4 Even if Gebhard Selz (2004: 196) is correct in interpreting the figure pouring water in the second register as a visual depiction of the rituals of the ki.a.naĝ ('place of pouring water'), where the dead were given sustenance, this does not require that ritual performance was driven by a fear of the dead. Nor does it mean that the dead in this register are the fallen soldiers of Lagash (as Selz insists). Furthermore, the ki.a.naĝ interpretation is not certain.

The contrast of corpses in the Stele of Vultures in fact involves the entire stele and is not limited to the second and fourth registers on the reverse side. The stele's front side (obverse) shows dead bodies filling Ningirsu's net, acknowledging that Lagash's victory was divinely granted. According to Zainab Bahrani (2008: 151), the image of Ningirsu shows that 'the act of controlling death is thereby attributed to the god, not the ruler'. Her reading is supported by the fact that E-annatum does not appear on the reverse standing victoriously upon Umma's corpses, a motif seen in other royal inscriptions (Bahrani 2008: 151). Yet as Winter (1985: 26) has observed, the repeated scenes of E-annatum in action effectively enforces his role as king in the narrative art of the reverse. This depiction complements the role of the deity on the stele's obverse. E-annatum leads his army as they trample Umma's corpses, and he oversees the burial of Umma's dead. If Ningirsu controls death, then E-annatum controls the dead. The 'iconic' presentation of Ningirsu on the obverse prefaces the reverse side's 'narrative' presentation of E-annatum's victory (following Winter 1985: 20). Anton Moortgat (1969: 43) once suggested that the two sides reflected Sumerian dualism, separating the 'divine world' from the 'mortal world'. But death plays a role on both sides of the stele regardless of whether one adopts the categories of myth and history. If the obverse is meant to present Lagash's victory as destiny, the reverse visualizes the realities of this victory. The stark portrayal of Umma's corpses and the vultures that feed upon them convey this reality.

Birds, corpses and Gog's burial in Ezekiel 39

The final example comes from the vision of Gog's defeat and burial in Ezek. 39.1-21. The vision contains multiple descriptions of birds and beasts feeding upon the dead (39.4-5, 17-21), and like the Stele of Vultures, the motif of carrion-feeding is presented alongside an image of burial.[5] In her comparative study of Ezekiel 39 and Mesopotamian literature, Francesca Stavrakopoulou (2010: 76–82) showed that Yahweh's mass burial of Gog's dead is a form of corpse abuse that parallels the destruction of the corpses by wild animals. Moreover, Stavrakopoulou has drawn attention to the passage's literary context within Ezekiel. Accordingly, Yahweh's appropriation of Gog's dead and the abuse of corpses in 39.1-21 contrasts with Yahweh's reburial of Israel two chapters earlier (37.1-14). In both chapters the remains of the dead play a critical role, and the depiction of their care and abuse serve as object lessons in the prophetic message. Set within this literary context, the birds and other carrion-feeding animals play a critical role in symbolizing divine control over the dead.

Ezekiel 39 begins by addressing Gog, which was already introduced in chapter 38 as an enigmatic nation and Israel's enemy (Zimmerli 1983: 299–302; Lust 1999; see Stavrakopoulou 2010: 69–70 n. 10). The oracle that follows describes Yahweh's victory over Gog and can be read as three scenes (cf. Stavrakopoulou 2010: 76). In the first scene (39.4-10), the fallen soldiers of Gog are left exposed and are preyed upon by carrion-feeding raptors and other animals. The bodies that litter the open field are also plundered

---

5 The use of graves as territorial markers and the prominent role of carrion birds in Ezek. 39.1-29 bears important similarities to the Stele of Vultures. The possible dating of Ezekiel ranges from the late neo-Babylonian through Achaemenid periods to the Hellenistic period, almost two thousand years later than E-annatum's victory stele. It is likely that the similarities are due to the Mesopotamian background of both. The motif of desecrating corpses was quite common in neo-Assyrian royal inscriptions not long before Ezekiel's time; cf. Richardson (2007).

by the Israelites. In the second scene (39.11-16), the Israelites will bury Gog's dead in the land of Israel at a place appointed by Yahweh. The third and final scene (39.17-21) involves birds and other animals feasting upon Gog's dead. Thus, the motif of birds feeding upon corpses begins and ends the pericope in the first and final scenes (39.4-5 and 17-21), effectively framing the depictions of plunder and interment. There has been a tendency among biblical scholars to read 39.11-16 as a later insertion because it seems out of place before the scene of the carrion feast that follows (Eichrodt 1970: 521, 526–9; Zimmerli 1983: 315; see Stavrakopoulou 2010: 81–2 and 81 n. 57 with sources), yet this redactional approach overlooks the overarching theme of 39.1-21. Gog is defeated by Israel's deity, and the abuse of corpses symbolizes this divine victory from start to finish.

Stavrakopoulou (2010: 81–2) has compared the different images in Ezekiel 39 with Jer. 7.32-33 and suggested that the scene of feasting carrion birds in Ezek. 39.17-21 represents an inversion of the burials in 39.11-16. Gog's dead, buried by Israel in the previous verses, are here disinterred to dishonour the nation further. The suggestion offers an enticing view of the literary motifs at work in the passage, but all the same, the carrion birds frame the scenes of corpse abuse and do not necessarily contradict the burials that are described in 39.11-16. The animal imagery is overarching. Similar to Irene Winter's reading of the narrative art in the Stele of Vultures, the carrion birds in 39.17-21 form the ultimate scene in a larger project of dishonouring the dead of a defeated enemy.

The references to carrion-feeders in Ezek. 39.4, 17 include birds and other animals, *ḥayyat haśśāde*, 'beasts of the field'. While both birds and beasts are mentioned categorically, the term used for the former begins with the more particular word for a bird of prey, which can also connote a carrion-feeding raptor: *'ayiṭ* (Kogan 2006: 286; Altmann 2019: 16–20; see Gen. 15.11; Isa. 18.6; Jer. 12.9). As in the case of the Sumerian text in the Stele of Vultures, the specific word 'vultures' is never used in Ezekiel 39. The collective birds are broadly termed *ṣippôr kol-kānāp* ('bird of every feather') in 39.17,[6] although the first reference in 39.4 specifically qualifies these birds as carrion-feeders: *'êṭ ṣippôr kol-kānāp* ('raptor of every feather'). It is possible that the verse indicates two types of birds, predatory and all other types (Altmann 2019: 16–17, citing GKC § 119, hh), yet throughout the Hebrew Bible vultures are referenced somewhat obliquely within such broad terms. The specific word for vulture in Biblical Hebrew, *nešer* can also mean 'eagle' (Driver 1955: 8–9; Kogan 2006: 286) and its nuance must be determined by context.[7] But in descriptions of carrion birds and corpses, biblical literature tends to prefer broad terminology.[8] While the word *'ayiṭ* in Ezek. 39.4 signifies a raptor of any

---

6 The Hebrew is literally 'bird of every wing'.
7 So, for example, the baldness of the *nešer* evoked in the image of mourning practices in Mic. 1.16 suggests the physical characteristic of the griffon vulture, the cinereous vulture or the lappet-faced vulture. See Driver (1955: 8–9); Altmann (2019: 79–84). Proverbs 30.17 describes the behaviour of vultures, along with ravens, pecking out and consuming eyes. Both types of birds typically begin feeding upon carcasses by devouring the soft tissue of the eyes; cf. Aharoni (1938: 468); Brichto (1973: 35). Moreover, the poetic image of nations flocking to consume spoil like the *nešer* in Hab. 1.8 (see also Deut. 28.49) fits the behaviour of vultures, which gather around carrion in large numbers – unlike the solitary behaviour of eagles.
8 Other words for 'vulture' are found in the dietary laws of the Pentateuch: *peres* and *ozniyyâ* in Lev. 11.13; Deut. 14.12; *rāḥām* in Lev. 11.18 (see also the Deir 'Alla Plaster Text [KAI 312:7–8]) and *rāḥāmâ* in Deut. 14.17. It is possible that this terminology reflects the various species of vulture that were once indigenous to the southern Levant, such as the griffon vulture, the cinereous vulture (*Aegypius monachus*), the lappet-faced vulture (*Torgos tracheliotos*), the Egyptian vulture (*Neophron percnopterus*) or the bearded vulture (*Gypaetus barbatus*). But the biblical references are lists, with no other context, so it is difficult to discern their precise meaning; see Driver (1955: 9–10); Kogan (2006); Altmann (2019: 79–116).

type, the curses of exposing the dead found in Deut. 28.26; 1 Sam. 17.44, 46 and Jer. 7.33 use a collective phrase that is even more generic: 'ôp haššāmayim, 'birds of the sky'.

The broad description of wildlife in the curses of Deut. 28.26 and Jer. 7.33 offers a general picture of exposed corpses. But this general image subtly builds a contrasting picture of nature versus humanity. In these divine curses, the birds and beasts will feed upon the dead bodies that litter the land because the dead will lack anyone to scare the animals away ('ên maḥărîd). The carrion birds are the effect caused by the inability of the living to care for their dead. There are a few instances in the Hebrew Bible that exemplify this problem. In the tragic story of Saul's executed sons, Rizpah keeps vigil over her sons' bodies and does not allow the birds of the sky ('ôp haššāmayim) to rest upon them (2 Sam. 21.10). Conversely, in Gen. 15.11 Abram/Abraham scares away the 'carrion bird' ('ayiṭ) that descends upon the carcasses of sacrificed animals. In these passages the carrion birds serve as object lessons for what happens to dead bodies that are left exposed. The control of the living over their dead is pre-eminent, and the birds become symbolic of the natural world that exists beyond human influence and that threatens the dead. This is an important function of mortuary practices, which are designed to control the uncontrollable nature of death (Suriano 2018: 51–3). As such, the tomb is a place where the corpse can be attended to and cared for and where human remains can be protected from vultures and other animals.

The element of control that underscores the appearance of carrion birds in the biblical passages reviewed above is configured differently in Ezekiel 39. The chapter begins by stating that Yahweh will defeat Gog (39.1–3), and that he will 'give them as food' to the carrion-feeders, both birds and beasts (39.4). That is, the chaotic aspect of nature is commanded by the God of Israel. This demonstration of divine power reaches its crescendo in 39.17, when the prophet is told to invite 'the birds of every feather and the beasts of the field' to feast upon Gog's dead. The dead are described as a sacrifice (Zimmerli 1983: 308–10). In this verse √zbḥ is used three times to describe Yahweh's actions and its results. At the beginning of the next verse, the animals are told explicitly to 'eat the flesh of the mighty and drink the blood of the princes of the land' (39.18). In 39.19 the instructions continue: 'And you shall eat fat until you are sated and drink blood until you are drunk from my sacrifice (mizzibḥî) that I have sacrificed (zābaḥtî) for you.' In 39.20, the wake of the battle is described as Yahweh's table. At this table, the carrion-feeding animals are told to sate themselves upon the defeated forces of Gog: 'horses and charioteers, mighty men and men of war'.

The theme of carrion-feeding animals devouring dead bodies that is introduced in Ezek. 39.4 is expanded upon in 39.17-20 (Zimmerli 1983: 308). As the scene of carrion-feeders becomes more explicit, so too does Yahweh's role in facilitating the abuse of Gog's corpses. Initially, Yahweh merely gives (√ntn) the defeated forces over to the carrion-feeders. But in 39.17, the corpses become a sacrificial feast and the carrion-feeders are specifically invited (Stavrakopoulou 2010: 80–1). Although zābaḥ can mean 'slaughter', factors such as the repeated use of the root and the implications of divine action suggest 'sacrifice'. This is not the only instance in the Hebrew Bible where human remains are used as a 'sacrifice' (Zimmerli 1983: 308–9; Stavrakopoulou 2004: 204–5). In 2 Kgs 23.16-18, Josiah defiles the high place at Bethel by exhuming burials and burning the bones upon the altar (hammizbēaḥ). Josiah's action is the fulfilment of the prophecy in 1 Kgs 13.2, which specifically states that Josiah 'shall sacrifice the priests of the high places upon you [the altar] who offer incense upon you, and human bones will be burned upon you'. The converted perfect wĕzābaḥ, 'and he shall sacrifice', establishes that the events that follow, Josiah's desecration of Bethel, go beyond tomb violation. Josiah uses the disinterred bones to ritually defile the altar (see *ṭimmē'* in 2 Kgs 23.16). Defilement is also a motif found throughout Ezekiel (see Ezek. 6.4-5; 9.6 cf. Lev. 26.30; Monroe 2011: 33–40). The slaughter of Gog's army likewise creates a problem of impurity in Ezek. 39.12-16, and although birds and other carrion-feeders are called upon to feast on the dead, Yahweh states that the Israelites will need to bury Gog's dead to remove corpse impurity from the land. Gog's dead are to be buried in Israel, in the Valley of Gog's Multitude (*gê' hămôn gôg*), near a city of the same name (*hămônâ*). As a result of this process of burial, the 'land will be cleansed' (39.16b).

The burial of Gog's dead is not the antithesis of the corpse abuse involving carrion-feeders. The scenes of carrion-feeders and interment complement each other. The process of burial lasts seven months (Ezek. 39.12, 14) and requires a concerted effort by the 'house of Israel' and 'all the people of the land' (39.12-13). The scene of corpses littering the landscape begins in 39.4-5 with the references to the fallen dead on the 'highlands of Israel' and who lie exposed in the fields. The slain soldiers of Gog's army will be left to be despoiled of their weapons by the Israelites in 39.9-10. The presence of Gog's dead will obstruct travel (39.11), as the place will be called the 'Valley of Travellers' (*gê hā'ōbĕrîm*) before being renamed the 'Valley of Gog's Multitude' (*gê' hămôn gôg*). The mass burial will also block the valley. People will be appointed to find remains (39.14) and bones will be discovered by those traversing the valley (39.15). The situation is such that the interment of Gog's dead is an ongoing event that hardly precludes animals such as vultures feeding upon human remains.

The mortuary practices in Ezekiel 39 symbolize control over the dead, as they involve the initial burial of Gog's remains in temporary sites with 'burial markers' (*ṣiyyûn*) and the reburial of these remains in a permanent place appointed by Yahweh. The element of control is important to note because the overarching image of corpse abuse is so stark. Throughout the passage, Gog's dead are referenced indirectly, 'Upon the highlands you shall fall ... and I shall give you to the carrion birds' (39.4). The one exception is in 39.15, which says that travellers who find a 'human bone' (*'eṣem 'ādām*) will set up a grave marker (*ṣiyyûn*) so that it can be reburied. In the few other occurrences of this construct in the Hebrew Bible, the term *'eṣem 'ādām* relates directly to problems of corpse impurity. It occurs in Num. 19.16 in a description of objects that bear defilement, while in 2 Kgs 23.14, 20 (cf. 1 Kgs 13.2) Josiah uses 'human bones' (*'aṣmôt 'ādām*) to defile sacred sites in Jerusalem and Bethel. Similarly, defilement due to human remains is cited as a problem in Ezek. 39.12, 14, 16. Although the origins of the problem differ, the scattered remains of the dead are due to Yahweh's victory. Moreover, unlike Josiah's actions, the people of Israel are called upon by their deity to remove the defilement through a complicated process of interment.

The complexity of Gog's burial relates to multiple themes such as territoriality, ritual purity and the propriety of the dead. While the predominant image is Yahweh's power over the living and the dead, this image is broken into separate yet intersecting categories (Stavrakopoulou 2010: 76–7). On the one hand there is the category of the natural world, which is demonstrated through graphic scenes of animals feeding upon human remains. Their consumption of the dead is divinely appointed and portrayed as a sacrificial meal. In this way, the otherwise chaotic forces of nature serve Yahweh's design in the destruction of Gog's dead. On the other hand, we have the category of human interaction with the dead, so that Gog's burial represents Israel's control over their defeated enemy. In Ezek. 39.11-15, the Israelites will collect dead bodies, locate identifiable human remains for reburial and construct a mass burial at a named site (Stavrakopoulou 2010: 78). The performance of funerary rites here empowers Israel as they appropriate the dead bodies of their enemy using Gog's dead as boundary markers (Stavrakopoulou 2010: 78–80). But the meticulous search for every human bone, together with the repeated references to cleansing the land, brings to the forefront the conceptual boundaries of ritual impurity that threatens the land of Israel. Gog's burial and the cleansing of the land of Israel is a necessary step in removing any barriers that can interfere with the dynamic of land, people and God.

Like the Stele of Vultures, the abuse of corpses in Ezekiel 39 is intended to assert the power of one group over another. Gog's dead are stripped of their weapons and their mortal remains are given a mass burial by the Israelites, which bears similarities to Umma's naked corpses that are amassed in burial mounds constructed by Lagash. The appearance of raptors, likewise, invokes the horrific realities of war and symbolizes Gog's inability to care for their own dead. Yet unlike the Stele of Vultures, the arrival of carrion birds in Ezekiel 39 is symbolic of divine control. In Ezekiel's imagery, the forces of nature serve a divine purpose. There is no divide separating a divine scene from the historical scene occupied by human actors, as depicted on the obverse and reverse sides of the Stele of Vultures. In Ezekiel 39, both humans and non-humans serve Yahweh's plan. This becomes more apparent when one compares Ezekiel 39 with the earlier scene of reburial and revivification in Ezekiel 37. In one chapter the interment of the enemy's dead serves as a form of corpse abuse (Ezekiel 39), in the other chapter the dead are disinterred in order to revive them (Ezekiel 37). One involves the creation of mass burials while the other involves the mass emptying of graves. The finality of death seen in Gog's defeat contrasts with the promise of new life through death's reversal given to the Israelite exiles (Suriano 2019). Bones and corpses play key roles in both prophetic images. The sky above the valley in Ezek. 37.9 becomes filled with the spirit of Yahweh, whereas raptors descend upon Gog's corpses. Even the dramatic scene of dry bones becoming refleshed and transformed into living bodies in 37.7-8 contrasts with the implied action of the raptors that deflesh the dead bodies of Gog throughout 39.4-20.

Conclusion

None of the three examples explored in this chapter have any direct connection with one another, but each shows how interaction with vultures can reveal the complexities involved in cultural responses to death. The three examples were chosen because they include both corpses and carrion-feeding birds. In each example the presence of one lends meaning to the other, yet the meanings can differ. For instance, the vultures at Çatalhöyük are never shown eating dead bodies. Their appearance flying above headless corpses draws upon the nature of the vulture as a carrion-feeder. The vulture symbolism at Çatalhöyük appears to be benign, serving as a mythological link to constructions of ancestry. In the other two examples, however, the vulture is used to indicate the unprotected nature and vulnerability of corpses. The remarkable thing about the vulture as symbol in all of these examples is how it serves multiple roles within various dichotomies of meaning: life and death, order versus chaos, myth and history, divine versus human.

As an image of death that is representative of the natural world, the vulture could stand for death's chaotic and uncontrollable aspects. The vulture as a carrion-feeding animal often served as a compelling symbol of both chaos and death. Again, this range of meaning is not inherently negative. Death is a natural part of the human experience, and the vulture could function as an enduring symbol of this experience. As a component of the natural landscape, the vulture was timeless. It existed in the past as it does in the present and its image lends itself to a mythologizing at Çatalhöyük that was paired with the dead in an early exercise in history-making. If we follow Ian Hodder's interpretation, the repeated scenes of vultures and corpses inside the history houses provide a timeless background for mortuary practices that formed ancestral discourses.

The negative portrayal of vultures and corpses can have the opposite effect in a myth and history dialectic. In the Stele of Vultures, the carrion birds on the reverse side of the stele form a key element in the artistic representation of a historical event. Here, the vultures are emblematic of the realities of war, as opposed to the mythic representation of divine victory portrayed on the stele's obverse side. In the Stele of Vulture's dialectic, the carrion birds play a part in a historical narrative that relates to the humanity of the events portrayed. By contrast, there is no myth and history dialectic in Ezekiel 39. The divide between human and divine is collapsed in the mythic trope of Yahweh's victory over Israel's enemy. This victory brings death into the land of Israel. Humans and non-humans alike are called upon by Israel's deity to respond to the dead, each in their own ways. The remains of Gog's defeated army bring ritual impurity upon the land of Israel, thus requiring the Israelites to bury Gog's dead. On the other hand, Gog's dead are treated as sacrificial victims, offered up to raptors and other animals that naturally feed upon carcasses. The vultures that gather around the corpses mark the natural end of all things, as in the saying from the Gospels. But in Ezekiel 39, the carrion-feeders also serve as powerful symbols of Yahweh's pervasive power over life and death. In each example, from Çatalhöyük through Sumer to the Hebrew Bible, the vulture serves as a guide, circling different responses and ways of coping with and controlling corpses. The vulture looms in the background of this diverse selection of human cultures, marking the ideological horizon of life and death.

References

Aharoni, I. (1938), 'On Some Animals Mentioned in the Bible', *Osiris* 5: 461–78.

Altmann, P. (2019), *Banned Birds: The Birds of Leviticus 11 and Deuteronomy 14*, Archaeology and Bible 1, Tübingen: Mohr Siebeck.

Andrews, P., T. Molleson and B. Boz (2005), 'The Human Burials at Çatalhöyük', in S. Hodder (ed.), *Inhabiting Çatalhöyük: Reports from the 1995–99 Seasons*, 261–78, Cambridge: McDonald Institute for Archaeological Research.

Bahrani, Z. (2008), *Rituals of War: The Body and Violence in Mesopotamia*, New York: Zone Books.

Bonogofsky, M. (2003), 'Neolithic Plastered Skulls and Railroading Epistemologies', *Bulletin of the American Schools of Oriental Research* 331: 1–10.

Bonogofsky, M. (2005), 'A Bioarchaeological Study of Plastered Skulls from Anatolia: New Discoveries and Interpretations', *International Journal of Osteoarchaeology* 15: 124–35.

Boz, B., and L. D. Hager (2013), 'Living above the Dead: Intramural Burial Practices at Çatalhöyük', in I. Hodder (ed.), *Humans and Landscapes of Çatalhöyük: Reports from the 2000–2008 Seasons*, 413–40, London: British Institute at Ankara.

Brichto, H. C. (1973), 'Kin, Cult, Land and Afterlife – a Biblical Complex', *Hebrew Union College Annual* 44: 1–54.

Cooper, J. S. (1983), *Reconstructing History from Ancient Inscriptions: The Lagash-Umma Border Conflict*, Sources from the Ancient Near East, Malibu, CA: Undena Publications.

Cooper, J. S. (1986), *Presargonic Inscriptions*, vol. 1 Sumerian and Akkadian Royal Inscriptions, New Haven, CT: American Oriental Society.

Dolce, R. (2018), *'Losing One's Head' in the Ancient Near East: Interpretation and Meaning of Decapitation*, Studies in the History of the Ancient Near East, New York: Routledge.

Driver, G. R. (1955), 'Birds in the Old Testament: I. Birds in Law', *Palestine Exploration Quarterly* 87: 5–20.

Düring, B. S. (2003), 'Burials in Context: The 1960s Inhumations of Çatalhöyük East', *Anatolian Studies* 53: 1–15.

Eichrodt, W. (1970), *Ezekiel: A Commentary*, The Old Testament Library, Philadelphia, PA: Westminster Press.

Frankfort, H. (1996), *The Art and Architecture of the Ancient Orient*, 5th edn, ed. M. Roaf and D. Matthews, Yale University Press Pelican History of Art, New Haven, CT: Yale University Press.

Frayne, D. (2008), *Presargonic Period, 2700–2350 BC*, Royal Inscriptions of Mesopotamia Early Periods, Toronto: University of Toronto Press.

Haddow, S. D., and C. J. Knüsel (2017), 'Skull Retrieval and Secondary Burial Practices in the Neolithic Near East: Recent Insights from Çatalhöyük, Turkey', *Bioarchaeology International* 1: 52–71.

Heuzey, L. (1884), *La stèle des vautours: étude d'archéologie chaldéenne d'après les découvertes de M. de Sarzec*, Paris: A. Lévy.

Hodder, I. (2006), *The Leopard's Tale: Revealing the Mysteries of Çatalhöyük*, New York: Thames & Hudson.

Hodder, I. (2016), 'More on History Houses at Çatalhöyük: A Response to Carleton et al', *Journal of Archaeological Science* 67: 1–6.

Hodder, I., and L. Meskell (2011), 'A "Curious and Sometimes a Trifle Macabre Artistry": Some Aspects of Symbolism in Neolithic Turkey', *Current Anthropology* 52: 235–63.

Ikram, S. (2012), 'An Eternal Aviary: Bird Mummies from Ancient Egypt', in R. Bailleul-LeSuer (ed.), *Between Heaven and Earth: Birds in Ancient Egypt*, 41–8, Chicago, IL: Oriental Institute of the University of Chicago.

Kogan, L. (2006), 'Animal Names of Biblical Hebrew: An Etymological Survey', in L. Kogan (ed.), *Babel und Bibel 3: Annual of Ancient Near Eastern, Old Testament, and Semitic Studies*, 257–320, Winona Lake, IN: Eisenbrauns.

Levtow, N. B. (2014), 'Monumental Inscriptions and the Ritual Representation of War', in B. E. Kelle, F. R. Ames and J. L. Wright (eds), *Warfare, Ritual, and Symbol in Biblical and Modern Contexts*, 25–46, Atlanta, GA: Society of Biblical Literature.

Lust, J. (1999), 'Gog', in K. van der Toorn, B. Becking and P. W. van der Horst (eds), *Dictionary of Demons and Deities in the Bible*, 2nd edn, 373–5, Leiden: Brill.

Macqueen, J. G. (1978), 'Secondary Burial at Çatal Hüyük', *Numen* 25: 226–39.

McMahon, A. (2016), 'The Encultured Vulture: Late Chalcolithic Sealing Images and the Challenges of Urbanism in 4th Millennium BC Northern Mesopotamia', *Paléorient* 42: 169–83.

Mellaart, J. (1964), 'Excavations at Çatal Hüyük, 1963, Third Preliminary Report', *Anatolian Studies* 14: 39–119.

Mellaart, J. (1967), '*Çatal Hüyük: A Neolithic Town in Anatolia*', New Aspects of Archaeology, New York: McGraw-Hill.

Meskell, L. (2008), 'The Nature of the Beast: Curating Animals and Ancestors at Çatalhöyük', *World Archaeology* 40 (3): 373–89.

Monroe, L. A. S. (2011), *Josiah's Reform and the Dynamics of Defilement: Israelite Rites of Violence and the Making of a Biblical Text*, New York: Oxford University Press.

Moortgat, A. (1969), *The Art of Ancient Mesopotamia: The Classical Art of the Near East*, London: Phaidon.

Morelli, F., A. M. Kubicka, P. Tryjanowski and E. Nelson (2015), 'The Vulture in the Sky and the Hominin on the Land: Three Million Years of Human–Vulture Interaction', *Anthrozoos* 28: 449–68.

Nadali, D. (2007), 'Monuments of War, War of Monuments: Some Considerations on Commemorating War in the Third Millennium BC', *Orientalia* 76: 336–67.

Parrot, A. (1961), *Sumer: The Dawn of Art*, Arts of Mankind, New York: Golden Press.

Pilloud, M. A., S. D. Haddow, C. J. Knüsel and C. S. Larsen (2016), 'A Bioarchaeological and Forensic Re-Assessment of Vulture Defleshing and Mortuary Practices at Neolithic Çatalhöyük', *Journal of Archaeological Science: Reports* 10: 735–43.

Richardson, S. (2007), 'Death and Dismemberment in Mesopotamia: Discorporation between the Body and Body Politic', in N. Laneri (ed.) *Performing Death: Social Analyses of Funerary Traditions in the Ancient Near East and Mediterranean*, 189–208, Chicago, IL: Oriental Institute of the University of Chicago.

Russell, N., and K. J. McGowan (2005), 'Çatalhöyük Bird Bones', in I. Hodder (ed.), *Inhabiting Çatalhöyük: Reports from the 1995–99 Seasons*, 99–110, Cambridge: McDonald Institute for Archaeological Research.

Selz, G. (2004), 'Early Dynastic Vessels in "Ritual" Contexts', *Wiener Zeitschrift für die Kunde des Morgenlandes* 94: 185–232.

Shonkwiler, R. (2012), 'Sheltering Wings: Birds as Symbols of Protection in Ancient Egypt', in R. Bailleul-LeSuer (ed.), *Between Heaven and Earth: Birds in Ancient Egypt*, 49–58, Chicago, IL: Oriental Institute of the University of Chicago.

Stavrakopoulou, F. (2004), *King Manasseh and Child Sacrifice: Biblical Distortions of Historical Realities*, Beihefte Zur Zeitschrift Für Die Alttestamentliche Wissenschaft, Berlin: Walter de Gruyter.

Stavrakopoulou, F. (2010), 'Gog's Grave and the Use and Abuse of Corpses in Ezekiel 39:11–20', *Journal of Biblical Literature* 129: 67–84.

Suriano, M. J. (2012), 'Ruin Hills at the Threshold of the Netherworld: The Tell in the Conceptual Landscape of the *Ba'al Cycle* and Ancient Near Eastern Mythology', *Die Welt des Orients* 42: 210–30.

Suriano, M. J. (2018), *A History of Death in the Hebrew Bible*, New York: Oxford University Press.

Suriano, M. J. (2019), 'No Rest for the Dead: The Reversal of Death in Ezekiel's Valley of Dry Bones', in A. Massmann and C. B. Hays (eds), *Deathless Hopes: Reinventions of Afterlife and Eschatological Beliefs*, 65–80, Zurich: Lit Verlag.

Testart, A. (2008), 'Des crânes et des vautours ou la guerre oubliée', *Paléorient* 34: 33–58.

Twiss, K. C. (2007), 'The Neolithic of the Southern Levant', *Evolutionary Anthropology* 16: 24–35.

Van Dooren, T. (2014), *Flight Ways: Life and Loss at the Edge of Extinction*, Critical Perspectives on Animals Theory, Culture, Science, and Law, New York: Columbia University Press.

Westenholz, A. (1970), '*berūtum, damtum*, and Old Akkadian KI.GAL: Burial of Dead Enemies in Ancient Mesopotamia', *Archiv für Orientforschung* 23: 27–31.

Winter, I. (1985), 'After the Battle Is Over: The *Stele of the Vultures* and the Beginning of Historical Narrative in the Art of the Ancient Near East', in H. L. Kessler and M. S. Simpson (eds), *Pictorial Narrative in Antiquity and the Middle Ages*, 11–32, Washington, DC: National Gallery of Art.

Zimmerli, W. (1983), *Ezekiel 2: A Commentary on the Book of the Prophet Ezekiel*, vol. 2, Hermeneia, ed. F. M. Cross and K. Baltzer, trans. P. D. Hanson, Philadelphia, PA: Fortress Press.

CHAPTER FOUR

'Know well the faces of your sheep': Animal bodies and human bodies

REBEKAH WELTON

Animals were essential in ancient Israel and Judah. Most non-elites were farmers who relied on an agropastoral survival subsistence strategy in order to mitigate the risks posed by drought, disease and famine (Sasson 2008; 2010: 60–1).[1] The lives of domesticated livestock – predominantly sheep, goats and cows – were enmeshed in the lives of their human keepers, much as humans were dependent on their animals. During their lifetimes, animals were a key component of the survival subsistence strategy: they were a direct source of food (milk) and ploughed the fields in which grain and other crops were cultivated.[2] While this fact hardly needs stating, what is rarely discussed is the social interaction arising from the interdependent relationship between animals and their keepers.[3]

Access to the 'lifetime products' of animals had likely motivated early humans to start keeping, breeding and rearing goats and sheep locally, rather than only hunting animals for meat.[4] This shift in the mode of animal exploitation seems to have impacted the way in which animals came to be regarded, so that certain species had not only been domesticated but were also integrated into the household in multiple ways – much as they continued to be in the ancient world.

---

1 The term 'survival subsistence strategy' is used in Sasson (2010: 120) to refer to the management of an ancient-world farmer's resource base in a way that mitigated against risk and instead made optimal use of land, water and livestock to ensure the survival of the household. This included careful management of the ratios of sheep to goats, limited use of cattle for ploughing, a dependence on the lifetime products of animals (such as milk, wool, traction power and dung for fuel) and culling patterns that ensured these lifetime products were in secure supply. Such a strategy was likely to have included transhumance, which both widened the overall resource base of the farmer and reduced the risk of over-pasturing, disease, insect infestation, drought and competition with other groups. See further Sasson (2010: 22–3).
2 For a detailed overview of the preservation of dairy products, drawing on a range of ethnographic sources, see London (2016: 120–3); cf. Abu-Rabia (1994: 75, 85–6). For the use of oxen in ploughing, see Potts (1997: 73).
3 I discuss the roles and relationships of animals in the Israelite and Judahite household in further detail in Welton (2020).
4 The designation 'lifetime products' is preferable to the more usual 'secondary products': such products were not secondary at all but rather the priority. Accordingly, so-called 'primary products', such as meat and bone, are best described as 'final products'. See Hesse (1984: 260); Helmer and Vigne (2007).

In ancient Israel and Judah, the most obvious evidence of the integration of animals into the human household is the so-called 'Israelite four-room house', which was a home to both animals and their keepers (Holladay 1997: 339; Ebeling 2010: 35; Dever 2012: 164). Given that they lived in such close proximity to humans, we can think of these household animals as 'companion species', which were active, if not central, participants in household life, rather than 'background' characters in the lives of humans (Stone 2018: 29). Indeed, animals contributed to nearly every aspect of human life and survival.

Animal excrement is a prime example of the contribution of animals to an array of household necessities. Given its fibrous structure, the dung of herbivores burns at an optimal rate and temperature, and thus was crucial for the conversion of raw grain into bread and porridge, in addition to its use as fertilizer for the fields (Kramer 1982: 45–7; Borowski 1987: 145–6; Abu-Rabia 1999: 26; Ebeling 2010: 51, 55; Dever 2012: 159). But dung was also utilized in other aspects of the material culture of the household. As a component in the production of plaster, it was used in the very walls and floors of the home (Shahack-Gross 2011: 31). Thanks to its gel-forming hydrated organic polymers, dung was also used in the production of pottery, for it increased the plasticity of clay (Sillar 2000: 46), while as a fuel, it powered kilns for the firing of pots and other clay vessels (London 2016: 162). Animal bodies thus manifested the very materiality of the household, from the physical construction of the house to the clay vessels from which humans ate and drank. Given the frequency of their physical presence in the house and the interwoven nature of their lifetime products in the materiality of daily life, it is reasonable to assume that animals were socially incorporated into the human home as fellow members of the household.

The care of household animals, and the processing of their lifetime products, was a constant and unrelenting aspect of household life which structured both daily routines and the social identities of the human household members. Pasturing and watering the flocks, ploughing fields with cattle, preparing extra fodder, tending to ill or injured animals and protecting flocks and herds from predators were activities most frequently carried out by the men of the house (Borowski 1997: 48; Holtzman 2009: 78–9, 84; Dever 2012: 172–3). Women likely made dung cakes for fires (Kramer 1982: 33, 89), processed wool into clothing (Meyers 2013: 133) and ground grain, an indirect product from the ploughing of cattle, for bread (Meyers 2002: 22). Like grain processing, dairy processing was likely performed within the domestic domain and was probably a component of women's household activities, as ethnographic examples illustrate (Watson 1979: 98, 259; Abu-Rabia 1994: 77; 1999: 23; Holtzman 2009: 103). Indeed, the zooarchaeologist Naomi Sykes notes the frequency with which dairying in the ancient world differentiated gender roles cross-culturally, providing women with social standing, personal esteem and connecting them with associated deities (Sykes 2014: 50). While the human contribution to the household in terms of time and energy was evident, the animals' contributions were at the forefront of the household's survival. As the very means by which the household gained the majority of its food, clothing and vessels, animals were regarded as key contributors – a reality witnessed and experienced every day by all human members of the home.

The reciprocal dependence of animals and humans likely elicited an emotional bond. Ethnographic analyses of similar pastoral societies suggest that the social status of household animals – such as goats and sheep – differs from that accorded to 'farm' animals within modern (and predominantly urban) Western cultures.[5] The Negev Bedouin, for

---

5 On the appropriate use of ethnographic studies in archaeological research, see Hodder (1982: 18, 26, 158); Sasson (2006: 33–40).

example, rely on their flocks of sheep and goats for their lifetime products of dairy, dung and fleece and reside in an environment similar to that of ancient Israelites and Judahites in terms of climate and landscape (Abu-Rabia 1994: 8–9, 75–7). Although the activities of the Negev Bedouin do not reflect a 'preservation' of Late Bronze or Iron Age activities, their lifestyles can be useful in drawing possible analogies based on the similarity of their circumstances and in shifting us from our urban, Western perspective (Sasson 2010: 18; Lyons and Casey 2016: 614). For the Negev Bedouin, the care and perpetuation of the flock is vital to the success of each household across its future generations, whose members will similarly depend upon the contribution of the beloved flock. A particularly expressive line from a Bedouin shepherding song displays this dependency: 'My destiny and that of the flock are bound together' (Abu-Rabia 1994: 62). The intertwining of human and animal fates gives rise to an emotional bond, so that the animals are not unlike kin to their shepherds. As such, the animals play an active role in the formation and maintenance of other social relationships across the household, as noted by the ethnographer Aref Abu-Rabia:

> The Bedouin are as devoted to their flock as they are to the family itself. Indeed, their bond with the flock is similar to the bond between members of the family. To them the flock is the centre of their interest, serving as the main focus of their conversation. Care of the flock dominates the minds of all members of the family, unifying them socially and economically. (Abu-Rabia 1994: 76)

The extent to which the Negev Bedouin regard animals as family members is also reflected in the fact that, like humans, individual animals are called by their own names and are easily distinguished from one another by their recognizable differences, such as their facial features, colouring, age, body-build and the size and shape of their udders (Abu-Rabia 1994: 25, 76, 89). In being perceived as a collection of individuals, the flock elicits emotional as well as practical care from humans, deepening the social bond between the Bedouin and their animals (Sykes 2014: 46).

Further examples of the affection displayed towards those animals on which humans depend are attested in an ethnographic report from rural Iran (Kramer 1982), where sheep, goats and cattle are relied upon for their hair, hide, milk, traction power and dung. Here, animals are rarely slaughtered for meat. Instead, they are 'maintained primarily for their milk and wool and are more useful alive than dead' (Kramer 1982: 42). Goats in particular are regarded as intelligent creatures, and young goats are treated to genuine acts of endearment, such as hugging and kissing (Kramer 1982: 45). The close social and emotional relationship between humans and their animals is also found among the Samburu of Northern Kenya, who are a similarly pastoral people and rely on milk as their primary staple food (Holtzman 2009: 97, 101–2, 158). Here, as the ethnographer Jon Holtzman (2009: 236) comments, 'herders have a great deal of genuine concern for the animals' well-being, out of intrinsic love for the animals and a recognition that their present and future well-being depends on them'. As all these examples suggest, the strategic and practical benefits of keeping animals cannot be disentangled from the emotional aspects of these human–animal relationships. In contrast to the ways in which livestock tend to be perceived in the modern-day, urban West, domesticated animals in traditional, pastoral societies are regarded as both economically and socially valuable members of the household, and akin in many ways to its human members.

Evidence from ancient Southwest Asian contexts similarly suggests that the economic, contributory value of household animals was inextricably bound to their social and emotional value. For example, an Old Babylonian (early second millennium BCE) document listing items for inheritance includes cows and oxen, but refers to them by their personal names: the first pair, an ox and cow, are called Minam-epuš-ilum and Taribatum, and two further cows are called Ili-dumqi and Ištar-rimti-ili (Postgate 1992: 97, §5.5). While the document is primarily concerned with detailing the division of property, its inclusion of these animals' names conveys the individual, social identities of the animals, demonstrating that they were not merely inheritable 'objects'. Instead, the document reflects the social – and not just economic – value of household animals as recognizable individuals.

Biblical texts similarly allude to the roles of individual sheep and goats in a pastoral household, as illustrated in Prov. 27.23-27:

23 Know well the faces of your sheep,
    and set your heart/mind (שׁית לבך) to your flock;
24 for riches do not last forever,
    nor a crown for all generations.
25 When the hay has been taken, and new grass appears,
    and the green plants of the mountains are gathered,
26 the lambs will be for your clothing,
    and the rams will be the value/reward of the field,
27 as there will be enough goats' milk for your food,
    for the food of your household,
    and nourishment for your young girls.[6]

This text emphasizes the need to know the faces of the household's sheep and to prioritize their care. This care is motivated not by the animals' value in death as a source of meat but because of their vitally important lifetime products of wool and milk. The call to know the faces of the sheep (v. 23) may also allude to the individuality of these animals – much as human individuality is intimately linked to the face of a person. Knowing the flock's faces implies an intimacy between human and animal; the keepers should be so well acquainted with their sheep that each face is familiar, highlighting the way in which the well-being of every member of the flock must be closely observed. The instruction to 'set your mind/heart' (שׁית לבך) to the flock not only signals the close attention shepherds must pay to their animals, so that their care can be properly prioritized and maintained, but also carries a more emotive nuance, suggesting that the animals' lives are of as great a concern as those of humans.[7]

The passage explicitly states that the value of the male and female goats lies in their production of sufficient nourishment for the herder, his household and specifically his young girls (v. 27). The specification of this last group may emphasize the way in which Israelite and Judahite farmers were dependent on their goats for the perpetuation of future generations. The household's success in producing and raising healthy young girls who would become fertile women, bear children and produce milk themselves was dependent on there being an adequate food supply. Additionally, given the likelihood that milking the flocks was primarily a female task, this passage in Proverbs seems to

---

6 All biblical translations are my own, unless otherwise stated.
7 See, for example, Exod. 13.20; 2 Sam. 13.20; Dan. 6.14, in which 'taking' something 'to heart' or 'setting' one's 'heart' on a matter is associated with an emotional distress or anxiety to resolve a particular concern.

encapsulate some of the ways in which animals and humans formed an entangled and interdependent household unit which perpetuated its own survival.

In 2 Samuel 12, a household animal is more explicitly portrayed as a family member. In this text, Nathan tells David a story about a rich man and a poor man. The rich man has many flocks but the poor man has only one little lamb. 'He brought her up, and she grew up with him and with his children; she used to eat of his morsels, and drink from his cup, and lie in his bosom, and she was like a daughter to him' (v. 3). The rich man kills the little lamb – a plot twist which angers David so much that he commands that the rich man shall be put to death (v. 5). In its narrative context, this story serves a wider rhetorical purpose, but its description of the lamb illustrates well the social value of household animals and the emotional dependency of human families on their animal members. This lamb is not described as being economically prized; instead, it is explicitly cast as a beloved member of the family: it is said to have grown up with the poor man's children and to have been treated as a daughter, receiving physical affection from her owner. The lamb is thus the focus of its human family's affection and care – an affection so powerful that David is moved to demand the rich man is punished.

This biblical passage offers a literary reflection of a broader social reality in which humans and animals were socially entangled, so that as members of the household, the lived experiences of animals and humans were emotionally and morally integrated.[8] Human household members likely developed a moral obligation to care for their animals as a part of the reciprocity by which animals secured the survival of the household. This duty of care to the animal probably elicited an emotional bond of 'kinship', and thus the animal effectively became a part of the family, underscoring its role as both an emotional and economic collaborator in the continued success of the household unit (Allentuck 2015: 108–9).

The social relationships between animals and their keepers should thus be taken into account when considering animal slaughter in an ordinary – pastoral – Israelite or Judahite context. Given that animals were not simply property to be exploited, and that they were not disconnected dispassionately from the family unit, the emotive and social impact of dispatching beloved household animals must be considered when discussing the relationship between humans as consumers of animals. Aharon Sasson (2010) draws on archaeological data and evidence from traditional pastoral societies to suggest that in ancient Israel and Judah, it was necessary to cull livestock at certain points in order to make the most efficient use of the resources available and to prevent them from becoming scarce. For example, most male lambs and kids were probably slaughtered to prevent them from consuming too much of the milk produced by the mature females – milk needed to feed their human owners. Were they to live to adulthood, they would also consume much of the pasture and brush required by females to be healthy enough to continue to produce both milk and offspring. Consequently, young males were likely slaughtered between the ages of 1 and 3 years, by which point they would have reached 70 per cent of their maximal body weight, and their pasture consumption threatened to outweigh their growth (Sasson 2010: 40–1). The herder thus gained more from the resources available by killing most males at this age and consuming the meat, but only after the animal had

---

8 Biblical laws against bestiality (Lev. 18.23; 20.15-16; Deut. 27.21) effectively acknowledge that the animals of the household are extensions of the human family, as discussed in Boer (2015: 93): 'the biblical laws assume that animals are on the same level, sexually, as a man's extended clan and his fellow men. The clan is not confined to human beings. Hence the laws on bestiality are located within a much-expanded range of incest taboos.'

already lived with the family for a year or more and was likely already a valued social member of the household. Additionally, and in line with the survival subsistence strategy, adult ewes and rams were probably killed at approximately 5 or 6 years of age in order to keep the herd size manageable in relation to the resources available and to protect the herd from disease by keeping the animals at optimum health (Sasson 2010: 41). By the time of slaughter, these adult animals would have spent at least five years living and collaborating with the household, during which extensive social and emotional relationships would have developed between the humans and their animal companions.

The emotional aspect of slaughtering a household animal must have been significant and very likely elicited certain practices to recognize the loss of the household member. Much as mortuary practices ritualize and 're-socialize' the death of a human (see Stavrakopoulou in this volume), the slaughter of domestic animals in Israel and Judah was ritualized as a form of sacrifice – although the extent to which it mapped directly onto biblical ideologies of sacrifice is uncertain. After all, although biblical texts tend to portray sacrifice as an action which effects transformations such as the atonement of sin, the removal of 'uncleanness', and the creation or maintenance of positive relationships between gods and humans, these texts are specialized in their ideologies, and thus do not necessarily reflect sacrifice in non-elite contexts.[9] Rather, sacrifice for ordinary Israelites and Judahites is better set within the context of what we know about the interdependent relationships between humans and their household animals. Given the affectionate emotional bond that grew between humans and their animals, it is very possible that guilt and grief were present when a beloved animal had to be slaughtered, combined with a grateful recognition of the animal's contribution to the household's survival and well-being during its lifetime. Such gratitude may have been expressed during the slaughter of the animal by ritualizing the act as an offering to the deities and venerated ancestors of the household, acknowledging the valued status of the animal. As Naomi Sykes comments,

> throughout time and space, most people have perceived animal killing to be an unpleasant experience, and where individuals have blood on their hands it has incurred feelings of guilt that need to be alleviated. Cue the soothing power of rituals and the supernatural. (Sykes 2014: 130)

Not only did the keepers 'give up' the beloved animal which had contributed so much during its life, but they also 'gave to' the supranatural powers which had granted (and thus might continue to grant) fertility and security to the household (cf. Stavrakopoulou 2016: 352–4). The zooarchaeologists Brian Hesse, Paula Wapnish and Jonathan Greer (2012: 219) have also noted the relationship between the role of animals while alive and the way humans may have dealt with their deaths: 'The slaughter of each animal, every one a beast of close familiarity, was an event that required thought and careful consideration.' It seems reasonable to assume that ancient Israelites and Judahites, who lived with animals in their own homes, would employ methods of marking and recognizing the death of an animal member of the household through the ritual of sacrifice as a means of socially managing their slaughter. This appears to have been a common strategy in the ancient world:

---

9 While I am not denying that non-elite sacrifice was transformative, it seems likely that the elite forms of sacrifice reflected in biblical traditions elaborated on pastoral/ordinary sacrifice and imbued sacrificial rites with a politically laden, ideological charge, which arguably implies a different transformative nuance. See Janzen (2004).

> Animals were powerful constituents in the cultural landscape ... never simply 'resources' manipulated as packages of fur, hide, protein and fat. Their deaths did not go unremarked. Complex ideologies emerged to 'naturalise' or even 'expiate' the deaths of animals even when these events were part of a necessary process of converting sheep, goats, cattle and other species to ingestible or otherwise consumable products ... Sacrifice is one part of the effort by human groups to make sense of their animal killing activities. By sacrificing, in either the sense of 'giving to' or 'giving up' animals and their products, humans create complex systems of exploitation, *but ones they can live with*. (Hesse, Wapnish and Greer 2012: 217; emphasis added)

In the urban West today, the 'complex systems of exploitation' enabling us to live comfortably with the mass consumption of animals are those which render the very *lives* of animals virtually invisible: the realities of life and death in farms, slaughter houses and food factories are hidden from view, so that most consumers see only the neatly packaged animal products they purchase from supermarkets.[10] But for ancient Israelites and Judahites, however, the emotional toll of animal slaughter and consumption was reconfigured and integrated into the larger narrative of the household and its relationship to the divine beings upon whom humans were also dependent. Sacrifice, in whichever form it took for ordinary Israelites and Judahites, allowed the human members of the household to 'live with' the slaughtering of their companionate animals.

This idea is brought into sharper focus by comparing the slaughter and consumption of domestic animals with wild animals. The butchered remains of gazelle and deer appear in the archaeological record only at low frequencies, indicating that while these animals were consumed occasionally, they were not a core component of the Israelite or Judahite diet.[11] This is unsurprising. As extremely skittish animals (particularly around humans), gazelle and deer are not easily domesticated and require very tall fences to prevent them from leaping out of pens – the sheer size of which panics the animals, leading to high levels of stress and a deterioration in their bodily condition (Davis 1987a: 141–2; Hodder 2012: 77). Therefore, when gazelle and deer were eaten in ancient Israel and Judah, they were hunted game rather than domesticated species, and their deaths were typically initiated by a long-range weapon such as a spear or a bow. Accordingly, no prior relationship existed between these animals and the humans who hunted them, rendering their deaths socially distinct from those of domesticated animals. Something of this distinction between wild animals and domestic animals is attested in the book of Leviticus. In 17.13, the blood of slaughtered game is to be directed into the earth: 'And anyone of the people of Israel, or of the aliens who reside among them, who hunts down an animal or bird that may be eaten shall pour out its blood and cover it with earth.' By contrast, goats, sheep and oxen are to be slaughtered in a sacrificial manner and have their blood dashed upon an altar (17.3-6). These differing regulations would thus seem to reflect a deeply rooted, conceptual difference between wild and domestic animals. But

---

10 Note, however, that a greater concern for animal rights and an increasing awareness of the stark realities of the dairy, poultry and beef industries (combined with anxieties about climate change) appear to account for the recent surge in vegetarianism and record numbers of people pledging to join Veganuary; cf. Jones (2020). Changing attitudes to the exploitation of animals are also reflected in recent theological work calling on Christians to reduce their consumption of animals, as illustrated by Clough (2018: 239–48).

11 For examples of sites at which gazelle and deer remains have been recovered, see Tchernov and Drori (1983: 219); Davis (1987b: 249–50); Kohler-Rollefson (1995: 98); Horwitz (1998: 110; 2000a: 227; 2000b: 67); Greer (2013: 60, 81).

in Deut. 12.20-24, this distinction appears to be modified by an alternative – and perhaps competing – instruction:

> [20] When Yahweh your God enlarges your territory, as he has promised you, and you say, 'I am going to eat some meat', because you wish to eat meat, you may eat meat whenever you have the desire. [21] If the place where Yahweh your God will choose to put his name is too far from you, and you slaughter as I have commanded you any of your herd or flock that Yahweh has given you, then you may eat within your towns whenever you desire. [22] Indeed, just as gazelle or deer is eaten, so you may eat it; the unclean and the clean alike may eat it. [23] Only be sure that you do not eat the blood; for the blood is the life, and you shall not eat the life with the meat. [24] Do not eat it; you shall pour it out on the ground like water.

Due to the ideology of centralization found in Deuteronomy, which demands that household animals are only to be sacrificed at the central cult place (by implication, Jerusalem), the scribes allow for domesticated animals further afield to be slaughtered as though they are 'merely' wild game: in the supposed absence of an altar (or to prevent the use of 'illegitimate' altars), their blood is to be poured out on the ground like water (cf. Lev. 17.13), rendering their deaths (and their meat) non-sacrificial (Gilders 2004: 15).[12] Despite their variations, the ritual regulations in Leviticus and Deuteronomy presuppose an underlying conceptual difference between domestic animals and wild game and the ways in which they are to be slaughtered. This difference likely reflects a social reality in which there was no emotional bond or mutual dependence between humans and wild game. Deer and gazelle did not regularly supply humans with milk, dung, traction power or fleece, and therefore were not viewed as part of the household. They did not collaborate with humans for mutual survival and as a result did not become like kin. Accordingly, their deaths did not elicit the emotional responses of grief or guilt evoked by the slaughter of domestic animals. There was no need to ritualize their deaths as a form of sacrifice – a practice deemed necessary only for those domesticated species upon whom their keepers had become dependent and with whom they had socially bonded.

Contributions to the household's survival, and the social ties that bound its human members as a distinct social unit, were also created and embodied by its domestic animals. In this sense, the life of an animal and the life of a human were similarly valuable. Something of this is evident in Lev. 17.3-4:

> If anyone of the house of Israel kills (ישחט) an ox or a lamb or a goat in the camp, or kills (ישחט) it outside the camp, and does not bring it to the entrance of the tent of meeting, to present it as an offering to Yahweh before the tabernacle of Yahweh, he shall be held guilty of bloodshed; he has shed blood, and he shall be cut off from the people.

In this text, killing a domestic animal without performing the appropriate social and ritual actions is tantamount to the spilling of human blood and may well point to the high social value of household animals. Although the narrator later specifies that this ruling prevents the offering of sacrifices to other deities (v. 7), the killing of the animal is treated

---

12 Contrary to the claims of Deuteronomy 12, the prevalence of four-horned altars and altar fragments unearthed across Israel/Palestine attests to the probability that Israelites and Judahites living pastoral lives ritually slaughtered their domesticated animals in their own locales; see Nelson (2002: 149–50). On the excavated remains of four-horned altars, see Zevit (2001: 298–314).

as a violent crime of bloodshed, rather than a ritual act of idolatrous or non-Yahwistic worship (Gilders 2004: 24). This suggests that in death, it is the very life of the animal which is of concern: the animal has not been treated in a way deemed to be socially and ritually acceptable, and as a result, the offender is rendered socially deviant and is to be excluded from the community.

In some ways, this portrayal of 'illegitimate' animal killing dovetails with the attitudes found in the story of the poor man's little lamb (2 Sam. 12.1-6), in which the killing and consumption of a household animal by a non-family member renders the lamb's slaughter an action distressingly dislocated from its appropriate socio-ritual context. It is thus pitched as a moral crime deserving of avenging, bloody justice, for the household has lost a beloved member of the family.[13] Although the dynamics of inappropriate animal slaughter differ in Lev. 17.3-4, these verses also problematize the killing of a domestic animal in inappropriate socio-ritual contexts. Consequently, this form of slaughter is similarly cast as a moral crime, and it too warrants retributive justice: the perpetrator is to be 'cut off' from his community, ensuring that his own family will similarly suffer the loss of a household member. Thus, to some extent, the punishment mimics the crime and, in doing so, signals the precious social entanglement of human and animal relationships.

In conclusion, human bodies and animal bodies were inextricably bound in the Israelite and Judahite household. Israelites and Judahites ate their domestic animals' dairy products and flesh, exploited their fleeces and hides for clothing, and used their traction power for producing grain. But these relationships between human bodies and animal bodies were socially negotiated – a negotiation that is variously reflected in the ethno-archaeological data and ritual regulations endorsed in the Hebrew Bible. At the point of its slaughter, an animal's death (and its body) had to be managed using a socially ordained set of ritualized practices. Humans and domestic animals interacted in such a way that their interdependence was recognized and acknowledged throughout each animal's life and death. Humans related to their animal household members as social beings because of their shared contribution towards a secure and stable future. Animals were not merely property or objects of exploitation, but were reciprocally engaged in the physical and emotional nourishment of the Israelite and Judahite household.

References

Abu-Rabia, A. (1994), *The Negev Bedouin and Livestock Rearing*, Oxford: Berg.

Abu-Rabia, A. (1999), 'Some Notes on Livestock Production among Negev Bedouin Tribes', *Nomadic Peoples* 3 (1): 22–30.

Allentuck, A. (2015), 'Temporalities of Human–Livestock Relationships in the Late Prehistory of the Southern Levant', *Journal of Social Archaeology* 15: 94–115.

Boer, R. (2015), *The Sacred Economy of Ancient Israel*, Louisville, KY: Westminster John Knox.

Borowski, O. (1987), *Agriculture in Iron Age Israel*, Winona Lake, IN: Eisenbrauns.

Borowski, O. (1997), *Every Living Thing: Daily Use of Animals in Ancient Israel*, Walnut Creek, CA: AltaMira Press.

---

13 The motivations behind this law are likely to be multifaceted, for there was probably an economic incentive also at play, which ensured that pastoralists did not carry out animal slaughter without contributing portions of meat to the 'legitimate' cult and its priests. Despite this, dressing an economic concern in the guise of a 'moral' concern about bloodshed may have enabled it to carry more currency in wider society, as it hit a nerve, so to speak, in the emotional and social lives of Israelite and Judahite households.

Clough, D. (2018), *On Animals: Volume Two, Theological Ethics*, London: T&T Clark.
Davis, S. (1987a), *The Archaeology of Animals*, New Haven, CT: Yale University Press.
Davis, S. (1987b), 'The Faunal Remains', in A. Ben-Tor and Y. Portugali (eds), *Tell Qiri: A Village in the Jezreel Valley*, 249–50, Jerusalem: Hebrew University.
Dever, W. G. (2012), *The Lives of Ordinary People in Ancient Israel: Where Archaeology and the Bible Intersect*, Grand Rapids, MI: Eerdmans.
Ebeling, J. R. (2010), *Women's Lives in Biblical Times*, London: T&T Clark.
Gilders, W. K. (2004), *Blood Ritual in the Hebrew Bible: Meaning and Power*, Baltimore, MD: Johns Hopkins University Press.
Greer, J. S. (2013), *Dinner at Dan: Biblical and Archaeological Evidence for Sacred Feasts at Iron Age II Tel Dan and Their Significance*, Leiden: Brill.
Helmer, D., and J. Vigne (2007), 'Was Milk a "Secondary Product" in the Old World Neolithisation Process? Its Role in the Domestication of Cattle, Sheep and Goats', *Anthropozoologica* 42: 9–40.
Hesse, B. (1984), 'These Are Our Goats: The Origins of Herding in West Central Iran', in J. Clutton-Brock and C. Grigson (eds), *Animals in Archaeology, Volume 3: Early Herders and Their Flock*, 243–64, Oxford: British Archaeological Reports.
Hesse, B., P. Wapnish and J. Greer (2012), 'Scripts of Animal Sacrifice in Levantine Culture-History', in A. M. Porter and G. M. Schwartz (eds), *Sacred Killing: The Archaeology of Sacrifice in the Ancient Near East*, 217–35, Winona Lake, IN: Eisenbrauns.
Hodder, I. (1982), *The Present Past: An Introduction to Anthropology for Archaeologists*, London: B. T. Batsford.
Hodder, I. (2012), *Entangled: An Archaeology of the Relationships between Humans and Things*, Malden, MA: Wiley-Blackwell.
Holladay, J. S. (1997), 'Four-room House', in E. M. Meyers (ed.), *The Oxford Encyclopedia of Archaeology in the Near East*, Volume 2, 337–42, Oxford: Oxford University Press.
Holtzman, J. (2009), *Uncertain Tastes: Memory, Ambivalence, and the Politics of Eating in Samburu, Northern Kenya*, London: University of California Press.
Horwitz, L. K. (1998), 'The Faunal Remains', in G. Edelstein, I. Milevski and S. Aurant (eds), *Villages, Terraces, and Stone Mounds: Excavations at Manahat, Jerusalem, 1987–1989*, 104–12, Jerusalem: Israel Antiquities Authority.
Horwitz, L. K. (2000a), 'Animal Exploitation – Archaeozoological Analysis', in Z. Gal and Y. Alexandre (eds), *Horbat Rosh Zayit: An Iron Age Storage Fort and Village*, 221–32, Jerusalem: Israel Antiquities Authority.
Horwitz, L. K. (2000b), 'The Contribution of Archaeozoology to the Identification of Ritual Sites', in S. Pike and S. Gitin (eds), *The Practical Impact of Science on Near Eastern and Aegean Archaeology*, 63–71, London: Archetype.
Janzen, D. (2004), *The Social Meanings of Sacrifice in the Hebrew Bible: A Study of Four Writings*, Berlin: Walter de Gruyter.
Jones, L. (2020), 'Veganism: Why are Vegan Diets on the Rise?', https://www.bbc.co.uk/news/business-44488051 (accessed 26 May 2020).
Kohler-Rollefson, I. (1995), 'The Animal Bones', in C. M. Bennett and P. Bienkowski (eds), *Excavations at Tawilan in Southern Jordan*, 97–100, Oxford: Oxford University Press.
Kramer, C. (1982), *Village Ethnoarchaeology: Rural Iran in Archaeological Perspective*, New York: Academic Press.
London, G. (2016), *Ancient Cookware from the Levant: An Ethnoarchaeological Perspective*, Sheffield: Equinox.

Lyons, D., and J. Casey (2016), 'It's a Material World: The Critical and On-Going Value of Ethnoarchaeology in Understanding Variation, Change and Materiality', *World Archaeology* 48: 609–27.

Meyers, C. (2002), 'Having Their Space and Eating There Too: Bread Production and Female Power in Ancient Israelite Households', *Nashim* 5: 14–44.

Meyers, C. (2013), *Rediscovering Eve: Ancient Israelite Women in Context*, New York: Oxford University Press.

Nelson, R. D. (2002), *Deuteronomy: A Commentary*, Louisville, KY: Westminster John Knox Press.

Postgate, J. N. (1992), *Early Mesopotamia: Society and Economy at the Dawn of History*, London: Routledge.

Potts, T. (1997), *Mesopotamian Civilization: The Material Foundations*, Ithaca, NY: Cornell University Press.

Sasson, A. (2006), 'Animal Husbandry and Diet in Pre-Modern Villages in Mandatory Palestine, According to Ethnographic Data', in M. Maltby (ed.), *Integrating Zooarchaeology*, 33–40, Oxford: Oxbow.

Sasson, A. (2008), 'Reassessing the Bronze and Iron Age Economy: Sheep and Goat Husbandry in the Southern Levant as a Model Case Study', in A. Fantalkin and A. Yasur-Landau (eds), *Bene Israel: Studies in the Archaeology of Israel and the Levant during the Bronze and Iron Ages*, 113–34, Leiden: Brill.

Sasson, A. (2010), *Animal Husbandry in Ancient Israel: A Zooarchaeological Perspective on Livestock Exploitation, Herd Management and Economic Strategies*, London: Equinox.

Shahack-Gross, R. (2011), 'Household Archaeology in Israel: Looking into the Microscopic Record', in A. Yasur-Landau, J. Ebeling and L. B. Mazow (eds), *Household Archaeology in Ancient Israel and Beyond*, 27–36, Leiden: Brill.

Sillar, B. (2000), 'Dung by Preference: The Choice of Fuel as an Example of How Andean Pottery Production Is Embedded within Wider Technical, Social, and Economic Practices', *Archaeometry* 42: 43–60.

Stavrakopoulou, F. (2016), 'Religion at Home: The Materiality of Practice', in S. Niditch (ed.), *The Wiley Blackwell Companion to Ancient Israel*, 347–65, Chichester: Wiley Blackwell.

Stone, K. (2018), *Reading the Hebrew Bible with Animal Studies*, Stanford, CA: Stanford University Press.

Sykes, N. (2014), *Beastly Questions: Animal Answers to Archaeological Issues*, London: Bloomsbury.

Tchernov, E., and A. Drori (1983), 'Economic Patterns and Environmental Conditions at Hirbet El-Msas during the Early Iron Age', in V. Fritz and A. Kempinski (eds), *Ergebnisse der Ausgrabungen auf der Hirbet el-Mšaš [Tel Masos] 1972–1975*, 213–22, Wiesbaden: Otto Harrassowitz.

Watson, P. J. (1979), *Archaeological Ethnography in Western Iran*, Tucson: University of Arizona Press for the Wenner-Gren Foundation for Anthropological Research.

Welton, R. (2020), *'He Is a Glutton and a Drunkard': Deviant Consumption in the Hebrew Bible*, Leiden: Brill.

Zevit, Z. (2001), *The Religions of Ancient Israel: A Synthesis of Parallactic Approaches*, London: Continuum.

PART TWO

Value, status and power

CHAPTER FIVE

Birthing new life: Israelite and Mesopotamian values and visions of the preborn child*

SHAWN W. FLYNN

Joseph Blenkinsopp, speaking of the Hebrew Bible, says: 'We can get some idea of the rather vague and ill-focused conception of childhood ... [but] it is consistent with Ariès' thesis that we do not find a clear consciousness of childhood as a distinct life phase' (Blenkinsopp 1997: 67; citing Ariès 1962). The scholarly characterization of childhood in ancient Israel and the Hebrew Bible has changed dramatically in just the past few years.[1] Following a trend that focused on children in Mesopotamia (Stol 2005), early Christianity (Betsworth 2015), Rome (Dasen and Späth 2010) and Egypt (Jassen and Jassen 2007), the study of children in ancient Israel has now become an important lens for interpreting biblical texts thanks to emerging work in this field (Fewell 2003; Michel 2003; Kunz-Lübcke 2007; Bergmann 2008; Koepf-Taylor 2013; Steinberg 2013; Parker 2013; Garroway 2014; Markl 2016; Bosworth 2016; Dewrell 2017; Flynn 2018). In particular, historical approaches have much to offer (Bergmann 2008; Garroway 2014; Bosworth 2016; Dewrell 2017; Flynn 2018). They can enrich our understanding of children in ancient Israel, nuance our understanding of the ways in which children are represented in the Hebrew Bible and provide some insight into how ancient cultures perceived children.

More specifically, we might ask how children were valued. Were children valued primarily for their economic contributions or did their value extend beyond economics and utility? Naomi Steinberg (2013: 103) has observed: 'In the economic sense, a child's value and identity was formed based on membership in the family.' For Steinberg, the contemporary idealization of the child in middle class and European contexts problematically 'obscures the economic conceptualizations of childhood and instances of

---

* This chapter is an adapted version of Flynn (2018: ch. 2). It is dedicated to all those who have lost children, even at the earliest stages.
1 In what follows, the designation 'ancient Israel' functions as a blanket term for the ancient societies in which the literature of the Hebrew Bible emerged.

violence against children in biblical texts' (Steinberg 2013: 121). Most who study children in the Hebrew Bible have been vague on the question of value but some have provided a bit of nuance (Parker 2013: 201–2). An approach that leverages the ancient Near Eastern context as a lens for understanding children's roles in the domestic cult, and applies this to the Hebrew Bible's representation of children, can clarify a child's value in both ancient Israel and its broader context. This line of questioning probes children's ritual and social roles in the domestic sphere and asks how the world of gods and goddesses factors into these expressions of the child's cultic contribution to the domicile. Let us explore this issue through one stage of a child's life that has not, beyond Claudia Bergmann (2008), received significant attention in the emerging secondary literature: an analysis of preborn and birthing children in biblical and Mesopotamian texts. Specifically, let us look at Mesopotamian constructions of preborn and birthing children, and the female bodies that birthed these children, gathering medical texts, letters and myth in Mesopotamian sources, and compare these with Jer. 1.4-5, Psalm 139 and Job 10.8-11.

When comparing Mesopotamian constructions with biblical sources one finds that biblical writers assume a commonly held domestic-cultic value of children beyond the economic value, and at times use this shared social value to say something unique in their own Levantine context. We also learn that the female body, only valued for its ability to produce the child, also reinforces the child's domestic-cultic value. We see that across Israel and Mesopotamia, value is expressed via a child–deity connection made during the prebirth stage, reinforced by female professionals and the role of the gods, as a foundational aspect of the child's cultic value in the household. In this expression, the female body that births the child often remains a secondary – and silenced – conduit or utility of this birthing process.

Exploring these questions via the comparative method not only advances the current discipline of childhood studies in the Hebrew Bible but also provides an important perspective on the stages of life and death in ancient Israelite thought and practice. In particular, the comparative study offered here will (1) help to reassess the social and cultic value of ancient children, (2) demonstrate how the broader cultural matrix can help us to better understand Israelite perceptions of children, (3) expand the scope of the emerging study of Israelite childhood by adding a new stage of the child's life and (4) provide some clarity on the socio-religious roles played by the smallest bodies that experienced life and death in ancient Israel, while offering some insights into the role of the bodies that birthed them.

The Mesopotamian child *in potentia*: Medical sources

Medical texts offer a helpful avenue into the Mesopotamian understanding of a child during the prebirth stage. Given high mortality rates in the ancient world, the threat of unsuccessful pregnancies, or losing newborn children, was considerable and likely motivated much of this medical focus and effort. Some studies suggest the infant mortality rate was as high as 50 per cent (Hübner 2009: 53). This was an important stage in a child's life from the ancient perspective. Assyria and Babylonia thus give substantial attention to gynaecology and obstetrics in the hopes of protecting the unborn child and increasing the possibility of successful births (Biggs 1995). For example, in anticipation of whether conception had been achieved, the ancients developed pregnancy tests: a makeshift tampon, to be used overnight and observed in the morning, measured changes in vaginal fluids (perhaps in an attempt to discern what we now know to be changes induced by oestrogen and progesterone levels and fluidic acidity) and thus functioned as a diagnostic tool (Scurlock and Andersen 2005: 262). Whether or not any changes accurately reflected pregnancy cannot be determined. Other medical texts suggest that one way a new mother might ensure subsequent successful conceptions was to use a wet nurse (*mušēniqtu*). In the ancient world, hiring a wet nurse was not an endeavour of the wealthy to avoid breastfeeding, but instead served a very specific purpose. The phenomenon addressed was likely 'lactational amenorrhoea': the absence of menstruation, and hence fertility, due to breastfeeding, a commonly known effect of nursing a baby (Diaz 1989; McNeilly 1993). Especially in the first six months after birth, breastfeeding on demand can act as natural birth control. In a contemporary context, with our improved knowledge of female physiology, this is a desirable method for spacing pregnancies to allow the body time to heal, especially for those in the developing world without ready access to modern medicine. Therefore, given the high mortality rates in the ancient Near East, times of infertility were not desirable and all knowledge available was leveraged towards helping the future child.

Motivated by these concerns, Mesopotamian medical knowledge developed entire diagnostic series dedicated to preborn children's medical care. These procedures used a variety of methods like palpitation, or vaginal examinations, and even cervical inspections (Scurlock and Andersen 2005: 259). For example, 'If a woman of childbearing age's womb (?) is shining, she was impregnated with a child that will not do well' (Scurlock and Andersen 2005: 260). This cervical inspection may or may not have been accurate but attests to the level of detail put into such examinations that may surprise contemporary readers. Such resources and texts necessarily imply the development of the relevant methods for such examinations, as well as an investment in the scribal resources to record them. No amount of resources or detailed investigation was spared.

In these medical examples, we see immediately that the woman's body is an important vehicle in the process of understanding the preborn child. But these medical examinations are concerned not for the overall health of the woman, as we might expect today, but focus instead on maternal health as it relates to the child and a safe delivery. The female body is thus a focal point only because of its connection to the child's life (cf. Hamori 2013). The medical focus is on the child, not the mother.

The medical concern for the preborn child at such an early stage can also be understood linguistically. Beyond early interventions to ensure healthy growth, medical texts also track the normal course of foetal development: 'A child (LÚ.TUR) is a half grain the day it is created in the womb of his mother ... On the tenth day, it is five grains. In a full month it is three fingers ... In ten months, it is a cubit' (Scurlock and Andersen 2005: 264). How was the LÚ.TUR perceived at this stage? The use of the logograms (here made up of two cuneiform signs) LÚ and TUR for 'child' demonstrates that the ancients considered this to be a normal stage of life but also hints at the child's value even at this stage. The term *ṣeḫrum*, 'child', comes from the logogram LÚ.TUR, which combines the sign LU = *amīlu* ('man') and the sign TUR = *ṣeḫru* ('small') (Labat 1951: 330), the latter also using part of the same logographic sign from DUMU (*māru*), 'son'. Thus the LÚ.TUR is literally a 'small man' from the earliest (half a grain) stage. The *ṣeḫerum* is then a generic lexeme for any state of smallhood in which the small thing has a corresponding larger state. This relates the earliest stage of childhood, here before birth, to what the child will be *in potentia* (Garroway 2014: 245). Thus, there is no negative judgement on the preborn child because of its early stage of development, nor because it is small. Rather, the child is acknowledged for what it could become in the domicile, even so early on. In the ancient mind, the 'child' begins as half the size of a piece of grain, growing to be three fingers in size, and has a potential to contribute to the household both economically and cultically. In supporting this view, Babylonian horoscopes take as their start-date the day of conception rather than the day of birth (Sachs 1952: 59).

All these medical texts show an immense concern for the preborn child, from investigations into the birthing female body on behalf of the child, and the tracking of the child's development and health, to developing the resources, texts and scribal support for recording and transmitting this knowledge, all of which articulate the preborn state as a valid stage of childhood in the ancient mind. Having catalogued an impressive collection of Mesopotamian gynaecology and obstetric medical texts, JoAnn Scurlock and Burton Andersen (2005: 283) conclude: 'the attention paid to maternal health and fetal development reflect both the importance of ... the labor pool for agriculture ... and [that] children were essential to the happiness and fulfillment of individual men and women'. Mesopotamian medical texts thus suggest that a child's value extended beyond its socio-economic utility to encompass its emotional, personal value. Is this personal value, hinted at in the medical data, confirmed by the Mesopotamian's own religious expression? And if so, what can this expression teach us about the child's cultic value?

The child and the gods in the Mesopotamian domestic cult

Our understanding of ancient perceptions of preborn and birthing children is improved by exploring the link between child and deity during this very early stage of Mesopotamian childhood. Personal prayers express the preborn/birthing child's value and are similarly stamped with approval in mythological literature. Medical practice and domestic ritual thus intersect with mythology to reveal a strong commentary on every child through the deity–child connection. In what follows, three broad examples help to demonstrate the child's domestic-cultic value: the connection between domestic rituals and mythology in their shared treatment of birth; examples of the language and metaphor used in prayers for the preborn/birthing child; and finally, a personal letter incorporating aspects of both.

First, the cultic-domestic value of children is evident in the rituals during birth and their connection to the mythological tradition. In *Atrahasis*, for example, the divine midwife (*šab–sa–ku*) is present at the birth of humanity (1. 290). Highlighting her place and role at the creation of humans, her role in the myth helps to solidify and honour the mortal midwife's role in domestic contexts at every human birth. Much like a priest or a diviner, the mortal midwife is equipped with the sacred tools of her divine counterpart to ensure a safe delivery (the birthing brick, the reed to cut the umbilical cord and the pail). The tools of birth in the domestic cult thus reflect those of mythological midwifery, so that the mortal midwife performs not only a practical role but a spiritual one, too: through her work, she invites the divine to be present at each human birth. We will see this later in a very personal prayer.

In a variety of texts the gods thus become part of every human birth, often through the midwife. Sometimes they come down with the water of labour (*na–ša–at mê*) and the oil from the jar (*na–ša–at šaman*) to help ensure a successful birth (*Ligabue*, lines 59–60; *Nimrud b Rm* 376, lines 31–2; cf. Bergmann 2008: 20–3), but in one Akkadian incantation used for childbirth, Asalluḫi (a male deity) becomes the midwife: 'I, Asalluḫi, am the midwife (*šab–sa–ku*)! I will receive you. Incantation formula' (for the text, see Veldhuis 1991: 61–2). In this incantation, the midwife's role in each human birth is justified and elevated through this particular deity, while at the same time, the deity himself is connected to the child and thereby promoted within the domestic cult. Given that Asalluḫi is the son of the head god Enki, this 'dialogue' between myth and domestic practice thereby brings a powerful god into the domestic cult for the child and family. The divine sphere thus reflects the human one (Scurlock 1991: 140, 166). Claudia Bergmann (2008: 33–59) has collected a variety of texts in which the gods are intimately involved in the birthing process. When discussing these divine assistants, Bergmann puts it this way: 'In the culture and literature of the ancient Near East, the gods and goddesses were seen as being involved in every aspect of conception, pregnancy and birth' (Bergmann 2008: 35). Prebirth rituals clearly connect deity and child with/in the domestic cult.

Prayers for the preborn child serve as a second source of material for our investigation into Mesopotamian perceptions of the earliest stage of childhood, for they too reinforce the role of the divine in the life of the child and point to the ways in which the child was valued. An Old Babylonian (1900–1600 BCE) incantation, for example, solidifies the divine and human connection in the prebirth stage:

> In the fluids of intercourse, bone (*lillidum*) was formed (*ibbani*),
> in the tissue of sinews, baby was formed.
> In the ocean waters, fearsome (*palḫūtim*) raging,
> in the distant waters of the sea,
> where the little one's (*ṣeḫrum*) arms are bound,
> there within, where the sun's eye can bring no brightness
> Asalluḫi, Enki's son, saw him.
> He loosed his tight-tied bonds,
> he set him on his way, he opened him the path.
> 'The path is [op]ened to you, the way is [made straight?] for you,
> the physician (?) ... is waiting for you,
> she is maker of [bl]ood (?), she is maker of us all'.
> She has spoken to the doorbolt, it is released.
> The lock is [fre]ed, the doors are wide. (YOS 11, 16.1-28)[2]

This incantation links the creation of a child in each domestic birth to the first creation in myth by using the same language found in the creation accounts, such as 'fearsome (*palḫūtim*) raging'. The child (*ṣeḫrum*) thus shares in the divine realm, since both humans and gods have a shared origin through the mother goddess: 'She is maker of [bl]ood (?) She is maker of us all' – a reference to the mother goddess who created both humans and the gods. Given this role, she is called on in the moment of every human birth. In *Atrahasis*, the goddess known as Mami, Belit–ili/Bēlet–kāla–ilī or Nintu is also the 'midwife' (*tab–sú–ut ilī^{meš}*) and in particular the 'creatress of mankind' (*ba–ni–a–at a–wi–lu–ti*) (1. 191, 193, 194; see Lambert and Millard 1999: 56). In myth, the deities are connected to the domestic cult through the birthing child. As a means of promoting a deity to the domestic cult, this is certainly a logical strategy. More generally, as Niek Veldhuis (1999: 40) observes, 'the description of the condition of the baby is skillfully connected with mythological allusions, so as to include the world of the gods into the problem. This is a common device.' As in medical literature, the child's cultic value is reinforced in mythological literature as a seal to common ritual-domestic practice.

---

2 For the translation, see Foster (2005: 171). The addition of relevant Akkadian lexemes is mine.

Another common motif evident in prayers for the preborn child is the metaphor of a ship, which is used to reinforce the deity–child connection and expresses the child's domestic-cultic value beyond economic gain. In this image, the ship's journey parallels the difficult journey of pregnancy and birth and supports a whole series of related analogies, like the waters of birth. Again, the utility of the ship reveals something of the way in which the female body is perceived, for it is inevitably presented as a vehicle for its cargo. Nonetheless, it remains a beautiful image: the mother carries the precious cargo of the preborn child during the long journey of pregnancy. Combining precious cargo with the reality of shipwrecks and the perils of ocean travel, the metaphor captures the hope for the baby's safe delivery amidst the risks, while the difficult journey of the child along the 'amniotic ocean' (Stol 2005: 11) communicates the child's fight for survival in the perilous, uncertain moments of its birth.

It is the notion of the preborn child as cargo that is of interest for our purposes. In describing the pregnant woman as a ship, one prayer declares: 'she is filled with carnelian and lapis lazuli (*sa–am–tim ù uq–ni–im*). (Yet) she does not know (if it is) carnelian (*sa–am–tim*); she does not know (if it is) lapis lazuli (*uq–ni–im*)' (for the text and discussion, see Cohen 1976). These precious stones anticipate the gender announcement upon birth, whereby the colour of lapis lazuli (blue) represents a boy and carnelian (red) a girl. But they also communicate much more. As an economic metaphor, the cargo of precious stones might communicate the child's socio-economic contribution to the household – although this interpretation does not map neatly onto the basic economic needs of a typical family (a more accessible metaphor might focus instead on a ship carrying an agricultural cargo like barley). Alternatively, the metaphor might communicate something of the family's ambitious desire for greater wealth and status. But in this prayer, the vehicle of the metaphor of lapis lazuli and carnelian communicates far more than the economic gains a child might bring to the family. Rather, the acquisition of this child is something precious, something rare and not commonly acquired.

Beyond their use as symbols of gender, these particular stones are likely used in the prayer's metaphor because they have divine and ritual connections. Lapis lazuli, a glassy blue stone well-known in the ancient world, was one of the most highly prized gifts offered to gods and kings, as is evident in its frequent association with royalty, votive vessels and the divine realm. In a neo-Babylonian text, a king discussing a tribute gift worries that if he were to carry off the lapis lazuli ($NA_4.ZA.GÌN$; *uqnû*), the people would revolt, since: 'does the king, my lord, not know that lapis lazuli is divine [*iluni*] to us?' (*ABL* 1240: 17; *CAD* U, 196). While we know artisans made highly desirable jewellery from it, lapis lazuli was also the source of votive objects and was used to line the temple of Ninurta (*CAD* U, 200). Its divine index and value beyond monetary gain is clear in its use for cultic service, rendering its metaphorical use in the prayer highly significant: casting the unborn child as lapis lazuli links deity to child in the prebirth stage. Likewise, carnelian (*sa–am–tim*) is a reddish stone – often described as the colour of blood – that seems to have had a particular association with high-status decoration and ornamentation, particularly within the cultic and divine realms. Like lapis lazuli, it is an approved gift to 'put in the basin of holy water' (*AMT* 71, 1.19; *CAD* S, 123); it is also a suitable stone for magical rituals and is even worn by the gods themselves (*CAD* S, 123). The metaphor of a precious cargo of lapis lazuli and carnelian clearly communicates the child's value beyond mere utility and economy; instead, it reinforces the connection between child and deity (already attested in myth and ritual), thus communicating the child's cultic value in the domicile.

Having considered medical texts, prayers and myth, one final example from a personal letter solidifies the connection between domestic birthing prayers and the mythological tradition and helps us to understand how the child–deity connection affected people's lives. This unusual text of the neo-Assyrian period appears to have been commissioned by a husband as a dedication to his dead wife, and it is her voice we hear. The opportunity to listen to the female voice, refracted through the grieving male voice, is a rare but rich interpretive moment, even if it is only an echo of that mother's voice we hear. The text displays the wider cultural tendency to cast the preborn child's value as paramount, while the woman's own voice communicates her value in relation to birthing. Here, the intertwining of the child's value in myth and prayer, and its connection to the divine, is apparent:

> 1. Why are you adrift, like a boat, in the midst of the river, 2. your thwarts in pieces, your mooring rope cut? ... 5. The day I bore the fruit, how happy (*ḫa–da–ak*) I was, 6. happy (*ḫa–da–ak*) was I, happy (*ḫa–da–ak*) my husband. 7. The day of my going into labour, my face became darkened, 8. the day of my giving birth, my eyes became clouded. 9. With open hands I pray to Belet–ili: 'You are the mother of the ones who give birth, save my life!' 10. Hearing this, Belet–ili veiled her face. 11. 'You [...], why do you keep praying to me? ...' [All] those [many] days I was with my husband, I lived with him who was my lover. Death came into my bedroom. (K.890; cf. Livingstone 1989: no. 15)

Here 'joy' (*ḫa–da–ak*) is an important word. Derived from *ḫadû*, it is a neo-Babylonian term that sometimes appears within the phrase *ina ḫadû libbīšu* ('joy in the heart/innermost being'). In this text, joy and sorrow collide as the expectation of a new child is juxtaposed with two deaths. The child, again using the boat imagery common in birthing metaphors, is adrift. It is not a boat set for a successful delivery, for it wanders, without course, direction or a final destination; it is lost. The child is motionless in the mother. This reality contrasts with the joy of the mother and her husband when they had learned that she was pregnant. This stark contrast compounds the loss, for now she must face giving birth to her dead child. This harrowing moment, devoid of the hope and joy of welcoming a living child, is now a life-threatening risk for the mother given all the complications such a difficult birth could imply. In this moment of grief and threat, she asks Belet–ili, the same deity involved in her own birth, as well as that of her lost child, to now save her life. The connection between child and deity is thus apparent in the mother's logical appeal to the mother goddess, demonstrating the intersection of mythology and the domestic cult in the life of the preborn child. But the call for divine help fails, and both child and mother die, leading a grieving father to commission this text. Once again, this final example demonstrates that the close connection between child and deity was intimately fostered in the context of household religion. As a focus of ritual activity in the home, the preborn child played an important role in the domestic cult.

This brisk but broad overview of select Mesopotamian texts, each engaging with the preborn/birthing child, brings into view the ways in which children were perceived within the wider cultural matrix of which ancient Israel was a part. Even at the prebirth stage, Mesopotamian children were valued for their contribution to economic life, but their value extended well beyond this: their cultic value in the domestic sphere hinged around the deity–child connection. Supported by mythological traditions, mediated through the midwife, and practised in the regular life of prayer, dedication and ritual, the close connection between deity and child was a prominent feature of household religion. This provides an important framework for assessing a child's value in the Hebrew Bible and the Israelite tradition. We might ask, for example, how biblical texts expressing violence towards children (such as Genesis 22) play with broader cultural perceptions of a child's value in the domestic cult? While we need not assume that Israelite scribes knew specific Mesopotamian texts and traditions, nor engaged with them directly, we can justifiably ask whether or not the Hebrew Bible reflects similar ideas.

The Hebrew Bible

Knowing now that the prebirth stage of life was well-defined – both socially and cultically – in Mesopotamian cultures, we can re-read biblical texts with a view to assessing the ways in which the social and ritual roles of preborn children are presented. As demonstrated above, the Mesopotamian material places a heavy emphasis on the divine–child connection within the household cult, which prompts us to ask: in the Hebrew Bible, what type of involvement does YHWH have with preborn children, and to what extent does this cohere or conflict with the Mesopotamian perspective?

Jeremiah 1.4-5

The most obvious starting point is Jer. 1.4-5, in which the prophet himself is portrayed as a preborn child. Recent scholarship on children in the Hebrew Bible, however, rarely engages this text.[3] Instead, these verses have received significant attention in biblical scholarship primarily because they offer a unique twist on what is commonly known as a prophetic call narrative (Habel 1965). But set against Mesopotamian perceptions of the prebirth stage and its associated rituals, Jer. 1.4-5 is not quite as distinctive as some would contend. The image of the preborn child in this text aligns well with the Mesopotamian portrayal of preborn children, suggesting that its author shared this broader cultural perception of earliest childhood and used it to communicate something about the Israelite prophet. It is only by comparing the image of the preborn child in Jer. 1.4-5 with Mesopotamian perspectives that we can better understand precisely what this text is trying to communicate about the prophet and his call.

The book of Jeremiah is a complex text. The Septuagint version is unusually shorter (by a seventh) than the MT, and there are also variances in section-ordering between the two. Thanks to the Qumran evidence (2QJer; 4QJer[a-e]), we know there were at least two versions of the book in antiquity. Both versions must be treated in any discussion of Jeremiah, but all this evidence likely demonstrates that the MT is a later version of the text. Despite these complexities, when it comes to our particular verses, the LXX is a relatively literal rendering of its *Vorlage* if the MT is representative, creating a relatively stable text for Jer. 1.4-5, which reads:

ויהי דבר יהוה אלי לאמר
בטרם אצורך בבטן ידעתיך
ובטרם תצא מרחם הקדשתיך
נביא לגוים נתתיך

---

3 A brief reference to Jeremiah 1 occurs only as a part of the word-study in Steinberg (2013: 112), and it is mentioned only in a footnote in Parker (2013:10 n. 33).

Καὶ ἐγένετο λόγος κυρίου πρός με λέγων Πρὸ τοῦ με πλάσαι σε ἐν κοιλίᾳ ἐπίσταμαί σε καὶ πρὸ τοῦ σε ἐξελθεῖν ἐκ μήτρας ἡγίακά σε, προφήτην εἰς ἔθνη τέθεικά σε.

4   The word of YHWH came to me, saying:
5   'Before I formed you in the womb I knew you,
    and before you were born I made you holy;
    a prophet to the nations I appointed you'.

While Jer. 1.4 echoes the biblical prophetic call genre, when we come to v. 5, the text seems unique only if read within this Israelite genre. But the images in v. 5 are now familiar after reviewing our selection of Mesopotamian medical texts, prayers, letters and mythological literature, in which the deity is linked with the preborn child. In its ancient context, the claim in Jer. 1.3-4 that YHWH was involved in this stage of a child's life was far from unique: commonly, a deity would come and assist in the moment of birth, to save the child and protect the birthing process (Stiebert 2012). Read without what we know of the Mesopotamian prebirth stage and the midwife's role connecting deity to child through domestic ritual practice and creation myths, the divine concern for the preborn Jeremiah seems exclusive to YHWH, but it is not. The divine concern for the child during the prebirth stage, reflecting the solidification of that deity in the domestic cult, was a widely held value across the cultural matrix – and it is this context that is operative for this biblical author.

Jeremiah's portrayal of this early life-stage is not dissimilar to the Mesopotamian portrayal of the preborn baby as precious cargo in the mother's womb in the incantations and prayers described above. Divine intervention is common, and even materially forming the child (as indicated by אצורך in Jer. 1.5) was already the Mesopotamian mother goddess's task in creation, re-echoed in each birth. Recall the language and imagery of one Old Babylonian incantation, discussed above: 'In the fluids of intercourse, bone (*lillidum*) was formed (*ibbani*) / in the tissue of sinews, baby was formed / In the ocean waters, fearsome (*palḫūtim*) raging' (YOS 11, 16.1-5). In these ways, Jer. 1.4-5 is thus unoriginal. While we can claim at least some emerging monotheistic perspective for these verses, it is not surprising that YHWH has subsumed something of the functions typical of other deities, combining key features of a head god and mother goddess. Jeremiah simply reflects and refracts the wider culture.

In keeping with the Mesopotamian portrayal of the prebirth/birthing stage of life, we must also acknowledge that the role of the mother is completely absent in Jer. 1.4-5. Just as the Mesopotamian tradition favours the deity, midwife and child more than the mother, in the Jeremiah text the birthing mother is completely absent in favour of the particular child. Only the mother's body is referenced (בטן), almost as an object disassociated from the woman herself. YHWH's relationship is with the child, not the mother. This is in notable contrast to the role of the deity in the neo-Assyrian letter giving voice to a dead wife, discussed above. In that text, the woman's relationship with the birth goddess underlies her plea for her own life as she dies in childbirth. The notable absence of the mother in Jer. 1.4-5 not only reinforces the broader cultural emphasis on the child's socio-religious value within the domestic cult but also exposes a lack of awareness – or even a denial – of the social value of the mother and her birthing body. Exhibiting the same ancient Near Eastern focus on the intimate connection between deity and child, the silencing of the female/birthing body in these verses effectively heightens the child's domestic-cultic value even further.

In the light of these observations, Jer. 1.4-5 initially appears unoriginal, for it communicates nothing distinctively new about the deity's care and concern for the preborn child (here the prophet Jeremiah himself). Although the author of this text was likely familiar with some of the ancient medical perspectives and practices underlying the socio-religious view of the preborn/birthing child,[4] there is no need to prove any familiarity or dependency on a particular Mesopotamian text. Rather, Jer. 1.3-4 simply reflects what was more broadly understood across both Mesopotamia and the Levant: that the divine played a role in the formation and development of the preborn child.

Despite this shared understanding, Jer. 1.4-5 does differ in one important way, although that difference relies on the shared cultural assumptions. Forming the preborn prophet does not occur by the divine hand while he is in the womb. Nor does YHWH come down to intervene at the moment of his birth – the 'moment of crisis' (Bergmann 2008) – as one might expect of the deity. No, YHWH subverts the entire and typical relationship between child and deity, already considered special, by beginning that relationship even before conception. The significance of this claim only makes sense in the light of the high domestic–cultic value placed on the child in the prebirth stage, well known in Mesopotamian literature and likely reflected across the Levant, too.

This remarkable shift is best understood as a means of distinguishing the baby prophet from all other children, in whose preborn lives the divine naturally intervened. Highlighting Jeremiah's extraordinary status in this way is accomplished not only by the appeal to the shared cultural perspective on the divine–child relationship but also by redactional shaping. Since Jer. 1.4-5 likely acts as an introductory frame for some older material, it provides a particular way to view the earlier layers. The existence of JerD (a Deuteronomistic redaction to the book) in Jer. 1.4-5 is well known (Theil 1973). Rainer Albertz (2003: 321) suggests Jer. 1.4-5 is part of the second layer of Jeremiah, JerD^2, which he dates to 545–540 BCE. Regardless of the date, the broader agenda in framing the older prophetic text is the concern to preserve and promote the uniqueness of this prophet. The frame of Jer. 1.4-5 casts YHWH's plan as more expansive than anything the gods have ever done before: the 'creation' of Jeremiah (and, by extension, the pre-planned divine endorsement of the prophet and his mandate during a national crisis) even before his conception.

The prophet Jeremiah thus claims all the traditional advantages of the child–deity relationship, but goes further in asserting that YHWH's involvement in his life goes beyond this. After all, had Jeremiah simply asserted that YHWH was there to ensure his safe birth, his claim would be far from unique (prompting the simple reaction, 'So what, the gods do that for every birth'). But in this later insertion, Jeremiah's material formation, his birth and his divine call are considered special not because of YHWH's participation – typical of other deities – but because YHWH has done what no other god has done before: YHWH involved himself in the life of the preborn child even before the child was conceived.[5] By both drawing upon and modifying widespread religious ideas about the divine concern and care for the preborn child (and all that implies about its cultic value), Jer. 1.4-5 thus legitimizes the prophet. In short, these verses harness the

---

[4] For examples of this sort of medical knowledge, including the use of pregnancy tests, see the Mesopotamian material collated and discussed in Scurlock and Andersen (2005).

[5] The redacted frame also renders Jeremiah special in another way: immediately before our text, Jer. 1.2-3 elevates the prophet's activity by giving his career a forty-year span, just like Moses (from the thirteenth year of Josiah until the fall of Jerusalem; c.627–587 BCE); see Blenkinsopp (1996: 135, 139).

high value of children in the domestic cult in order to elevate the specialized social status of the prophet and to endorse the prophetic (and national temple cult) aims of the book of Jeremiah.

Psalm 139.13-15 and Job 10.8-11

Do the texts of the Hebrew Bible reflect the deity–child connection only with reference to figures of importance, such as prophets and kings, or do they agree with Mesopotamian evidence in assuming that the divine participated in every human birth? While some biblical texts exhibit the same common cultural foundation on which the imagery in Jer. 1.4-5 is built, others do not modify or redirect that common matrix to establish some strategic point. The connection between child and deity does not reflect a concern for a particular child of a predestined social status, but is a common expression of each child's value in the domestic cult. Consider Ps. 139.13-15:

כי אתה קנית כליתי תסכני בבטן אמי
אודך על כי נוראות נפליתי נפלאים מעשיך ונפשי ידעת מאד
לא נכחד עצמי ממך אשר עשיתי בסתר רקמתי בתחתיות ארץ

13   For it was you who formed (קנית)[6] my inward parts;
      you knit me together in my mother's womb.
14   I praise you, because wonderfully you separated me out,[7]
      your works are wonderful,
      you know me well.
15   My frame was not hidden from you,
      when I was made in secret,
      woven in the lower parts of the earth.

And note Job 10.8-11:

ידיך עצבוני ויעשוני יחד סביב ותבלעני
זכר נא כי כחמר עשיתני ואל עפר תשיבני
הלא כחלב תתיכני וכגבנה תקפיאני
עור ובשר תלבישני ובעצמות וגידים תסככני

8   Your hands have formed me and fashioned me;
     will you then turn and destroy me?
9   Oh, remember that you fashioned me from clay!
     Will you then bring me down to dust again?
10   Did you not pour me out as milk,
     and thicken me like cheese?
11   With skin and flesh you clothed me,
     with bones and sinews you knit me together.

---

6 The Ugaritic cognate is important in creation narratives. When Kirta wants to have sons, he says, 'give me sons so I may procreate' (*KTU* 1.14 ii 4). Here, '*aqny* means 'I will create' and is used much the same way in other Ugaritic texts (e.g. *KTU* 1.19 iv 58); see Sivan (2001). While there is no creation myth at Ugarit, El's epithets reinforce his role as 'creator of created things'; see Mullen (1980: 12–22).
7 A variant is attested in 11QPs^a, which reads, 'you are awesome', directing the wonder to YHWH, not to the self, and thus expanding on the reason to praise YHWH.

In these texts, the use of creator language to describe the divine formation of the preborn child emphasizes the child's value, just as it does in the Mesopotamian material. But this use of creator language to describe the deity's actions also serves another purpose: the creative act in the womb is likened to the first moments of cosmic creation. It is worth recalling again the opening lines of the Old Babylonian incantation discussed above: 'In the fluids of intercourse, bone was formed (*ibbani*) / in the tissue of sinews, baby was formed / In the ocean waters, fearsome (*palḫūtim*) raging' (YOS 11, 16.1-5). Compare this with our psalm: 'For it was you who formed (קנית) my inward parts; you knit me (תסכני) together in my mother's womb' (Ps. 139.13). This text also matches the image of YHWH forming the preborn child in Job 10.8 ('your hands shaped me and made me'), with the *piel* of עצב emphasizing this ongoing and constant work. While the Mesopotamian mother goddess 'is maker of [bl]ood (?) She is maker of us all' (YOS 11, 16.19-20), YHWH understandably takes over that female role, so that in Ps. 139.13, he forms the child's inward parts (קנית כליתי) within the mother's womb.

The parallel between creation myths and YHWH's involvement in the creation of preborn children is rich in Psalm 139. The connection is more noticeable if v. 14, likely a later addition (cf. *BHS*), is removed, for v. 13 forms a conceptual parallel with v. 15b, drawing out the connection between the two types of creation. Thus,

כי אתה קנית כליתי תסכני בבטן אמי
אשר עשיתי בסתר רקמתי בתחתיות ארץ

13   For it was you who formed my inward parts;
       you knit me together in my mother's womb.
15b ... when I was made in secret,
       woven in the lower parts of the earth.

In many ways, vv. 14 and 15a are a narrative interruption to the parallelism that is more at home in the broader cultural context. References to the כלית ('inward parts') and בטן אם ('mother's womb') in v. 13 find a suitable parallel with the תחתיות ארץ ('lower parts of the earth') in 15b. The psalmist therefore casts an imaginative eye not only to the womb as the mother's lower parts but also to the fecund lower parts of the earth, and thus recalls the first creation, evoking the mother goddess and her own womb. Thus the psalmist shares with the Mesopotamian material the sense that the same deity is responsible for creating both the world and each child – especially if v. 14 is a gloss. Indeed, it may be that the close association of the womb and the lower parts of the earth motivated the addition of v. 14, for in the ancient Near East this natural association would have pointed, entirely logically, to the female deity. With the insertion of v. 14, the psalmist's praise of YHWH suddenly interrupts the paralleling of cosmic creation and the creation of the preborn child, dissuading the reader from thinking of the mother goddess. The Hebrew Bible is always careful to mitigate such associations in its editorial history.

Within its Israelite and biblical context, the creation imagery of Psalm 139 could refer to any of the creation traditions attested in the Hebrew Bible (Gen. 1; 2.4b; Prov. 8.22-31; Ezek. 28.12-17) or even one now lost to us. The closest conceptual parallel to the psalmist's reference to the תחתיות ארץ ('lower parts of the earth') is the second story of creation in Genesis, in which YHWH forms Adam from the 'ground' (Gen. 2.7). Although the language differs somewhat from Ps. 139.13-15, and while the story of Adam certainly does not use the ארץ ('earth') of the Priestly creation account, the imagery is the same: just as YHWH forms every child in the mother's womb in Ps. 139.13-15, so YHWH also formed Adam from the lower parts of the earth and breathed the breath of life into him in Gen. 2.7. The lack of the term ארץ in this story is understandable if it is earlier than the Priestly narrative (the latter repeats ארץ twenty-two times), since the establishment of the land is central to the post-exilic concerns of the Priestly account. There is thus ample time for the ארץ language to have been filtered into Psalm 139. Ultimately, however, Ps. 139.13-15 reflects the same cultural assumptions attested in the Mesopotamian material, with minimal developments or innovations: the deity–child connection was not confined to extraordinary individuals but extended to all preborn children.

Much like Ps. 139.13-15 and its Mesopotamian parallels, the portrayal of the preborn child in Job 10.8-11 draws on creator language to describe the relationship between the deity and the child, without reference to any special birth or status. There is thus nothing unique about this portrayal. Indeed, the language and imagery of Job 10.8-11 comes very close to that commonly employed in the Mesopotamian texts we have examined. In v. 8, for example, the expression ידיך עצבוני ויעשוני ('your hands formed and fashioned me') parallels the imagery of the opening phrase of the childbirth incantation we have already seen ('In the fluids of intercourse, bone (*lillidum*) was formed (*ibbani*)'), while in v. 11, עור ובשר תלבישני ובעצמות וגידים תסככני ('with skin and flesh you clothed me, with bones and sinews you knit me together') parallels the imagery of the incantation's subsequent line ('in the tissue of sinews, baby was formed').

All this commonality admitted, and recognizing the innovative twist in Jer. 1.4-5, heightening Jeremiah's prophetic legitimacy, there is perhaps one feature that distinguishes the biblical tradition. In Mesopotamia, the connection between deity and child is made during the birthing and incantation rituals in order to help the birthing process. For this reason, Mesopotamian reflections on the preborn child often take the form of prayers or incantations uttered in the domestic cult at the actual time of the child's delivery. These incantations and prayers seamlessly correspond with the motif of birth in the wider mythological tradition of divine creation. By contrast, in the Hebrew Bible, the connection between YHWH and the preborn child occurs as part of a prayer relating to the life of an adult, when the supplicant recalls the moment of his or her own birth to emphasize or re-establish their connection with the deity. The petitioner implores the deity to hear them by reminding the deity of the close relationship they enjoyed at the moment of their birth. Thus, in Job 10.8-11, Job mounts a defence against YHWH's actions by reminding YHWH of the child–deity connection he and YHWH shared while Job was in the womb.

Likewise, the poet of Psalm 139 recalls the deity–child connection later in adulthood. In the first part of the psalm, the speaker seeks to understand why YHWH knows the thoughts and actions of the speaker (vv. 1-6); the speaker considers escaping YHWH (vv. 7-12) and reflects on the darkness of isolation (v. 11). But that darkness is paralleled with the darkness of the womb, leading the supplicant to remember the child–deity connection experienced by every preborn child. Many have interpreted this psalm as a petition before YHWH in the temple, or even a judgment scene (Mowinckel [1962] 2004: 74–5; Allen 1983: 260–1; Goulder 1998: 241–2). Connecting with the deity of birth in order to legitimize one's petition certainly makes sense in the genre of supplication to that same deity.

Other Hebrew Bible texts share this use of the child–deity connection. In Ps. 131.2, the person at prayer uses the relationship between child and mother as a metaphor for the relationship of the supplicant to YHWH (Zenger 2006). Likewise, Psalm 22 makes a similar connection. YHWH's involvement in the life of each person (vv. 10-11) links YHWH to the deliverance of the people to come (לעם נולד) in v. 32. The child–deity relationship in the prebirth stage becomes foundational for religious expression at a later stage of life (Jer. 1.4-5; cf. TIM 1.15). In this early poem, the supplicant's painful anguish triggers the appeal to YHWH as the deity involved in his birth, so that a connection is made between YHWH and the labour pains of each birth.

It would therefore seem that, through some forms of prayer, the Hebrew Bible offers a small insight into the ways in which the preborn child was perceived in the Israelite household, demonstrating that the child was valued in ways similar to those attested of the child in the Mesopotamian household. In Israel, the adult worshipper could call upon the religious significance of their prebirth stage of life to advance a claim with YHWH. The penitent need not stand before YHWH in any special capacity as priest or prophet; rather, their plea was founded on the understanding that they had been shaped by YHWH in the womb. These prayers and petitions not only offer an insight into domestic-cultic practice and beliefs about children but also suggest that recalling the deity of childhood – the deity of the household cult – played a part in the religious lives of adults.

Within their biblical context, household prayers like these have been used to great effect by the writers and editors of the Hebrew Bible, for they function as promotional material for the central YHWH cult. Their inclusion and adaptation in biblical material sends a clear theological message: not only was YHWH the deity who was there for the worshipper in earliest childhood, and there for the worshipper's parents in the domestic cult, but YHWH remains similarly effective throughout the worshipper's life *because* of that initial bond. YHWH, the deity of the central cult, is thus cast as the ideal deity for the domestic cult. In part, these texts therefore engage in a programmatic promotion of the central YHWH cult beyond the Jerusalem temple, in the hope that it will be disseminated to each household.

Conclusions

This comparison of biblical and Mesopotamian perceptions of the preborn child offers new ways to further current work in the study of childhood in ancient Israel and the Hebrew Bible. First, this study makes it apparent that the preborn stage was considered a logical category of childhood, and that this life-stage is reflected in biblical texts. A focus on the preborn stage draws in biblical texts missing from current analyses in childhood studies, which can now be used, I hope, to confirm or refine recent conclusions reached by means of other texts. At the very least, this discussion opens up prebirth as another important dimension of childhood to be considered in scholarship, broadening our knowledge of ancient children for future discussions.

Second, the specific discussion of the preborn child in this study sets up new and important interpretive directions. The close examination of the prebirth stage reveals a different way in which children were valued in Israelite and Mesopotamian cultures: even before its birth, the child was an important focus of the domestic cult. Its high value, however, exposes the religious undervaluing of birthing bodies in both Israelite and Mesopotamian texts, in which the pregnant and birthing mother is cast merely as a vehicle for her child. Although birthing mothers are certainly given attention in Mesopotamian medical and incantation texts (and may well have received similar ritual attention in ancient Israel), they nonetheless take a back seat to the midwife, the gods and the expected child. In biblical portrayals of the preborn/birthing child, the mother's body is similarly overlooked or downplayed; it is the deity–child connection that is paramount.

Indeed, even in those petitionary texts in which an adult recalls the prebirth stage later in life (perhaps a distinct feature of the Hebrew Bible), the birthing mother remains unrecognized.

Finally, this study has suggested that the preborn child was highly valued within the context of the domestic cult. Although children served an important role in the economic realities of the household in both Israel and Mesopotamia, it was their cultic value during the prebirth stage that seems to have resonated in particular. Not only did the preborn child enrich the domestic cult, but as a focus for interaction with the divine, the preborn child might facilitate the promotion and growth of a particular deity in the domestic sphere – much as certain biblical texts suggest of YHWH. Given the importance of children, and their essential role and value in the fabric of domestic cults, it may be that the successful promotion and growth of a deity's cult in ancient societies relied less on cultic expression at the temple, or the textual traditions of scribal culture, and rather more on the life of the child in the family home.

References

Albertz, R. (2003), *Israel in Exile: The History and Literature of the Sixth Century B.C.E.*, Atlanta, GA: Society of Biblical Literature.

Allen, L. (1983), *Psalms 101–150*, Word Biblical Commentary 21, Waco, TX: Word Books.

Ariès, P. (1962), *Centuries of Childhood: A Social History of Family Life*, trans. Robert Baldick, New York: Vintage Books.

Bergmann, C. D. (2008), *Childbirth as a Metaphor for Crisis: Evidence from the Ancient Near East, the Hebrew Bible, and 1QH XI, 1–18*, BZAW 382, Berlin: Walter de Gruyter.

Betsworth, S. (2015), *Children in Early Christian Narratives*, Library of New Testament Studies 521, London: Bloomsbury.

Biggs, R. (1995), 'Medicine, Surgery, and Public Health in Ancient Mesopotamia', in J. Sasson (ed.), *Civilizations of the Ancient Near East* III, 1911–24, New York: Scribner.

Blenkinsopp, J. (1996), *A History of Prophecy in Israel*, Louisville, KY: Westminster John Knox Press.

Blenkinsopp, J. (1997), 'The Family in First Temple Israel', in L. Perdue, J. Blenkinsopp, J. J. Collins and C. Meyers (eds), *Families in Ancient Israel*, 48–103, Louisville, KY: Westminster John Knox Press.

Bosworth, D. (2016), *Infant Weeping in Akkadian, Hebrew, and Greek Literature*, Critical Studies in the Hebrew Bible, Winona Lake, IN: Eisenbrauns.

Cohen, M. E. (1976), 'Literary Texts from the Andrews University Archaeological Museum', *Revue d'Assyriologie et d'Archéologie Orientale* 70: 129–44.

Dasen, V., and T. Späth, eds (2010), *Children, Memory, and Family Identity in Roman Culture*, Oxford: Oxford University Press.

Dewrell, H. (2017), *Child Sacrifice in Ancient Israel*, Winona Lake, IN: Eisenbrauns.

Diaz, S. (1989), 'Determinants in Lactational Amenorrhea', *Supplement to International Journal of Gynecology and Obstetrics* 1: 83–95.

Fewell, D. (2003), *The Children of Israel: Reading the Bible for the Sake of Our Children*, Nashville, TN: Abingdon Press.

Flynn, S. W. (2018), *Children in Ancient Israel: The Hebrew Bible and Mesopotamia in Comparative Perspective*, Oxford: Oxford University Press.

Foster, B. (2005), *Before the Muses: An Anthology of Akkadian Literature*, Bethesda, MD: CDL Press.
Garroway, K. (2014), *Children in the Ancient Near Eastern Household*, Explorations in Ancient Near Eastern Civilizations 3, Winona Lake, IN: Eisenbrauns.
Goulder, M. (1998), *The Psalms of the Return (Book V, Psalms 107–150): Studies in the Psalter, IV*, Journal for the Study of the Old Testament Supplement Series 258, Sheffield: Sheffield Academic Press.
Habel, N. (1965), 'The Form and Significance of the Call Narratives', *Zeitschrift für die alttestamentliche Wissenschaft* 77: 297–323.
Hamori, E. (2013), 'Heavenly Bodies: Pregnancy and Birth Omens in Israel', *Hebrew Bible and Ancient Israel* 2 (4): 479–99.
Hübner, U. (2009), 'Sterben, überleben, leben. Die Kinder und der Tod im antiken Palästina', in C. Grube, J. Krispenz, T. Kruger, C. Rose and A. Schellenberg (eds), *Sprachen – Bilder – Klänge: Dimensionen der Theologie im Alten Testament und in seinem Umfeld*, 49–73, Münster: Ugarit-Verlag.
Jassen, R., and J. Jassen (2007), *Growing Up and Getting Old in Ancient Egypt*, London: Golden House.
Koepf-Taylor, L. (2013), *Give Me Children or I Shall Die: Children and Communal Survival in Biblical Literature*, Minneapolis, MN: Fortress Press.
Kunz-Lübcke, A. (2007), A. *Das Kind in den antiken Kulturen des Mittelmeers: Israel – Ägypten – Griechenland*, Neukirchen-Vluyn: Neukirchener.
Labat, R. (1951), *Traité Akkadien de Diagnostics et Pronostics Médicaux*, 2 vols, Paris: Academie Internationale d'Histoire des Sciences.
Lambert, W., and A. Millard (1999), *Atrahasis: The Babylonian Story of the Flood*, Winona Lake, IN: Eisenbrauns.
Livingstone, A. (1989), *Court Poetry and Literary Miscellanea*, Helsinki: Helsinki University Press.
Markl, D. (2016), 'Infant, Infancy. I. Hebrew Bible/Old Testament', *Encyclopedia of the Bible and Its Reception* 12: 1135–9.
McNeilly, A. (1993), 'Lactational Amenorrhea', *Endocrinology and Metabolism Clinics of North America* 22 (3): 59–69.
Michel, A. (2003), *Gott und Gewalt gegen Kinder im Alten Testament*, Forschungen zum Alten Testament 37, Tübingen: Mohr Siebeck.
Mowinckel, S. ([1962] 2004), *The Psalms in Israel's Worship*, trans. D. R. Ap-Thomas, Grand Rapids, MI: Eerdmans.
Mullen, E. (1980), *The Divine Council in Canaanite and Early Hebrew Literatures*, Chico, CA: Scholars Press.
Parker, J. (2013), *Valuable and Vulnerable: Children in the Hebrew Bible, Especially the Elisha Cycle*, Brown University Judaic Study Series, Providence, RI: Brown University.
Sachs, A. (1952), 'Babylonian Horoscopes', *Journal of Cuneiform Studies* 6: 49–75.
Scurlock, J. (1991), 'Baby-Snatching Demons, Restless Souls and the Dangers of Childbirth: Medico-Magical Means of Dealing with Some of the Perils of Motherhood in Ancient Mesopotamia', *Incognita* 2: 137–85.
Scurlock, J., and B. Andersen (2005), *Diagnoses in Assyrian and Babylonian Medicine: Ancient Sources, Translations, and Modern Medical Analyses*, Illinois: University of Illinois Press.
Sivan, D. (2001), *A Grammar of the Ugaritic Language*, Handbook of Oriental Studies 28, Atlanta, GA: Society of Biblical Literature.
Steinberg, N. (2013), *The World of Children in the Hebrew Bible*, Sheffield: Sheffield Phoenix Press.

Stiebert, J. (2012), 'Human Conception in Antiquity: The Hebrew Bible in Context', *Theology and Sexuality* 16 (3): 209–27.
Stol, M. (2005), *Birth in Babylonia and the Bible: Its Mediterranean Setting*, Groningen: Styx.
Theil, W. (1973), *Die deuteronomistische Redaktion von Jeremia 1–25*, Wissenschaftliche Monographien zum Alten und Neuen Testament 41; Neukirchen-Vluyn: Neukirchener Verlag.
Veldhuis, N. (1991), *A Cow of Sîn*, Groningen: Styx.
Veldhuis, N. (1999), 'The Poetry of Magic', in T. Abusch and K. van der Toorn (eds), *Mesopotamian Magic: Textual, Historical, and Interpretative Perspectives*, 35–48, Groningen: Styx.
Zenger, E. (2006), '"Wie das Kind dei mire ...": Das weibliche Gottsbild von Ps 131', in I. Riedel-Spangen and E. Zenger (eds), *Gott bin ich, kein Mann: Beiträge zur Hermeneutik der biblischen Gottesrede*, 177–95, Paderborn: Scöningh.

CHAPTER SIX

Persons with disabilities, unprotected parties and Israelite household structures

JEREMY SCHIPPER

This chapter tries to answer a question that Saul Olyan describes as 'not an easy question to answer'. His remark occurs in a lengthy endnote in his book *Disability in the Hebrew Bible* (2008), in which he discusses the difficulty in accounting for the fact that 'blind, lame, and deaf persons do not typically appear in the most commonly attested versions of the formulaic list of dependent/protected persons' (Olyan 2008: 136 n.35). It is worth considering Olyan's endnote more fully. As he observes, these formulaic lists occur repeatedly in the Pentateuch, especially in Deuteronomy. When discussing the commands that prohibit the abuse of persons with certain disabilities in Lev. 19.14 and Deut. 27.18, he writes,

> Why there are so few passages like Lev. 19:14, Deut. 27:18, and Ps. 146:8, given the many texts challenging the stigmatization of the widow, the orphan, and the resident alien, and, to a lesser degree, the poor and afflicted, is not an easy question to answer. A text such as Job 29:12–15 suggests that these persons (including the blind and the lame) share a common weakness, vulnerability, and dependence, and that treating them justly and generously is the appropriate and expected response of the powerful. Psalm 146 suggests Yhwh himself has a special concern for such persons, including the blind. Given this, it is perhaps surprising that blind, lame, and deaf persons do not typically appear in the most commonly attested versions of the formulaic list of dependent/protected persons. The widow, the fatherless, and the resident alien are frequently listed together; occasionally, they are joined by the poor, the afflicted, and even the Levite (in Deuteronomy). However, persons with disabilities are usually not present. At the very least, it seems fair to say that although disabled persons such as the blind, lame, and deaf are sometimes brought into association with the poor, the widow, and other persons cast as vulnerable and dependent, the most commonly attested version of the formulaic list of dependent sufferers, for whatever reason, includes only the widow, fatherless, and the resident alien. It may be that these particular persons have come to represent all who are

cast as vulnerable and dependent for the writers of the texts in which the formula occurs. (Olyan 2008: 136 n.35)

This chapter engages Olyan's important question and expands on his observations. To anticipate my conclusion, I argue that the widow (or 'unprotected woman'),[1] the fatherless, the resident alien and even the Levite are listed not because they are representative of all who are cast as vulnerable and dependent for the writers of the relevant texts but because they are representative of those parties who would be understood as otherwise unprotected and without allotted land as an inalienable inheritance within the Israelite household structure as idealized by these writers.[2] By contrast, persons with disabilities are not considered unprotected parties or without allotted land as an inalienable inheritance within the idealized Israelite household structure, even if they are characterized as potentially vulnerable or dependent in some texts.

First, I provide a brief overview of the Israelite household structure as idealized in Pentateuchal legislation, particularly Deuteronomy. Second, I discuss the parties that appear in the most commonly attested version of the formulaic list of 'dependent sufferers' (to use Olyan's terminology). I argue that the lists include those who are representative of unprotected parties without allotted land as an inalienable inheritance within the household structure, rather than representative of all who are cast as vulnerable and dependent. Third, I provide examples of parties who may be considered potentially vulnerable and dependent but are not on the formulaic lists because they would be considered protected or as having access to allotted land as an inalienable inheritance within the structure of the household. These examples include, but are not limited to, persons with certain disabilities. Fourth, I argue that Lev. 19.14, Deut. 27.18, Ps. 146.8 and Job 29.12-15 are not comparable to the formulaic lists of unprotected parties without allotted land as an inalienable inheritance because the former texts serve different rhetoric purposes or address different social issues than the formulaic lists.

The idealized Israelite household structure in the Pentateuch

In his influential book *The House of the Father as Fact and Symbol* (2001), J. David Schloen argues that a patrimonial 'household' framework served as a foundational building block for social organization in ancient Israel. He explains:

> In the absence of the rather abstract idea that an impersonal political constitution or universal egalitarian social contract underpins the social order, personal relationships patterned on the household served to integrate society and to legitimate the exercise of power ... Far from being merely banal or euphemistic, the use of [kinship terminology] expressed a basic understanding of political and social relations that was derived from familiar household relationships. This model of society was quite simple, to be sure, but it was also quite flexible and extensible

---

1 For the purposes of this chapter, 'widow' is better understood as 'unprotected woman', as I explain in n. 8.
2 The question of whether the biblical depictions of the Israelite household structure reflect historical realia in ancient 'Israel' (here serving as a cultural designation) is beyond the scope of this chapter – in part because I focus on the textual representations of persons with disabilities, unprotected parties and Israelite household structures (much as Olyan does). For detailed discussions of the Israelite household structure, consult Gottwald (1979); Lemche (1985); Ben-Dor (1996); van der Toorn (1996); McNutt (1999); Schloen (2001); Chapman (2016); Schipper (2016a).

to encompass personal relationships at many different levels from the affairs of the humblest family to the dealings between kings. (Schloen 2001: 255, 258)[3]

In the Hebrew Bible, this patrimonial household structure is often, but not always, referred to as the 'house of the father'. For example, in Gen. 24.38, Abraham instructs his servant to travel to the extended family of his birth as follows: 'go to my father's house, to my kindred' (אל בית אבי תלך ואל משפחתי).[4] In Gen. 28.21, Jacob, while fleeing the wrath of his brother Esau, expresses a desire to return to his birth household. He desires to 'come again to my father's house in peace' (ושבתי בשלום אל בית אבי). Leviticus 22.13 sets out provisions to be made for a priest's daughter who is 'widowed or divorced, without offspring, and returns to her father's house, as in her youth' (אלמנה וגרושה וזרע אין לה ושבה אל בית אביה כנעוריה).

In its idealized form in the Hebrew Bible, the house of the father represents a socio-economically integrated unit consisting of three or four generations,[5] who live together on allotted land that is considered its inalienable 'inheritance' (נחלה).[6] In addition to livestock and material goods, these households include a senior living male ('the father'), his wives, their unmarried daughters, their sons and their wives, and their sons' children. This household structure is conceptualized through asymmetrical relationships on the basis of the relative social seniority of the parties involved. Members have varying degrees of authority and can simultaneously have authority over and be under the authority of other parties depending on the nature of the relationship.[7]

Unprotected parties without allotted land as an inalienable inheritance in the household structure

In addition to people who are either born into or married into the household, the household can include other dependents such as unprotected women, the fatherless, enslaved women or men, or resident aliens who are not allotted land as an inalienable inheritance but rely on the household for material support. For example, in Exod. 20.10, Moses instructs the senior members of Israelite households that 'the seventh day is a Sabbath to YHWH your God; you shall not do any work – you, your son or your daughter, your enslaved men or women (עבדך ואמתך), your livestock, or the alien resident in your towns (וגרך אשר בשעריך).' In Exod. 22.22, Moses instructs the senior members to 'not abuse any unprotected woman or fatherless person' (כל אלמנה ויתום לא תענון).[8] In Exod.

---

3 Although Schloen's study concentrates on the Bronze and Iron Ages, this model of social organization was not necessarily limited to those time periods but was used (as he notes at 2001: 255) 'for all manner of political and social relationships throughout the Near East in the pre-Hellenistic period'.
4 All biblical quotations follow the New Revised Standard Version (NRSV) and its versification, although I have modified the translation when necessary.
5 For further examples, consult Gen. 38.11; Josh. 2.12; Judg. 9.18; 1 Sam. 22.15; 2 Sam. 14.9; Isa. 7.17; Ps. 45.11; 2 Chron. 21.13.
6 See, for example, Num. 26.52-56; 33.54; Josh. 13.23, 28; 15.20; 16.8; 18.20, 28; 19.8, 23, 31, 39, 48.
7 Consult the discussion of heterarchy in Meyers (2013: 196–9); Schipper (2016a: 46–9).
8 Although the NRSV translates אלמנה in this verse as 'widow', it refers more precisely to a woman outside of the protection of the household or clan into which she was married. For detailed discussion, consult Hiebert (1989) and Steinberg (2004). Similarly, although the NRSV translates יתום in this verse as 'orphan', it does not always refer a person whose mother and father have both died. Rather, it refers more precisely to a person other than a senior male who is otherwise outside of the protection of the household structure, even if the person's mother is still alive. In other words, it refers to a person who is not otherwise part of a 'house of a father'. Thus, יתום is sometimes more accurately translated as 'fatherless' or 'fatherless person'.

23.6, he states, 'You shall not pervert the justice due to your poor (אבינך) in their lawsuits' (cf. Deut. 24.14).

Deuteronomy frequently includes various combinations of these parties as examples of unprotected people who depend on the household in part because they have no allotted land or inheritance. Deuteronomy 27.19 declares, 'Cursed be anyone who deprives the resident alien, the fatherless, and the unprotected woman (גר יתום ואלמנה) of justice. All the people shall say, "Amen!".' Other texts associate the provision of justice for these parties with divine behaviour. In Deut. 10.18, Moses describes YHWH as a deity 'who executes justice for the fatherless and the unprotected woman (יתום ואלמנה), and who loves the alien (גר), providing them food and clothing'.

Unprotected women, fatherless persons, enslaved women and men, and aliens are all listed as examples of dependents without allotted land or an inheritance in Deut. 24.17-22, which reads as follows:

> You shall not deprive an alien (גר) or a fatherless person (יתום) of justice; you shall not take the garment of an unprotected woman (אלמנה) in pledge. Remember that you were an enslaved person (עבד) in Egypt and YHWH your God redeemed you from there; therefore I command you to do this. When you reap your harvest in your field and forget a sheaf in the field, you shall not go back to get it; it shall be left for the alien, the fatherless, and the widow (לגר ליתום ולאלמנה), so that YHWH your God may bless you in all your undertakings. When you beat your olive trees, do not strip what is left; it shall be for the alien, the fatherless, and the unprotected woman (לגר ליתום ולאלמנה). When you gather the grapes of your vineyard, do not glean what is left; it shall be for the alien, the fatherless, and the unprotected woman (לגר ליתום ולאלמנה). Remember that you were an enslaved person (עבד) in the land of Egypt; therefore I am commanding you to do this.

In this passage, the repeated rationale for the just treatment of these parties is that the Israelites, as enslaved people (עבד) in Egypt, would have qualified as dependents according to the household model (cf. 16.11-12). Similarly, Deut. 23.8b (Eng. v. 23.7b) also depicts the Israelites as dependents while in Egypt as a justification for why they should not abhor Egyptians: 'You shall not abhor any of the Egyptians, because you were an alien (גר) residing in their land.'

One finds similar legislation in Holiness literature in Leviticus, although it references the poor (עני), who presumably would not have allotted land or an inheritance, alongside the alien, instead of the unprotected woman or the fatherless alongside the alien. For example, Lev. 19.10 commands those with an allotted land holding as follows: 'You shall not strip your vineyard bare, or gather the fallen grapes of your vineyard; you shall leave them for the poor and the alien (לעני ולגר): I am YHWH your God.' Similarly, Lev. 23.22 reads, 'When you reap the harvest of your land, you shall not reap to the very edges of your field, or gather the gleanings of your harvest; you shall leave them for the poor and for the alien (לעני ולגר): I am YHWH your God.' According to Deut. 24.14, the poor (עני), as well as the needy (אביון), could be either a kin person (אח) or an alien (גר) residing in an Israelite household.

Certain texts in Deuteronomy also include Levites among the various types of household dependents. For example, Deut. 26.11-13 instructs the senior members of the household as follows:

> Celebrate with all the bounty that YHWH your God has given to you and to your household (ולביתך) – you, together with the Levites and the aliens (אתה והלוי

והגר) who reside among you. When you have finished paying all the tithe of your produce in the third year (which is the year of the tithe), giving it to the Levite, the alien, the fatherless, and the unprotected woman (ללוי לגר ליתום ולאלמנה), so that they may eat their fill within your towns, then you shall say before YHWH your God: 'I have removed the sacred portion from the house, and I have given it to the Levite, the alien, the fatherless, and the unprotected woman (ללוי ולגר ליתום ולאלמנה), in accordance with your entire commandment that you commanded me; I have neither transgressed nor forgotten any of your commandments'.

This text positions the Levites as dependents within the household structure. Another list of household members and their dependents occurs in the instructions concerning the festival of booths in Deut. 16.11-14, which reads as follows:

Rejoice before YHWH your God – you and your sons and your daughters, your enslaved men and women, the Levite resident in your towns, as well as the alien, the fatherless, and the unprotected woman who are among you (ועבדך ואמתך והלוי אשר בשעריך והגר והיתום והאלמנה אשר בקרבך) – at the place that YHWH your God will choose as a dwelling for his name. Remember that you were an enslaved person (עבד) in Egypt, and diligently observe these statutes. You shall keep the festival of booths for seven days, when you have gathered in the produce from your threshing floor and your wine press. Rejoice during your festival, you and your sons and your daughters, your enslaved men and women, as well as the Levite, the alien, the fatherless, and the unprotected woman resident in your towns (ועבדך ואמתך והלוי והגר והיתום והאלמנה אשר בשעריך).

Likewise, in addition to the senior male member of the household, Deut. 12.18 lists 'your son and your daughter, your enslaved men and women, and the Levites resident in your towns (ובנך ובתך ועבדך ואמתך והלוי אשר בשעריך)'. A rationale for why the Levite is included alongside the resident alien, the unprotected woman and the fatherless appears a few verses earlier, in 12.12:

And you [the senior male household members] shall rejoice before YHWH your God, you together with your sons and your daughters, your enslaved men and women, and the Levites who reside in your towns (since they have no allotment or inheritance with you) (אתם ובניכם ובנתיכם ועבדיכם ואמהתיכם והלוי אשר בשעריכם כי אין לו חלק ונחלה אתכם).

Deuteronomy 14.27, 29 use the same rationale for why the Levite is included along with the alien, the unprotected woman and the fatherless. These verses read as follows:

As for the Levites resident in your towns, do not neglect them, because they have no allotment or inheritance with you (הלוי אשר בשעריך לא תעזבנו כי אין לו חלק ונחלה עמך) ... the Levites, because they have no allotment or inheritance with you, as well as the alien, the fatherless, and the unprotected woman in your towns (הלוי כי אין לו חלק ונחלה עמך והגר והיתום והאלמנה אשר בשעריך), may come and eat their fill so that YHWH your God may bless you in all the work that you undertake.[9]

One may ask why the Levites are listed alongside household dependents who are not allotted inalienable land as an inheritance of their own. Numbers 26 may provide a clue, for after a lengthy census-list of the Israelite tribes and clans, v. 53 concludes, 'To these the land shall

---

9 The Levites' lack of a land allotment and inheritance is also noted in Deut. 10.19; 18.1, 6-8; cf. Gen. 31.14.

be apportioned for inheritance according to the number of names.' The preceding list of names, however, does not include the Levites, who are only discussed in vv. 57-61. Joshua 14.3-4, 7 state more explicitly that the Levites did not hold an ancestral land inheritance:

> For Moses had given an inheritance to the two and one-half tribes beyond the Jordan; but to the Levites he gave no inheritance among them. For the people of Joseph were two tribes, Manasseh and Ephraim; and no portion was given to the Levites in the land, but only towns to live in, with their pasture lands for their flocks and herds.

A rationale for the Levites' lack of ancestral land appears in Josh. 18.7a: 'The Levites have no portion among you, for the priesthood of YHWH is their heritage.' Along similar lines, Deut. 10.8-9 states: 'YHWH set apart the tribe of Levi to carry the ark of the covenant of YHWH, to stand before YHWH to minister to him, and to bless in his name, to this day. Therefore, Levi has no allotment or inheritance with his kindred; YHWH is his inheritance, as YHWH your God promised him' (cf. 18.5). Other texts suggest that the Levites' priestly duties required a renouncement of kinship ties. For example, in Deut. 33.8-10, Moses blesses the Levites as follows:

> And of Levi he said: Give to Levi your Thummim, and your Urim to your loyal one, whom you tested at Massah, with whom you contended at the waters of Meribah; who said of his father and mother, 'I regard them not'; he ignored his kin, and did not acknowledge his children. For they observed your word, and kept your covenant. They teach Jacob your ordinances, and Israel your law; they place incense before you, and whole burnt offerings on your altar.

This text suggests that the Levite should renounce kinship ties and devote himself to his priestly duties (cf. Exod. 32.26–29). This lack of kinship ties could explain why the Levites are not apportioned ancestral land holdings as an inheritance. It could also explain why a Levite would live among those Israelite households who do have land holdings and rely on them for material support, as assumed in Deut. 14.27, 29.

Noting the Levites' lack of inherited land holdings and kinship ties in certain texts, some scholars have argued that the term 'Levite' does not necessarily designate the hereditary descendants of Jacob's son Levi, as one might otherwise conclude from Gen. 46.11 or Exod. 6.16.[10] In Gen. 29.34, the popular etymology for the proper name 'Levi' creates a pun on a niphal inflection of the root לוה when, upon Levi's birth, his mother Leah states: 'Now this time my husband will be joined (ילוה) to me, because I have borne him three sons.' The verse continues: 'therefore he was named Levi (לוי)'. Elsewhere, niphal inflections of this root describe an individual or group 'joining' or 'attaching' with another group for a variety of reasons (e.g. Isa. 14.1; 56.3, 6; Jer. 50.5; Est. 9.27). Employing a similar pun to that in Gen. 29.24, Num. 18.2 describes Levites as those who join with Aaron's descendants from the same ancestral household in priestly service: 'So bring with you also your brothers of the tribe of Levi (לוי), your ancestral tribe, in order that they may be joined (וילוו) to you, and serve you while you and your sons with you are in front of the tent of the covenant' (cf. ונלוו in v. 4). Elsewhere, the term 'Levite' describes a man from the clan of Judah who serves as an itinerant priest apart from the household of his birth or their inherited land. Judg. 17.7-13 reads:

---

10 For a helpful and concise overview of scholarship on this issue, consult the discussion and works cited in Leuchter (2013: 24–31).

Now there was a young man of Bethlehem in Judah, of the clan of Judah (ממשפחת יהודה). He was a Levite residing there. This man left the town of Bethlehem in Judah, to live wherever he could find a place. He came to the household of Micah (בית מיכה) in the hill country of Ephraim to carry on his work. Micah said to him, 'From where do you come?' He replied, 'I am a Levite of Bethlehem in Judah, and I am going to live wherever I can find a place'. Then Micah said to him, 'Stay with me, and be to me a father and a priest, and I will give you ten pieces of silver a year, a set of clothes, and your living'. The Levite agreed to stay with the man; and the young man became to him like one of his sons. So Micah installed the Levite, and the young man became his priest, and was in the household of Micah (בבית מיכה). Then Micah said, 'Now I know that YHWH will prosper me, because the Levite has become my priest'.

In this text, the term 'Levite' does not describe a biological descendant of Jacob's son Levi, since the unnamed priest is from 'the clan of Judah', rather than the tribe of Levi. Instead, the term describes a man who severs his ties to his tribal kin (the Judahites) and their land holdings and serves as a priest supported by Micah, the senior male member of a household in the hill country of Ephraim. This text fits with the Deuteronomic passages discussed earlier that instruct the senior members of the Israelite household to support the Levites in their towns (e.g. Deut. 12.18; 14.27, 29). This may explain why the Levites are depicted as dependents alongside unprotected women, the fatherless and the resident alien among other examples of dependents without inalienable land as an inheritance.

Vulnerable and dependent but protected parties within the Israelite household structure

Aside from persons with disabilities, there are other parties that are cast as vulnerable or dependent which do not appear in the formulaic lists discussed in the previous section. For example, even if we follow Kristine Garroway (2014: 18) in understanding childhood in ancient Israel as the period from birth until marriage (cf. Flynn in this volume), children could still qualify as vulnerable, as Judg. 21.21 (among others) suggests.[11] Along these lines, the term 'daughter' (בת) could refer to an unmarried woman within the household structure (as in Ruth 1.11-13; 2.2, 8, 22; 3.1, 10-11, 16, 18). Yet, under normal circumstances, children were usually understood to be protected members of patrilocal Israelite households with access to the household's alienable land as an inheritance. It is only those children, broadly defined, who were not members of a patriarchal house and were not allotted land as an inalienable inheritance – and therefore considered 'fatherless' (יתום) – who appear on the formulaic lists discussed earlier, because the criteria for the lists include dependents or vulnerable parties who would not otherwise be protected by the household structure. One could make a similar argument regarding a married woman (אשה) as opposed to an unprotected woman (אלמנה). Both types of women may be potentially vulnerable or dependent. The former, however, would be protected members of the household without the need for specific legal mandates, whereas the latter's protection must be legally mandated.

Deuteronomy 32.19-25 imagines the destruction of Israel. The text reinforces the comprehensive nature of this destruction through the gender inclusiveness and wide

---

11 For other recent treatments of children in the Hebrew Bible, consult Parker (2013); Steinberg (2013); Flynn (2018).

age range of the victims, encompassing a 'young man (בחור) and young woman (בתולה) alike, nursing child (יונק) and old grey head (איש שיבה)' (v. 25). The victims listed could also represent dependents within an ancient Israelite household, since a 'young man' (בחור) and 'young woman' (בתולה) were often unmarried and thus considered dependents within the extended family household structure. One might also find nursing children and elderly men included as the household could encompass up to three or four generations at any one time. The four parties listed as representative victims in this text could also be considered vulnerable. Yet, none of these parties appear in the formulaic lists discussed earlier because their protection or their access to allotted land as an inalienable inheritance would be assumed within the household structure. In other words, the various combinations of parties on those lists of people without allotted land as an inalienable inheritance are not representative of all who are cast as vulnerable and dependent by the writers of the relevant texts.

Similarly, having a disability in ancient Israel may have resulted in increased dependency or vulnerability. And yet, disabilities alone would not affect one's protected status or access to allotted land as an inalienable inheritance unless the person was also an unprotected woman, or fatherless, an alien or poor. Hebrew Bible narratives do not tend to depict characters with disabilities as unprotected women, fatherless, aliens or poor. For example, if we consider infertility as a disability, every named woman described as infertile (עקר) is a protected member of a household (Gen. 11.30; 25.21; 29.31; Judg. 13.2-3). The same holds true for prose texts that describe long-term or short-term female infertility without using the word עקר (Gen. 16.2; 20.17-18; 1 Sam. 1.5-6). Moreover, if one interprets Leah as having a visual impairment (Gen. 29.17), one could note that she is a wife of Jacob, the senior male member of a large household.[12]

Male characters who develop visual impairments in old age include Isaac (Gen. 27.1), Jacob/Israel (Gen. 48.10), Eli (1 Sam. 3.2; 4.15) and Ahijah (1 Kgs 14.4). Eli is the senior member of a prominent priestly family in Shiloh. Although his priestly household ('the house of your father'; 1 Sam. 2.31) is ultimately cut off (1 Sam. 2.27-36; 3.11-14), he retains his position of authority within this priestly household even after he develops a visual impairment (1 Sam. 3.1–4.18). His visual impairment in and of itself does not affect his authority within the household structure. Like Eli, the prophet Ahijah is also from Shiloh. While he is not as clearly situated in a household structure, his impairment does not seem to have an explicitly negative impact on his prophetic status. This does not mean that a visual impairment could not affect one's status in other contexts, such as the cult (e.g. Lev. 21.18) or situations involving human captivity (e.g. Samson in Judg. 16.21 and Zedekiah in 2 Kgs 25.7). As Karel van der Toorn (1986) and Tracy Lemos (2006) have shown, in the ancient Near East, captors often forcibly blinded their victims as a way of physically marking their status as captives. Yet, these two contexts are different from the contexts addressed in the formulaic lists of household dependents without allotted land as an inalienable inheritance. Moreover, while Lev. 21.18-23 prohibits a priest with blemishes from altar service, he is still understood as a priest from Aaron's household.[13]

---

12 In Gen. 29.17, the description of Leah's eyes as רכות could indicate that her eyes were 'weak' (JPS; NIV) or that her eyes are 'lovely' (NRSV).
13 Similarly, the book of the Covenant (Exod. 20.22–23.33; cf. 24.7) discusses acquired impairments that may result from applications of the principle of *lex talionis* in contexts that address organization of the household in ancient Israel (Exod. 21.23-25; cf. Lev. 24.19-20; Deut. 19.21).

As for Isaac, he continues to function as the senior member of his household after he develops his visual impairment, as is indicated when his sons seek his blessing (Gen. 27.1-40). Although Jacob and Rebekah trick him in order to secure the blessing, the fact that they still recognize that they must seek the blessing from Isaac because of his senior status within the household indicates that his impairment has not affected his status within that household. As Kerry Wynn observes,

> Indeed, we see no loss of social authority or power on the part of Isaac as a result of his disability. Isaac retains both his social status as head of the clan and his theological import as the heir of the promise regardless of his loss of vision. While his family takes advantage of his disability to further their own ends, there is no judgment or ridicule associated with his disability ... It is the status of Jacob and Esau that is at stake. The status of Isaac as patriarch and his power to grant the blessing are never brought into question in light of his age or blindness. (Wynn 2007: 95–6)

One may make a similar point about Israel, who is sometimes called Jacob. In Gen. 48.8-22, Israel blesses his sons after he develops a visual impairment. Once again, the visual impairment does not have an effect on his senior status within the household structure.

Likewise, one could interpret the hip injury that Jacob/Israel sustains during the wrestling match in Gen. 32.24-32 as resulting in a chronic impairment, since this was not uncommon in the ancient world. For example, in 2 Samuel, Mephibosheth's leg injury results in permanent mobility impairment (2 Sam. 4.4; 9.3, 13; 19.26 [MT v. 27]; cf. Schipper 2016b; Wynn 2007). This may have been the norm rather than the exception regarding leg or hip injuries in the ancient world. Yet, if one follows this interpretation with regard to Jacob, there is no indication that this mobility impairment alters his status as the senior member of the house. One may make a similar point about Mephibosheth. He has a son (2 Sam. 9.12; 1 Chron. 8.34; 9.40), which may imply that he is a married adult rather than a fatherless person (יתום), although his exact status within the household structure remains uncertain. Although he is supported by the house of Machir (בית מכיר; 2 Sam. 9.4), this may be a result of the political upheaval in the house of Saul rather than Mephibosheth's mobility impairment. At any rate, his birth household has inherited land which David returns to him (2 Sam. 9.7) and he is not without protection within the household structure.

Overall, there are a number of parties, including but not limited to persons with disabilities, that could have qualified as vulnerable or dependent in ancient Israel but are not on the formulaic biblical lists discussed above – presumably because they would have already been considered protected, or would have had access to allotted land as an inalienable inheritance, within the structure of the household.

Rhetorical goals and issues addressed in Lev. 19.14, Deut. 27.18, Job 29.12-16 and Ps. 146.8

Job 29.12-16 is the only text in the Hebrew Bible in which persons with disabilities appear alongside some of the standard examples of unprotected persons without allotted land as an inalienable inheritance. Olyan (2008: 135 n.35) cites Job 29.12-15, along with Lev. 19.14, Deut. 27.18 and Ps. 146.8, as texts that 'suggest both Yhwh's special concern for such persons and their status as weak, vulnerable, and dependent'. While these parties are potentially vulnerable or dependent, they do not serve as examples of unprotected parties without allotted land as an inalienable inheritance in these texts.

In Job 29.12, 15-16a, the titular character views himself as a model senior member of the household, exemplified by his aid of vulnerable or dependent persons (Newsom 2012: 213). He claims: 'I delivered the poor (עני) who cried, and the fatherless (יתום) who had no helper ... I was eyes to the blind (לעור), and feet to the lame (לפסח). I was a father to the needy (אב אנכי לאביונים).' Nevertheless, Job's inclusion of persons with disabilities among those he aids may be a way of presenting himself as the model patriarch in hyperbolic terms. Even if persons with disabilities do not appear on the formulaic lists of unprotected parties without allotted land as an inalienable inheritance, their appearance alongside the fatherless, poor and needy in Job 29.12-16 adds rhetorical force to Job's defence of his piety. The possibility that Job lists examples of vulnerable or dependent parties for a different rhetorical purpose than the formulaic lists in the Pentateuch could explain the unique combination of persons with disabilities and unprotected parties without allotted land as an inalienable inheritance.

Leviticus 19.14 reads, 'You shall not revile the deaf (חרש) or put a stumbling block before the blind (עור); you shall fear your God: I am YHWH.' This text is addressed to all the Israelites (v. 2). As Rebecca Raphael notes (2008: 36 n.21), the command mitigates cruelty towards those with certain sensory impairments but does not address issues of inclusion or make material provisions for persons with disabilities as the laws regarding unprotected parties without allotted land as an inalienable inheritance do. In this sense, while both types of laws address potentially vulnerable parties, they address very different issues. The same holds true for Deut. 27.18a, which is part of a series of curses addressed to all the Israelites (vv. 14-26). It reads, 'Cursed be anyone who misleads a blind person (עור) on the road.' Like Lev. 19.14, this text addresses cruelty towards a person with a visual impairment. It does not mandate the inclusion of, or material provisions for, an unprotected party without allotted land as an inalienable inheritance. To be sure, a formulaic list of such parties appears in the following verse: 'Cursed be anyone who deprives the alien, the fatherless, and the unprotected woman (גר יתום ואלמנה) of justice' (Deut. 27.19). Yet, the two curses address different issues, cruelty and legal justice, respectively. The various curses in this series in Deut. 27.14-26 do not necessarily address similar parties or subjects. For example, v. 17 involves a curse against moving the boundary marker of one's neighbour (רע) rather than the parties addressed in either v. 18 or v. 19.

Similar to Deut. 27.18-19, references to aliens, the fatherless and the unprotected woman follow a reference to persons with visual impairments in Ps. 146.7b-9, which reads as follows:

> YHWH sets the prisoners (אסורים) free;
> YHWH opens the eyes of the blind (יהוה פקח עורים).
> YHWH lifts up those who are bowed down;
> YHWH loves the righteous.
> YHWH watches over the aliens (יהוה שמר את גרים);
> he upholds the fatherless and the unprotected woman (יתום ואלמנה יעודד),
> but the way of the wicked he brings to ruin.

Unlike any of the other texts considered thus far, this text depicts the healing of impairments. The reference to released prisoners immediately before the healing imagery may explain this difference. As mentioned earlier, blindness is often associated with captivity in ancient Near Eastern literature. For example, in Isa. 42.7, the servant's teaching is intended to 'to open the eyes that are blind (לפקח עינים עורות), to bring out the prisoners (אסיר) from the dungeon, from the prison those who sit in darkness' (consult further Schipper 2015: 325). Despite pointing to aliens, the fatherless and the unprotected woman in the following verse, the references to the healing of visual impairments in Ps. 146.7b-9 fit the captivity imagery in this text more so than the examples of unprotected parties without allotted land as an inalienable inheritance in pentateuchal legislation.

Conclusions

The concept of the household governs many aspects of the biblical depiction of Israelite social organization, including its perspectives on bodies in relation to the household. I have argued that a reason why persons with disabilities do not usually appear in what Olyan describes as 'the many texts challenging the stigmatization of the widow, the orphan, and the resident alien, and, to a lesser degree, the poor and afflicted' may be that it is the concept of the household which structures the social organization reflected in many of these texts. The formulaic lists in these texts address provisions for otherwise unprotected parties without allotted land as an inalienable inheritance. The parties on these lists do not serve as representative of all who are cast as vulnerable and dependent. Although persons with disabilities may qualify as potentially vulnerable or dependent parties, disabilities in and of themselves usually do not affect a person's status within the household. In fact, certain characters who develop impairments maintain their status as senior members of the household. This may also explain why there are relatively few passages like Lev. 19.14, Deut. 27.18 and Ps. 146.8 when compared to those discussing provisions for unprotected parties without allotted land as an inalienable inheritance. When interpreted against the backdrop of the concept of the household, one finds that Lev. 19.14, Deut. 27.18 and Ps. 146.8 do not address the same social concerns for the household that are addressed in texts containing the formulaic lists of unprotected parties without allotted land as an inalienable inheritance.

References

Ben-Dor, S. (1996), *The Social Structure of Ancient Israel*, Jerusalem: Simor.
Chapman, C. (2016), *The House of the Mother: The Social Roles of Maternal Kin in Biblical Hebrew Narrative and Poetry*, New Haven, CT: Yale University Press.
Flynn, S. (2018), *Children in Ancient Israel: The Hebrew Bible and Mesopotamia in Comparative Perspective*, Oxford: Oxford University Press.
Garroway, K. (2014), *Children in the Ancient Near Eastern Household*, Winona Lake, IN: Eisenbrauns.
Gottwald, N. K. (1979), *The Tribes of Yahweh: A Sociology of the Religion of Liberated Israel, 1250–1050 B.C.E.*, Maryknoll, NY: Orbis.
Hiebert, P. S. (1989), '"Whence Shall Help Come to Me?": The Biblical Widow', in P. L. Day (ed.), *Gender and Difference in Ancient Israel*, 125–41, Minneapolis, MN: Fortress Press.
Lemche, N. P. (1985), *Early Israel: Anthropological and Historical Studies on the Israelite Society before the Monarchy*, Leiden: Brill.
Lemos, T. M. (2006), 'Shame and Mutilation of Enemies in the Hebrew Bible', *Journal of Biblical Literature* 125: 225–41.
Leuchter, M. (2013), *Samuel and the Shaping of Tradition*, Oxford: Oxford University Press.
McNutt, P. (1999), *Reconstructing the Society of Ancient Israel*, Louisville, KY: Westminster John Knox.

Meyers, C. (2013), *Rediscovering Eve: Ancient Israelite Women in Context*, New York: Oxford University Press.

Newsom, C. A. (2012), 'Job', in C. A. Newsom, S. H. Ringe and J. E. Lapsley (eds), *Women's Bible Commentary*, 3rd edn, 208–15, Louisville, KY: Westminster John Knox Press.

Olyan, S. M. (2008), *Disability in the Hebrew Bible: Interpreting Mental and Physical Differences*, New York: Cambridge University Press.

Parker, J. F. (2013), *Valuable and Vulnerable Children in the Hebrew Bible, Especially the Elisha Cycle*, Brown Judaic Studies, Providence, RI: Brown University Press.

Raphael, R. (2008), *Biblical Corpora: Representations of Disability in Hebrew Biblical Literature*, Library of the Hebrew Bible Series 445, New York: T&T Clark.

Schipper, J. (2015), 'Why Does Imagery of Disability Include Healing in Isaiah?', *Journal for the Study of the Old Testament* 39: 319–33.

Schipper, J. (2016a), *Ruth: A New Translation with Introduction and Commentary*, Anchor Yale Bible 7D, New Haven, CT: Yale University Press.

Schipper, J. (2016b), 'Plotting Bodies in Biblical Narrative', in D. N. Fewell (ed.), *The Oxford Handbook to Biblical Narrative*, 389–97, New York: Oxford University Press.

Schloen, D. J. (2001), *The House of the Father as Fact and Symbol: Patrimonialism in Ugarit and the Ancient Near East*, Studies in the Archaeology and History of the Levant 2, Winona Lake, IN: Eisenbrauns.

Steinberg, N. (2004), 'Romancing the Widow: The Economic Distinction between the *"almānâ"*, *"iššâ-'almānâ"*, and the *"ēšet-hammēt"'*, in D. L. Ellens, E. Kalimi, R. Knierim and J. H. Ellens (eds), *God's Word for Our World*, vol. 1, 327–46, Sheffield: T&T Clark.

Steinberg, N. (2013), *The World of the Child in the Hebrew Bible*, Hebrew Bible Monographs, Sheffield: Sheffield Phoenix Press.

Toorn, K. van der (1986), 'Judges XVI 21 in the Light of Akkadian Sources', *Vetus Testamentum* 36: 248–53.

Toorn, K. van der (1996), *Family Religion in Babylonia, Syria and Israel: Continuity and Change in Forms of Religious Life*, Leiden: Brill.

Wynn, K. H. (2007), 'The Normate Hermeneutic and Interpretations of Disability within Yahwistic Narratives', in H. Avalos, S. J. Melcher and J. Schipper (eds), *This Abled Body: Rethinking Disabilities in Biblical Studies*, 91–101, Semeia Studies 55, Atlanta, GA: Society of Biblical Literature.

CHAPTER SEVEN

Modifying manly bodies: Mourning and masculinities in Ezra 9–10

ELISABETH COOK

When Ezra is confronted with the news that a group of men belonging to the community of 'returned' exiles (*golah*) have taken daughters from the 'peoples of the land' as wives (Ezra 9.1-2), he responds by performing rituals of mourning, lament and penitence: he tears his garments, pulls at his hair and beard, falls to the ground (9.3-4), extends his arms to Yhwh (9.5), prays and confesses (9.6-15; 10.1), weeps and throws himself before the temple (10.1) and then retreats into a temple chamber, where he refrains from food and drink (10.6). Although these numerous mourning rites occupy a significant portion of Ezra 9–10, they are often overlooked in favour of enquiries concerning the 'foreign' women, whose identities, actions and traits have been the object of extensive scholarly debate.

The curiosity generated by these women is aptly summarized by Bob Becking (2011: 58): 'What intrigues me is the question of the identity of these women. Who were they? Why did they evoke the anger of the community?' Their simultaneous roles in the narrative as daughters of indigenous inhabitants of the land, 'foreign' wives of *golah* men and mothers of the community's new members are brought to the fore as elements that render them threatening and problematic.[1] As Claudia Camp (2011: 306) observes, the insistent scholarly focus on the women as the key to unlocking the motivations and mysteries of the story – and even its assumed historical referents – takes at face value the 'textual claim that the problem [with intermarriage] lies only with foreign wives'. This line of enquiry has drawn a quasi-voyeuristic gaze to the women of Ezra 9–10, whose ethnicity, assumed religious and sexual proclivities, and gendered social roles are examined in search of clues to decipher this unsettling text (e.g. Janzen 2002; Brown 2005; Johnson 2011; Moffat 2013: 146–54). Even feminist and gender-critical studies, which tend to critique the narrative's marginalization of

---

1 For example, Moffat (2013: 152) argues that the foreign women serve to symbolize 'outsiders who were resistant to Yahwism ... agents of apostasy, contagious impurity and an alluring temptation that carried destruction for the community'.

the women or 'recover' their presence and social roles in the community (Eskenazi 1992; Karrer-Grube 2012; Maier 2017), continue to perpetuate the 'problematic' status of these characters in the text.[2]

Ezra 9–10, however, offers little information about the women, who are granted no speech or action in the story. Their identities are not given, their cultural and religious practices are not described and their sexual proclivities are not a matter of critique.[3] Rather, it is the men – specifically *golah* men – who are the primary actors in this narrative and for whom identities, religious practices and social roles are expanded upon in the story-world of the text. It is the men who take wives and bring them into the *golah* (9.2). It is men who accusingly designate other men's marriages an act of infidelity (9.1-2). It is men of the *golah* who gather around Ezra (9.3; 10.1, 12), mourn, pray, tremble, fall to the ground, weep (9.3–10.1), fast (10.6), propose covenants (10.3), swear (10.5), issue orders that affect the property and status of other men (10.8), assemble (10.9), plan (10.13-14), voice dissenting opinions (10.15), carry out enquiries (10.15-17), make pledges (10.19) and occupy all the social and cultic roles in the text. As readers, we encounter men, not women, in the text: it is these men's relationships that are disputed; their cultural memory of captivity and plundering that is memorialized (9.6) and their relationship with Yhwh that is called into question (10.2).

The men, however, are not subjected to forensic analysis in scholarship, and neither are their gendered roles as fathers, sons and husbands explored. Scholars and readers have not problematized or otherwise considered how these men are constructed and deployed in the text as *men*. Nor have the masculine performances and attributes, much less the bodies of these narrative players, been the object of gendered analysis.[4]

In this chapter, I shift the focus of analysis from the 'foreign' women to the men of the *golah* and the masculinities that are produced, performed and embodied in the culture conjured within the text. I consider masculinities as constituted in relation to other men and as socially and culturally prevalent imaginaries of 'manliness' in the world of the narrative. I address, moreover, Ezra's performance of mourning and body modification rituals (largely overlooked dimensions of Ezra 9–10) and explore the ways in which this performance configures bodies, gendered identities and socio-religious power relations in this narrative world.

Ezra the man

In the book of Ezra, the eponymous hero is introduced with a series of exceptional roles and attributes (Ezra 7). He is a priest of the highest pedigree (7.1-5), who is charged by the Persian king to transport prized vessels to the Jerusalem temple and given access to local treasuries (7.16-19, 21-23). He is both an expert scribe (7.6), who is to inspect

---

2 As Kelso (2013: 269) rightly notes, these approaches do not 'attend to the complexities of the absence and silence of women'; cf. Boer (2005); Fuchs (2008).
3 These women are not accused of leading Yhwh-worshippers after other deities as other women are in several biblical texts (e.g. Exod. 34.15-16; Num. 25.1-2; Deut. 7.3-4; 1 Kgs 11.1, 8). And contrary to scholarly claims, neither does Ezra 9.11 single out the women as bearers of impurity: impurity is attributed to the 'peoples of the land', the social group to which the women belong, and not specifically to the women themselves.
4 As Økland (2015: 481) notes, while men are viewed as 'generic representations of the human norm and condition', women are analysed as 'particularities and deviations' to be problematized and recovered; cf. Sawyer (2004); Creanga (2014).

the region concerning obedience to the Torah (7.14), and a Persian emissary, granted authority over the legal administration of the province of Abar-Nahar (7.25-26).

While Ezra's many roles may appear disparate and even hyperbolic, they serve to establish Ezra as a man who has authority over other men in matters of the cult, as well as civil and judicial management and administration over Jerusalem and local political elites (cf. Fried 2001; Leuchter 2010). The skills and responsibilities attributed to Ezra are particularly significant, for as Martti Nissinen (2016: 342) observes, manhood appears in biblical and other ancient texts as a vulnerable quality that has to be 'demonstrated, done, and accomplished by means of proper male performance'. The authority granted Ezra by both Yhwh and the Persian king Artaxerxes, as well as that derived from his lineage and scribal skill, speaks to a way of being a man, performing masculinity and embodying 'manliness' in the cultural world of the narrative.

One might indeed wonder, then, why the writer or redactor bothered to include such a grandiose presentation of Ezra, only to have him fall to the ground with weeping when a problem requires his attention (9.3-5; 10.6). Ezra's response to the report of intermarriage is to engage in a series of rituals consistent with biblical and ancient West Asian mourning rites (Olyan 2004: 68–9; cf. Pham 1999: 16–24). These rituals purposefully and radically transform his body, as described in the character's first-person account: 'I tore my garment and my mantle, and I made bare the hair from my head and my beard, and I sat appalled' (9.3). This intense sequence of actions, presumably accompanied by sounds (Levine 1993; Olyan 2004: 30–1), ends with a man lowered in desolation (אשבה משומם), perhaps finally silent (9.3, 4); he is dishevelled, shaved, bareheaded and at least partially unclothed. In short, when considered in terms of biblical and ancient West Asian ideals of dominant masculinity, Ezra does not act 'like a man'.

Perhaps not unexpectedly, Ezra's response has been perceived by many scholars and readers as inadequate, problematically emotional and unseemly for a man of his status. In the face of the transgression of the *golah*, Ezra does not read or teach the Torah, he does not initiate judicial proceedings, he does not offer sacrifices. Nor does he employ the authority of his position to punish the guilty men. His apparent inadequacy as a man appears even more pronounced when viewed in tandem with Nehemiah's retort against Yehudite men who had married Ashdodite, Moabite and Ammonite women (Neh. 13.23). Nehemiah admonishes the guilty men and bares their heads, exerting power over them and humiliating them by forcing them into a 'ritual stance of penitential mourning' (Olyan 2019: 102; see also Olyan 2012). Ezra, on the other hand, acts upon his own body and debases himself before Yhwh (Ezra 9.3-4). Lester Grabbe highlights these contrasting responses in his evaluation of Ezra's behaviour:

> He has been given the power and authority to teach and enforce the law over the entire satrapy ... Yet when confronted with an actual situation, there is only stupefaction instead of decisive action. Ezra tears his garment and hair and sits on the ground in the square (Nehemiah, on the contrary, tears the hair of his opponents) ... with all that religious and imperial authority behind him, he has trouble dealing with a relatively minor problem in Jerusalem. (Grabbe 2004: 314, 330)

Joseph Blenkinsopp (1988: 177) is likewise unimpressed with Ezra, whose actions he describes as 'almost absurdly intemperate', while Charles Fensham (1982: 124) accuses him of engaging in insincere dramatism.

Such evaluations of Ezra's ritual acts evidence a prevalent scholarly tendency in biblical studies to locate such acts solely in the realm of the 'symbolic' – that is, as referencing meanings external to the body and embodied performance itself.[5] This referential role assigned to ritual problematically renders the body an empty 'acting object' that serves merely to communicate, transmit or represent externally constituted meanings (Bell 1992: 47–9). But as David Morgan (2017: 33–4) posits, the study of religious phenomena, including ritual, should not be limited to ideas or beliefs but must focus on their 'embodied, physical and felt forms', including the 'images, emotions, sensations, spaces, food, dress or the material practices of putting the body to work'. Ritual, therefore, is neither solely nor simply a symbolic act but rather a social process by which power relations, social ties and bodies are restructured 'in the very doing of the act itself' (Bell 1992: 100).

This approach to ritual envisions a body that is continually under construction, a body that Francesca Stavrakopoulou (2013: 532, 535) describes as a 'recursively engaged social project' that is brought into being through 'practices, social relations, and cultural performances'. Masculinity, masculine bodies and embodied performances cannot be understood, therefore, as solely discursive or social constructs but more broadly as socially engaged, practised and embodied productions that are inevitably constituted within the constraints, as well as the possibilities, of their material, cultural and social contexts (so Butler 1999; Hearn 2014).

The referential contexts for considering the gendered effects of Ezra's ritual performance are the idealized constructs and performances of politically dominant masculinity in biblical and ancient West Asian representations, primary aspects of which include dominance over women and inferior men, physical strength, forceful speech, clothed, upright bodies and full beards and heads of hair, as well as emotional self-control (Cifarelli 1998: 210–28; Chapman 2004: 26–7; Llewellyn-Jones 2015; Assante 2016; Lipka 2016: 271–304; Wilson 2016; cf. Root 1979). Shaving, garment rending, donning sackcloth, weeping, fasting and prostration necessarily alter these cultural markers of dominant masculinity, so that their ritual performance within petitionary contexts renders men self-debased and physically diminished before a superior figure (whether divine or mortal). In essence, male mourners intentionally compromise or downgrade their masculinity: their bodies are rendered prone, exposed and vulnerable, not unlike those of punitively humiliated 'foreign enemies, domestic offenders, or political rivals' (Olyan 2019: 75).

These are precisely the ways in which Ezra enacts his masculinity in Ezra 9–10: he modifies his body in ways that evoke the less-than-masculine, even feminized, images of enemies, foreigners, subject peoples and fallen soldiers in political and military contexts. Ezra's body modifications and the manipulation of postures and gestures, all practices common to mourning and petitionary contexts in the Hebrew Bible, deliberately deconstruct normative performances of masculinity in order to reconfigure socio-religious power within the *golah*.

Ezra the mourner

Body modification practices are widely attested in ancient and modern cultures; they are ways in which embodied identities are materially and physically produced, configured

---

5 For critiques of these approaches, see Gorman (1994); Lemos (2013); Stavrakopoulou (2013).

and marked (Olyan 1998; Stavrakopoulou 2013). Common body modification practices in the Hebrew Bible, including circumcision and body cutting, produce permanent alterations, while others temporarily modify the head and face, clothing and skin and alter body postures (Stavrakopoulou 2013: 535–6). Male mourning practices include modifications that are easily reversible, such as the removal or tearing of clothes, placing ashes on the head, wearing sackcloth and temporary, highly visible but not immediately reversible modifications of the head and beard (Olyan 2004: 114–16). Such bodily practices function not only to communicate but also to produce and perform status, identity or affiliation (Stavrakopoulou 2013: 539). As Saul Olyan (2004: 59) argues, mourning rituals do something: they produce a mourner by creating a 'distinct ritual status' that separates the mourner from non-mourners. They also produce a specialized configuration of the body: a mourning body.

Modifying manly bodies

The actions that introduce Ezra's performance of mourning – tearing his garment and mantle (קרעתי את בגדי ומעילי), making his head and chin bare (ואמרטה משער ראשי וזקני) – materially and physically transform his body in very evident and visible ways (Ezra 9.3). In the Hebrew Bible, these ritual acts are performed in contexts of lament and distress by numerous characters (primarily men)[6] and are often described by commentators as 'symbolic' expressions of grief or loss (so Janzen 2002: 62; Lipka 2016: 295 n.51). But they are so much more: they modify the mourner's body and social position by acting upon and diminishing or transforming culturally privileged markers of masculinity.

The social and gendered effects of these self-inflicted rites are more clearly evidenced where they are imposed on unwilling others to punish, subordinate or humiliate them (cf. Niditch 2008: 96–9; Olyan 2015; 2019: 71–84). Such is the case when Hanun, the King of Ammon, humiliates David's envoys by shaving their beards and cutting their garments to the buttocks (2 Sam. 10.4; 1 Chron. 19.4). The significance of these acts is not limited to the humiliation they signal or symbolize; by altering culturally coded physical and material markers of masculinity they produce 'less-than-masculine' bodies.[7] As Susan Niditch observes, the sexual and gender nuances are inescapable as David's envoys are forced into a feminizing position of submission:

> To have the beard or half the beard removed against one's wishes by foreign enemies, together with the symbolic ripping of the clothes up to an erogenous zone, betokens exposure, vulnerability, and being turned into a womanlike figure who is sexually used by male enemies. (Niditch 2008: 96)

David addresses this offence by going to war, where the Israelites 'reclaim' their former masculinity by displaying appropriately 'male' bravery and might in battle (2 Sam. 10.12-19). This text is a potent example of the ways in which body modification practices, with their associated gendered effects, are involved in the negotiation of power relations (Lemos 2006; 2017: 28–60).

---

6 E.g. Reuben (Gen. 37.29); Jephthah (Judg. 11.35); David (2 Sam. 13.31); Ahab (1 Kgs 21.27); Hezekiah (2 Kgs 18.27); pilgrims (Jer. 41.5); Job (Job 1.20); Mordecai (Est. 3.15).
7 Lipka (2015: 280) notes that an 'effective means of undermining masculine performance in biblical texts was by destroying, altering, or otherwise tampering with biological markers that served as attributes of masculine identity'.

The gendered effects of garment tearing and manipulation are evident in prophetic texts that feminize Jerusalem, depicting the city as a woman who is punished for her infidelity to Yhwh: 'your skirts are lifted up and you are violated' (Jer. 13.22; cf. Ezek. 16.39). Similar threats are levelled against Nineveh and Babylon, as well as male Egyptian captives, who are depicted as sexually exposed (and abused) women (Isa. 20.4; 47.3; Nah. 3.5). Such exposure of male genitalia, in Tamar Kamionkowski's analysis (2003: 64), 'does not simply shame, but exposes a man's weakness, his vulnerability'. A similar feminizing strategy is employed in neo-Assyrian reliefs, in which the 'sexual exposure, penetration and bodily mutilation of enemy men' is repeatedly attested (Chapman 2004: 160). While not imposed by others, the tearing of garments in biblical contexts of mourning has similar gendered effects on the mourner, as it generally involves or evokes partial or full nakedness. As male genitalia are to be covered and protected, especially in ritual contexts (Exod. 28.42-43), the mourner's exposure of his nakedness renders him socially and physically exposed and sexually vulnerable to the gaze and touch of other men. He becomes 'like a woman', whose body may be viewed, acted upon and penetrated (Nissinen 1998: 52).

Along with clothing, the hair and beard, whether grown long or cut and shaved, also index identity and social status and function as privileged sites for the negotiation and contestation of masculinity (Niditch 2008; Lipka 2016). Beards distinguish men from women, non-dominant men and boys (Wilson 2016). In neo-Assyrian and Achaemenid iconography, kings – emblematic figures of politically dominant masculinity – sport ornate beards that distinguish them from inferior men, vassals and subordinate peoples (Winter 1996; Llewellyn-Jones 2015: 221–4). Likewise, in Judg. 16.16-21, Samson's uncut hair is a measure of his hyper-masculinity: once his hair is cut, he is weak and easily captured (see Niditch in this volume).

Self-inflicted ritual alterations of the hair and beard are commonly performed in contexts of mourning, as in the case of Ezra (9.3-4), Job (1.20) and the pilgrims from Shechem (Jer. 41.5). Several prophetic texts include shaving and haircutting among the mourning rituals to be performed in the face of the destruction of Jerusalem as well as neighbouring peoples (Isa. 15.2; Jer. 7.29; 47.5; 48.37; Ezek. 27.31; Mic. 1.16). Like garment rending and nakedness, hair and beard cutting are punitive acts when imposed upon others. A helpful contrast is an already mentioned distinction between Ezra's self-imposed hair-tearing and chin-baring and that which Nehemiah inflicts upon the men guilty of intermarriage (Neh. 13.25). An even more dramatic image is the announcement of Israel's destruction at the hands of Assyria in Isa. 7.20: 'Yhwh will shave with a razor hired beyond the river – with the king of Assyria – the head and the hair of the feet [genitals], and it will take off the beard as well' (cf. Isa. 3.24). Given that beards are only grown and cultivated by men, their removal is a 'special affront with gendered connotations' (Niditch 2008: 98). Masculine hair mutilation is thus a body modification that both 'unmanes' and 'unmans'.

Ezra is not 'unmanned' by others, however; rather, he voluntarily tears his own garment and cloak, pulls his hair and shaves his face (9.3-4). In contrast to the book's earlier image of Ezra as priest, scribe and emissary, who presumably would have been appropriately clothed and bearded (cf. Exod. 28.42; Lev. 19.27), the mourning Ezra denudes himself of prominent material markers of masculinity. His acts effect an immediate change in both his body and the gendered and social configurations of the social body. As he sits on the ground appalled, even as he prays and confesses before Yhwh, Ezra's body is exposed and open for all to see (Ezra 9.3-4). And yet, while these body modifications alter Ezra's masculine status, they are not imposed upon him by other men. Rather, they are self-imposed acts of humiliation manifesting and pointedly embodying his obeisance to Yhwh.

A more subtle form of body modification performed by Ezra is fasting: he withdraws from before the house of God into one of the temple chambers, where he 'does not eat bread and does not drink water' as he mourns the infidelity of the *golah* (Ezra 10.6). Like others who variously fast to mourn the dead, seek divine intervention or enact penitence or lament in the face of calamity, Ezra withdraws from a critical physical, social and cultural activity of daily life: eating and drinking.[8] The hunger and thirst that result from fasting echo the bodily sensations provoked by famine, drought and military siege (Deut. 28.48; 2 Kgs 6.25; 7.4; 25.3). While in such cases hunger and thirst are the felt effects of disasters and suffering external to the body, in the case of fasting, they are deliberately brought into the body. Whether involuntary or self-inflicted, fasting is a form of body modification provoking sensory and physical changes in the body: it renders the person weak, diminished and has socially restrictive and restricting effects (cf. Dietler 2011).

The location of Ezra's fasting is particularly significant, for his move into the precincts of the Jerusalem temple locates him directly in the realm of priestly and Levitical privilege and sacrificial functions. He does not, however, prepare the evening sacrifice or participate in it. A contrast is evoked between priestly 'feasting' and Ezra's fasting, between his penitential, diminished masculinity and the normative masculinity of the priests who officiate and share in the sacred feasts. Ezra's embodied performance of mourning outside the temple (10.1) and his denial of food and drink within its chambers (10.6) have social effects: they are disruptive of the temple's economy, its ritual sociality and the status of the priests who serve in it.

Embodying subordination

Ezra not only materially modifies his body but also manipulates his postures, gestures and bodily position in ways that configure his body and his status both in relation to those around him and in relation to Yhwh. In Ezra 9.3b, having torn his garment and bared his head and chin, Ezra sits appalled (אשבה משומם), 'reduced to shuddering' (Becking 2013: 14), while in 10.1, he is vividly described throwing himself (מתנפל) before the house of Yhwh. These verbs indicating Ezra's physical diminishment are frequently used in contexts of mourning in the Hebrew Bible.[9] They likewise describe the bodily posture of men fallen in battle (2 Sam. 1.19; Isa. 21.9; Amos 5.2) and feminized cities that are bowed to the ground under Yhwh's judgement (Isa. 3.26; 47.1). The gendering of these relational bodily postures in contexts of warfare is similarly highlighted in neo-Assyrian iconography, in which the image of the victorious king is contrasted with that of the defeated enemy who 'lies helpless at his feet, literally fallen ... stripped of his weapons and often his clothing' (Assante 2016: 78–9), evidencing the inferior masculinity of the defeated and the superior masculinity of the victor (Cifarelli 1998). In the Hebrew Bible, inferior parties fall before their superiors in a variety of other social contexts: Ruth falls before Boaz (Ruth 2.10); Joseph's brothers fall before him (Gen. 44.14); the king's subjects fall before him (2 Sam. 1.2; 19.18). Whether forced by others or self-imposed, these

---

8 Cf. 1 Sam. 21.13; 2 Sam. 1.12; 12.21; 1 Kgs 21.27; Ezra 8.21; Neh. 1.4; Isa. 58.3; Jer. 14.12; Est. 4.16; Joel 2.12; Jon. 3.5.
9 See Deut. 9.25; Josh. 7.6-7; Job 1.20; Ps. 44.25; Lam. 2.10; Ezek. 9.8; 26.15-17; Jon. 3.6; 1 Macc. 4.36-40.

bodily postures of submission and subordination configure gendered power relations in the world of the narratives.

Ezra falls, but not before any superior mortal to whom he is beholden. Nor is his prostration induced by the power of other men over him – not even that of the Persian king. Rather, Ezra falls before the temple, before Yhwh; it is also before Yhwh that he kneels in preparation for prayer and extends his hands (אפרשה כפי אל יהוה אלהי), a gesture often reserved for an address to the deity (9.5).[10] This embodied performance removes him from the referential political context of Persian imperialism and his role as an emissary of the king and locates him instead in the socio-cultic realm of Yhwh. It is to Yhwh that Ezra directs his prayer, and it is the commands of this god, rather than the edicts of the Persian king, that Ezra presents as the basis for community practice (9.10-12). Ezra's performance of penitential masculinity positions him, therefore, as a privileged servant of Yhwh, the deity who moves the Persian kings to accomplish his own purposes (Ezra 1.1-2; 6.22; 7.27-28; 9.9).

The power of mourning

The nuanced gendered and political effects of Ezra's body modification and self-debasement parallel (perhaps quite intentionally) those of other, high-profile and authoritative male figures in the Hebrew Bible, such as Moses (Deut. 9.9, 18), Hezekiah (2 Kgs 19.1) and Josiah (2 Kgs 22.11, 19; 2 Chron. 34.19, 27). In the face of the consequences of transgression, these men weep, fast, tear their garments and fall to the ground, physically diminishing their bodies – and their masculinity – in subordination to Yhwh.

Like Moses before Yhwh in the matter of the golden calf (Deut. 18.9, 25), Ezra prostrates himself (מתנפל; Ezra 10.1) and refrains from food and drink (לחם לא אכל ומים לא שתה; 10.6). Not insignificantly, Ezra's mourning rituals liken him to this authoritative figure to whom the biblical texts attribute the exodus from Egypt, the giving of the Torah, the organization of the Israelite community and the establishment of the Tabernacle. Moses is the chosen mediator *par excellence* of Yhwh's will and words for his people. Both Ezra and Moses derive and demonstrate their authoritative status from their subordination to Yhwh.[11]

The Judahite kings Hezekiah and Josiah also engage in rituals of mourning and self-debasement. When faced with the imminent destruction of Jerusalem by Sennacherib, Hezekiah tears his clothes, covers himself in sackcloth and goes to the house of Yhwh (2 Kgs 19.1; Isa. 37.1). In response to the king's self-imposed humbling, Isaiah announces that Yhwh will save Jerusalem (2 Kgs 19.6-7; Isa. 37.5-6). In this way, Hezekiah's authority and his ability to protect and provide for his subjects – key markers of royal masculinity (Chapman 2004: 83–4) – are made possible by this voluntary deconstruction of his own masculinity and subjection to Yhwh's superior might. Similarly, Josiah tears his garments upon hearing the words of the newly discovered scroll of the Torah, which

---

10 See Exod. 9.33; 1 Kgs 8.22, 38; 2 Chron. 6.12, 13, 29; Ps. 44.21; Isa. 1.15; Jer. 4.31. Similar postures of subordination are attested in neo-Assyrian iconography, where inferior combatants kneel in surrender and stretch out their hands in supplication, much as kings extend their arms to beseech the gods. See further Cifarelli (1998: 216–17).
11 On the portrayal of Ezra as a second Moses in Ezra 7–10 and Nehemiah 8, see Fried (2014: 45–53). She highlights the shared images of court official and Torah scribe associated with both biblical figures but makes no mention of the mourning rituals they share.

spells out Yhwh's imminent punishment (2 Kgs 22.11; 2 Chron. 34.19). His physical act of debasement lowers his status before Yhwh, as evidenced in the words of the prophetess Huldah: 'because your heart was penitent, and you humbled yourself before Yhwh ... because you have torn your clothes and wept before me, I also have heard you, says Yhwh' (2 Kgs 22.18-19).[12] Josiah's 'less-than-masculine' behaviour locates him in a privileged position before, and in relationship to, the deity, without diminishing his power over others, as evidenced in his ambitious cultic purge (2 Kings 23). Self-abasement before Yhwh legitimates and sustains the power of these kings over other men, especially the men of Judah. It is perhaps no surprise, then, that similar gendered nuances and social complexities are present in Ezra 9–10. Before Yhwh, Ezra's embodiment of inferior social and gendered types legitimates his mediation of the deity's words and commands – and specifically the divine prohibition of marriages which will blend Yhwh's people with the 'foreign' peoples of the land (Ezra 9.10-12; 10.3). Ezra's mourning, likewise, powerfully reconfigures *golah* identity, power relations, masculine performance and even male bodies, as the men of the *golah* are drawn to Ezra and mourn with him.

Reconfiguring community

The first to gather around Ezra are those who 'tremble (חרד) at the words of the God of Israel' (9.4; 10.3) and who sit with Ezra in mourning until he addresses Yhwh in prayer (9.5). In 10.1b, a second group, a 'very great assembly of men, women, and children' from 'out of Israel', gathers around him and weeps intensely with him as he cries, mourns and confesses. Finally, while Ezra fasts inside the temple chambers (10.6), 'all the men of Judah and Benjamin (כל אנשי יהודה ובנימן)' gather in the square before the temple where they stand trembling (רעד) in the rain (10.9). The gathering of the *golah* around Ezra that begins with a few 'tremblers' (9.4) continues until all the men (אנשים) of the *golah* are gathered in fearful trembling before the house of Yhwh. Saul Olyan describes this dynamic as one of group affiliation:

> Their acts of entering Ezra's physical proximity and embracing his ritual stance realize and signal an affiliation between Ezra and his supporters and between the individual members of the newly formed group. The group itself is created in the context of penitential petition by the very behaviour of the individuals who choose to rally to Ezra and embrace mourning rites, thereby declaring their affiliation with him and his cause. The mourning and petition of Ezra and his followers separate them ritually from all others who are worshipping in the sanctuary and communicate to others their distinct political stance. (Olyan 2004: 90)

Even more significantly, I would add, this dynamic suggests the ritualization of this community, a process by which 'bodies are restructured in the very doing of the acts' (Bell 1992: 100). The gendered identities and social status of the *golah* are performatively enacted as a growing number of bowed, weeping, trembling men gather towards Ezra and before Yhwh in submission, vulnerability and fear.[13]

---

12 For an insightful and considered analysis of Josiah's body and ritual acts, see Stavrakopoulou (2018).
13 While the community that gathers around Ezra in 10.1 includes women and children, they are displaced by the 'men of the *golah*' who gather in Jerusalem (10.7) and stand in the square where decisions are to be made concerning 'foreign' women and their children (10.14).

Ezra's mourning, and that of those who gather around him, constitutes an example of what Catherine Bell (1992: 570) has described as 'a specific embodiment and exercise of power'. That is, power relations are reconfigured, and distinctions are enacted and deployed within the group: mourners separate themselves from the quotidian activities of non-mourners, the guilty are set apart from the rest, women and children are displaced from the assembly and a group of men determines the fate of the wives and children of their transgressive *golah* fellows.[14]

The fundamental problem in Ezra 9–10, as suggested in 9.1, is that there are men who have taken 'foreign' women in marriage, an act that is labelled an infidelity (מעל) to Yhwh (9.2, 4; 10.2, 6). A closer look at the actions carried out by these men reveals that the rejection of these marriages and the call to expel the women and children may well be a matter of disputed masculinities. The daughters of the 'peoples of the land' are not 'taken' (לקח), as might be expected.[15] Rather, they are 'lifted' (נשא), a verb that in other biblical texts associates marriage with strength and political status. Its use here emphasizes the active, even forceful, role of *golah* men in acquiring daughters as wives (9.2, 12; 10.44).[16] Furthermore, the women are 'settled' (הושיב) by the men of the *golah* (10.2, 10, 14, 17, 18). While used for marriage only here and in Neh. 13.23, the hiphil of ישב frequently describes an action performed upon inferior parties that settles them in a place or territory.[17] Like נשא, therefore, הושיב highlights the active role of the *golah* men who have taken wives from the 'peoples of the land'. This terminology, more usually understood by various scholars to discredit the marriages in Ezra 9–10 (Japhet 2007; Bautch 2009: 99–103; Southwood 2012: 166–8), functions as a pointed statement concerning the masculine performance of the 'guilty' men. They are assertively active, for they 'lift' the daughters of other men (the 'peoples of the land') to acquire wives and 'settle' them – and thereby themselves – in the land. Furthermore, the men have engendered children, for their wives have given birth (10.3, 44).[18]

A fundamental rift between men of the *golah* comes to the fore: some have acted upon the 'foreign' women and their kin, others have not. The terminology used to describe the marriages draws attention to these actions and to the dominant and assertive role of the men who have performed them. Most problematically, however, these terms and the actions to which they refer call into question the masculine status of the *golah* men who have *not* taken 'foreign' women in marriage, who have *not* 'settled' women and have *not* produced descendants. Thus, when the Ezra group declares the marriages to be unacceptable, and a transgression of the relationship with Yhwh, it is an attempt to bring

---

14 Curiously, these distinctions do not privilege either the priests or the Levites who are notably included among the accused and head the list of the guilty men (Ezra 9.2; 10.17-19). It is only they who offer a sacrifice for their guilt (10.19). This offering (אשם), viewed by some as a sign of their repentance, highlights the severity of their transgression. See Milgrom (1976: 73 n.262).

15 The most common phrase used for marriage in the Hebrew Bible is 'to take a wife' (לקח אשה), e.g. Gen. 24.3, 4, 7, 37, 38, 40; Lev. 21.14; Judg. 14.3; 1 Kgs 16.31.

16 The verb נשא is used for marriage in various texts in which the 'lifting' of daughters does not involve consent or reciprocity between kinship groups (cf. Judg. 21.21-23) or where the marriages are associated with the superior masculinity, virility and military or political status of the men (cf. 2 Chron. 11.21-22; 13.19-21; 24.3). See Guenther (2005: 399–401); Eskenazi (2006: 509–29).

17 See Gen. 47.6; 2 Kgs 17.6, 24, 26; 2 Chron. 8.2; Jer. 32.37. On the spatial resonances of this term as used in Ezra 10, see Eskenazi (2006); Clauss (2011).

18 Ezra 10.3 calls for the expulsion of the women and 'those born from them' (הנולד מהם), while 10.44, an arguably difficult verse, indicates that the 'foreign' women had 'put sons' (וישימו בנים), which is rendered in Williamson (1985: 145) as 'and some of the women had even borne children'.

the unfettered masculinity of the guilty men under control. They consequently advocate a corrective masculinity of mourning, self-abasement and subordination – a masculinity that derives its status from obedience to Yhwh – as the appropriate masculinity for the *golah*.

The Ezra group thus seeks to 'manage' the unfettered masculinity of the unfaithful men, a move articulated most fundamentally by Shecaniah's exhortation in 10.3: 'And now, let us make a covenant with our God (נכרת ברית לאלהינו) to expel (להוציא) the women and those born from them ... and let it be done according to the law (תורה).'[19] This call to covenant-making is premised on the guilt of the *golah* – 'we have been unfaithful' (10.2) – for having transgressed Yhwh's commands, as emphasized in Ezra's prayer (9.10b-12), and demands of all the *golah* men a masculinity of penitence and humbling before the deity.

Not all the men, however, are directly affected by the covenant in 10.3. It is only those who have seemingly over-asserted their masculinity and taken 'foreign' wives who must reject their wives and offspring to choose Yhwh. The 'guilty' men of the *golah* are humiliated and 'unmanned', obliged to fail at the fundamental masculine task of protecting their wives and children.[20] The covenant with Yhwh places them under the management of Ezra, wielder of the Torah on which the covenant is grounded (10.3b), and of those who mourn before the temple and tremble with Ezra 'at the commands of our God' (10.2; cf. 9.3).[21]

'Rehabilitating' divine masculinity

Ezra's ritual actions inevitably index anxieties about Yhwh's own masculinity. The deity's dominant masculinity and unrivalled status is likely assumed by most readers of the text, and indeed appears to be the premise for Ezra's mourning in the wake of the transgression of the *golah* and the call to a covenant with this god. But as gender-critical studies suggest, dominant masculinity is neither an essential trait nor an accomplished state; it is a relational performance that is negotiated, contested and in need of continual affirmation in the face of other forms of masculinity (Boer 2010; Nissinen 2016).[22] Dominant masculinity is constituted, produced, upheld and legitimated within a network of culturally situated performances and relations. It is a precarious social location:

> Once a man did succeed in achieving hegemonic masculinity, there was always the fear that something or someone could come along and undermine his masculine performance ... those who don't perform the hegemonic masculine ideal satisfactorily are viewed as being associated with lesser, sometimes subordinate masculinities on the spectrum, which means in practical terms a loss in social power and prestige. (Lipka 2016: 276)

---

19 That the call to action comes from Shecaniah, identified only as the son of Jehiel and a descendant of Elam, is not only in keeping with Ezra's character in this book, it evidences too the incorporation of the *golah* into the interpretation of events enacted in Ezra's mourning rituals. On the nature of the covenant in Ezra 9–10, see Nykolaishen (2015).
20 Chapman (2004: 47) describes a strikingly similar scene on a neo-Assyrian palace relief depicting Sennacherib's siege of Lachish: 'The women of Lachish are depicted neatly filing out of the city gate ... and their children accompany them ... Their own king and husband failed the masculine contest of battle.'
21 On the Hebrew Bible's concern with 'managing' men and 'regimenting' their bodies, relationships and performance of masculinity, see George (2010).
22 Drawing on Connell (2005), Nissinen (2016: 341) describes hegemonic masculinity as that which 'corresponds to the cultural ideal of male performance in a male-dominated society, defined and legitimated by those in privileged positions of power'. On the relational quality of masculinities, see further Connell and Messerschmidt (2005); Zsolnay (2016: 16–21).

Claims to Yhwh's dominant masculinity both in Ezra 9–10 and the rest of the book sit uncomfortably, however, against the backstory of exile and temple destruction and the current state of foreign domination in which the *golah* resides. Problematically, Yhwh's actions are not in evidence in Ezra 9–10, nor does he intervene in the affairs of the *golah*. While the deity is the (alleged) aggrieved party in Ezra 9–10, no direct speech is attributed to Yhwh by the narrator.[23] There is no indication that he is aware of, much less affected by, the marriages that have taken place. Furthermore, the self-afflicted, humiliated and deconstructed bodies of Ezra and the *golah* appear not to receive a response from the deity.[24] Instead, it falls to the human players, and Ezra in particular, to 'produce' and represent Yhwh's words, will, actions and even his gendered status – his masculinity.

The silence of Yhwh often triggers concern in the Hebrew Bible, and while it does not necessarily signal his absence, it does raise doubts concerning his interest, involvement and commitment to his people.[25] It may even suggest that he has abandoned them or was forced to do so (cf. Kutsko 2000). It is in this context that the 'rehabilitation' of Yhwh's masculinity becomes a pressing matter.[26] As Ilona Zsolnay (2016: 19) argues, a patriarch or ruler 'can only maintain his authority if he has convinced his family as well as his society that he is worthy/able to embody, maintain, and sustain that power'. The overassertive masculinity of the men who have taken wives from the 'peoples of the land', however, challenges the authority of Yhwh and undermines his 'ability to be a male god' (Stone 2005: 125), one able to provide for the needs of his subjects. These men have chosen wives, produced offspring, and settled a territory without divine participation and outside the bounds of divine control. They have usurped the role of Yhwh. The masculinity of mourning and obeisance to the deity enacted by Ezra and affirmed as the appropriate configuration of masculinity for the *golah* (most vividly enacted in the covenant that requires the expulsion of women and children) reasserts the dominant masculinity of Yhwh. The land is to be entered, possessed and inhabited, and children are to be engendered, on Yhwh's terms and under his aegis.[27]

Ezra's mourning rituals and body modification constitute the *golah* as the subject people of Yhwh, to whom the obeisance and obedience of the community is due: not to Persia or to local governing elites but to the deity. Even as Ezra positions himself in humiliation to Yhwh, he elevates the deity as the sovereign of the *golah*: Ezra mediates the commands of Yhwh, not the דת ('law') of the Persian king, and it is the infidelity of the *golah* to Yhwh, not to Persia, that provokes Ezra's mourning (9.3-4). It is before Yhwh that he falls and to Yhwh that he directs his prayer (9.5). It is the wrath of Yhwh, not that of the Persian king, that the *golah* fears and in the face of which they fall trembling to the ground and decree the expulsion of wives and children (9.14-15; 10.2-3, 14). Ezra's mourning rituals re-signify the silence and apparent absence of Yhwh, casting the god

---

23 On the silence of Yhwh in the book of Ezra, see Becking (2013).
24 Olyan (2004: 73) describes Ezra's mourning as petitionary mourning, which has various purposes, all of which involve a response from the deity: 'to reverse the deity's decision to punish the people, or to seek Yhwh's guidance by means of an oracle or revelation, or to solicit the deity's help in a situation of personal difficulty'; cf. Grol (1998: 32-3).
25 See, e.g. 1 Sam. 28.6-7; 2 Sam. 12.22-23; Ps. 44.24-25; Isa. 54.8; 58.3; Lam. 5.20.
26 Diamond (2003: 38) uses the phrase 'the rehabilitation of Yhwh' to refer to a 'complex of operations designed to prevent at any price the failure of Israel's patron deity and the cultural oblivion of Israel'.
27 Camp (2011: 308-9) argues that the problem with strange women, and in fact with all women in the Hebrew Bible, is the threat they present to male patrilineage by virtue of their active role in procreation. However, men's virility is likewise a challenge to the masculinity of the deity; cf. Sawyer (2004: 162); Hooker (2014: 22-7).

of a small territory as an imperial overlord. Like the Persian kings in the book of Ezra, Yhwh remains distant, his presence mediated by authorized representatives, his scribes and servants.[28] Like Persia's kings, Yhwh issues edicts and commands that are sought out, studied and implemented (9.10-12; 10.3). And it is Yhwh who, through the Persian kings, rather than despite them, ensures the well-being of the *golah*, providing a 'stake in this holy place', sustenance and relief (9.8-9).

In the book of Ezra, the implicit inadequacy of Yhwh's masculine performance is ultimately addressed and corrected, although not on the geopolitical landscape of Persian imperialism, nor on worldly or mythic battlefields in which he might display warrior skills.[29] Yhwh produces no sponsored dynasty through which to order the world, execute justice or provide for his people. He requires, rather, that the men of the *golah* cede their masculinity to Yhwh – and to those who speak for Yhwh – even to the point of turning over their wives and their offspring. As Deborah Sawyer (2004: 164–71) aptly notes in her study of Abraham's masculinity, in the face of Yhwh, 'male power is emasculated' so that the masculinity of the male god is 'triumphant and unchallenged'. This 'emasculation' ultimately and simultaneously serves to prove that Yhwh is good at being a male god, that the *golah* group is the 'chosen' people of Yhwh and that the future of the community, and its possession of the land, depends on obedience to the commands of Yhwh, as wielded by Ezra, the mourning man.

Conclusion

While the focus of this chapter has been the men of the *golah* and the embodiment and performance of *golah* masculinities, I do not suggest that the women, and their silencing and expulsion, as well as the structures, systems and institutions that perpetuate and naturalize their subordinated status, are not important. The question I have addressed is not who the women are and why are they expelled, but why their silence and expulsion 'seem necessary to this particular version of the past' (Kelso 2013: 288).

Shifting the object of analysis and problematization from the 'foreign' women to the men of the *golah* reveals that, contrary to scholarly assumptions, the primary issue in Ezra 9–10 is not the desired expulsion of the women and children; much more grievously, the dispute does not directly concern them. At issue instead is the men of the community, their masculinities and the power relations between these men. Ezra 9–10 is about men's bodies and their embodiment of fealty to Yhwh. It is about Yhwh's masculinity and its rehabilitation in the wake of exile and the spectre of divine abandonment, or even impotency. The women play a key role not as agents or actors in the narrative[30] but as the site by which, and in relation to which, men's bodies are modified and deconstructed, masculinities are negotiated and, ultimately, doubts concerning Yhwh's masculinity and power are addressed.

---

28 In the book of Ezra, the Persian kings are never present in Jerusalem but are represented by local elites, scribes and other representatives who speak for them, proclaim and implement their decrees, and transmit information to them (see especially Ezra 4–6). Ezra is one of these representatives, but he deliberately diminishes that role and embraces the role of mediator for Yhwh.
29 On Yhwh's inadequacy in Ezekiel 16, see Zsolnay (2010).
30 In numerous biblical texts, men dispute power and status on the body of a woman (Genesis 34; Judges 19–21; 2 Sam. 3.6-11; 13.1-22; 16.20-33). See further Stone (1996: 85–127). Gedalof (1999: 44, 202) rightly observes that women's exclusion and subordination do not render them 'inert or consenting targets' of power but 'always also the elements of its articulation'. Cf. Molloy (1995).

References

Assante, J. (2016), 'Men Looking at Men: The Homoerotics of Power in the State Arts of Assyria', in I. Zsolnay (ed.), *Being a Man: Negotiating Ancient Constructs of Masculinity*, 76–134, New York: Routledge.

Bautch, R. J. (2009), *Glory and Power, Ritual and Relationship: The Sinai Covenant in the Postexilic Period*, Library of Hebrew Bible/Old Testament Studies, New York: T&T Clark.

Becking, B. (2011), *Ezra, Nehemiah, and the Construction of Early Jewish Identity*, Tübingen: Mohr Siebeck.

Becking, B. (2013), 'Temple Vessels Speaking for a Silent God: Notes on the Divine Presence in the Books of Ezra and Nehemiah', in B. Becking (ed.), *Reflections on the Silence of God: A Discussion with Marjo Korpel and Johannes de Moor*, 14–28, Leiden: Brill.

Bell, C. M. (1992), *Ritual Theory, Ritual Practice*, New York: Oxford University Press.

Blenkinsopp, J. (1988), *Ezra-Nehemiah: A Commentary*, The Old Testament Library, Philadelphia, PA: Westminster John Knox Press.

Boer, R. (2005), 'No Road: On the Absence of Feminist Criticism of Ezra-Nehemiah', in C. Vander Stichele and T. C. Penner (eds), *Her Master's Tools? Feminist and Postcolonial Engagements of Historical-Critical Discourse*, 233–52, Leiden: Brill.

Boer, R. (2010), 'Of Fine Wine, Incense and Spices: The Unstable Masculine Hegemony of the Book of Chronicles', in O. Creanga (ed.), *Men and Masculinity in the Hebrew Bible & Beyond*, 20–33, Sheffield: Sheffield Phoenix Press.

Brown, A. P. (2005), 'The Problem of Mixed Marriages in Ezra 9–10', *Bibliotheca Sacra* 162: 437–58.

Butler, J. (1999), *Gender Trouble: Feminism and the Subversion of Identity*, New York: Routledge.

Camp, C. V. (2011), 'Feminist- and Gender-Critical Perspectives on the Biblical Ideology of Intermarriage', in C. Frevel (ed.), *Mixed Marriages: Intermarriage and Group Identity in the Second Temple Period*, 303–15, New York: T&T Clark.

Chapman, C. R. (2004), *The Gendered Language of Warfare in the Israelite-Assyrian Encounter*, Harvard Semitic Monographs, Winona Lake, IN: Eisenbrauns.

Cifarelli, M. (1998), 'Gesture and Alterity in the Art of Ashurnasirpal II of Assyria', *Art Bulletin* 80 (2): 210–28.

Clauss, J. (2011), 'Understanding the Mixed Marriages of Ezra-Nehemiah in the Light of Temple-Building and the Book's Concept of Jerusalem', in C. Frevel (ed.), *Mixed Marriages: Intermarriage and Group Identity in the Second Temple Period*, 109–31, New York: T&T Clark.

Connell, R. W. (2005), *Masculinities*, 2nd edn. Berkeley, CA: University of California.

Connell, R. W., and J. W. Messerschmidt (2005), 'Hegemonic Masculinity: Rethinking the Concept', *Gender & Society* 19 (6): 829–59.

Creanga, O. (2014), 'Introduction', in O. Creanga and P.-B. Smit (eds), *Biblical Masculinities Foregrounded*, 3–14, Sheffield: Sheffield Phoenix Press.

Diamond, A. R. P. (2003), 'Deceiving Hope', *Scandinavian Journal of the Old Testament* 17 (1): 34–48.

Dietler, M. (2011), 'Feasting and Fasting', in T. Insoll (ed.), *The Oxford Handbook of the Archaeology of Ritual and Religion*, 179–94, Oxford: Oxford University Press.

Eskenazi, T. C. (1992), 'Out from the Shadows: Biblical Women in the Postexilic Era', *Journal for the Study of the Old Testament* 54: 25–43.

Eskenazi, T. C. (2006), 'The Missions of Ezra and Nehemiah', in O. Lipschitz and M. Oeming (eds), *Judah and the Judeans in the Persian Period*, 509–29, Winona Lake, IN: Eisenbrauns.

Fensham, F. C. (1982), *The Books of Ezra and Nehemiah*, New International Commentary on the Old Testament, Grand Rapids, MI: Eerdmans.

Fried, L. (2001), '"You Shall Appoint Judges": Ezra's Mission and the Rescript of Artaxerxes', in J. W. Watts (ed.), *Persia and Torah: The Theory of Imperial Authorization of the Pentateuch*, 63–89, Atlanta, GA: Society of Biblical Literature.

Fried, L. (2014), *Ezra and the Law in History and Tradition*, Columbia: University of South Carolina Press.

Fuchs, E. (2008), 'Reclaiming the Hebrew Bible for Women: The Neoliberal Turn in Contemporary Feminist Scholarship', *Journal of Feminist Studies in Religion* 24 (2): 45–65.

Gedalof, I. (1999), *Against Purity: Rethinking Identity with Indian and Western Feminisms, Gender, Racism, Ethnicity*, London: Routledge.

George, M. K. (2010), 'Masculinity and Its Regimentation in Deuteronomy', in O. Creanga (ed.), *Men and Masculinity in the Hebrew Bible & Beyond*, 64–82, Sheffield: Sheffield Phoenix Press.

Gorman, F. (1994), 'Ritual Studies and Biblical Studies: Assessment of the Past, Prospects for the Future', *Semeia* 67: 13–37.

Grabbe, L. L. (2004), *A History of the Jews and Judaism in the Second Temple Period: Volume I*, London: T&T Clark.

Grol, H. van (1998), 'Exegesis of Exile – Exegesis of Scripture? Ezra 9: 6–9', in J. C. de Moor (ed.), *Intertextuality in Ugarit and Israel*, 31–61, Leiden: Brill.

Guenther, A. (2005), 'A Typology of Israelite Marriage: Kinship, Socio-Economic, and Religious Factors', *Journal for the Study of the Old Testament* 29 (4): 387–407.

Hearn, J. (2014), 'Men, Masculinities and the Material(-)Discursive', *NORMA* 9 (1): 5–17.

Hooker, A. (2014), '"Show Me Your Glory": The *Kabod* of Yahweh as Phallic Manifestation?', in O. Creanga and P.-B. Smit (eds), *Biblical Masculinities Foregrounded*, 17–34, Sheffield: Sheffield Phoenix Press.

Janzen, D. (2002), *Witch-Hunts, Purity and Social Boundaries: The Expulsion of the Foreign Women in Ezra 9–10*, Sheffield: Sheffield Academic Press.

Japhet, S. (2007), 'The Expulsion of the Foreign Women (Ezra 9–10): The Legal Basis, Precedents, and Consequences for the Definition of Jewish Identity', in F. Hartenstein and M. Pietsch (eds), *'Sieben Augen auf einem Stein' (Sach 3,9): Studien zur Literatur des Zweiten Tempels*, 141–61, Neukirchen-Vluyn: Neukirchener Verlag.

Johnson, W. M. (2011), *The Holy Seed Has Been Defiled: The Interethnic Marriage Dilemma in Ezra 9–10*, Sheffield: Sheffield Phoenix Press.

Kamionkowski, S. T. (2003), *Gender Reversal and Cosmic Chaos: A Study on the Book of Ezekiel*, New York: Sheffield Academic Press.

Karrer-Grube, C. (2012), 'Ezra and Nehemiah: The Return of the Others', in L. Schottroff, M.-T. Wacker and M. Rumscheidt (eds), *Feminist Biblical Interpretation: A Compendium of Critical Commentary on the Books of the Bible and Related Literature*, 192–206, Grand Rapids, MI: Eerdmans.

Kelso, J. (2013), 'Reading Silence: The Books of Chronicles and Ezra-Nehemiah, and the Relative Absence of a Feminist Interpretative History', in S. Scholz (ed.), *Feminist Interpretation of the Hebrew Bible in Retrospect: I. Biblical Books*, 268–89, Sheffield: Sheffield Phoenix Press.

Kutsko, J. F. (2000), *Between Heaven and Earth: Divine Presence and Absence in the Book of Ezekiel*, Winona Lake, IN: Eisenbrauns.

Lemos, T. M. (2006), 'Shame and the Mutilation of Enemies in the Hebrew Bible', *Journal of Biblical Literature* 125 (2): 225–41.

Lemos, T. M. (2013), 'Physical Violence and the Boundaries of Personhood in the Hebrew Bible', *Hebrew Bible and Ancient Israel* 2 (4): 500–31.

Lemos, T. M. (2017), *Violence and Personhood in Ancient Israel and Comparative Contexts*, New York: Oxford University Press.
Leuchter, M. (2010), 'Coming to Terms with Ezra's Many Identities in Ezra-Nehemiah', in L. C. Jonker (ed.), *Historiography and Identity (Re)Formulation in Second Temple Historiographical Literature*, 41–64, New York: T&T Clark.
Levine, B. (1993), 'Silence, Sound, and the Phenomenology of Mourning in Biblical Israel', *Journal of Ancient Near Eastern Studies* 22: 89–106.
Lipka, H. (2016), 'Shaved Beards and Bared Buttocks: Shame and the Undermining of Masculine Performance in Biblical Texts', in I. Zsolnay (ed.), *Being a Man: Negotiating Ancient Constructs of Masculinity*, 271–304, New York: Routledge.
Llewellyn-Jones, L. (2015), '"That My Body Is Strong": The Physique and Appearance of Achaemenid Monarchy', in D. Boschung, H. A. Shapiro and F. Wascheck (eds), *Bodies in Transition: Dissolving the Boundaries of Embodied Knowledge*, 211–48, Paderborn: Wilhelm Fink.
Maier, C. M. (2017), 'The "Foreign" Women in Ezra-Nehemiah: Intersectional Perspectives on Ethnicity', in L. J. M. Claassens and C. J. Sharp (eds), *Feminist Frameworks and the Bible: Power, Ambiguity, and Intersectionality*, 79–97, New York: T&T Clark.
Milgrom, J. (1976), *Cult and Conscience: The Asham and the Priestly Doctrine of Repentance*, Leiden: Brill.
Moffat, D. P. (2013), *Ezra's Social Drama: Identity Formation, Marriage and Social Conflict in Ezra 9–10*, London: T&T Clark.
Molloy, M. (1995), 'Imagining (the) Difference: Gender, Ethnicity and Metaphors of Nation', *Feminist Review* 51: 94–112.
Morgan, D. (2017), 'Material Analysis and the Study of Religion', in T. Hutchings and J. McKenzie (eds), *Materiality and the Study of Religion: The Stuff of the Sacred*, 14–32, London: Routledge.
Niditch, S. (2008), *'My Brother Esau Is a Hairy Man': Hair and Identity in Ancient Israel*, New York: Oxford University Press.
Nissinen, M. (1998), *Homoeroticism in the Biblical World: A Historical Perspective*, Minneapolis, MN: Fortress Press.
Nissinen, M. (2016), 'Relative Masculinities in the Hebrew Bible/Old Testament', in I. Zsolnay (ed.), *Being a Man: Negotiating Ancient Constructs of Masculinity*, 340–79, New York: Routledge.
Nykolaishen, D. J. E. (2015), 'Ezra 9–10: Solemn Oath? Renewed Covenant? New Covenant?' in R. J. Bautch and G. N. Knoppers (eds), *Covenant in the Persian Period: From Genesis to Chronicles*, 371–89, Winona Lake, IN: Eisenbrauns.
Økland, J. (2015), 'Requiring Explanation: Hegemonic Masculinities in the Hebrew Bible and Second Temple Traditions', *Biblical Interpretation* 23: 479–88.
Olyan, S. M. (1998), 'What Do Shaving Rites Accomplish?', *Journal of Biblical Literature* 117 (4): 611–22.
Olyan, S. M. (2004), *Biblical Mourning: Ritual and Social Dimensions*, Oxford: Oxford University Press.
Olyan, S. M. (2012), 'Theorizing Violence in Biblical Ritual Contexts: The Case of Mourning Rites', in S. M. Olyan (ed.), *Social Theory and the Study of Israelite Religion: Essays in Retrospect and Prospect*, 169–80, Leiden: Brill.
Olyan, S. M. (2015), 'Ritual Inversion in Biblical Representations of Punitive Rites', in J. J. Collins, T. M. Lemos and S. M. Olyan (eds), *Worship, Women, and War: Essays in Honor of Susan Niditch*, 135–43, Providence, RI: Brown University.
Olyan, S. M. (2019), *Violent Rituals of the Hebrew Bible*, New York: Oxford University Press.

Pham, X. H. T. (1999), *Mourning in the Ancient Near East and the Hebrew Bible*, Sheffield: Sheffield Academic Press.

Root, M. C. (1979), *The King and Kingship in Achaemenid Art: Essays on the Creation of an Iconography of Empire*, vol. 19, *Acta Iranica*, Leiden: Brill.

Sawyer, D. F. (2004), 'Biblical Gender Strategies: The Case of Abraham's Masculinity', in U. King and T. Beattie (eds), *Gender, Religion, and Diversity: Cross-Cultural Perspectives*, 162–74, London: Continuum.

Southwood, K. E. (2012), *Ethnicity and the Mixed Marriage Crisis in Ezra 9–10: An Anthropological Approach*, Oxford: Oxford University Press.

Stavrakopoulou, F. (2013), 'Making Bodies: On Body Modification and Religious Materiality in the Hebrew Bible', *Hebrew Bible and Ancient Israel* 2 (4): 532–53.

Stavrakopoulou, F. (2018), 'The Prophet Huldah and the Stuff of State', in C. A. Rollston (ed.), *Enemies and Friends of the State: Ancient Prophecy in Context*, 277–96, University Park, PA: Eisenbrauns.

Stone, K. (1996), *Sex, Honor, and Power in the Deuteronomistic History*, Sheffield: Sheffield Academic Press.

Stone, K. (2005), 'Lovers and Raisin Cakes: Food, Sex, and Manhood in Hosea', in K. Stone (ed.), *Practicing Safer Texts: Food, Sex and Bible in Queer Perspective*, 111–28, London: T&T Clark.

Williamson, H. G. M. (1985), *Ezra-Nehemiah*, Word Biblical Commentary, Nashville, TN: Thomas Nelson.

Wilson, S. M. (2016), *Making Men: The Male Coming-of-Age Theme in the Hebrew Bible*, New York: Oxford University Press.

Winter, I. J. (1996), 'Sex, Rhetoric and the Public Monument: The Alluring Body of the Male Ruler in Mesopotamia', in N. Kampen and B. A. Bergmann (eds), *Sexuality in Ancient Art: Near East, Egypt, Greece, and Italy*, 11–26, Cambridge: Cambridge University Press.

Zsolnay, I. (2010), 'The Inadequacies of Yahweh: A Re-Examination of Jerusalem's Portrayal in Ezekiel 16', in S. T. Kamionkowski and W. Kim (eds), *Bodies, Embodiment, and Theology of the Hebrew Bible*, 57–74, New York: T&T Clark.

Zsolnay, I. (2016), 'Introduction', in I. Zsolnay (ed.), *Being a Man: Negotiating Ancient Constructs of Masculinity*, 16–31, New York: Routledge.

CHAPTER EIGHT

The wisdom of ageing

HUGH S. PYPER

HP: 'Now that you're a hundred-and-one years old, do you think it's true that you get wiser as you get older?'

JP: 'I don't recall ever being particularly stupid.'[1]

The relationship between wisdom and age is not a simple one, either now or in the biblical accounts of ageing. Old age gives one the opportunity to gain experience, but if you start out a fool, no amount of experience will make you wise. Only the wise can learn from their experience. Sadly, however, age may rob even the wise of the faculties they need to remember, use or express that wisdom and, wise or foolish, virtuous or wicked, eventually decline and death come to all. If that is the case, a further question arises as to whether living longer, beyond a certain point, is itself a wise thing to do. Is the very fact that the old have let themselves grow old a sign that they are not wise, but foolish? To put it another way, is living into extreme old age a sign of blessing, or a curse?

Although the dilemmas of age have always been with us, the study of old age is more pertinent now than ever. In most industrialized societies, increasing life expectancy means that the proportion of those over 65 in the population is steadily increasing. Diseases of the elderly such as Alzheimer's and other degenerative conditions place an increasing burden on health services and on the younger generations of carers. The problems of ageing are becoming a major issue in public discourse.

In the light of this, it is surprising how little has been published in academic circles about the treatment of ageing in the Hebrew Bible or the role of the elderly in ancient Israelite society.[2] We may speculate that the causes of this neglect are similar to those that led to the comparable lack of studies of women or children in the biblical world until recently. Women, children and the elderly are doubly disadvantaged: first, through their low status in their ancient-world context and their consequent neglect in ancient texts and, second, through the prejudices and structures of the academic communities that study these texts. In the ancient world, these groups are not the ones who write – although we need to qualify that statement in the case of the elderly – and on the whole they are not authoritatively active participants in the public realm of social and political

---

1 This epigraph is a verbatim – and highly characteristic – extract from a conversation between the writer and his mother, the late Mrs Jean Pyper, on her 101st birthday, 16 June 2015. She died on 10 March 2018. I should like to dedicate this chapter to her memory.
2 In what follows, 'Israel' and 'Israelite' function as convenient blanket terms for the ancient societies in which the literature of the Hebrew Bible emerged.

life.³ Where they appear, they are exceptions and either vanish quickly from the record or are subordinated or assimilated to the societal norm of the male in his prime. This means that we are not rich in direct accounts of their lives and experience and have to work by inference and analogy in a way that has to take account of the biases of ancient sources while being sensitive to the effects of our own societal preferences and prejudices on our interpretations.

That there were elderly people in ancient Israel is not in question. The Hebrew Bible is full of characters who are represented as long-lived. Archaeological evidence of burials shows that, even if average life expectancy in the ancient Near East was much shorter than it is now, individuals could live into advanced old age (Blenkinsopp 1997; Knight 2014: 139–41). Two periods of life accounted for the majority of deaths in the young: infancy and the dangerous period of mid-to-late adolescence, which for men brought military service and exposure to other violent and perilous situations, and for women was the likely time of their first pregnancy and childbirth. Those who survived these threats could expect to live well past their forties.

Psalm 90.10 gives seventy or eighty years as the lifespan one could reasonably expect, which is not the same as holding it out as a norm. Most would not reach that age but no one could claim that they had been short-changed by life if they did. The possibility of living until the age of 120 is mentioned in Gen. 6.3 but in the light of West Semitic parallels that figure seems to function as an idealized maximum (Eng 2011: 114–22). Once we are past the patriarchal period in the biblical story, Moses is the only major figure recorded as achieving that age (Deut. 31.2; 34.7), a mark of his exceptional status.⁴

Age is not simply a matter of numbers, however. Time marches on for everyone, but the consequences of this for one's health, social status and influence are not the same. This suggests an important distinction between what we could describe as 'chronological age' and 'functional' or 'social' age; two people aged 70, even of the same social class and gender, can be very different in what they are able to do and how they are regarded by the rest of their social group. That said, the consequences of ageing for, say, a female slave and a male patriarch were very different: the effects of differences in gender, economics and social role ensure that (cf. R. Harris 2000).

Studying the elderly in ancient Israel is thus not simple, whether we are considering the lives elderly people led or the ideas about age and the ageing process that are at work in Israel's literature. Not many books or even articles that deal with the subject have been written; much of what does exist has been produced not by biblical scholars but by pastoral theologians seeking to find a biblical basis for the care of the elderly. The best-known of such works is Gordon Harris's pioneering *Biblical Perspectives on Ageing: God and the Elderly* (1987). Such works do offer useful expositions of the biblical material, but there are inevitable limitations in the questions that they pose. Sociological questions over the role of the elderly in family and village life in ancient Israel, for instance, may be mentioned, but they are seldom the object of extended discussion.

---

3 Given what we understand of the production and compilation of the texts comprising the Hebrew Bible, we may surmise that the bulk of the writers were older members of the scribal class and most likely male. Even for those, however, age could take away the ability to write or the social status of having one's writing acknowledged. The voices of the very elderly and those living with the infirmities of age are not likely to be heard.
4 According to Num. 33.39, Aaron manages to go on until the age of 123. In 2 Chron. 24.15, Jehoiada lives to 130, and Job 42.16 suggests Job reaches 140, double the usual measure, as pointed out in Knight (2014: 145).

One more explicitly biblical study that is directly relevant to the title of this chapter is Joel Ayayi's monograph *A Biblical Theology of Gerassapience* (2010), which assembles much relevant material. It is, however, as it states, a study in biblical theology rather than the sociology of ageing. Ayayi's main purpose is to explore the theological implications of the wisdom of the elderly in the biblical tradition. This does require him to discuss the socio-anthropological aspects of both age and wisdom in the biblical literature, but these are not his main concern. The term 'gerassapience', which is Ayayi's coinage, is a hybrid word, derived from the Greek *geras* ('old age') and Latin *sapientia* ('wisdom'). Unfortunately, it is unlikely to occur to researchers as a search term in databases on the subject and therefore risks being overlooked in the study of the topic.

Another recent work that gives a particularly thorough overview of the biblical vocabulary and treatment of ageing and compares this helpfully with what can be learned from Ugaritic sources is Jason Bembry's *Yahweh's Coming of Age* (2011). Again, however, Bembry's interest is not primarily in the experience of ageing in ancient Israel but in tracing the reasons behind what he claims is a shift in Israel's conception of Yahweh. Earlier biblical material, he argues, depicts Yahweh as a young and vigorous warrior equivalent to Baal in Ugaritic mythology. This contrasts with later material, particularly with the description of Yahweh as 'the Ancient of Days' in Daniel 7. He attributes this change of image at least in part to the growing significance of the metaphor of Yahweh as Israel's father in post-exilic writing and the adoption of language that relates him to the elderly, if not senescent, El rather than Baal.

More pertinent to the concerns of this chapter is Douglas Knight's wide-ranging and informative article 'Perspectives on Aging and the Elderly in the Hebrew Bible' (2014). He provides a more extensive overview of the wider social context and the archaeological evidence than is possible in this article and refers to many of the same biblical passages, but one of the chief points he wishes to get across is that in his view many of those counted as elderly in biblical texts are actually in their 30s, given that he sees 40 as the assumed average life expectancy. That is a timely reminder of the need to distinguish social or functional age from chronological age, but the fact remains that many characters in the Hebrew Bible live much longer than that, and it is with those in particular that we are concerned here. His paper interestingly ends at the point that the present chapter begins, with a statement of the expectation that the elderly will be the source of communal wisdom and memory and so are due veneration. In what follows, however, we will see that this undoubtedly important aspect of the Hebrew Bible's treatment of the topic is, typically, subject to critique in the biblical texts themselves and open to question. The relationship between age and wisdom, and the motivation for the apparent insistence in certain biblical books on this relationship, bears further investigation.

These publications, especially the last, are all important contributions. None of them provides, however, a study of the elderly in ancient Israel on the lines of those provided for the classical world by Tim Parkin's *Old Age in the Roman World: A Cultural and Social History* (2003) and Karen Cokayne's *Experiencing Old Age in Ancient Rome* (2003). The simple reason for this is that the range of materials available to students of classical society is much wider than that available to biblical scholars.

Cokayne gives a helpful overview of these sources while noting that they do have limitations. There are treatises by classical writers that explicitly take old age as their subject, but only a few. The main sources are more incidental and tangential. Rhetorical treatises and medical tracts, legal documents, letters and memoirs all supply data, as do literary works that deal with ageing characters. She cautions, however, that all these sources, especially the literary ones, may reflect more of the stereotypical attitudes of authors and audiences than they do of the lived reality of the lives of the elderly.

Despite these limitations, both of these detailed investigations of the available literary and archaeological evidence from the Roman world suggest many questions, and perhaps some answers, which are pertinent to the study of the elderly in ancient Israel. So too do Marten Stol and Sven Vleeming in their edited collection *The Care of the Elderly in the Ancient Near East* (1998). The essays in this volume demonstrate the usefulness of records of actual legal cases which deal with inheritance and property laws in ancient Mesopotamia and Egypt in providing glimpses of the tensions that existed between generations, and the economic problems and solutions to which these gave rise. Again, such documents do not address the issues of ageing directly but provide data from which inferences can plausibly be made.

That said, in all these scholarly discussions the authors draw attention to how sparse explicit reference to the experience of the elderly themselves is in any ancient records, Classical or Near Eastern alike. In Israel's case, the problem is compounded by the lack of surviving legal documentation. In addition, Cokayne's cautions about the potential problems of literary sources certainly apply in the case of the biblical texts. In the absence of direct evidence, however, these studies of other ancient societies point to issues that, by analogy, are likely to have arisen in ancient Israelite society and can inform speculation on the references to these problems and their solutions that may lie implicit in Israel's writings.

In this chapter, I shall review the evidence the biblical texts provide and then, drawing on the analogies that the study of the wider ancient world provides, make some suggestions about the status of the elderly in ancient Israel, and, in particular, the association between age and wisdom. A brief review of the vocabulary used to designate the elderly and some of the implications of this, especially for the all-important question as to whether old age is a blessing or a curse, will come first, followed by an investigation into the biblical understanding of what causes old age and its symptoms. We will then look at the ways in which old age is used in characterization in the Hebrew Bible; what are we led to expect of a character who is designated as 'old'? Finally, we will return to what we may conclude about the relationship between wisdom and age in the Hebrew Bible and suggest reasons why promoting that relationship may have been particularly significant for ancient Israel and for the composition of the biblical writings themselves.

The vocabulary of ageing

Any investigation of the vocabulary for old age in the Hebrew Bible immediately comes across a condign example of what David Clines refers to as 'the scandal of a male Bible'.[5] The most commonly used word for 'old' in the Hebrew Bible is זָקֵן (*zāqēn*), which is transparently related to the word זָקָן (*zāqān*) meaning 'beard'. To be old is to be bearded in a context where a beard was the mark of male maturity (see Niditch in this volume). The masculinist implications of this hardly need to be pointed out.

Milton Eng's study *The Days of Our Years: A Lexical Semantic Study of the Life Cycle in Biblical Israel* (2011) contains a useful chapter on the variety of words and expressions

---

5 The phrase forms the title of his Ethel M. Wood lecture of 2015, delivered in King's College London, available online at https://www.academia.edu/10977758/The_Scandal_of_a_Male_Bible (accessed 1 March 2019).

that are used to describe old age.⁶ There he points out that the noun זקן ('old') is used in two discrete ways. It can designate an elderly man, often in contexts where there is an implied contrast with younger men in their prime or where a whole population is designated by the hendiadys 'old and young'. There are, however, only three instances where a character is described as זקן ('old') modified by the word מאד ('very'): Eli in 1 Sam. 2.22, Barzillai in 2 Sam. 19.32 and David in 1 Kgs 1.15. We shall return to these instances later.

In the plural זקנים, however, the word most often refers to a discrete social group who have some jurisdiction within a particular community or township and is translated as 'elders' (Eng 2011: 114–22; see also Reviv 1989; Knight 2014: 146). The two usages may overlap, but not necessarily; membership of the social group of 'elders' cannot be taken to imply a particular chronological age. Indeed, this is a clear instance of the difference between chronological and functional age. A younger man of sufficient status who is capable of wise leadership could be deemed suitable to become an elder. Jephthah, for instance, is deemed to be worthy of leading the elders of Gilead while still clearly in his physical prime (Judg. 11.8) and, although the circumstances are explicitly exceptional, and the narrative is a fiction, the clearly young Daniel is rewarded for his acumen in exposing the seducers of Susannah by being invited to sit among the elders (Sus. 1.50).

The details of what functions the elders performed and how one became recognized as an elder in general are not so clear. The picture is clouded further by the fact that 'the elders' often perform an explicit literary function, somewhat reminiscent of the chorus in Greek plays. Just as it is misleading to imagine that crowds of people moving synchronously and reciting in one voice well-composed epodes were part of the daily scene in ancient Athens, the impression that we gain in some biblical passages of a cohesive and identifiable body of elders may not reflect social reality, but serves nonetheless as a very handy device for the biblical narrator to give voice to a representative group who articulate public opinion or traditional values in certain scenarios.

Once we begin to examine these biblical narratives more closely, we may also begin to question just how wise the elders were. While in some cases they are presented as giving counsel and support to key figures and standing up for Yahweh's causes, in others they represent the voice of timid or unimaginative conservatism and parochial self-interest, hindering rather than helping the heroes of the biblical stories. In Numbers 11, seventy elders of the people have some of the spirit of Moses bestowed upon them, but the narrative is also clear that this gift has only very limited effects (v. 25). In later narratives, the elders offer no resistance to the schemes of Jezebel (1 Kgs 21.11) or to the campaign of extermination waged against Ahab's family by Jehu (2 Kgs 10.5). Ezra may commend the obstinacy of the elders in insisting on prioritizing the rebuilding of the temple (Ezra 5), but Isaiah and Ezekiel see the elders as part of the problem that led to the destruction of the temple in the first place (Isa. 3.14; 9.15; Ezek. 20.3). Indeed, Ezekiel 8 highlights another group of seventy elders; these, however, are implicated in the pollution of the temple under the leadership of Jaazaniah son of Shaphan. The apocryphal story of Susannah revolves around the hypocrisy and lust of two elders who seek first to seduce and then to silence the innocent young woman.

Other terms relating to the elderly are less frequent. The book of Job uses the distinctive term ישיש ('aged') four times (12.12; 15.10; 29.8; 32.6) in contexts where it expresses the

---

6 Bembry (2011: 8–15) also offers a useful review of what he calls the 'lexicon of old age'.

positive side of old age and the opportunity that it gives to gain wisdom. Derivatives of the root שיב, 'to be grey', also occur around twenty times, often in parallel with זקן ('old'). This can connote both the positive and negative sides of old age. Grey hairs command respect in Gen. 15.15 or 25.8, for instance, but may equally be a sign of the decline and impotence of old age, as in Hos. 7.9.

In addition to the expressions above, Eng (2011: 114) lists the following idioms, with acknowledgement to Malamat (1982: 215):

ארך ימים: 'length of days'
ימים רבים: 'many days'
ימים שבע: 'sated with days' or 'full of days'
מלא ימים: 'full of days'
בא בימים: 'advanced in days' often rendered as 'well on in years'
שיבה טובה: 'a ripe old age'

With all of these, the question arises as to whether the positive or negative implications of age are being stressed.

Eng suggests that the expression בא בימים, 'advanced in years', seems to be used in contexts where the limitations of age are being highlighted, whereas ימים שבע, 'sated with days', is used in cases where the blessings of old age are the focus (Eng 2011: 118–19). He points to the way which 1 Kgs 1.1 introduces the elderly king David as being 'advanced in years' whereas the parallel verse in 1 Chron. 23.1 uses the expression 'sated with days'. He argues that the differences perhaps encapsulate the very different pictures of David's last days in the two books. However, there may be more ambiguity in both these terms than Eng allows. Friedrich Delitzsch (1869: 132) unusually but intriguingly translates the expression ימים שבע ('sated with days' or 'full of days') when it occurs as the final words of the book of Job as 'weary of life'; to be sated, after all, may denote contentment, but it may also denote that one has come to one's limit and enough is enough. Is it a blessing or a curse to be granted 'fullness of days'?

The Hebrew Bible is divided on this. 'Fullness of days' or length of life may well be a blessing; to live and see one's grandchildren is often put forward as the fulfilment of life, especially given the apparent lack of interest in the afterlife in this literature (see n. 12). By the same token, the wicked are threatened with an early death. Yet this understanding is in tension with three intractable contraindications. One is that the good and the evil alike are finally subject to death; the second, that length of life and standing with Yahweh do not seem to be correlated; the third, that prolongation of life may simply mean the prolongation of suffering, again with no correlation between those who suffer and those whom we might judge deserve to suffer. Ageing in such a case looks more like a form of punishment than a blessing.

The causes of bodily ageing and its symptoms

However we evaluate it, ageing appears to be inevitable and affects the good and the bad, the deserving and the undeserving, alike, although at different rates and with different consequences in different people. In this section, I want to turn to the question of how biblical writers may have understood the process of ageing itself. What is happening to the human body as it ages and why does it seem inevitable, with little regard for the moral or social standing of a person?

Here our recourse once again must be to analogies in other ancient cultures, given the absence of a direct account in extant Hebrew literature. In the medical tracts that have come down to us through the Classical tradition, ageing tends to be linked to two concurrent processes: the gradual drying up and cooling down of the vital liquids or humours that sustain the human organism (Cokayne 2003: 34–40).

Without making any claim that ancient Israelites had a developed theory of humours as it appears in Hippocrates or Galen, the Hebrew Bible does seem to associate the ageing of the human body with the effects of desiccation. If human bodies go from dust to dust (Gen. 3.19) or, as in Ezekiel 37, to dry bones, the implication is that what makes the difference that constitutes the living body is its moisture. Inevitably, as time goes by, just as wet clay becomes brittle and eventually crumbles as it dries, so the human body, formed of damp earth according to Gen. 2.5-7, becomes stiffer, cracks and is reduced to dust as it ages. Alternatively, to pick up a botanical metaphor that reappears throughout the Hebrew Bible, the fresh and vital juiciness of young well-watered plants in spring contrasts with the dry withered stems and chaff of autumn, soon reduced to dust and carried off by the wind.[7] As an example of this metaphor of drying, we can cite the description of Moses – whose vigour in old age contrasts with that of other patriarchs – as one who had not lost לֵחֹה (Deut. 34.7). This word is usually translated as 'strength' or 'vigour', but its root meaning is 'moistness'; in Ezek. 17.24 and 21.3, the same root is used in a context where a 'green' tree is contrasted with a dry one.

As to the cooling effect of old age, we can turn to the example of David. In 1 Kgs 1.1, as we embark on the story of his last days, we read that 'though they covered him in bedclothes, he never felt warm'. To counter this, the vital, warm young Abishag is sent to bring heat to the old king. David's coldness marks his loss of vitality, but he exhibits another important side effect of the cooling and drying up of the vital humours. As the text laconically states, although the girl was exceedingly beautiful, 'the king did not know her' (1 Kgs 1.4).

Ancient medical texts suggest that in both men and women, an important consequence of the drying and cooling of age is the loss of the capacity to reproduce. In women this was expressly marked by the menopause and the so-called 'drying up' of the womb,[8] but men too could age to a point beyond which they were no longer capable of impregnating a woman.

Indeed, one of the important markers of the boundary between maturity and old age was the loss of fertility. Genesis 18.11 could not be clearer: 'Now Abraham and Sarah were old, advanced in age; it had ceased to be with Sarah after the manner of women. So Sarah laughed to herself, saying, "After I have grown old, and my husband is old, shall I have pleasure?"' Note that both she and Abraham are implicated here. The idea that infertility affects men too is reinforced, for instance, by Gehazi's reply in 2 Kgs 4.14 when Elisha asks what favour they can do for the Shunammite woman. Gehazi replies, 'The fact is, she has no son and her husband is old.' Elisha reads between the lines and promises that she will have a son within the year. The implication is clear that an old husband means the end of hopes for progeny.

---

7 Both Galen (*Mixtures* 2.581-582) and Seneca (*Epistulae* 121.15-17) explicitly compare human ageing to the withering of plants.

8 2 Esd. 5.53 states explicitly that the child of old age is not the equal of the child of youth as the womb has become old. This explains why successive generations of human beings have become smaller as they are 'born of a creation that already is ageing and passing the strength of youth'.

This association between entering old age and losing fertility had the consequence, however, that the elderly, both men and women, were to some extent no longer bound by the conventions that constrained the behaviour of the fertile. In that sense they became once more like prepubertal children.[9] For women, this could be in some circumstances liberating as it allowed them to take more part in public activities, for instance, trading in the market place or travelling.[10]

For men, concomitantly, the loss of fertility and vigour meant that they posed less of a threat to the women of a household and so they could find themselves a place, again like prepubertal children, in the female-dominated domestic economy of the camp or the homestead in a new way, although no doubt resentfully. In the Hebrew Bible, the elderly Isaac is a case in point. He is also one case of the frequent reference to blindness or the dimming of sight as a sign of age (Gen. 27.1), often attributed to the effects of the drying up of the eyes, yet another symptom of the drying and cooling of the whole body.

Qoheleth 12

The Hebrew Bible's most memorable account of the effects of these processes of desiccation and ageing is the poem in Qoheleth 12, by any standards a wonderfully evocative piece of writing. It is addressed by implication to an audience still in its youth as it begins with the injunction that the hearer should remember his creator (or, indeed, his vigour – literally his 'wells')[11] in the days of his youth. This needs to be done before the onset of the days of sorrow and years when one will say 'I have no pleasure in them' (v. 1).

The signs of this are related to the creation and particularly to the heavens: the dimming of the sun and other heavenly bodies and the return of clouds after rain. The poem then proceeds as a complex multiple allegory where the decay of the body, the decay of a household, the signs of mourning in the village and the ravages of a storm are intertwined. Michael Fox (1999: 343) writes of this passage, 'In one sense this is the extinction of an individual life; in another the extinction of a universe. Every individual is a microcosm and every death the end of a world. For the person who dies, the stars blink out, the sun goes dark (only the living "see the sun"), rigor mortis sets in, and all sound ceases.'

While the allegorical readings that have been offered for this chapter are many and various and, as always, reveal as much about the decoders of the allegory and their assumptions as they do about the intentions of the writer, the impulse to map this passage onto bodily decline is at least as old as the Targum. In v. 3, the guards of the house who become shaky or tremble may indicate the loss of strength in the arms and the onset

---

9 2 Esd. 5.49 is explicit in making this link: 'For as an infant does not bring forth, and a woman who has become old does not bring forth any longer, so I have made the same rule for the world that I created.'
10 Such an observation may put a slightly different construction on the book of Ruth, for instance, and may explain Naomi's decision to travel back to her home country and her apparent reluctance to have Ruth accompany her. Naomi explicitly points to the fact that she is no longer likely to conceive sons (Ruth 1.12). One implication may be that, as an older woman, she is less likely to attract the attentions of men on the public road; a postmenstrual woman was of little interest to potential suitors or assailants. Being accompanied by a marriageable woman like Ruth, however, might expose them both to more dangers; Ruth's best place to avoid such threats was her mother's house. On the social roles of maternal kinship, see Chapman (2016).
11 The peculiar expression בוראיך in Qoh. 1.1 (MT) has proved difficult for commentators, ancient and modern. For its derivation from באר ('well'), see Crenshaw (1987: 184–5).

of tremors. The men of valour or strong men who become bent may refer to the legs and so on.

In the same verse, the effects of age on the body parts of one human body are described in metaphors that involve the effects of time on once vigorous communities in a kind of *mise en abyme* of metaphor. The maids that grind, taken to be the teeth, become few and are idle, evoking the desertion of a household where decline means that the need for serving girls is less; those who have not moved away to seek a more prosperous household are left idle and are themselves, no doubt, ageing.

Those looking through windows 'grow dim' (v. 3); this is readily interpreted as referring to the dimming eyes of the elderly but also invokes the biblical trope of the woman at the window (e.g. Judg. 5.28; 2 Sam. 6.16; 2 Kgs 9.30; Prov. 7.6), for those who are looking out are grammatically feminine. They too are losing their strength. The loss of hearing seems to be behind the figure of the closed street doors (v. 4), but this also invokes a house where the traffic with the outside world is ceasing. Closed doors may also be a sign that sickness or death is present.

The sound of the grinding (v. 4) has been related to the enfeebled sound of the pumping of the heart and it may be that the rather difficult references to bird songs and singing birds are to the changes in pitch and volume characteristic of the voice of the elderly. A fear of heights and an increasing sense of vulnerability when abroad are also evident in this portrait of old age (v. 5).

In v. 6, the images of the golden bowl and silver thread can all be related to the breaking of the jar and the failure of the pump as pointing to the return of the body to dust as part of the understanding of ageing as a process of drying up and withering (v. 7). All these images point to the breakdown of the systems for accessing and controlling water, both in terms of a failing household and in terms of the individual body of the elderly, contributing to the central trope of the body returning to the dust from which it came.

Elsa Tamez (2000: 135) regards the poem as 'three-dimensional' in that it is 'using old age as a metaphor for brokenness' in the three dimensions of the cosmos, society and humanity. This adds the insight, one that Qoheleth would be eager to emphasize, that the effects of old age are not only felt by the one who is ageing but by all those who have depended on his or her strength and support in their own lives, or who have chafed under his or her authority; family members, of course, but also slaves, servants and employees as well as members of the local community. If the person dying has had significant responsibilities and power, that circle may extend much further. It is a moot point whether this offers us consolation in showing the influence that can be attained in one human life or, conversely, further confirmation of the vanity of all human effort in that so many other lives can be adversely affected by the death of one individual.

Trying to extract a single coherent reading from this passage is rather like trying to find 'the' melody in a Bach fugue; the whole point of fugue is that multiple melodic lines are interacting in a complex play of variation and imitation. The way in which a household can decline as its head declines, and the way in which the frailty of an ageing householder may be visible in the neglect and decline of his house and his retainers, reflects vital aspects of how, for Qoheleth, the body is a social rather than personal construct. Throughout the book, there is also the continual evocation of mourning rituals, which points up the way in which they seek to accommodate death and ageing by imitating yet opposing their effects (cf. Olyan 2004). Ageing in Qoheleth is not a personal tragedy; it is the outworking of an unfathomable but inexorable tendency to decay built into the structure of human bodies, human societies and the created natural order that meets a forlorn resistance in human understanding.

Qoheleth, of all biblical books, gives the impression of having been written with the hindsight of the elderly. It has that characteristic sense that the beginnings of stories give little indication of their ends. Unpredictably, fools prosper and the promising youth is cut off in his prime. All that is sure is that good and bad alike face the prospect of death sooner or later; an early death may seem a tragic waste of potential, but the later it comes the more likely it is preceded by a time of decline, leading to the dissolution of all the physical and mental riches that had been carefully accumulated and guarded in a lifetime.

Social problems for the elderly

The problems that beset the elderly are not simply those of bodily decline and increasing frailty, however. They also lose the ability to fend for themselves and risk ending up being net consumers rather than producers of the food and the wealth of the community, again reverting to the status of children. Children are a drain on the resources of the community when they are young, but of course the expectation is that they will become the next generation of contributors through their labour. The old have no such future value. Each year, each month, they become less productive and more needy.

What they do have, however, is experience. They have seen things before and they have seen people's stories through to their conclusion, or to the lack of conclusions. They, like Qoheleth, have seen young men and women that started out with potential either become successful parents and householders themselves or, out of the blue, become the victims of disease, misfortune and violence or self-destructive behaviour. Some who they despised as youths have risen to positions of power and responsibility; they may turn out to be unexpectedly effective or they may increasingly abuse that power, while others with more potential are sidelined.

The elderly also remember and have time to tell and recreate the stories and the law codes that ensure the continuity of the clan (cf. Deut. 32.7). It is little wonder, then, that these stories and law codes for the main part enjoin respect and care for the elderly as they become increasingly dependent on the ministrations of their children and families (e.g. Lev. 19.32; cf. Isa. 3.5).

The legal materials from Mesopotamia and Egypt show us that the elderly with property could enter into legally binding agreements with relatives that ensured that they would be fed and housed for life in return for promised legacies on their death (Westbrook 1998: 246–50). The fact that such provisions were thought necessary does also suggest, however, that not every family could look after their elderly relatives and indeed that some may have refused to do so. The power and wealth that the elderly have gained over their lifetime may end by making them vulnerable at a time when they can no longer defend themselves. 2 Kings 8.7-15 tells the cautionary tale of Hazael, who, told by Elisha that he would succeed King Ben-Hadad of Aram, hurries the process along by smothering the king with a wetted bedcover the next day. The legislation enjoining respect of the elders points as much to anxiety on behalf of the elderly who can no longer physically defend themselves as it does to the filial respect of the younger generation.

One way that this status was defended in many ancient cultures was through the system of ancestral worship. If you believe that your elderly relatives may have considerable power over your good fortune once they die, the chances are that you will treat them with more respect and care while they are alive. Any grudges they bear will come home to roost. The peculiar (and perhaps deliberate) disinterest in the biblical text over any question concerning the active role of the dead in the lives of the living seems to militate against that possible line of protection for the vulnerable elderly.[12]

For those with no families, the problems are increased. One route to try and secure a future, again for the propertied, was to adopt other family members, or orphans or even slaves, as nominal heirs, again on condition that the old person would be looked after until their death (Stol and Vleeming 1998). Another was to throw oneself on the mercy of a wealthy patron in return for services rendered in one's prime.

But what of the poor and landless, the childless widow of a peasant or a slave who had become too old to earn their keep? There is some evidence that the destitute and vulnerable could seek help not only from local communities (see Schipper in this volume) but temples, too, especially if they were of a priestly caste, as seems to have been the case in other ancient Near Eastern contexts (Avalos 1995: 176–7). Much later, of course, Luke places two elderly people, Simeon and, even more to the point, Anna, in the Jerusalem temple. Anna, indeed, 'was of a great age' – at least 84 – and 'never left the temple but worshipped there with fasting and prayer night and day' (Lk. 2.36-37). Given that, it is tempting to wonder if the phrase in Ps. 23.6 'and I shall dwell in the house of YHWH my whole life long' may not be simply metaphorical but point to at least the possibility that food and lodging could be found for the elderly in the temple.

Could it be that in earlier centuries, local temples were a place of refuge for the elderly with no family willing or able to support them? Psalm 27.4-6, 10 might support this, and Ps. 92.13-15 (Eng. vv. 12-14) speaks specifically of the righteous who flourish like a palm tree and are planted in the house of YHWH. The association we have made between old age, drying up and sterility is reinforced by the contrasting picture of these righteous in v. 15: 'In old age they still produce fruit; they are always green and full of sap.'

The lessons of the 'very old'

Some further illumination on the perception and experience of the elderly in ancient Israel comes through the accounts involving older characters in the narrative books. We can distinguish two sorts of characters here. The first are those whom we meet when they are younger and whom we watch ageing. We have already alluded to David, who may be the best example, but the lives of many of the patriarchs are also traced through to their end, and so too are many of the kings, although details of their life in old age may be sparing.

A second group are those characters who are introduced to us as elderly people: Eli and Barzillai would be prime examples here. As we have seen, these two share with David the distinction of being the only biblical characters that are accorded the epithet זקן מאד, 'very old' (1 Sam. 2.22; 2 Sam. 19.32; cf. 1 Kgs 1.15). Given that space precludes an analysis of every elderly biblical character, it may prove instructive to concentrate on these three as examples of what the biblical writers conceived of as the possibilities and limitations of the very elderly. The question of their wisdom will also bear examination.

---

12 As several scholars have shown, allusions to ancestor veneration or a 'cult of the dead' can be detected in some biblical texts, although the extent to which these reflect the religious realities of ancient Israel, rather than pointed polemic, continues to be debated. See Suriano (2018) and Wyatt in this volume.

In David's case, we have already discussed the evidence of physical decline. There is poignancy in the picture of the old king, once so vigorous and full of life, now confined to bed and at the mercy of his courtiers, having to decide the succession of his kingdom on the basis of what they tell him.

Opinions differ on whether David ever actually made the vow that Solomon would be his successor that Nathan and Bathsheba invoke in 1 Kgs 1.13, 17. Are they inducing the elderly king, whose memory is now no longer to be trusted, to make a retroactive promise? Or is he aware of their ploy and content to play along with it? There is also cynical wisdom in his advice to Solomon to get rid of several characters to whom David had sworn protection as long as his own life lasted (1 Kgs 2.5-9). His death will release Solomon from any need to respect those vows. Yet how wise is that? The ruthlessness with which Solomon inaugurates his rule is carried on throughout his reign, leading to the disaffection of the people that comes to a head in their rebellion against Rehoboam. The seeds of the division of David's kingdom might be found in his words of wisdom.

The final words attributed to David in 1 Kings concern Shimei whom he had sworn not to put to death (2 Sam. 19.23). Speaking to Solomon, he says, 'You are a wise man; you will know what you ought to do to him, and you must bring his grey head down with blood to Sheol' (1 Kgs 2.9). Shimei's grey head is no protection and this is a grim play on the idiom of bringing one's grey head in sorrow to the grave. One dying man seals the fate of another. 'Is the old David wiser than the young?' we might ask. More experienced, surely, but wiser?

In the case of Eli, his old age is stressed (1 Sam. 2.22), as is his resultant blindness (1 Sam. 3.2; 4.15); his age is given as 98 in the notice of his death (1 Sam. 4.15-18). As a result, he is dependent on others, principally his family, of course, to carry out many of his duties and for his daily sustenance and care. Frail as he is, his continued life is in their hands, whatever outrages his scoundrelly sons may commit. Before we simply condemn him as a weak father doting on his sons, we should consider how restricted his options are at this stage of his life, although we may wonder why he failed to instil a respect for proper conduct in his sons earlier in life. When he does stand up to them (1 Sam. 2.23-25), his age and infirmity mean that he lacks the strength to enforce his will.

The elderly Eli is portrayed as an interesting mixture both of wisdom and folly. In 1 Sam. 1.12-14, he foolishly mistakes Hannah's silent prayer for drunken ravings, but, assuming his fading eyesight and, at least conceivably, his failing hearing, this may be forgivable. On the other hand, he is wise enough to counsel Samuel soundly and to show considerable equanimity when confronted with the news of the end of his priestly line.

Significantly, in the speech attributed to the unnamed man of God which conveys this news, it is twice repeated that he is told 'no-one in your family will live to old age' (1 Sam. 2.21-22). This is usually read as a curse, but what good has Eli's prolonged life done him? He lives to see his sons not only desecrate their inherited office but also has to live with the knowledge that they are fated to die on the same day. Explicitly, part of the sentence passed on his house is that one member of his family will in fact be spared early death. However, that is no cause for congratulation as the reason he will be spared is 'to weep out his eyes and grieve his heart' (1 Sam. 2.33). Long life is not necessarily a reward; it may be a punishment.

In the end, Eli's death is explicitly connected to his age: 'Eli fell over backwards from his seat by the side of the gate and his neck was broken and he died, for he was an old man, and heavy' (1 Sam. 4.18). The cause of his death is the shock of the news not only that his sons are dead but that the ark is captured. A life dedicated to preservation of the ark ends with its loss and the snuffing out of his progeny. Eli lives long enough to learn that his life will leave no legacy except a memory of failure and loss, hardly an outcome to be wished for.

By contrast, another elderly character, Barzillai, represents a more positive but still enigmatic picture of the fruits of experience. In 2 Sam. 19.31-40, he is one of the procession of people who come down to meet David in the course of his return to Jerusalem after Absalom's revolt. In these verses, we are told Barzillai too is not just old, but very old, 'the son of eighty years' as the Hebrew idiom puts it (v. 32). He is also a very great, or wealthy, man as he had been able to provide for David when he was in Manahaim (cf. 2 Sam. 17.27-29).

When they meet on David's return, the king offers to provide for Barzillai in Jerusalem if he comes with him (v. 33). On the face of it, this is a simple reciprocation of Barzillai's generosity. It raises the question, however, as to why David considers Barzillai as in need of his care. Is this a recognition of his age? Is it evidence that some part of the largesse of kings or those in positions of power and wealth was to offer refuge to faithful elderly companions and followers once they were no longer to take care of their own affairs?

Intriguingly, Barzillai declines the offer. Given that he is unlikely to live long, he asks what benefit he would gain from a move to Jerusalem and then catalogues the deficiencies of age. First, he claims he no longer knows the difference between טוב and רע, literally between 'good' and 'evil' (2 Sam. 19.35). For readers aware of Genesis 2–3, the resonance of this with the story of the forbidden fruit of the tree of the knowledge of 'good' and 'evil' is striking, all the more so as this particular phrase is otherwise remarkably rare in the biblical corpus, despite its subsequent cultural importance. The link is disguised in many English versions, as the two terms are often rendered as 'pleasant' and 'unpleasant' in this context, perhaps because readers are so attuned to the idea of the wisdom of the elderly that the suggestion that the elderly Barzillai has now lost his moral compass is not to be entertained.

What if he means this literally, however? It may imply not so much that he is incapable of knowing whether he is doing good or evil but that he cannot be sure what the outcome of any course of action may be. For the reader, and presumably Barzillai himself, the careers of Saul and David as set out in the books of Samuel rather complicate any simple notion of good and evil and certainly show that actions do not always have the consequences that those involved would have anticipated. Like Qoheleth, by this time of life he has seen too much to believe in simple retribution. At a practical level, would allying himself with David at this point in his career be 'good' or 'evil' for Barzillai, who of course does not have the benefit of hindsight that we do?

Another link to Qoheleth is to be found when Barzillai lists his infirmities and the implied pleasures of the court that he can no longer enjoy. This is very reminiscent of the list of pleasures accumulated but then found empty by the king in Qoh. 2.3; indeed, the expression שרים ושרות, 'singing men and women', only occurs otherwise in 2 Samuel 19 and Qoheleth 2. A suspicious mind might even wonder whether Barzillai's mention of his loss of the sense of taste could be related to the possibility that the food in a royal court may not always be trustworthy.

In this light, his admission that he can no longer tell the difference between טוב and רע, itself a distinction fundamental to the wisdom tradition, may be a demonstration of the wisdom that a shrewd man has accrued through his long life and his experience with kings and courts. Canny old fellow that he is, he knows only too well that, for him at least, there may be more רע than טוב in David's offer. Age may bring the wisdom to realize that the platitudes that pass for wisdom are hollow.

Conclusion

The Hebrew Bible offers no simple answer if we press it for anything like a theology of ageing or a single so-called 'biblical' view of ageing. Is age a curse or a blessing? Does it lead to wisdom or does it rather put in question all human aspirations to wisdom, if even the wisest may find that their wisdom slips away from them along with everything else life brings? In the end, only one sure result comes through, which we stated in the beginning: age will not make a fool wise, though it may make a fool of a wise man.

However, the biblical writers have a vested interest in promoting the norm that the aged are due respect from the young. As we have argued above, the degree to which they insist on this is likely to reflect a sense of vulnerability rather than power. Tim Parkin (2003: 275) suggests in the context of the Roman world that 'in spite of the theoretical dominance of the *paterfamilias*, ... in reality the aged members of the family were often in a situation of dependence on the younger generations, and a dependence without security at that, because the obligation to support elderly parents rested more on *pietas* than strict law' and furthermore that 'although criteria of age played an important part in public and private life alike, old age, the inevitable conclusion of a long life and the precursor to death, was not accorded in practice the esteem or authority that people such as Cicero and Plutarch in their own old age felt it merited'.

The aged have little to offer the young except in terms of experience, especially if the threat of their influence beyond the grave is diminished or ruled out. Is it a coincidence that the literature of ancient Israel which so firmly rules out communication with the dead (e.g. Deut. 18.11; Isa. 8.19-20) at the same time insists on its own importance and ties the survival of Israel as an entity to the preservation and remembrance of the traditions handed down from the past? Those who committed Israel's traditions to writing also insisted that the continuity of Israel depended on its care for the repositories of that tradition, whether as written texts or in the memories of the older generation. As the writers themselves were aware of approaching old age, they had all the more a vested interest in shoring up the customs and institutions that might ensure them of the respect and care that they foresaw they might need.

If this life is our only concern, then it is understandable that length of days, together with the prospect of descendants, is read as divine favour. Yet, as we have seen, the biblical tradition also knows that a long life that simply prolongs suffering or forces one to live through the collapse and decay of all one had struggled to build is more like a curse than a blessing. One of the things that age teaches is that the most cherished of human traditions can be suspect and that no exercise of wisdom can predict the vagaries of life or guarantee its length.

For Qoheleth, this indeterminacy of life, coupled with the inevitable deterioration that comes with age, is a mystery to be accepted. In the book of Psalms, however, there is a different perspective. In Psalms 31, 32, 38 and 102, very similar symptoms to ageing are described using similar metaphors of desiccation, but there they are explicitly the punishment for sin which the Psalmist pleads to have lifted from him. Those who are subject to old age, however, have no hope of rescue.

It is in the Apocrypha that we see this tension dealt with most explicitly. Wisdom of Solomon attempts to assuage such apparent injustice by a readjustment in the afterlife as follows (Wis. 4.16): 'The righteous who have died will condemn the ungodly who are living, and youth that is quickly perfected will condemn the prolonged old age of the unrighteous.' Perhaps, but that is not the message of other books in the Hebrew canon. A better summary, or response, to the question of the relationship between wisdom and age is that of the most grandfatherly of books, Ecclesiasticus. Ben Sirach asks, reasonably, 'If you gathered nothing in your youth, how can you find anything in your old age?' (Ecclus. 25.3). But he also enters a plea that may make a fitting last word for this chapter: 'Do not disdain one who is old, for some of us are also growing old' (Ecclus. 8.6).

References

Avalos, H. (1995), *Illness and Healthcare in the Ancient Near East: The Role of the Temple in Greece, Mesopotamia and Israel*, Atlanta, GA: Scholars Press.

Ayayi, J. A. A. (2010), *A Biblical Theology of Gerassapience*, New York: Peter Lang.

Bembry, J. (2011), *Yahweh's Coming of Age*, Winona Lake, IN: Eisenbrauns.

Blenkinsopp, J. (1997), 'Life Expectancy in Ancient Palestine', *Scandinavian Journal of the Old Testament* 11: 44–55.

Chapman, C. R. (2016), *The House of the Mother: The Social Roles of Maternal Kin in Biblical Hebrew Narrative and Poetry*, New Haven, CT: Yale University Press.

Cokayne, K. (2003), *Experiencing Old Age in Ancient Rome*, London: Routledge.

Crenshaw, J. L. (1987), *Ecclesiastes: A Commentary*, Philadelphia, PA: Westminster John Knox Press.

Delitzsch, F. (1869), *Biblical Commentary on the Book of Job II*, Edinburgh: T&T Clark.

Eng, M. (2011), *The Days of Our Years: A Lexical Semantic Study of the Life Cycle in Biblical Israel*, New York: T&T Clark.

Fox, M. V. (1999), *A Time to Tear Down and A Time to Build Up: A Rereading of Ecclesiastes*, Grand Rapids, MI: Eerdmans.

Harris, J. G. (1987), *Biblical Perspectives on Ageing: God and the Elderly*, Philadelphia, PA: Fortress Press.

Harris, R. (2000), *Gender and Aging in Mesopotamia: The Gilgamesh Epic and Other Ancient Literature*, Norman: University of Oklahoma Press.

Knight, D. A. (2014), 'Perspectives on Aging and the Elderly in the Hebrew Bible', *Interpretation* 68: 136–49.

Malamat, A. (1982), 'Longevity: Biblical Concepts and Some Ancient Near Eastern Parallels', *Archiv für Orientforschung* 19: 215–24.

Olyan, S. M. (2004), *Biblical Mourning: Ritual and Social Dimensions*, Oxford: Oxford University Press.

Parkin, T. G. (2003), *Old Age in the Roman World: A Cultural and Social History*, Baltimore, MD: Johns Hopkins University Press.

Reviv, H. (1989), *The Elders in Ancient Israel: A Study of a Biblical Institution*, trans. J. Smith, Jerusalem: Magnes Press.

Stol, M., and S. P. Vleeming, eds (1998), *The Care of the Elderly in the Ancient Near East*, Leiden: Brill.

Suriano, M. J. (2018), *A History of Death in the Hebrew Bible*, Oxford: Oxford University Press.

Tamez, E. (2000), *When the Horizons Close: Rereading Ecclesiastes*, trans. M. Wilde, Maryknoll, NY: Orbis Books.

Westbrook, R. (1998), 'Legal Aspects of Care of the Elderly in the Ancient Near East: Conclusion', in M. Stol and S. P. Vleeming (eds), *The Care of the Elderly in the Ancient Near East*, 241–50, Studies in the History and Culture of the Ancient Near East 14, Leiden: Brill.

PART THREE

Extended sociality

CHAPTER NINE

Immortality and the rise of resurrection

NICOLAS WYATT

It is probably true to say that all human cultures have entertained some notion of an 'afterlife' from at least the Palaeolithic to the present – with views, however inchoate their conception, on the continuance, beyond the point of biological death, of the life of individual humans – and have treated their engagement with it in ritual fashion. That is, they have not believed that life was simply extinguished at death, but that in some manner, a part of the individual was carried over into a post-mortem existence. In the ancient Near East, this further state might be a generally dreary persistence in the underworld, as expressed in poignant lines in the *Gilgamesh* epic,[1] though the widespread observance of *kispum* rites shows that provided the correct ritual procedures were observed, the dead lived in a state of relative tranquillity, in continuing solidarity with their surviving kin (Tsukimoto 1985; see also Bayliss 1973).[2] In Egypt, a process of apotheosis by identification with Osiris, limited originally to the king and then expanded to his entourage, was eventually adopted widely with a gradual percolation of belief down to the general population; a variety of other destinies, from identification with various deities to astral ascent and bodily resurrection, were also available, in a kaleidoscope of beliefs.[3]

This ritualization of death means that some meaning and purpose has probably been felt to be present – or has been invested in it – and that its negative quality can somehow be tempered. Ritual confers meaning. A belief in some kind of survival of an element of individual identity seems to have been universal (perhaps due to encountering dead relatives in dreams). The idea of total annihilation ('the second death'), whenever mentioned in ancient texts, came to be understood from early times to be a terrible punishment for unforgivable sin[4] or for failure to observe the appropriate rites, with survival as otherwise normative.

---

1 *Gilgamesh* VII 182–210 (Enkidu's dream); cf. *Descent of Ishtar* 1–12. See also Achilles' words to Odysseus in *Iliad* 11: 488–91.
2 With regard to the West Semitic world see also Lewis (1989); Sanders (2012); Suriano (2016, 2018); Wyatt (2012).
3 There are also statements in the Pyramid Texts (PT), Coffin Texts (CT) and Book of the Dead (BD) which appear to be describing a form of resurrection. See below, §5.
4 Targum Isa. 22.14; 65.6; Targum Jer. 51.17; Rev. 2.11; 20.6, 14; 21.8. The term is surely misused by Korpel (1996: 105; cited below, n. 9).

If we turn to the West Semitic peoples, a variety of belief systems was probably observed, reflected in the different local means for the disposal of the dead. Archaeology has had an important part to play in advancing a modern understanding of ancient beliefs, which has enabled recent scholarship to offer important correctives to older perceptions, particularly with regard to Israel and Judah. The conventional histories of 'Israelite religion' of a few decades ago, when they even bothered to address the topic,[5] gave a negative account of a people who despite having what the writers considered to be the most elevated religion of antiquity, the precursor of Christianity, nevertheless denied them any post-mortem consolation – a bleak future indeed for 'God's chosen people'! Johannes Pedersen (1959: 460–70) painted a dismal picture, though he offered the important concession that there was a solidarity between the dead and living members of the family. John Gwyn Griffiths observed, in discussing the idea of judgement in Israel and Judah, that

> it may be doubted whether a stage in a future life is envisaged. The confident statement that God *will requite every man for what he does* (Prov. 24:12) probably implies compensation in the present life. If there is no full-hearted belief in life after death, there is obviously no place for a judgement of the life record ... without a belief in an afterlife, the act of recording lacks the motive which concerns us ... We look in vain for any clear evidence that early Hebrew religion embraced a belief in immortality. (Griffiths 1991: 300–1; emphasis original)

John Day observed that

> Until the postexilic development of belief in a more worthwhile afterlife it was held by the ancient Israelites that the destination of all human beings after death, irrespective of moral quality or social status, was a dark, gloomy underworld cavern akin to the Greek Hades, known as Sheol. (Day 1996: 231)[6]

And in his relatively recent and wide-ranging study of Israelite religion, Ziony Zevit (2001) devoted scarcely any discussion to post-mortem beliefs and practices.[7] To be

---

5 Many studies even in the later twentieth century failed to address the issue and had no appropriate entries in their indices. Note von Rad (1965: 349–50), entirely in accordance with contemporary assessments:

> The dead were excluded from fellowship with Jahweh and were in the highest degree unclean ... We find in Ps. LXXXVIII a definition of the state of being dead which, theologically speaking, leaves practically nothing more to be said: the dead were cut off from praising Jahweh and from hearing him proclaimed, and above all, they were cut off from him himself. On the other hand, since Israel was strictly forbidden to ascribe any numinous power to the dead lying outside the possibilities of Jahwism, i.e. by way of an additional private cult, an extremely odd theological vacuum resulted. Jahwism's tendency to destroy myth in all its forms was not abandoned in its understanding of death. What is astounding is the way in which this mysterious word is entirely divested of its sacral character.

With the benefit of hindsight afforded by later scholarship – quite apart from the egregious remark on myth – this now reads as a serious misunderstanding of the complex reality of Israelite–Judahite religion. Rowley (1956: 155) was very restrained. And even so innovative a study as Albertz (1994) ignored the topic. In contrast, see Oesterley and Robinson (1930: 58–61, 317–32); de Vaux (1961: 56–61); Tromp (1969); Brichto (1973).
6 On the concept see Johnston (2002).
7 Zevit (2001: 242–7) briefly dealt with the tomb at Tel ʿEton, where he made the interesting suggestion that some of the relief carvings were of birds, which he called *nešārîym* (sc. *nešārîm* – 'raptors'), and associated with the Egyptian avian representation of the Ba, the freely moving soul of the dead (on the concept see Korpel 1996). Unfortunately, the site has now been identified as a Philistine settlement (Faust 2015), which rather reduces its immediate value as a guide to 'Israelite' practice! Astour (1998: 59) shared this view, writing of 'the pessimistic view of the hereafter' in relation to Mesopotamian and Levantine thought, though with a recognition of a 'selective immortality' restricted to certain persons, mostly in a proto-Greek ambit. Note too Brichto (1973: 2–3)

sure, annihilation was not an issue; instead, he also recognized a shadowy existence in a rather grim subterranean zone, 'Sheol' (šĕ'ôl, šĕ'ōl),⁸ as described by Day, characterized by separation from God (or at least from Yahweh). There is certainly some textual support for this view, but it is not the whole story. Obvious examples apparently supporting this assessment are the following passages, probably spread over many centuries, which lament the loss of communication with Yahweh:

Psalm 6.6:

kî 'ên bammāwet zikrekā	For in death there is no remembrance of you;
biš'ôl mî yôdeh-lāk	In Sheol who will give you thanks?

Qoheleth 9.10:

kol 'ăšer timṣā' yādĕkā	Whatever your hand finds to do,
laʿăśôt bĕkōḥăkā ʿăśēh	do it with your might;
kî 'ên maʿăśeh wĕḥešbôn	for there is no work or device
wĕdaʿat wĕḥokmâ	or knowledge or wisdom
biš'ôl 'ăšer 'attâ šāmâ	in the grave where you are going.

Isaiah 38.18:

kî lō' šĕ'ôl tôdâ	For Sheol cannot thank you,
māwet <lō'> yĕhalĕlekā	death cannot praise you;
lō' yĕśabĕrû yôrĕdê-bôr	those going down to the pit cannot hope for
'el-'ămittekā	your truth.

Psalm 115.17:

lō' hammētîm yĕhalĕlû-yāh	The dead do not praise Yahweh,
wĕlō' kol-yōrĕdê dûmâ	Nor any who go down into silence.

Job 10.20b-22:

yĕšît mimmennî wĕ'ablîgâ mĕʿāṭ	Leave me, and allow me a little happiness
bĕṭerem 'ēlēk wĕlō' 'āšûb	until I go away and do not return,
'el-'ereṣ ḥōšek wĕṣalmāwet	to the dark and gloomy underworld,
'ereṣ ʿēpātâ kĕmô 'ōpel	to the murky, pitch-black underworld

Many further similar passages could be cited. Citations such as these are not, however, to be construed (in somewhat jaundiced terms) as formal statements of 'doctrine'. And it is certainly unwarranted to see them as privative statements set against the 'fullness' of a later Christian conception. Rather, they are to be understood in either (or both) of two ways.

---

for his remarks concerning the confused situation, not least with regard to imprecision in the terminology scholars employ. Zevit (2001: 627 n. 36) briefly notes Brichto's study.

8 The etymology of the term is disputed and not entirely clear. See *HALOT* (iv) 1368–70. Day (1996: 231) cites with approval the view of Koehler (1946: 71–4), that it is a final –*l* formation on √*šā'â*, on the analogy of *gbʿ–gbʿl* and *krm–krml*, with the sense of (place of) 'devastation', 'ruination'. *HALOT* 1368 endorsed this as 'the most likely proposal'. On the concept in general see Tromp (1969: 21–3, and for various aspects 23–79); Barstad (1999); Johnston (2002: 69–124); Suriano (2016). Lipiński (2016: 139–41) (with supporting references) makes a convincing case that the Hurrian underworld goddess Šuwala underlay the biblical concept (a feminine noun), since it has no convincing Semitic etymology. There is an important Hurrian substrate to early Israelite and Judahite religion.

First, they may be described broadly as the natural psychological response of resignation to the inevitability of one's mortality. Second, they may be reflecting particular dark moments in the experience of the poet after bereavement, or in moments of unbelief and depression, or even such experience expressed communally through the form of liturgy.

In the polytheistic milieu which was probably their original context – for we should certainly not *assume* a monotheistic background as the default – it may be that since the underworld was the domain of other divine powers (such as Reshef, Horon and Mot), what the poets were lamenting was specifically alienation from *Yahweh*, who was supposed to have no jurisdiction there. But this third option is not entirely convincing in view of our further discussion, for the passages just cited offer no evidence that we are to consider such a divine division of labour: these passages despair at the absence of the deity, Yahweh, to whom they are wholly devoted, with no sense of divided loyalties. There is no escape from the despair. But despair is a state of mind, not a doctrine. Psychology rather than metaphysics should be read in (but not *into*!) these passages.

The various dismal expressions such as these are also to be qualified in the face of the archaeological evidence, which shows a well-structured process of transition into death: from the cessation of life to primary burial on a bench in the tomb, to secondary (collective) burial at the back of the tomb, once natural excarnation and disassembly of bones has taken place. This was routine, in the sense that it operated as a regular, accepted process of transformation of the living individual into a member of the ancestral group, to whom one was 'gathered' or 'added'. This pattern was well-established, with minor variations in development, throughout Iron Age Palestine (see most recently Suriano 2018).

It is in this broader context that Sheol should be assessed. Rather than a place of ultimate misery,[9] it is to be seen as an intermediate stage in the journey made by the dead, a liminal condition between the initial rites of burial on the bench and those accompanying the final deposition of the bones with those of earlier generations at the back of the tomb, in which one's lonely post-mortem condition gave way to a communal rest with the ancestors. This is what is meant by the biblical expression 'being gathered (or "added") to one's kinsmen' (*yēʾāsep ʾel-ʿammāw*: Gen. 25.8; 35.29; cf. 49.29). It is the final fulfilment of life's process and should not be seen through modern eyes, as somehow deficient (Tromp 1969: 21–3, 102–7; Barr 1993: 28–36; Barstad 1999; Olyan 2005; Suriano 2016). The dead on whom the appropriate rites had been performed passed beyond Sheol. Furthermore, the Iron Age biblical evidence suggests that an analogue of the *kispum* was an integral part of this belief system (Tsukimoto 1985; Lewis 1989; Wyatt 2012). Key elements in the understanding of this institution were family identity (integration into the 'communion of saints') and the transmission of property. Probably not unrelated to the institution and social pattern is the view that one somehow lived on in one's descendants, so that as an individual one bridged the past (the ancestors) and the future (the descendants). The perpetuation of one's name (*šēm*) in descendants is a related idea, and these three concepts – being 'gathered' or 'added' to the ancestors, *kispum*-like practices and the perpetuation of the name – may be regarded as different aspects of the same reality (Sanders 2012). The picture evoked in such negative passages as are cited above requires, therefore, to be qualified in the light of other textual evidence

---

9 So Johnson (1964: 94): 'This foul region of virtual annihilation'! And Korpel (1996: 105): 'eternal imprisonment in Sheol, the second death from which even the inhabitants of the hereafter were not exempt'.

and archaeological analysis of practice in the two kingdoms (Bloch-Smith 1992, 2002 [cf. Tappy 1995]; Suriano 2018), particularly in the Iron Age II period, when we are on reasonably secure historical grounds concerning the reality of the polities described in the Hebrew Bible.

If we bear in mind the observation above, regarding the communal identity and destiny of the dead, we should think, so far as the pre-exilic era is concerned, that the prevailing world view did not necessarily see the need for further enquiry into ideas such as resurrection. However, while the idea of divine resurrection, such as that of Baal in the Ugaritian tradition, need not be related directly to that of human resurrection (except in the special case examined below), it does indicate a world view in which the possibility was acknowledged and the concept had taken root. And we would be wise not to assume the purely coincidental nature of this. When Christianity developed the theme, it was Christ's resurrection (which is presented in the New Testament as a complete surprise to his disciples) which 'proved' the validity of the common hope, and he was increasingly seen as divine.[10]

Left unqualified, the idea of resurrection is actually rather woolly. What does it mean for a spiritual being, that is, a god: how can a physical concept apply to deities? The woolliness will persist when we turn to the idea of human resurrection. Does resurrection mean coming back to physical life? If so, what of Jesus' word of warning to Mary on Easter morning (Jn 20.17), or Paul's 'spiritual' body as expounded in 1 Cor. 15.35-54 (especially v. 44)? Against this can be set the sound of Lazarus shuffling forth from his tomb after four days in Jn 11.44, and Thomas putting his finger into the hole in Jesus' side in Jn 20.24-28 (but does he actually *do* it?). A sophist might call the former option 'pseudo-resurrection', the form, without the substance.[11] And in John, these are 'signs' (σημεῖα: parabolic, not literal), proofs of Jesus' divine status rather than expositions of current belief. Indeed, the witness of the gospels and Acts suggests that resurrection was the last thing Jesus' disciples expected to happen!

When we consider the idea of resurrection, we should think of it as primarily a physical one,[12] since this epitomizes the social aspect, as a communal, collective motif. In nascent Judaism it represented a belief in the vindication and triumph of an oppressed minority, so was communally orientated, and not just an expression of individualism. The very improbability and even inconceivability of resurrection is in direct proportion to its value as a symbol of *national* survival, as in its powerful early expressions in Isa. 26.19 and Ezekiel 37, considered below.[13] This was certainly its original conception in the

---

10 On Baal, see further discussion below. One important caveat should be noted. The myth of Baal's death and resurrection does not reflect any known older or wider tradition to this effect. It belongs exclusively within the literary world of the Ugaritic text, and its ritual association within the context of royal ideology, as discussed below. We have no *evidence* that this ideology had other comparators.

11 See the excellent study in Elledge (2017), which surveys the bewildering range of beliefs in post-exilic Jewish society. See also Wyatt (2020). One area discussed in Elledge (2017: 175–98) but not covered here is the significance of the work of Josephus.

12 As we shall see, a precise understanding of what is or was involved is difficult to pin down.

13 Charlesworth (2006c: 2–3) denies that Ezekiel 37 had anything to do with resurrection: 'The raising of the nation Israel from disgrace or defeat has too often been confused as "resurrection" of mortals who have died ... For centuries, this passage was, and in many synagogues and churches today is, misrepresented as referring to the resurrection of individuals to eternal life.' Of course, Ezekiel 37 predated the developments in the Hellenistic period by some centuries, but the fact that it used the metaphor of resurrection for national revival certainly would not go unnoticed. Elledge (2017: 68–71) shows how these prophetic texts had an afterlife, slowly becoming proof-texts for developing ideas among various social sub-groups, which, as so often with 'Scripture' used as an authority, were read back into them. The actual process was often an unconscious assimilation of the prophetic language in the composition of the new texts.

Maccabaean crisis and its expression of a resurgence of Jewish nationalism in the second century BCE. Its transformation into a 'spiritual resurrection' – whatever such an idea was supposed to mean, being strictly oxymoronic in nature – is perhaps to be explained as a consequence of the privatization of religion in the new Christian dispensation, which was always challenged by Greek metaphysical presuppositions. Whether we are to see an adumbration of this new mental disposition in the shifts taking place in the exilic period, as hinted at by Carol Newsom (see below), remains difficult to quantify but is a proposal deserving attention.

The question of resurrection is distinct from the general notion of some kind of survival (i.e. continuance of conscious life or of some spiritual dimension) after death. It is a sub-category, and a particularly interesting one, because it arises as an issue for discussion as both a divine and a human concept. The separation of the two categories seems to be unwarranted (Elledge 2006: 23), except perhaps for analytical purposes.[14] The one is paradigmatic for the other and really would have little significance except for its cross-referential nature. We shall therefore consider the two in tandem in this discussion. It is worth reflecting for a moment on the question of priority, if one application of the idea was indeed historically earlier than the other. In other words, was it the theological exploration which triggered the rise in ritual and credal systems presupposing resurrection, and was the divine context the mythical legitimization of the social reality, or was it vice versa, with the probably unconscious urge to make some positive sense of life (i.e. that it need not all come to an end but might lead to greater things), which only later took the form of legitimizing myths?

Or was it perhaps a mutually influential development? While the idea of a bodily, human survival, expressed in terms of resurrection, may have developed independently of the divine category, or the other way round, it is hard to believe that they did not become closely linked, with a cross-fertilization in the thought process. It is also evident that the idea of divine resurrection would not necessarily involve any corporeal element, in that the gods had a spiritual life independent of their embodied forms in icons and statues. It is this element which suggests that the divine conception is older and probably led to the development of the concept of human resurrection. This is perhaps supported by the fact that resurrection is generally conceived as an individual rather than a collective experience in the divine realm, so that the human concept was arguably a generalized development from that singular idea.

Though it is unlikely that either of these arguments can be proved, we shall proceed with them as a working hypothesis. But it is also worth noting that the widespread institution of the *kispum* and analogues throughout the ancient Near East, involving the feeding of the dead, and a belief in their continuing force for good or ill in the land of the living, even if it did not necessarily imply it, could nevertheless be understood to mean that the dead continued to have a quasi-corporeal existence of some kind, if they needed, and could benefit from continued sustenance. Feeding the dead suggests a notion of corporeality. It is perhaps no accident that the institution of the *kispum* was closely analogous to the continued feeding of the gods in the cult, which to a modern Western mind might seem superfluous if they were really supernatural beings.[15]

---

14 The term *'ĕlōhîm* in Hebrew texts can denote the dead, as in 1 Sam. 28.13.
15 Such an argument could converge with the greater argument, of how deities were originally conceptualized with the Neolithic religious revolution (I have in mind the assessment in Cauvin 1994), when a case can be, and often has been, made, though unprovably, that the gods originated in the psychological reality of perceiving one's ancestors in dreams and hallucinations, and concluding that they were supernatural realities.

The development of the idea of resurrection in Second Temple Judaism

There has long been a broad consensus that belief in resurrection developed very late in the Jewish experience in the pre-Christian era. There remained even with the first century CE a profound dichotomy between those who accepted and those who rejected the new concept: the conflict between Sadducees and Pharisees, reflected in the New Testament (Mt. 22.23; Mk 12.18; Lk. 20.27; Acts 4.1-2; 23.8; 1 Cor. 15.12), shows that ideas were still fluid, and still the subject of active theological debate and disagreement.

The catalyst for change from the old Iron Age conventions, which probably survived even the catastrophe of the exilic experience, was the political and social upheaval caused by the Seleucid conquest of the Levant and the imposition of vigorous anti-Jewish policies by Antiochus IV Epiphanes. James Charlesworth (2006c: 138) summarizes the discussion of his edited volume on resurrection in these words: 'It was during the time of the Maccabees that the final editorial work on the book of Daniel and the concept of resurrection finally makes a clear and unmistakable impact on the biblical books.'[16] This is a well-crafted assessment, worthy of a diplomatic résumé: it avoids the trap of dating the origin of an idea to its first surviving textual expression, allows an earlier editorial process and concedes a prior impact of the resurrection concept before it became 'clear and unmistakable'. So it allows for the kind of anticipation we shall see below. But against this consensus we should set the following observation of Stephen Cook:

> Far from mere metaphor, Isaiah 26 anticipates a vision of actual resurrection that forms a basis for the well-known resurrection faith of Daniel 12:1–3. Israel was long familiar with the idea that the dead could be awakened (cf. 1 Kings 17:17–24; 2 Kings 4:8–37; 13:21; Hosea 6:2; Ezekiel 37; Isaiah 53:9–10). So too, from early on, a core biblical ideal entailed the joy and fulfillment of embodied human community. In the Second Temple period, in texts such as Daniel 12:1–3, these ideas and ideals joined up and surfaced in Israel's conscious faith. Deep currents within Israelite tradition flowed together and poured forth in an explicit expectation of eschatological resurrection. God's reign would only come in fullness, the scriptures now declared, when earth finally beholds a collective end-time raising of the dead. (Cook 2007: 10)

This illustrates rather nicely the tension between different assessments of the evidence. If Cook is right, then while the nuances of many of the analyses currently in play have much to offer about the way in which beliefs were developed and refined, the question of origins must be reopened. Earlier (indeed, *all*) texts must always be open to re-examination, to allow any necessary corrective (unlike a Brexit vote, they are renegotiable), even though it is in the nature of the composition and transmission of biblical materials that dating always remains an open question, and always with the proviso that later glosses and additions may be embedded in older texts. And in principle, there should be no restriction on which texts are to be considered. Thus, as well as earlier biblical texts such as those which Cook cites, various key Ugaritic texts and other intellectual currents abroad in the world of Israel and Judah may also be relevant to any reappraisal, as we shall see below.

---

16 Cf. Tappy (1995: 64): 'Generic notions of an afterlife and a judgment of the dead, then, do not appear to have entered the mainstream of Israelite tradition until the later periods (Dan 12.2; Eccl. 12.14?; compare the Ethiopic Apoc. of Enoch 47.3; 50; 90.20 and 2 Esdras 7; note that Daniel, as a transitional text, includes continuing national judgment and incipient individual judgment).'

What is the content of the idea of 'resurrection'? We saw above the range of options which have been entertained. Charlesworth (2006b) notes that it is wrong to restrict enquiry to the meaning of one word; rather, we should examine a whole nexus of interrelated themes ('a cluster of words'), since the term is something of a portmanteau. Before enlarging on a variety of beliefs, he offers the following primary definition:

> Resurrection denoted the concept of God's raising the body and soul after death (meant literally) to a new and eternal life (not a return to mortal existence). This belief should not be confused with the Hellenistic concept of the immortality of the soul. (Charlesworth 2006b: 2)[17]

He goes on to identify sixteen different ways in which the term or its equivalent is used, mostly occurring in an essentially metaphorical sense, with only his fifteenth, the 'raising of the individual from death to eternal life', strictly qualifying for the sense he wishes to be considered (Charlesworth 2006b: 12).[18] Perhaps wisely, he does not at this point differentiate between types of resurrection. He also leaves out of account the vision in Ezekiel 37, and the similar oracle in Isa. 26.19, since the usage in these passages is a metaphor for national revival. Contrasting with Cook's assessment cited above, he notes that only later exegesis in the Hellenistic period saw this as a prefiguration of individual destiny (Charlesworth 2006b: 2–3).

Daniel 12.2-3, composed at some point during the Maccabaean rebellion, is widely regarded as the earliest unambiguous biblical reference to a belief in individual resurrection.[19] It reads:

wĕrabbîm miyyĕšēnê 'admat-ʿāpār yāqîṣû *'ēleh lĕḥayyî ʿôlām wĕ'ēleh laḥărāpôt lĕdirʾôn ʿôlām:* *wĕhammaśkilîm yazhirû kĕzōhar hārāqîaʿ ûmaṣdîqê hārabbîm kakôkābîm leʿôlām wāʿed*	Then many of those sleeping in the Land of Dust[20] will awake, some to everlasting life, and the rest to contempt and everlasting disgrace. And the wise shall shine like the splendour of the firmament, while those who make many people righteous (shall shine) like the stars, for ever and ever.

It is important to recognize what this passage does not say as well as what it does. It is reasonable to take *'ēleh … wĕ'ēle …* here to refer to everybody, dividing humanity neatly between the righteous and the wicked, but it is wrong to claim universality for the sentiment. It refers rather to those within Yehud, presumably distinguishing persecuted loyalists from time-serving collaborators, its primary concern being therefore theodicy. It may not even be universal within Jewish culture, since its primary concern is those who

---

17 Elledge (2017: 3) offers this useful preliminary minimal definition: 'resurrection is to be defined by the new, qualitatively different life into which the dead are raised'. See also next note.
18 Charlesworth (2006b: 18) summarizes the list with the following useful observation: 'the varieties and differing taxonomies … represent not a system but an expression of the common human hope that God has the last word, and the future of the righteous will be blessed'. See also the nicely succinct definition in Elledge (2006: 24): 'to qualify as a resurrection, something must happen to the lifeless body of one who has died'.
19 See Elledge (2006: 25–6) ('the earliest definitive literary evidence … in the Bible') and Nickelsburg (2006: 23), originally published in 1972, and now qualified by his further observation at 2006: 5–6 on the priority of 1 Enoch 1–36, though this is an extrabiblical composition. This is also the assessment of Elledge (2017: 130–49), who examines the *Book of Watchers* (1 Enoch 1–36) in detail.
20 Thus JB: a more sensitive rendering of *'admat-ʿāpār* than the usual 'dust of the earth' (RSV, JPS, NEB); see also Tromp (1969: 41, 91).

have been punished unjustly for fidelity and those who have avoided having to account for their impiety. The silent majority, who neither sinned nor were persecuted, may not be the focus of attention here (Nickelsburg 2006: 5). And the nature of the 'everlasting life' on offer is not formally stated to be bodily resurrection, but may rather be an astralization, involving a spiritual 'body'. Nor is it obvious that this is an eschatological transformation (sc. at the end of history, as distinct from the end of the life of those concerned); it may be an imminent irruption by Michael (v. 1) within historical time to redress the moral balance. The passage is thoroughly opaque if we seek a clear teaching, allowing contradictory interpretations along these alternative lines. Casey Elledge (2006: 27–8) makes an important point regarding the formulaic nature of v. 2: 'it declares in abbreviated form a belief that had already enjoyed an extended prehistory in the author's historical context. The author of Daniel, therefore, did not invent the resurrection hope.'[21]

The immediate 'prehistory' to which Elledge refers is to be sought in a number of passages in extrabiblical Jewish literature, which explore various possibilities about life after death, themselves almost certainly inspired by critical and threatening events in history (just as Isa. 26.19 and Ezekiel 37 have similar contexts, in the exilic catastrophe). The literary and theological context of Dan. 12.2-3 has been thoroughly explored by George Nickelsburg (2006). His exhaustive study also examines every other relevant text. The chief ones predating Daniel are *Jub.* 23.16-31,[22] *Testament of Judah* 25 and *1 Enoch* (Nickelsburg 2006: 5 n. 14),[23] to which Elledge (2017: 160–9) adds the important Qumran compositions nicknamed 'Pseudo-Ezekiel' (4Q385) and the 'Messianic Apocalypse' (4Q521).

Types of resurrection

There was no generally agreed understanding of resurrection in early Judaism (Nickelsburg 2006; Elledge 2017). Some passages appear to anticipate a physical resurrection (a 'spiritual body' not being specified in the following cases): *2 Bar.* 50.2-4; *4 Bar.* 6.7; *1 En.* 51.1-5; *Liv. Proph.* 3.12 (Ezekiel < Ezekiel 37); *2 Macc.* 7.9, 11, 14 (the righteous), 23, 29; *Syb. Or.* 221–26; *T. Abr.* (B) 7.16; *Test. XII Patr.* 10.2 (Zebulun); 10.7 (Benjamin) and 25 (Judah). Some passages envisage bones remaining in the ground and spirits rising: *Jub.* 23.31 (though see Wintermute 1985: 102); *T. Mos.* 10.28; *4 Macc.* 16.13; 17.12; 18.23; *T. Abr.* (A) 20.11-12; while some passages offer no details of what is entailed: *T. Jud.* 25.4; *2 En.* 42.5; *Hist. Rech.* 15.1–16.8; *LAE* 41.2-3; *Liv. Proph.* 2.15 (Jeremiah); *Pss. Sol.* 3.12; *T. Job.* 4.9; 39.12.

In his study on the subject, Oscar Cullmann (1956) addressed primarily New Testament issues but assumed a Jewish background. He argued that the concepts of the immortality of the soul and the resurrection of the body were in fundamental opposition, and that the former, a Greek idea, was alien to biblical thought. It was perhaps his insistence on there

---

21 Elledge is a bit optimistic in immediately continuing, 'Daniel is far clearer on this matter than its Enochic predecessor.'
22 'Roughly contemporary with and perhaps slightly earlier than Daniel and the Testament of Moses': Nickelsburg (2006: 47).
23 The view that *1 Enoch* predates Daniel is not universal; see Goldstein (1983: 212): 'The "Parables of Enoch" (1 En. 37-71) are difficult to date, but I think the mention at *1 Enoch* 56.5 of the Parthians as menace to Judaea excludes their having been written before the first century BCE', cited with approval by Zinner (2014: 119); cf. Charlesworth (2006b: 2–3).

being no room for flexibility which brought sharp responses from various scholars.[24] James Barr (1993) in particular used Cullmann as a foil for his altogether more satisfying analysis of the material, though more recently, Matthew Suriano (2016) has drawn attention to shortcomings in *his* treatment.[25]

Possible contexts for the rise of resurrection beliefs

How is the initial appearance of belief in resurrection in Judaism to be accounted for? Here are some possibilities. I list them in receding historical order, from the Maccabaean period, with the exception of the last (below, §7). We should bear in mind that the belief may have developed incrementally, with hints and suggestions, expressions of wishful thinking, the adoption of fashionable views (expressed, for example, in the influence of neighbouring cultures in burial practice). The diversity of views expressed in the passages cited above indicates a fluidity of views from the earliest forms down into the early Christian era. In some quarters debate and doctrinal disagreement have still not ceased!

§1 Theodicy in the Maccabaean period

Theodicy seems to be the whole point behind Dan. 12.2-3. The idea developed in the face of palpable injustice, as a way of maintaining God's integrity in the face of evil, especially in the particularly difficult context of people being martyred for their beliefs and practices. It had the added advantage of achieving a kind of justice for the victims of oppression. But this really has a weakened explanatory value if the idea was already present in earlier compositions. It must have been building on foundations already present. So we are forced to go further back.

§2 Persian influence

Yehud was under Persian political control for two centuries.[26] We should expect at least some Iranian impact on theological matters, on either of two fronts: the general absorption of new intellectual ideas and a specific theological reaction to any perceived threats (as with Genesis 1, which is probably a challenge to the appeal of the theology of Marduk in Babylon). This does not seem likely, in the view of most scholars. There is certainly little evidence of Persian religious ideas filtering through, though something of its dualistic cosmology has been discerned in some Qumran material. It should be

---

24 E.g. Barr (1993: 1–3, 21–4) (where he criticizes Cullmann's view that death was viewed as unnatural in biblical thought); Nickelsburg (2006: 219–23) ('[Cullmann] appears to assume that there was a single Jewish view on the subject' [219]); revisited by Grappe (2014: 15–18); Suriano (2016).
25 Suriano (2016: 2): 'neither Cullmann nor Barr were able to offer any specific insight into the cultural practices that informed the depiction of death in the Hebrew Bible'.
26 See Wyatt (2009: 174): 'While scholars have broadly sought in vain to find clear evidence of any influence, it should be remembered that post-exilic Judaism developed during two centuries of Persian imperial control of Jehud. It is scarcely possible that the Jews remained entirely unaware of the Zoroastrian interest in eschatology, a concept hitherto alien to Jewish thought.' Note too Wyatt (2009: 174 n.20), citing Zaehner (1961: 57–8, 307–8):

> [Zaehner] was right to point out that we know next to nothing about general developments in Zoroastrian thought in the Achaemenid period, so that the debt remains unquantifiable; but he considered that in eschatological matters there is a case to answer. Fire, as in the Lake of Fire, was strictly part of a judgmental process rather than a destination for the damned, whose abode was rather icy coldness ... Hell was in any case temporal in Zoroastrian thought, since the final Rehabilitation (*Frashkart*) redeemed all souls.

remembered, however, that our surviving texts belong to communities particularly opposed to any 'foreign' influence. But perhaps Iranian ideas did effect beliefs among the wider population. Later Zoroastrianism had a clear teaching of physical resurrection, but for the Achaemenid period, our information is sketchy in the extreme, so that little more can be said.[27]

But there are other more positive assessments of the matter. The *Encyclopædia Iranica* also offers a rather different perspective, according to which the rather abrupt appearance of developed eschatological ideas in Jewish texts of the second to first centuries BCE are better understood as Iranian imports via Persian cultural dominance in both Palestine and wider Southwest Asia. As such, the motifs which would come to dominate subsequent Jewish and Christian constructs of resurrection and immortality (including cosmic dualism, individual and universal judgement, raising the dead at the end-time and constructs of 'hell') have their origins in Zoroastrianism:

> The emergence of a fully developed eschatology in Jewish circles, and one that displays such great resemblance to the complex of Persian ideas, cannot be a coincidence and must be explained as a result of contact between the two cultures. It seems rather unlikely that these ideas were originally developed among Jews, and that they were borrowed by the Persians, who constituted the dominant culture. The many eschatological allusions in the Gāθās and in the Younger Avesta, although they are not always entirely unequivocal, seem to guarantee a certain measure of antiquity and continuity to these ideas in Persia, while we lack similar indices in Judaism. The strong dualistic character of Jewish eschatology seems also to suggest the likelihood of a borrowing from Iran. Zoroastrian eschatology seems to possess a certain coherence and structure, given the large role that the dichotomy between the notions of *mēnōg* and *gētīg* plays in it. This can explain many of the duplications in the narrative, while no similar mechanism is available in the complex of eschatological notions in Judaism.[28]

In particular, the remarkable similarities between several rabbinic writings and the Zoroastrian books are highly suggestive of a continued and powerful influence of the latter on the former, as is evident in rabbinic discussions about spirits accompanying the soul on its journey and the fate of those whose virtues and sins are equally balanced. It

---

27 Note this passage from *Encyclopædia Iranica*, drawing on Oldenberg (1917: 546–7), at http://www.iranicaonline.org/articles/indo-iranian-religion (accessed 6 February 2020):

> Some idea, at least an embryonic one, of a paradisiacal existence was not altogether unfamiliar to the primitive [sic] Iranian mind, although it cannot have been marked by strictly ethical values. A happy life after death must have been reserved for an elite of priests and warriors, while the background of individual eschatology must have been dominated by the belief in a grey, shadowy survival of the spirits of the dead in a nether region, which was approached along the paths trodden by deceased ancestors ... There is an echo of a similar afterlife, which is neither good nor bad, in the Zoroastrian concept of an intermediate zone, halfway between heaven and hell, for those who have deserved neither too much nor too little in their life on earth ... while those who succeed in possessing Truth (Av. *Aša*; Ved. *ṛta*) and who are therefore *ašavan* or *ṛtāvan* ... are assured of a state of blessedness.

This may be supplemented by the further passage at http://www.iranicaonline.org/articles/eschatology-i (accessed 6 February 2020; emphasis added):

> Faith in the events beyond life on this earth is attested in the Zoroastrian scriptures from the very first, from the Gāθās. This faith developed and became central to later Zoroastrianism so that it colors almost all aspects of the religious life. It also seems to have had *a deep impact on neighboring religions, notably on Judaism*, and through it on Christianity and Islam, as well as on Manicheism.

28 http://www.iranicaonline.org/articles/eschatology-i (accessed 6 February 2020).

is perhaps no coincidence that the *Ascension of Moses* exhibits a structure strikingly akin to the *Ardā Wirāz-nāmag*, for several Hebrew versions of this book exist, and it is also attested as a Judaeo-Persian text (see further Böklen 1902; Shaked 1971; Hultgård 1979; Netzer 1990; Winston 1996).[29]

Some of the judgments expressed here concerning the late development of Jewish eschatology will not bear scrutiny in the light of our discussion, in view of the extensive revaluation of the subject in modern archaeological studies. But the matter of indebtedness is still one for which a case can be made.

Christian Grappe also argues for the influence of Zoroastrian thought on the development of the Jewish concept:

> So we can say that from the perspective of the history of religions, the concept of the resurrection of the dead appears for the first time in Iran, and further, that vertical, spatial eschatology and linear, temporal eschatology, are superimposed, a superimposition which we shall encounter again in ancient Jewish and Christian representations. (Grappe 2014: 37–9; my translation)[30]

Elledge (2017: 46–50) offers a well-nuanced assessment of the Iranian question in examining the views of Mary Boyce ([1975–91] 1996). She had argued for a debt to Zoroastrian eschatological ideas mediated through Hellenistic thought.[31] 'Boyce', he observes, 'walks the fine line between Judaism's indebtedness to Zoroastrianism and its own unique reinterpretation thereof' (Elledge 2017: 50).

Another factor of possible significance to be dated to the Persian period (specifically the early post-exilic period) may be explored in the light of Carole Newsom's (2017) Tyrwhitt Lecture, in which she argued that evidence of a growth in the capacity for introspection in biblical literature was a feature of compositions datable to this era.[32] She noted Robert di Vito's interesting paper (1999), which had stressed (in her view, overstressed) the 'embeddedness' of the individual Israelite psyche (my term, not his, for *nepeš*).[33] If some cultural and psychological development is to be discerned in the transition from pre-exilic to post-exilic society, is it not possible to see in the evolution of beliefs concerning the afterlife, the transition from the essentially collective destiny of being 'gathered' (or 'added') to one's forefathers (or people, kinsmen, clan, etc.), which is reflected in the collective burials of the Iron Age (Bloch-Smith 1992, 2002; Suriano 2016, 2018),[34] to a more individualistic pattern in the post-exilic period, perhaps reflecting incipient ideas about individual resurrection? A shift towards individualism had

---

29 Against the assumption of Persian influence on Judaism, see König (1964).
30 'On peut dire ainsi que, du point de vue de l'histoire des religions, le concept de resurrection des morts apparaît pour la première fois en Iran et aussi que s'y superposent eschatologie verticale, spatiale, et eschatologie linéaire, temporelle, superposition que nous retrouverons plus tard en abordant représentations juives et chrétiennes anciennes'. See also Zaehner (1961: 316): 'Of all the doctrines of Christianity that the modern scientific mind finds hard to swallow, the resurrection of the body is the hardest. This dogma, which Christianity inherited from Zoroastrianism, the Zoroastrians themselves find hard.' Earlier, he had touched on Zoroastrian influence on Judaism (Zaehner 1961: 20–1, 51–2, 57–8). Martin-Achard (1960: 186–205 [esp. 186–95]) cautiously allowed some Iranian influence.
31 Cf. Boyce (1987) (not available to me).
32 I am very grateful to Professor Newsom to be given access to a PDF of this study, as I approached the deadline for this paper before hers would be published.
33 She also noted the critique offered by Frevel (2017a, b).
34 Suriano (2018) offers a detailed analysis of the tombs with relation to biblical texts and other Iron Age inscriptions. Following on from a considerable diversity of tomb-types, tombs in later Iron Age Judah were overwhelmingly of the multiple occupancy bench-tomb type; see also Bloch-Smith (2002: 127). Judahite society, as the main source of the Hebrew Bible tradition, provides the bulk of our textual information about mortuary

already emerged within the Iron Age, according to Baruch Halpern (1991, 1996) and Israel Finkelstein (1999), attributed by them to the trauma of the Assyrian invasion of the Levant at the end of the eighth century. This analysis is rejected by Elizabeth Bloch-Smith (2002: 121–3), but more by way of delaying such a transition than denying it. The matter of individual consciousness, by which I mean a consciousness of oneself in opposition or distinction from the collectivity of one's community, is somewhat elusive but may be discerned in legal developments (i.e. regarding such concepts as individual responsibility and liability) as reflected in passages like Ezek. 18.2 and Jer. 31.29-30, where the proverb of the sour grapes in the former leads on to Jeremiah's reference to a legal principle.[35]

The interesting argument of Joseph Blenkinsopp (1995) should also be noted. He proposed that the objection of Deuteronomy towards the cult of ancestors was politically motivated: 'The laws concerning death rites and forbidding commerce with the dead in Deuteronomy were therefore part of a broader strategy of undermining the lineage system to which the individual household (*bêt 'āb*) belonged' (Blenkinsopp 1995: 1). The state stood to benefit from what could amount in some circumstances to an expropriation of private (family) property, the social tension incurred showing nicely in the narrative of Naboth's vineyard (1 Kgs 21.1-15). If this argument is sustainable, then insofar as the Deuteronomic strategy probably contributed to (a) a breakdown of the clan in favour of the individual and (b) an undermining of the old family–land tenure nexus, a process already underway in both Israel and Judah by the eighth century (according to Blenkinsopp), then it provides an interesting example of the law of unforeseen consequences.[36] On the other hand, it is clear that there was resistance to such a programme, as particularly illustrated in the land-claim element in the (exilic) patriarchal narratives and their burial traditions (cf. Stavrakopoulou 2010). The continued use of family burial plots might also be construed as passive resistance against the encroachments of the state.

§3 Exilic influence

The trauma of the exile, with its deportations, sack of the Jerusalem temple and hugely destructive effects on Judah's fabric, altogether more substantial regarding the destruction of the community, is generally agreed to be a watershed in the development of Judahite (henceforth developing into Jewish) religion. Much of the early literature in the Hebrew Bible was either written or re-edited in its shadow. Traces are seen in most of the compositions. Interesting examples in the light of the present discussion are the two prophetic passages noted above, Isa. 26.19 and Ezekiel 37. The former reads:

yiḥyû mētêkā nĕbēlātî yĕqûmûn	May your dead live! May their bodies rise!
hāqîṣû wĕrannĕnû šōkĕnê ʿāpār	Awake and sing for joy, you who dwell in the dust!
kî ṭal 'ôrōt ṭallĕkā	For your dew is a dew of light,
wā'āre rĕpā'îm tappîl	and the earth will give birth[37] to the shades.[38]

---

belief and practice, and the correlation of this tomb-type with the patrimonial clan-system of the dead, after protracted rituals, being gathered (or added) to the ancestors (in the literal sense of added to a pile of bones!).
35 Contrast the strict group solidarity presupposed in the Achan narrative, Josh. 7.16-26. For another passage addressing the issue see Ezek. 14.12-23.
36 Blenkinsopp (1995: 15) envisaged the codification he had in mind taking place in Judah, and therefore supposedly after 621 BCE, if Ur-Deuteronomy was the 'book' 'discovered' in the temple (2 Kgs 22.8).
37 The earth is Adam's mother in Gen. 2.7; cf. Job 1.21.
38 Whether or not any ideological dimension should be discerned in *rĕpā'îm* here is imponderable. But the term is certainly intended to contrast with its appearance in v. 14, referring to foreign oppressors. On the background to the Rephaim, see Rouillard (1995, 1999); Wyatt (2007b); Doak (2012).

This certainly has the appearance of a declaration of belief in physical resurrection, especially since the second colon speaks in terms of waking up, and the fourth in terms of birthing. But we should avoid drawing conclusions more in line with later disputes on the process, if the individual text does not *require* such an interpretation. And Nickelsburg, even while drawing attention to the similarity between this verse and Dan. 12.2, rather qualifies such an assessment:

> In [the] context of judgment and restoration, the passage uses language of the resurrection of the dead. But the literal understanding of this language is not *a priori* certain, for such imagery appears in pre-exilic and exilic literature not as a description of a people who were literally dead, but as a picture of the restoration of Israel. According to Hosea [5.15-6.3], the people were saying that YHWH would bring them to life again. Ezekiel [37] pictures the exile and restoration of Israel in his vision of the valley of the dry bones. (Nickelsburg 2006: 31)

The passage from Ezekiel describes the prophet's vision of the valley of dry bones. The narrative is the form of a dialogue, in which Yahweh asks the prophet what he sees and, in response to the description of the bone-strewn valley, instructs Ezekiel to 'prophesy' (*hinnābē'*). The bones rearticulate themselves, and then on further instruction, breath comes from the four winds (*rûaḥ* is used in both instances) to reanimate them.

I would not dispute the collective nature of either of these passages: both are indeed metaphors for national revival, all the more poignant for hoping for a future event. But to use that view as somehow negating their relevance to the idea under discussion here, of individual resurrection, would be premature (and see n. 13). The best way to consider the necessary linkage between the communal and the individual is to see the changes in mortuary practice which occurred over the same period (see most recently Suriano 2018).

§4 Egyptian practice

So far our discussion has addressed ideas which relate to society as a whole. Kings throughout the ancient Near East were the subject of complex rituals, which not only consolidated their power but also encapsulated national aspirations. They would all have endorsed Louis XIV's assertion, 'L'état, c'est moi!' The king was the epitome of society.[39] In Egypt, the mortuary belief system was very complex, involving identification with various deities, notably Osiris and the Sun, spiritual ascent among the stars, a continuing subterranean life in avian form (Korpel 1996), divine rebirth (mothered by Isis and Nephthys) and resurrection. We know little of mortuary beliefs concerning the majority of society in the Old Kingdom: individual burials in simple tombs contained a few grave-goods, but no textual material. The nobility had massive mastabas, modelled on their estates while alive, and implying some hope for a continuance of some of the benefits of opulence (Emery 1961). With kings, the Pyramid Texts from the tombs of Unas, Teti, Pepi I and II, Merenre and various queens give us an insight into the details of belief. Resurrection (often in combination with other ideas) was one of the many options, as illustrated in PT 373:

---

39 This is expressed in Genesis 2 in the figure of representative Adam, who is described in royal terms; see Wyatt (2014).

Aha! Aha! Raise yourself, Teti!
Receive your head,
assemble your bones for you,
collect your limbs for you,
clear away the earth on your flesh for you,
receive for you your unmouldering bread
and unrotting beer sour.[40]

Over centuries, into the Middle and New Kingdoms, the beliefs represented by the Pyramid Texts filtered down by way of the Coffin Texts (originally restricted to the nobility) into the Book of the Dead, which gave a fairly democratic expression to the hopes.[41] The overriding theme in all the recensions of the tradition was the identification of the deceased with Osiris. He was 'raised', even physically reconstituted after his dismemberment by Seth, but his restored state was confined to the Underworld (*du3t*), where he ruled as judge of the dead. So there was a fundamental distinction between this and other conceptions of resurrection. While there is no direct evidence of Egyptian eschatology filtering through into nascent Jewish belief, Late Bronze Philistine and Iron Age Phoenician (recycled!) anthropoid coffins suggest that some Egyptian beliefs may have had an influence in the southern Levant in the Late Bronze and Early Iron; later, in the post-exilic period, several Jewish communities lived in Egypt – Elephantine (already, preceding the exile), Daphne (Tahpanhes), Memphis, Leontopolis and Alexandria – and would certainly have come into (at least) informal contact with Egyptian mortuary practice.

§5 *Ugaritian royal beliefs*

The Ugaritic evidence has given rise to two positive claims for a blissful afterlife, with implications for the interpretation of the biblical evidence. Mitchell Dahood (1960, 1965a, 1965b [1973], 1970) insisted that the term *ḥayyîm* (Ugaritic *ḥ*, *ḥym*) regularly had the sense of a blissful post-mortem 'life', while Klaas Spronk (1986), endorsing his view, wrote of a 'beatific afterlife'. But there is no serious justification on the basis of the evidence we have (see discussion of *Aqhat* below) for seeing this 'life' as a post-resurrection or even post-mortem experience (so Vawter 1972; Smith and Bloch-Smith 1988). However, having said that, if we concede that the intellectual grasp of the idea was perhaps being explored in the *Baal* Cycle and *Aqhat*, it is not impossible that the materials analysed by Dahood and Spronk reflect further such explorations. I referred to these views in a previous discussion (Wyatt 2009; citing Johnston 2002; Levenson 2006;

---

40 Allen (2015: 87), my verse arrangement. See also PTs 355, 364–7, 412, 437, 457, 459, 482, 483, 536, 537, 548, 556, 576, 577, 578, 596, 603, 604, 611, 612, 619, 620, 662, 665, 665abc, 666, 667c, 670, 676, 677, 694, 697, 700, 701, 703 among others. Many passages blend the resurrection with alternative or complementary destinies. Resurrection generally became specifically Osirian in nature, involving a bodily resurrection, though experienced as a continuing subterranean existence, with the estate, furniture, pastimes and servants to ensure a comfortable afterlife.

41 English translations in Allen (1974); Faulkner (1985, 2004). In CT 761 the corpse is told to raise itself, its members identified with various gods: resurrection and apotheosis. BD 89 is a spell enabling the soul (*b3*) to regain the corpse; BD 92 opens the tomb to allow egress. The *b3* is comparable to the Hebrew concept of the *nepeš*, a key element in understanding human post-mortem destiny. Recent discussions relevant to the present study are Johnson (1964: 3–22); Barr (1992: 36–43, 102–15); Nutkowicz (2006: 244–55): Steiner (2015 *passim*). See also the implications of the Katumuwa stele raised by Steiner (2015: 10–22, 128–62); cf. Herrmann and Schloen (2014).

Cook 2007).[42] For non-royal ideas we should turn in the absence of directly relevant textual evidence to that of the archaeological record (Salles 1987; Marchegay 2007). In the Late Bronze, both individual and communal tombs were used (Marchegay 2007), which leaves us, on the basis of how different funerary systems are generally supposed to reflect differing ideologies, with no firm basis for an overall assessment. The duties of the son listed in *Aqhat* provide general principles of filial piety, and some of the contents are best explained as having a funerary reference (Wyatt 2002: 255–9; 2012: 76–8). As a catalogue of duties, while it has royal overtones (since Danel is a king), it probably nevertheless represents a stereotypical view of filial duties in a patrimonial household.

Ugaritian royal ideology has a number of points in common with Judahite ideology and so should also be considered here, in spite of the temporal and geographical distance. Again, it is not a matter of claiming direct influence, but rather of seeing a broader West Semitic range of beliefs and practices, attested elsewhere, as perhaps at Qatna, and in the Levantine kingdoms to which we have witness in the Amarna letters (Akko, Ashkelon, Beirut, Byblos, Gezer, Hazor, Jerusalem, Lachish, Megiddo, Shechem, Tyre), to which the later Palestinian kingdoms were natural heirs, despite the disruption of the 'crisis years' (Joukowsky and Ward 1992; Cline 2014).[43]

In a previous study (Wyatt 1997) I examined the relationship of some passages in the *Baal* Cycle with the same formulations in *Kirta*, which indicated, I suggested, that the Ugaritian king 'shared in the ontology of Baal'.[44] Two subsequent studies, by Mark Smith (1998) and Matthew Suriano (2009), have examined the restoration to life of Baal (*KTU* 1.6 iii 0-[1]-21) in the light of the implications of the royal funerary text *KTU* 1.161, which would appear to confirm this assessment (cf. Wyatt 2017: 831–7). Though 'dying and rising' gods have been seen at every turn in some older scholarship, Baal is the only ancient Near Eastern deity whose restoration to life survives scrutiny (Smith 1998; Suriano 2009; cf. Mettinger 2001). For Baal himself, the death and resurrection sequence is part of the plot of the *Baal* Cycle, peculiar to Ugarit, and without other parallels among storm-gods. The close relationship of king and god in this context lends a peculiar importance for our present discussion to this passage from the funerary text

---

42 As I observed in Wyatt (2009: 164): 'Dahood's valiant attempt to discern a beatific afterlife not only in the Hebrew Psalms, but in the older Ugaritic literature, is to be considered a magnificent failure', and in Wyatt (2012: 259 n. 3) (citing Dahood 1960 and 1970: xli–lii):

> The attempt of Dahood ... to see a primitive form of the beatific vision in the Bible and even in Ugaritic literature seems seriously to overstate the case, though he provided a useful counter to the common perception that later Israel never had any belief in an afterlife until the Maccabaean crisis forced an eschatological theology upon the Jews ... [though critical of Dahood] Spronk was fairly positive about later intra-biblical developments in this direction.

Note also Cook (2007: 2):

> Whereas many mainline biblical scholars of the twentieth century tended to see living souls of the dead nowhere in the Hebrew Bible, this new camp tends to see them hidden throughout ... It is fair to say that biblical scholars are currently divided between the position that ancient Israelites had no belief in spirits and the position that they had rather pronounced dealings with them.

The writing of this chapter, and in particular the appearance of Lang (2017) (taken into account below), has obliged me to consider the case reopened, at least with regard to the biblical evidence. I think that Dahood and Spronk are too optimistic concerning the Ugaritic material, but the biblical material is another matter. However, a complete reappraisal is beyond the scope of this chapter.

43 For an excellent recent survey of Levantine conditions from the Late Bronze into the Iron Age, see Benz (2016).
44 Baal's fate and Kirta's are compared in the formulaic usage in *KTU* 1.5 vi 3–5 || 1.5 vi 26–28 || 1.6 ii 15–17 || 1.16 iii 2–4. See Wyatt (1997) and (2007a).

IMMORTALITY AND THE RISE OF RESURRECTION

(*KTU* 1.161.20-l.e.). It appears to contain the instructions for the rites, though it also appears to cite excerpts from the liturgy:

[ ]aṯr.[b] ʿlk.l.k[i].aṯr	'After your lords, from the throne,
bʿlk.arṣ.rd.	After your lords into the underworld go down:
arṣ rd.	into the underworld go down
w.špl.ʿpr	and fall into the dust,
tḥt sdn.w.rdn.	down to Sidanu-and-Radanu,
tḥt.tr ʿl{.}imn.	down to the eternal one, Tharu,
tḥt.rpim.qdmym	down to the ancient *Rapi'ūma*,
tḥt.ʿmṯtmr.mlk	down to ʿAmmithtamru the king
tḥt.unq[md].mlk	and also down to Niqmaddu the king'.

Smith and Suriano both argue, rightly in my view, that the person addressed here is the living king, ʿAmmurapi, who is burying his father and *at the same time* assuming power as his successor. ʿAmmurapi's descent and later ascent constitute an integral part of the rite of power-transference from one generation to the next. We may reasonably think that Baal's descent and ascent in *KTU* 1.5–1.6 is modelled on that of the successor king in the rites. We may almost say that kingship has died with Niqmaddu IV (the monarch named in the last line cited here) and is reborn in the person of ʿAmmurapi II.[45] Do we perhaps have here an early form of the belief in resurrection? While the Ugaritic texts tell us nothing on the subject (though see next paragraph), that in itself is scarcely proof of the absence of the idea. It is comparable to the Egyptian idea of the Ka, in which this divine element ('[royal] power') is incarnate in each successive king.

One Ugaritic passage *does* appear to deal directly with the concept of resurrection, if that is what 'immortality' (*blmt*) here means, and may conceivably be conceptually related to the present context. This is the episode of ʿAnat's offer to Aqhat while trying to persuade him to part with his bow. His response, however, is a firm rejection of what is on offer:

[y]irš.ḥym.laqhat.ǵzr	'Ask for life, O hero Aqhat:
irš.ḥym.watnk	Ask for life and I shall give (it) you,
blmt wašlḥk.	immortality and I shall bestow (it) on you:
ašsprk.ʿm.bʿl šnt	I shall make you number years with Baal:
ʿm.bn.il.tspr.yrḥm	With the son of El you shall number months.
kbʿl.kyḥwy.	"Like Baal he shall live indeed!
yʿšr.ḥwy.	Alive, he shall be feasted,
yʿš r.wyšqynh.	he shall be feasted and given to drink.
ybd.wyšr.ʿlh nʿmxx	The minstrel shall intone and sing concerning him"'.
tʿnynn.	[She] said to him:
ap.ank.aḥwy aqht[.ǵz]r.	'Thus shall I make Aqhat the hero live!'
wyʿn.aqht ǵzr	But Aqhat the hero replied:
al.tšrgn.ybtltm	'Do not deceive me, O Virgin,
dm.l ǵzr šrgk. ḫḫm.	for to a hero your deceit is rubbish!
mt.uḥryt.mh.yqḥ	Man, (at his) end, what will he receive?
mh.yqḥ.mt.aṯryt.	What will he receive, a man (as his) destiny?
spsg.ysk [l]riš.	<S>ilver² will be poured on his head,

---

45 For the revised numbering of the kings of Ugarit, see Freu (2006: 23).

ḥrṣ.lzr.qdqdy	gold² on top of his skull,
[ap]mt.kl.amt.	[and] the death of all I shall die,
wan.mtm.amt	and I shall surely die.

This passage has proved rather controversial in Ugaritic exegesis. As observed above (n. 42), Dahood and Spronk wished to see in it a serious adumbration of later ideas.[46] Others have seen in it a vacuous, flattering offer by ᶜAnat, which Aqhat rightly rejects. Aqhat's response is not to be seen as pessimistic, a sad acceptance of the human lot. It is rather an allusion to the type of royal burial which was common in Bronze and Iron Age contexts.[47] But its contrast with the material cited above (*KTU* 1.6, 1.161) is puzzling. If ᶜAnat's offer can be squared with that (because Baal died and rose, and 'kingship' dies and rises, a 'ritual metaphor', a performative gesture for the successor king's legitimate accession) which is perhaps to be expected, and therefore is not vacuous within the context of royal ideology, why does *Prince* Aqhat scornfully reject what is on offer? The overall plot of the story is perhaps the key: it is a study of impetuous hubris on the part of a prince who is not prepared to accept the constraints of his position, to say nothing of basic courtesy to a goddess, just as Yaṣibu, with singularly bad timing, forgets himself in challenging Kirta for the throne. In other words, Aqhat's words are not a rejection of funerary norms (after all, his description is part of the process) but an outburst of emotional immaturity.

§6 *Judahite royal beliefs*

While we have no certain Judahite parallel to *KTU* 1.161 as ritual practice, it is likely that we should consider the satirical passage in Isa. 14.9-20 to be conceptually related to it. The *rapi'ūma* (deified dead kings) of the Ugaritic text are the exact ideological counterparts to the *rĕpā'îm* of Isa. 14.9, who are also identified as kings (vv. 9-10); the twist in Isaiah is that the solemn rite is turned into a monstrous charade, mocking the dead king and denying him a proper burial. I have suggested that the Isaianic passage is actually modelled on the same procedures – that is, a historical Judahite funerary rite based on the same principles as the Ugaritic example (Wyatt 2010: 73–5).[48] If this interpretation is correct, then we should envisage the new king accompanying his father's corpse into the tomb (so too Shipp 2002: 124–5).[49]

Isaiah 14 focuses on a royal funeral. A recent study of the royal psalms has proposed a striking incidental parallel to this: David Beadle (2017) has noted that a number of psalms exhibit a ritual complex involving descent into the underworld, followed by ascension to heaven (primarily Psalms 2, 18, 24, 89.2-38 and, for part of the pattern, Psalm 110). This ritual process, if real, would take place at the king's accession, thus conforming to the double aspect of *KTU* 1.161. In their present form, Beadle argues, these psalms are post-exilic, and part of his analysis considers the final product to be a critique of monarchy, the ideology 'subverted' by its formulation. The quasi-shamanistic

---

46 Smith and Bloch-Smith (1988: 279) remark, writing of Spronk's interpretation of this passage: 'Unlike most scholars Spronk takes this claim seriously.' In their conclusion they further remark, 'Ultimately the sparseness of the data prevents scholarship from conclusively establishing beliefs in resurrection or "beatific afterlife" in Iron Age Israel' (Smith and Bloch-Smith 1988: 284).

47 For discussion of the 'gold ... silver ...' problem, see Wyatt (2017: 829–30 n. 36). On Aqhat as royal (Danel his father being a king) see Wyatt (1999: 249–51) and (2002: 307 n. 250). For Ugaritian funerary practice see Salles (1995); Marchegay (2007).

48 The view expressed there that it is simply the dead king who descends is to be modified in view of Smith (1998) and Suriano (2009).

49 Although note that in Shipp (2002: 124) 'the "lord"' must now be identified as Niqmaddu IV.

pattern of this material, recognized by Beadle, is similar to such echoes discerned in the Hekhalot literature by James Davila (2001).[50] If the analyses offered by Beadle and Davila are cogent, then we should perhaps see outliers of a largely submerged ferment of ideas, which later burst into the open in the late Hellenistic period, by then probably enriched by Iranian ideas.

§7 Levitical beliefs

An entirely unexpected avenue of enquiry was opened up by a perceptive new study by Bernhard Lang (2017). This raised the possibility of the Levites having a significant role in the development of a new way of considering death and its aftermath. Lang begins his discussion with the observation that 'domestic religion, essential to the household but closed to all others, was the constituent principle of the ancient family' (Lang 2017: 65; drawing on Fustel de Coulanges 1864; Brichto 1973). This is in accord with the discussion above concerning mortuary practices, particularly as observed in pre-exilic Judah, along patrimonial (extended family) lines. The Levites were an exception, being outside the normal domestic clan–ancestors–landownership framework (Brichto 1973; see also Schipper in this volume). They were thus disqualified from participation in the normal processes.[51] Their inheritance (*naḥălāh*)[52] was not in land (giving access to the conventional sharing with ancestors), but with Yahweh (Num. 18.20). Lang argues that Psalm 16 – a psalm with many textual problems – reflects the initiation of the Levite into membership of the group and describes his rejection of the conventional land-based *mores* in favour of the distinctive Levitical devotion to the deity. Here is my translation of the psalm, informed by Lang's insights:

šāmrēnî 'ēl kî-ḥāsîtî bāk	Keep me, El, for I take refuge in you.
**'āmart<î> layhwh*	I say to Yahweh
'ădōnāy 'attā ṭôbātî	my Lord are you, my benefactor.
bal-ᶜāleka {lî} qĕdôšîm	Not above you[53] are the holy ones,
'ăšer bā'āreṣ hēmāh	those who are in the underworld;
**wĕ'arûrîm kol-*ḥapṣê-bām*	and cursed[54] are all those who are devoted to them:
yirbû ᶜaṣṣĕbôtām 'aḥēr māhārû	the idols multiply, of those who hasten[55] after them!
bal-'assîk niskêhem middām	I shall not pour out their libations of blood,[56]

---

50 See also Alexander (1977: 172) on 3 Enoch. Note that Blenkinsopp (1995: 14) called the 'witch' of Endor 'a woman who commands the spirits, a female shaman'.
51 Lang (2017: 66): 'By not owning landed property, the Levites opted out of the cultural complex of "kin, cult, land, and afterlife in Sheol" and created their own cultural and religious pattern. However, this pattern remains unexamined, leaving a gap in the relevant secondary literature.' As is indicated in the discussion above, it seems that we can now qualify Sheol as an intermediate stage on the journey of the dead. If this is the case, then the frequent biblical references to it as a place of fear presumably express the anxiety of the living that they will be caught there, without being able to complete their journey to the ancestral ingathering.
52 See Lewis (1991) for the legal and social significance of the technical term, and his discussion of the link between landownership and burial rights (resuming Brichto 1973 and anticipating Stavrakopoulou 2010).
53 MT: implying rank, allowing them to be subordinate. Or (*BHS* app.) {*bal*} *bil-ᶜādêkā*, 'apart from you', denying their existence.
54 Reading *wĕ'arûrîm* for MT *wĕ'addîrê*.
55 'Devoted ... hasten ...': translating 'travail pains ... lust ...', Dahood's intertextual reference to *KTU* 1.12 i 38–39 is interesting (Dahood 1965a: 88; cf. Wyatt 2002: 164 n.12). Opponents of a Dahoodian approach should remember that in poetry, many allusive elements beside the niceties of modern philology may inform a writer's choice of words (cf. my remarks in Wyatt: forthcoming n. 40).
56 As a number of commentators have observed, libations of water would sustain the dead; libations of blood suggest a cult of the dead, or involvement in necromancy; cf. Odysseus offering blood libations to bring up

ûbal-'ăšer 'et-šĕmôtām ʿal-śĕpātāy	and their names will never be on my lips![57]
yhwh mĕnot-ḥelqî wĕkôsî	Yahweh, the portion of my heritage[58] and my cup (are you);
'attāh tômîk gôrālî	you hold my destiny (in your hands).
ḥăbālîm nāpĕlû-lî bannĕʿimîm	The threads[59] have fallen in my favour in the paradisal places.[60]
'ap-naḥălāt šāpĕrāh ʿālāy	and my inheritance falls to me.
'ăbārēk 'et-yhwh 'ăšer yĕʿāṣānî	I shall bless Yahweh who counsels me,
'ap-lēlôt yissĕrûnî kilyôtāy	and by night my heart shall instruct me.
šiwwîtî yhwh lĕnegdî tāmîd	I keep Yahweh ever before me;
kî mîmînî bal-'emôṭ	indeed, (with him) at my right hand, I shall not be moved.
lākēn śāmaḥ libbî wayyāgel kĕbôdî	So my heart rejoices, and my liver is joyful;
'ap-bĕśārî yiškōn lābeṭaḥ	even my body remains secure.
kî lō'-taʿăzōb napšî liš'ôl	For you will not abandon my soul to Sheol;
lō'-tittēn ḥăsîdĕkā lir'ôt šaḥat	you will not allow your faithful one to see the pit.
tôdîʿēnî 'ōraḥ ḥayyîm	You will teach me the path of life.
śōbaʿ śĕmāḥôt 'et-pānêkā	(There is a) surfeit of joy in your presence;[61]
nĕʿimôt bîmînĕkā neṣaḥ	The paradisal delights at your right hand[62] are for ever!

'Paradisal places' in v. 6 translates Hebrew *nĕʿimîm* (note also the 'paradisal delights' – *nĕʿimôt* – of v. 11) which must have some technical sense. On my reading, the term echoes the similar usage in Ugaritic, which may be a useful guide to the Hebrew. In *KTU* 1.5 vi 6–7 it denotes the threshold of the underworld:

mġny lnʿmy.arṣ.dbr	we came to Paradise, the land of pasture,
lysmt.šd.šḥlmwt	to Delight, the steppe by the shore of death.

And in *KTU* 1.3 iii 28–31 (cf. 1.10 iii 27–31) it denotes the threshold of the divine mountain, the former reading:

atm.wank ibġyh.btk.ġry.il.ṣpn	Come, and I shall reveal it in the midst of my divine mountain, Saphon,

---

the dead (*Odyssey* 11.23-36). The ritual probably falls short of cult, in the sense of worship of a deity, except in the mind of the psalmist! The text reflects the mentality of fierce devotion to a jealous god, which tends to intemperance of language. This could be a libel on ancestral devotion.

57 Naming the dead (and so implicitly remembering them) is part of the whole complex of giving the dead substance and an inheritance with the living; see Sanders (2012).
58 √ḥlq II: the term anticipates *naḥălāh* in v. 6. The three terms *ḥelqî*, *nĕʿimîm* and *naḥălāt*, belong together, the two legal terms framing the substance of the inheritance: here a paradisal home. The mythological root of this language is the deity gaining a temple.
59 Cf. the Greek motif of the thread of the Moirai ('Measurers'), spun by Clotho, measured by Lachesis and cut by Atropos, signifying a person's destiny.
60 I have translated the term *ad contextum* (Wyatt 1996: 40; 2002: 126 n. 50, 160 n. 32) to indicate the nuances.
61 The language of the cult, originally before an image.
62 'At your right hand': a specifically royal trope, as suggested by Ps. 110.1. This could explain the attribution of the psalm *lĕdāwid*.

bqdš.bġr.nḥlty	in the sanctuary, on the mountain of my inheritance,
bnᶜm.bgbᶜ.tliyt	in Paradise, on the hill of victory.

There may be a euphemistic dimension to this usage. After all, in both instances here, it denotes a liminal place, both dangerous and potentially destructive, the threshold of the underworld or the threshold of a temple. But euphemistic usage can imbue a term with richer, more positive nuances, and the psalm reflects such a development.

A close reading of Psalm 16 requires a partial reappraisal of the line taken by Dahood and Spronk on the matter of 'eternal life' – the translation Dahood (1965a: 86, 91) offered for *ḥayyîm* in v. 11. Not to be separated from this so far as the ideology is concerned is an important point: the (here, implicit) garden image belongs to temple architectural forms and in many Bronze Age sites appears to have functioned both as a temple garden and as a (collective) royal tomb, as at Ebla, Qatna and Ugarit – and is likely reflected in the *gan-hammelek* in Jerusalem (Wyatt 1990, 2012: 284–6; cf. Stavrakopoulou 2006). The templates of Eden in Genesis 2 and Ezekiel 28 require each to be superimposed on the other, and both on the Jerusalem temple – and this in turn with the garden tomb of John 20 (Wyatt 1990, 2014), suggesting a continuity of tradition and ideology between the first temple and the New Testament period: this is how intertextuality works! It is in this nexus of developing ideas that the geography of the dwelling place of the resurrected is to be set, and it is the framework of the rich pseudepigraphical literature on the trope.

Psalms 49.15 and 73.24-25 express similar sentiments to those of Psalm 16. Psalm 49.15-16 (Eng. vv. 14-15) reads as follows:

kaṣṣ'ōn liššĕ'ôl šattû	Like sheep they are bound for Sheol;
māwet yirᶜēm	Death is their shepherd.
*wayyardû bām yĕšārîm lĕbāqār	And they shall go down into his throat like a calf,[63]
wĕṣîrām lĕballôt {šĕ'ôl} mizzĕbul lô	and their bodies will be devoured by the Prince himself.[64]

---

[63] Ps. 49.15c (MT) offers no coherent meaning. Modern versions (e.g. JPS, 'the upright shall rule over them at daybreak') try rather desperately to deal with it, but misread the context. Dahood (1965a: 300), still having difficulties, especially with *bām yĕšārîm*, which he construed as *bĕmēšārîm*, citing Prov. 23.31-32 and Song 7.10, came up with 'when they descend into his gullet like a calf', reading *wayyārĕdû* for *wayyirdû* and *lĕbāqār* for *labbōqer*. This is an intelligent approach to a crux, and I have been guided by it. If Lang's (2017) approach has substance, then the critique of Dahood in Vawter (1972: 162–3) with regard to Psalms 49 and 73 misses the mark.
[64] Text *wĕṣîrām lĕballôt {šĕ'ôl} mizzĕbul lô*: meaning conjectural. Cf. Dahood (1965a: 301). Whatever *lĕballôt* strictly means, Dahood's account is not very convincing. To √*blh*, cf. Arb *baliya*, OSAr *blwt*, 'grave', Eth. *balaya*, 'be consumed', Akk. *balû*, 'fade, pass away', all cited in *HALOT* i 132 (note too Wehr (1976: 75): *balīy*, 'worn, old, shabby … decomposed etc.'; *balīya*, 'tribulation etc.'). Wilfred Watson also drew my attention to Aram-Syr. *bly* = 'hurry, frighten away, stun'. Perhaps more to the point here, we should consider Hebrew *bālaᶜ*, with cognates, including Ugaritic, meaning 'swallow'. It would be going too far perhaps to alter the word, but perhaps it plays on the assonance of the latter, especially in view of the Ugaritic motif of Mot as swallower in *KTU* 1.4 viii 15–20, 1.5 i 12-20. Cf. Num. 16.31-34. I take *šĕ'ôl* here to be intrusive (brought down from the first colon in the verse). It overloads the present colon. As for *zĕbul*, 'prince', it appears frequently as a divine title in Ugaritic, of Yariḫu (*KTU* 1.15 i 4, etc.), Rašpu (*KTU* 1.15 i 6), Yam (*KTU* 1.2 iii 8, etc.) and Baal (in the formula *zbl bᶜl arṣ*, 'the Prince, lord of the earth', *KTU* 1.2 i 43, etc.). I take it that here it is a title of Death. Cf. the kingdom of Death (Mot) in *KTU* 1.4 viii 11–14 = 1.5 ii 15–16. In 1 Kgs 8.22 = 2 Chron. 6.2 the expression *bêt-zĕbul (lāk)* may denote 'the house (= temple) of (your) princeship', referring to Yahweh. The use of *mi-* remains problematic. Wilfred Watson has suggested to me that the *m* may be an enclitic on *šĕ'ôl*. In this case it would belong to the

| *'ak-'ĕlōhîm yipdeh napšî* | But God will redeem my soul: |
| *miyyad šĕ'ôl kî yiqqāḥēnî* | From the grasp of Sheol he will surely[65] snatch me. |

Psalm 73.24-26 reads thus:

ba'ăṣātĕkā tanĕḥēnî	With your counsel you console me,
wĕ'aḥar kābôd tiqqāḥēnî	and afterwards you will take me[66] in glory!
mî-lî baššāmayim wĕ'immĕkā	Whom else do I have in heaven beside you?
(wĕ'immĕkā) lō'-ḥāpaṣtî bā'āreṣ	And beside you[67] I desire nothing in the underworld.
kālāh šĕ'ērî ûlĕbābî	My flesh and my heart will come to an end,
ṣûr-lĕbābî wĕḥelqî 'ĕlōhîm lĕ'ôlām	(but) the rock of my heart and my heritage is God, forever.

All three psalms are 'Levitical', Lang argues, being assigned respectively to Korah (Psalm 49) and Asaph (Psalm 73; cf. Buss 1963), while Psalm 16 he interprets, on the strength of parallels between the three texts, as celebrating the induction of a Levite into office. What emerges clearly from the text in each case is a clear alternative to the conventional expectation of an underworld post-mortem existence, vigorously asserted.

Lang's discussion does not contain any specific mention of resurrection, although this is where the logic of his exegesis leads us. Instead, he speaks in these terms:

> Unlike the other Israelites, who expected to spend life after death in Sheol, a vast underground realm inaccessible to the living but inhabited by their ancestors, the Levites entertained the presumably secret, esoteric notion of an afterlife with God in heaven. A heavenly afterlife would be the exclusive privilege of the landless Levites, granted to none of the landowners. (Lang 2017: 77)[68]

If we consider this to be at an early stage in the development of the idea, so far as acceptance within Israelite–Judahite eschatology is concerned, then we do not have to demand consistency with later developments. Perhaps no differentiation was yet understood between different nuances. Perhaps none had yet arisen.

Lang then goes on to emphasize the opposition between conventional (land-based) and Levitical beliefs:

> Psalm 16 is marked by a clear binary opposition between 'ancestor worship and post-mortem existence in the netherworld' and 'worship of Yahweh and post-mortem existence in God's abode, heaven'. This binary opposition does not juxtapose two equally inviting prospects but privileges one prospect over the other, taking heaven to be the better place. Heaven is above and takes precedence on the scale of values. Heaven, moreover, is only for an elite minority, whereas Sheol for all the others, the masses. After this life, the Levite expects to be promoted to a heavenly abode,

---

intrusive *šĕ'ôl* (perhaps giving it an adverbial force) on my construal, and therefore also require excision in order to recover an original text. I concede that we can never be certain that this or that version of a text is the Ur-text!
65 Emphatic *kî*.
66 The same verb *lāqaḥ* is used of God's 'taking' of Enoch in Gen. 5.24.
67 The particle *wĕ'immĕkā* appears to be performing double-duty.
68 'Heaven' appears throughout the article. The function of Sheol as indicated here perhaps goes beyond the evidence, being either the destiny of those who fail to be gathered/added to the community of ancestors or (and perhaps in addition to) a transit point on the way to that gathering – a forerunner to the later ideas of limbo and purgatory.

presumably to continue work in the service of his divine master. Levites would die a normal death, and have a normal burial, but their soul would not descend to the netherworld; instead, it would find its way upwards, to heaven. (Lang 2017: 79)

He makes a further important point regarding the matter of individuality, which I raised above as a possibly significant factor in the development of later ideas:

> Heaven, by contrast, belongs to a different, theocentric complex of ideas – 'God, cult, and afterlife in heaven', where the individual relates to God alone, to the exclusion of all human relationships or attachment to the land. Human relationships exist in levitical everyday life, but they are weaker than in other societal groups, and when they conflict with the theocentric complex they are completely denied. When such conflict arises, the Levite must say of each relative, be it father or mother, brother or son, 'I do not see him' (Deut 33:9), I do not recognise any relationship. The Levite belongs to heaven where no human relationships exist. (Lang 2017: 79)

Now if a celestial rather than an infernal destiny was on offer, it evidently has a conceptual link with resurrection, whether seen in spiritual or physical terms. Perhaps the lack of an indication of which nuance is intended indicates that the idea as formulated in Psalm 16 predates its later refinement. Certainly, Lang's citation (2017: 80–2) of Acts 2.25-28 (to which add v. 31) and 13.35, which quote Psalm 16 in support of claims about Jesus' resurrection, is eloquent testimony to the continuing interpretation of the psalm.[69]

Conclusion

This survey of diverse currents influencing beliefs over a long period of history leads to the conclusion that it is wrong to identify any single cause for the rise in resurrection belief. Violent political upheavals in the second century BCE, the time of the Maccabaean crisis, appear to have concentrated minds on the theodicial problem of righteous suffering and martyrdom. But as we have seen, currents of thinking, both within Judah–Yehud and among neighbouring peoples, go back centuries, with Palestine at the heart of the great Afro-Asiatic mercantile and geopolitical zone. The Levitical belief system, if Lang's analysis is correct, certainly owed something to landownership issues, but formed in a world where developments in eschatological thought transcended political and social boundaries. Where once the dead had enjoyed (or endured) a post-mortem existence in their graves, some would rise up from the earth to move towards the heavens.

References

Albertz, R. (1994), *A History of Israelite Religion in the Old Testament Period*, 2 vols, London: SCM Press.

Alexander, P. S. (1977), 'The Historical Setting of the Hebrew Book of Enoch', *Journal of Jewish Studies* 28: 156–80.

Allen, J. P. (2015), *The Ancient Egyptian Pyramid Texts*, Writings of the Ancient World 38, Atlanta, GA: Society of Biblical Literature.

---

[69] In the same discussion, he also considered assumption (Jesus, Moses, Enoch, Elijah) as representing the scope of Levitical beliefs.

Allen, T. G. (1974), *The Book of the Dead or Going Forth by Day: Ideas of the Ancient Egyptians Concerning the Hereafter as Expressed in Their Own Terms*, Studies in Ancient Oriental Civilizations 37, Chicago, IL: Oriental Institute.

Astour, M. C. (1998), 'RDMN/RHADAMANTHYS and the Motif of Selective Immortality', in M. Dietrich and I. Kottsieper (eds), *'Und Mose schrieb dieses Lied auf ...'. Studien zum Alten Testament und zum Alten Orient. Festschrift für O. Loretz zur Vollendung seines 70. Lebensjahres mit Beiträgen von Freunden, Schülern und Kollegen*, 55–89, Alter Orient und Altes Testament 250, Münster: Ugarit-Verlag.

Barr, J. (1993), *The Garden of Eden and the Hope of Immortality*, Minneapolis, MN: Fortress Press.

Barstad, H. (1999), 'Sheol', in K. van der Toorn, B. Becking and P. van der Horst (eds), *Dictionary of Deities and Demons in the Bible*, 2nd edn, 768–70, Leiden: Brill.

Bayliss, M. (1973), 'The Cult of Dead Kin in Assyria and Babylonia', *Iraq* 35: 115–25.

Beadle, D. N. (2017), 'The "Divine" Confused and Abused: Cultural Memories of Royal Ritual Netherworld Descent and Heavenly Ascent in the Hebrew Bible', PhD thesis, University of Exeter, UK.

Benz, B. C. (2016), *The Land before the Kingdom of Israel: A History of the Southern Levant and the People Who Populated It*, History, Archaeology, and Culture of the Levant 7, Winona Lake, IN: Eisenbrauns.

Blenkinsopp, J. (1995), 'Deuteronomy and the Politics of Post-Mortem Existence', *Vetus Testamentum* 45: 1–16.

Bloch-Smith, E. (1992), *Judahite Burial Practices and Beliefs about the Dead*, Sheffield: Sheffield Academic Press.

Bloch-Smith, E. (2002), 'Life in Judah from the Perspective of the Dead', *Near Eastern Archaeology* 65: 120–30.

Böklen, E. (1902), *Die Verwandtschaft der jüdisch-christlichen mit der parsischen Eschatologie*, Göttingen: Vandenhoeck & Ruprecht.

Boyce, M. A. ([1975–91] 1996), *A History of Zoroastrianism*, Section 1, The Near and Middle East, Handbook of Oriental Studies, Leiden: Brill.

Boyce, M. (1987), *Zoroastrianism: A Shadowy but Powerful Presence in the Judaeo-Christian World*, London: Dr Williams' Trust.

Brichto, H. C. (1973), 'Kin, Cult, Land and Afterlife – A Biblical Complex', *Hebrew Union College Annual* 44: 1–54.

Buss, M. J. (1963), 'The Psalms of Asaph and Korah', *Journal of Biblical Literature* 82: 382–92.

Cauvin, J. (1994), *Naissance des divinités, naissance de l'agriculture*, Paris: Centre National de la Recherche Scientifique/Institut Français du Proche-Orient.

Charlesworth, J. H., ed. (2006a), *Resurrection: The Origin and Future of a Biblical Doctrine*, Faith and Scholarship Colloquies, London: T&T Clark.

Charlesworth, J. H. (2006b), 'Where Does the Concept of Resurrection Appear and How Do We Know That?', in J. H. Charlesworth (ed.), *Resurrection: The Origin and Future of a Biblical Doctrine*, Faith and Scholarship Colloquies, 1–21, London: T&T Clark.

Charlesworth, J. H. (2006c), 'Resurrection: The Dead Sea Scrolls and the New Testament', in J. H. Charlesworth (ed.), *Resurrection: The Origin and Future of a Biblical Doctrine*, Faith and Scholarship Colloquies, 138–86, London: T&T Clark.

Cline, E. H. (2014), *1177 B.C. The Year Civilization Collapsed*, Princeton, NJ: Princeton University Press.

Cook, S. L. (2007), 'Funerary Practices and Afterlife Expectations in Ancient Israel', *Religion Compass* 1: 2–24.

Cullmann, O. (1956), *Immortalité de l'âme ou résurrection des morts? Le témoignage du Nouveau Testament*, L'actualité protestante, Neuchâtel: Delachaux & Nestlé.
Dahood, M. J. (1960), 'Immortality in Proverbs 12:28', *Biblica* 41: 176–81.
Dahood, M. J. (1965a), *Psalms I*, Anchor Bible 16, New York: Doubleday.
Dahood, M. J. ([1965b] 1973), *Psalms II*, 2nd edn, Anchor Bible 17, New York: Doubleday.
Dahood, M. J. (1970), *Psalms III*, Anchor Bible 17a, New York: Doubleday.
Davila, J. (2001), *Descenders to the Chariot: The People behind the Hekhalot Literature*, Journal for the Study of Judaism Supplements 70, Leiden: Brill.
Day, J. (1996). 'The Development of Belief in Life after Death in Ancient Israel', in J. Barton and D. Reimer (eds), *After the Exile: Essays in Honor of Rex Mason*, 231–57, Macon, GA: Mercer University Press.
Di Vito, R. A. (1999), 'Old Testament Anthropology and the Construction of Personal Identity', *Catholic Biblical Quarterly* 61: 217–38.
Doak, B. E. (2012), *The Last of the Rephaim: Conquest and Cataclysm in the Heroic Ages of Ancient Israel*, Boston, MA: Ilex.
Elledge, C. D. (2006), 'Resurrection of the Dead: Exploring Our Earliest Evidence Today', in J. H. Charlesworth (ed.), *Resurrection: The Origin and Future of a Biblical Doctrine*, 22–52, Faith and Scholarship Colloquies, London: T&T Clark.
Elledge, C. D. (2017), *Resurrection of the Dead in Early Judaism, 200 BCE – CE 200*, New York: Oxford University Press.
Emery, W. B. (1961), *Archaic Egypt*, Harmondsworth: Penguin.
Faulkner, R. O. (1985), *The Ancient Egyptian Book of the Dead*, London: British Museum.
Faulkner, R. O. (2004), *The Ancient Egyptian Coffin Texts*, Oxford: Aris and Phillips/Liverpool University Press.
Faust, A. (2015), 'The "Philistine Tomb" at Tel ʿEton: Culture Contact, Colonialism, and Local Responses in Iron Age Shephelah, Israel', *Journal of Anthropological Research* 71: 195–230.
Finkelstein, I. (1999), 'State Formation in Israel and Judah: A Contrast in Context, a Contrast in Trajectory', *Near Eastern Archaeology* 62 (1): 35–52.
Freu, J. (2006), *Histoire Politique du Royaume d'Ugarit*, Kubaba Antiquité 11, Paris: L'Harmattan.
Frevel, C. (2017a), 'Von der Selbstbeobachtung zu inneren Tiefen – Überlegungen zur Konstitution von Individualität im Alten Testament', in A. Wagner and J. van Oorschott (eds), *Individualität und Selbstre exion in den Literaturen des Alten Testaments*, 13–43, Veroffentlichungen der Wissenschaftlichen Gesellschaft für Theologie 48, Leipzig: Evangelische Verlagsanstalt.
Frevel, C. (2017b), '"Quellen des Selbst"? Charles Taylors Einfluss auf die alttestamentliche Anthropologie', in R. Althaus, J. Hahn and M. Pulte (eds), *Im Dienste der Gerechtigkeit und Einheit: Festschrift für Heinrich J.F. Reinhardt zur Vollendung seines 75. Lebensjahres*, 447–63, Beihefte zum Münsterischen Kommentar zum Codex Juris Canonici, Essen: Ludgerus Verlag.
Fustel de Coulanges, N. D. (1864), *La Cité Antique: étude sur le culte, le droit, les institutions de la Grèce et de Rome*, Paris: Durand.
Goldstein, J. A. (1983), *II Maccabees: A New Translation with Introduction and Commentary*, New York: Doubleday.
Grappe, C. (2014), *L'au-delà dans la Bible. Le temporel et le spatial*, Le Monde de la Bible, 68, Geneva: Labor et Fides.
Griffiths, J. G. (1991), *The Divine Verdict: A Study of Divine Judgement in the Ancient Religions*, Leiden: Brill.
Halpern, B. (1991), 'Jerusalem and the Lineages in the Seventh Century BCE: Kinship and the Rise of Individual Moral Liability', in B. Halpern and D. Hobson (eds), *Law and Ideology*

in Monarchic Israel, 11–107, Journal for the Study of the Old Testament Supplement 124, Sheffield: Sheffield Academic Press.

Halpern, B. (1996), 'Sybil, or the Two Nations? Archaism, Kinship, Alienation, and the Elite Redefinition of Traditional Culture in Judah in the 8th-7th Centuries B.C.E.', in J. Cooper and G. Schwartz (eds), *The Study of the Ancient Near East in the Twenty-First Century: The William Foxwell Albright Centennial Conference*, 291–338, Winona Lake, IN: Eisenbrauns.

Herrmann, V. R., and J. D. Schloen, eds (2014), *In Remembrance of Me: Feasting with the Dead in the Ancient Middle East*, Oriental Institute Museum Publications 37, Chicago, IL: Oriental Institute.

Hultgård, A. (1979), 'Das Judentum in der hellenistich-römischen Zeit und die iranische Religion. Ein religionsgeschichtliches Problem', *Aufstieg und Niedergang der Römischen Welt* 19 (1): 512–90.

Johnson, A. R. (1964), *The Vitality of the Individual in the Thought of Ancient Israel*, 2nd edn, Cardiff: University of Wales Press.

Johnston, P. S. (2002), *Shades of Sheol: Death and Afterlife in the Old Testament*, Downers Grove, IL: InterVarsity Press.

Joukowsky, M., and W. A. Ward, eds (1992), *The Crisis Years: The 12th Century B.C.: from beyond the Danube to the Tigris*, Dubuque, IA: Kendal-Hunt.

Koehler, L. (1946), 'Alttestamentliche Wortforschung. Sche'ol', *Theologische Zeitung* 2: 71–4.

König, F. (1964), *Zarathustras Jenseitsvorstellungen und das Alte Testament*, Vienna: Herder.

Korpel, M. C. A. (1996), 'Avian Spirits in Ugarit and in Ezekiel 13', in N. Wyatt, W. G. E. Watson and J. B. Lloyd (eds), *Ugarit, Religion and Culture. Proceedings of the International Colloquium on Ugarit, Religion and Culture, Edinburgh July 1994. Essays in Honour of Professor J. C. L. Gibson*, 98–113, Ugaritisch-Biblische Literatur 12, Münster: Ugarit-Verlag.

Lang, B. (2017), 'New Light on the Levites: The Biblical Group That Invented Belief in Life after Death in Heaven', in E. M. Becker, J. Dietrich and B. K. Holm (eds), *What Is Human? Theological Encounters with Anthropology*, 65–85, Göttingen: Vandenhoeck & Ruprecht.

Levenson, J. D. (2006), *Resurrection and the Restoration of Israel: The Ultimate Victory of the God of Life*, New Haven, CT: Yale University Press.

Lewis, T. J. (1989), *Cults of the Dead in Ancient Israel and Ugarit*, Harvard Semitic Monographs 39, Atlanta, GA: Scholars Press.

Lewis, T. J. (1991), 'The Ancestral Estate נַחֲלַת אֱלֹהִים in 2 Samuel 14:16', *Journal of Biblical Literature* 110: 597–612.

Lipiński, E. (2016), 'Hurrians and Their Gods in Canaan', *Rocznik Orientalistyczny* 69: 125–41.

Marchegay, S. (2007), 'Les pratiques funéraires à Ougarit à l'Age du Bronze', in J.-M. Michaud (ed.), *Le royaume d'Ougarit de la Crète à l'Euphrate. Nouveaux axes de recherche*, 423–47, Proche-Orient et Littérature Ougaritique 2, Sherbrooke, QC: Éditions GGC.

Martin-Achard, R. (1960), *From Death to Life: A Study of the Development of the Doctrine of the Resurrection in the Old Testament*, Edinburgh: Oliver and Boyd.

Mettinger, T. N. D. (2001), *The Riddle of Resurrection: 'Dying and Rising Gods' in the Ancient Near East*, Coniectanea Biblica, OT Series 50, Stockholm: Almqvist and Wiksell International.

Netzer, A. (1990), 'A Midrash on the Ascension of Moses in Judeo-Persian', in A. Netzer and S. Shaked (eds), *Irano-Judaica II: Studies Relating to Jewish Contacts with Persian Culture Throughout the Ages*, 105–43, Jerusalem: Ben-Zvi Institute.

Newsom, C. A. (2017), 'Sin-consciousness, Self-alienation, and the Development of the Introspective Self in Second Temple Judaism', Tyrwhitt Lecture delivered at the University of Cambridge, 8 March.

Nickelsburg, G. W. E. (2006), *Resurrection, Immortality and Eternal life in Intertestamental Judaism and Early Christianity*, Cambridge, MA: Harvard University Press.

Nutkowicz, H. (2006), *L'Homme Face à la Mort au Royaume de Juda. Rites, pratiques et representations*, Patrimoines Judaïsme, Paris: Cerf.

Oesterley, W. O. E., and T. H. Robinson (1930), *Hebrew Religion, Its Origin and Development*, London: SPCK.

Oldenberg, H. (1917), *Die Religion des Veda*, 2nd edn, Stuttgart: J. G. Cotta.

Olyan, S. M. (2005), 'Some Neglected Aspects of Israelite Interment Ideology', *Journal of Biblical Literature* 124: 601–16.

Pedersen, J. (1959), *Israel, Its Life and Culture*, 2 vols. London: Oxford University Press.

Rad, G. von (1965), *Old Testament Theology*, Volume 2, Edinburgh: Oliver and Boyd.

Rouillard, H. (1995), 'Rituel mortuaire et rituel social à Ras Shamra/Ougarit', in S. Campbell and A. Green (eds), *The Archaeology of Death in the Ancient Near East*, Oxbow Monograph 51, 171–84, Oxford: Oxbow.

Rouillard, H. (1999), 'Rephaim', in K. van der Toorn, B. Becking and P. van der Horst (eds), *Dictionary of Deities and Demons in the Bible*, 2nd edn, 692–700, Leiden: Brill.

Rowley, H. H. (1956), *The Faith of Israel: Aspects of Old Testament Thought*, London: Westminster John Knox Press.

Salles, J.-F. (1987), 'Deux nouvelles tombes de Ras Shamra', in M. Yon (ed.), *Le Centre de la Ville. 38ᵉ-44ᵉ campagnes (1978–1984)*, 157–95, Ras Shamra-Ougarit 3, Paris: Editions Recherche sur les Civilisations.

Sanders, S. (2012), 'Naming the Dead: Funerary Writing and Historical Change in the Iron Age Levant', *Bulletin of the Schools of Oriental Research* 19: 11–36.

Shaked, S. (1971), 'The Notions *mēnōg* and *gētīg* in the Pahlavi Texts and Their Relation to Eschatology', *Acta Orientalia* 33: 59–107.

Shipp, R. M. (2002), *Of Dead Kings and Dirges. Myth and Meaning in Isaiah 14:4b-21*, Academia Biblica 11, Atlanta, GA: Society of Biblical Literature.

Smith, M. S. (1998), 'The Death of "Dying and Rising Gods" in the Biblical World: An Update, with Special Reference to Baal in the Baal Cycle', *Scandinavian Journal of the Old Testament* 12: 257–313.

Smith, M. S., and E. Bloch-Smith (1988), 'Death and Afterlife in Ugarit and Israel [Review of Spronk 1986]', *Journal of the American Oriental Society* 108: 277–84.

Spronk, K. (1986), *Beatific Afterlife in Ancient Israel and in the Ancient Near East*, Alter Orient und Altes Testament 219, Neukirchen-Vluyn: Neukirchener Verlag.

Stavrakopoulou, F. (2006), 'Exploring the Garden of Uzzah: Death, Burial and Ideologies of Kingship', *Biblica* 87: 1–21.

Stavrakopoulou, F. (2010), *Land of Our Fathers: The Roles of Ancestor Veneration in Biblical Land Claims*, London: T&T Clark.

Steiner, R. C. (2015), *Disembodied Souls: The Nefesh in Israel and Kindred Spirits in the Ancient Near East, with an Appendix on the Katumuwa Inscription*, Ancient Near Eastern Monographs 11, Atlanta, GA: Society of Biblical Literature.

Suriano, M. J. (2009), 'Dynasty Building at Ugarit: The Ritual and Political Context of *KTU* 1.161', *Aula Orientalis* 27: 105–23.

Suriano, M. J. (2016), 'Sheol, the Tomb, and the Problem of Postmortem Existence', *Journal of Hebrew Scriptures* 16: article 11.

Suriano, M. J. (2018), *A History of Death in the Hebrew Bible*, New York: Oxford University Press.

Tappy, R. E. (1995), 'Did the Dead Ever Die in Biblical Judah?' *Bulletin of the American Schools of Oriental Research* 298: 59–68.

Tromp, N. J. (1969), *Primitive Conceptions of Death and the Netherworld in the Old Testament*, Bibbia e Oriente 21, Rome: Pontifical Biblical Institute.

Tsukimoto, A. (1985), *Untersuchungen zur Totenpflege* (kispum) *im Alten Mesopotamien*, Alter Orient und Altes Testament 216, Neukirchen-Vluyn: Neukirchener Verlag.

Vaux, R. de (1961), *Ancient Israel: Its Life and Institutions*, London: Darton, Longman and Todd.

Vawter, B. (1972), 'Intimations of Immortality and the Old Testament', *Journal of Biblical Literature* 91: 158–71.

Wehr, H. (1976), *A Dictionary of Modern Written Arabic*, 3rd edn, ed. J. M. Cowan, Ithaca, NY: Cornell University Press.

Winston, D. (1996), 'The Iranian Component in the Bible, Apocrypha, and Qumran. A Review of the Evidence', *History of Religions* 5: 183–216.

Wintermute, O. S. (1985), 'Jubilees, ii 35–142', in J. H. Charlesworth (ed.), *The Old Testament Pseudepigrapha*, Volume 2, Anchor Bible Reference Library, New York: Doubleday.

Wyatt, N. (1990), '"Supposing Him to Be the Gardener" (John 20, 15): A Study of the Paradise Motif in John', *Zeitschrift für die Neutestamentliche Wissenschaft* 25: 21–38.

Wyatt, N. (1996), *Myths of Power: A Study of Royal Myth and Ideology in Ugaritic and Biblical Tradition*, Ugaritisch-Biblische Literatur 13, Münster: Ugarit-Verlag.

Wyatt, N. (1997), 'Ilimilku's Ideological Programme: Ugaritic Royal Propaganda, and a Biblical Postscript', *Ugarit-Forschungen* 29: 775–96.

Wyatt, N. (1999), 'The Story of Aqhat', in W. G. E. Watson and N. Wyatt (eds), *Handbook of Ugaritic Studies*, 234–58, Leiden: Brill.

Wyatt, N. (2002), *Religious Texts from Ugarit*, 2nd edn, Biblical Seminar 53, London: Continuum.

Wyatt, N. (2007a), 'The Religious Role of the King at Ugarit', in K. Lawson Younger Jr (ed.), *Ugarit at Seventy-Five*, 41–74, Winona Lake, IN: Eisenbrauns.

Wyatt, N. (2007b), 'À la recherche des Rephaïm perdus', 579–613 in J. M. Michaud (ed.), *Le royaume d'Ougarit de la Crète à l'Euphrate. Nouveaux axes de recherche*, 579–613, Proche-Orient et Littérature Ougaritique 2, Sherbrooke, QC: Éditions GGC.

Wyatt, N. (2009), 'The Concept and Purpose of Hell: Its Nature and Development in West Semitic Thought', *Numen* 56: 161–84.

Wyatt, N. (2010), 'Royal Religion in Ancient Judah', in F. Stavrakopoulou and J. Barton (eds), *Religious Diversity in Ancient Israel and Judah*, 61–81, London: T&T Clark.

Wyatt, N. (2012), 'After Death Has Us Parted: Encounters between the Living and the Dead in the ancient Semitic world', in G. del Olmo Lete, J. Vidal and N. Wyatt (eds), *The Perfumes of Seven Tamarisks: Studies in Honour of Wilfred G. E. Watson*, 257–91, Alter Orient und Altes Testament 394, Münster: Ugarit-Verlag.

Wyatt, N. (2014), 'A Royal Garden: The Ideology of Eden', *Scandinavian Journal of the Old Testament* 28: 1–35.

Wyatt, N. (2017), 'The Problem of "Dying and Rising" Gods: The Case of Baal', *Ugarit-Forschungen* 48: 819–45.

Wyatt, N. (forthcoming), 'Distinguishing Wood and Trees in the Waters: Creation in Biblical Thought', in R. Watson and A. H. W. Curtis (eds), *Conversations on Canaanite and Biblical Themes: Creation, Chaos and Monotheism*, Berlin: Walter de Gruyter.

Wyatt, N. (2020), Review of Elledge 2017, *Ancient Near Eastern Studies* 57: 360–2.

Zaehner, R. C. (1961), *The Dawn and Twilight of Zoroastrianism*, London: Weidenfeld and Nicolson.

Zevit, Z. (2001), *The Religions of Ancient Israel: A Synthesis of Parallactic Approaches*, London: Continuum.

Zinner, S. (2014), *Textual and Comparative Explorations in 1 & 2 Enoch*, Ancient Scripture and Texts Series 1, Salt Lake City, UT: Eborn.

CHAPTER TEN

Forming divine bodies in the Hebrew Bible

DANIEL O. McCLELLAN

A number of publications in recent years have significantly strengthened the case that the biblical texts consistently conceptualize an embodied deity. There is frequently a tendentiousness accompanying the relevant scholarship, however, which perdures for a number of reasons. Among the most salient of these is the embeddedness of a dichotomous view of deity and humanity. Rudolph Otto famously developed a theoretical framework for the holy around the conceptualization of deity as *das ganz Andere*, or 'the wholly other' (Otto 1917). Otto did not innovate this view of deity, but he and others have helped it become firmly entrenched within biblical scholarship's methodological foundations, and it has become one of the most significant obstacles to a more robust and productive understanding of biblical conceptualizations of deity, particularly of divine bodies. While a number of publications have significantly advanced the discussion regarding the conceptualization of embodied deity (especially Hamori 2008; Sommer 2009; Wagner 2010; Knafl 2014; Smith 2015; Markschies 2016), much of that discussion remains anchored to ontological frameworks and to theological systematization.

These methodological anchors prioritize clear lines of demarcation and in many ways endure because they support the structuring of values and power within the academy and the church or synagogue. In an effort to spur this discussion into more productive spaces, this chapter will apply social and cognitive lenses to this line of enquiry, interrogating the ways cognitive ecologies and predispositions influenced and informed the conceptualization of divine embodiment and the curation of its socio-material manifestations. The discussion will settle on two specific manifestations of presencing media: the ark of the covenant and the written Torah.

Throughout this chapter, I will make an important distinction between intuitive reasoning and reflective reasoning. By these terms, I refer to two types of reasoning that occupy a spectrum of cognition. Intuitive reasoning is automatic, subconscious and rapid and is more closely linked with our cognitive architecture and conditioning. Reflective reasoning is slower, more deliberate and more directly based on conscious reasoning (Evans and Frankish 2009; Oviedo 2015; Morgan 2016). The two frequently come into conflict, resulting in two general types of resolutions (Järnefelt, Canfield and Kelemen 2015; Pennycook, Fugelsang and Koehler 2015). Decoupling is the process by which an *intuitive* response is constrained or overridden by *reflective* reasoning (for instance, when initial alarm at noises in our home at night is ameliorated by the conclusion that it must be the house settling). Rationalization is the process by which the person applies *reflective* reasoning to the justification, explanation or elaboration of an *intuitive* response (for instance, when our tribalism compels us to justify voting for an immoral or unfit candidate for office because we belong to the same political party). Understanding the distinction of the two types of cognition can help us to more carefully parse socioculturally contingent reflective explanations and accounts of deity from the far more consistent underlying intuitive motivations.

Bodies, human and divine

There are a number of different dimensions involved in today's conceptualizations of the human 'body', but in broad terms, we intuitively understand the body to be the primary visible and material locus of a person's identity and agency. Now, that is not to identify the body *with* a person's agency or identity, it is only to say the body is where a person's agency and identity are intuitively *located*. We also intuitively understand these different elements of personhood to be separable from the body in certain circumstances, and even to be capable of permeating other bodies. This is why stories about things like minds switching bodies, multiple identities inhabiting bodies, and spirits possessing and controlling bodies are so common – they rely on intuitive reasoning about agency and bodies. This has direct relevance to how the Hebrew Bible represents the formation and curation of divine bodies, but some unpacking is necessary for a fuller picture.

To be perhaps recklessly succinct, our evolutionary history and cognitive architecture predispose us to think of our bodies as containers for the separable loci of our selves (Sharifian et al. 2008: 3–24; Chudek et al. 2017). This is not to assert ontological binaries or a Cartesian conceptualization of the self but to refer to the ubiquitous conceptual metaphor THE BODY IS A CONTAINER, which frames our understanding of the body according to the notion of internal and external spaces mediated by a boundary that can have varying degrees of permeability and extension inward and/or outward. Cognitive and anthropological research suggest the CONTAINER image schema naturally starts developing in preverbal infant cognition (Mandler 1992; Tilford 2017: 17, 23). As we grow, have more and more experiences in the world and participate in discourse about ourselves and the world around us, we get a sense for interiority and exteriority – things are put *into* our bodies and things come *out of* our bodies – and we recognize that our skin functions in numerous ways as a boundary that separates us from the world around us and keeps the things inside us on the inside, and the things outside us on the outside.

This conceptual metaphor also influences other reasoning about our sense of self. Because injury to parts of the body like the head, the chest and the abdominal region tend to be the most life-threatening, these regions and the organs within them have become highly salient to our concepts of self and have become identified in societies around the world with internal loci of agency, cognition, emotion and animation (Sharifian et al. 2008; Berendt and Tanita 2011). As an example, in the Western world today, the heart is commonly identified as the seat of emotion, while the brain is identified as the seat of intelligence. These associations contribute to the common motif of one's heart and brain being in conflict with each other. The general autonomy of these loci of agency and cognition also contributes to stories about brains being surgically implanted in other bodies, or people feeling reunited with a deceased loved one by listening to the heartbeat of a recipient of that loved one's donor heart (Earl 2015). In certain circumstances, these loci can intuitively reify identity on their own.

Death raises another influential dynamic. Bodies die and observably deteriorate, but we do not intuitively perceive the body to be strictly coterminous with the person. The loci of their agency and identity are often perceived to be separate, so it can take that intuitive cognition some time to restructure our perceptions and expectations regarding the presence and agency of deceased loved ones (Bennett and Bennett 2000; Keen, Murray and Payne 2013). As a result, we might feel they are still with us or 'out there' in some way. This contributes to the perception attested across cultures that unseen and socioculturally curated loci of cognition, animation and agency can survive the deterioration of the body (Bering 2002; Bering, McLeod and Shackelford 2005). In Western cultures, among the most salient of these loci are the mind, the soul and the spirit (Bering 2006; Roazzi, Nyhof and Johnson 2013). These intuitions about unseen loci of agency and their continuation after death lead to sociocultural elaborations such as disembodied spirits, spirit possession, out-of-body experiences and reincarnation (Cohen 2008; Cohen and Barrett 2008; Craffert 2015). This unseen agency is usually conceptualized ambiguously and inconsistently, even within these culturally conventional frameworks, but material media provide a tangible, visible locus for engagement. This is connected with a phenomenon that provides a helpful segue into discussions of divine bodies: the 'animated' gravestone. Even in thoroughly secularized societies, people commonly speak with the dead, and gravestones, in particular, often function to facilitate and focus these discussions. As Elizabeth Hallam and Jenny Hockey explain,

> The highly personalized graves of loved ones have been transformed into spaces in which the 'living' deceased reside and receive visitors and gifts ... The headstone is, in a sense, animated as the body of a person in that it is washed, cared for, gazed at, dressed with flowers, offered drinks, and surrounded by household and garden ornaments. (Hallam and Hockey 2001: 151)

In the ancient world, mortuary spaces performed much the same functions. Meals were provided for the deceased and shared with the deceased, while stelae served as proxy bodies for the unseen agency of the deceased. One of the clearest articulations of this framework was found in the so-called mortuary chapel of Katumuwa at Sam'al (Sanders 2013; Herrmann and Schloen 2014; Steiner 2015). The space included a stele that depicts Katumuwa in a banquet scene and is inscribed with a text prescribing meal offerings for his *nbš* ('self' or 'life'), which, according to the inscription, will be 'in this stele' (*bnṣb.zn*).[1] These meal offerings, associated with primary burial/memorialization and then repeated at intervals, were among a series of actions perpetuating the afterlife of the deceased through ritual memorialization.[2] The inscription or utterance of the deceased's name was one of the most salient mechanisms for perpetuating their existence, as personal names were symbolic of identity and thus intuitively linked with agency. Where remains were inaccessible or buried at a distance, a stele or other ritual objects could host the deceased's locus of agency. Katumuwa's patron in life, Panamuwa, for instance, arranged for his own post-mortem welfare by having the following inscribed on a statue of Hadad that

---

1 On the relationship of the Sam'alian *nbš* to the Hebrew נפש, see Steiner (2015: 137–9).
2 For archaeological evidence of meal offerings to the deceased in ancient Israel and Judah, see Bloch-Smith (1992: 218). These offerings appear to have played a role in maintaining social relationships with the dead of the household, as discussed by Stavrakopoulou (2016). While the Hebrew Bible prohibits offerings to the dead in some places (Ps. 106.28), in others it seems to treat them favourably or at least neutrally, as long as food offerings to YHWH do not come from the same source as offerings to the deceased (Deut. 26.14).

was discovered at a cultic installation in Sam'al: '[May the *n*]*bš* of Panamuwa [eat] with you, and ma[y the *nb*]*š* of Panamuwa dri[nk] with you' (Donner and Röllig 2002: 49). As Matthew Suriano (2014: 403) states, 'The establishment of Panamuwa's *mqm* for his name and soul right beside (and along with) Hadad's stele insured that his defunct-soul would be fed so long as the storm god received food and drink offerings.'[3]

Suriano's comment highlights the consonance between the treatment of the dead and the treatment of deities.[4] Like deceased kin, deities had partible loci of agency and were provisioned through offerings made in special cultic installations and to cultic objects that functioned to presence the deities. Indeed, the care and feeding of deities is likely an elaboration on the care and feeding of deceased kin (Pyysiäinen 2009: 68; Barrett 2011: 103–4). Like deceased kin, deities were understood to be partible and permeable (Sommer 2009; Pongratz-Leisten 2011), but because divine bodies were unavailable for direct observation, there were fewer restrictions on the reflective reasoning about that partibility and permeability, as well as about the deterioration of divine bodies. Without these restrictions, divine bodies were still most commonly conceptualized in anthropomorphic terms, but they were thought to be far more durative, far less susceptible to damage, far more luminous and fantastical and, in many circumstances, far larger (Moore 1996; Hamori 2008: 129–49; Smith 2015). They were also distant and inaccessible, which meant some manner of materially accessible 'body' would have to be provided in order to reify and directly engage with the presence and agency of the deity.

Forming divine bodies in ancient Southwest Asia

The larger societies of ancient Southwest Asia developed a variety of material media for the presencing of deities and divine agency, but they reflect socioculturally mediated variations on very similar underlying themes. In general, these societies reflectively developed authoritative knowledge regarding certain materials that were considered appropriate or necessary for presencing deities and divine agency. These materials could be transformed through prescribed processes and by authorized agents into conventionalized types of cultic images, which could be 'animated' or 'enlivened' by the deity's presence through ritual acts.

The most explicit discussions of these rituals are limited to a few surviving Akkadian fragments from first millennium BCE Mesopotamia (Boden 1998; Walker and Dick 1999, 2001; McDowell 2015). The number and order of incantations and ceremonies differ between the surviving fragments, but the core of the process was the ceremonial washing of the mouth, which purified the image for contact with the deity, and the ceremonial opening of the mouth,[5] which enabled the image to breathe, smell, eat and drink. As lines in the incantation preserved on the Sultantepe tablet (STT 200) illustrate, 'This

---

3 Related conceptualizations of the material presencing of the deceased and their provisioning are found among elite burials in Egypt and Mesopotamia and are obliquely attested in the biblical texts; see further Asher-Greve (1997); Taylor (2001); Wyatt (2012); MacDougal (2014).
4 As an example, the *mis pî* and *pit pî* rituals (discussed below) were used for the animating of divine images as well as cultic images of deceased kings, as discussed in Winter (1992); Walker and Dick (1999: 58); Machinist (2006).
5 The opening of the mouth could also be performed for images representing living kings and other persons; see Walker and Dick (2001: 13).

statue without its mouth opened cannot smell incense, cannot eat food, nor drink water' (Walker and Dick 1999: 96–100).⁶ Both the secondary references to the ritual and the ritual texts themselves use language and symbols related to gestation and birth (as well as manufacturing) as part of a lengthy ritual process involving a tamarisk trough, symbolic of a divine womb (the *buginnu*), which transitioned the deity into the cultic image. According to one text, after reciting an incantation that includes, 'Go, do not tarry', the performer 'makes (him) enter the form' (Walker and Dick 1999: 96–7).⁷ The Ninevite Ritual Text instructs the artisan to whisper 'into the ear(s) of that god', saying, '"You are counted among your brother gods"' (Walker and Dick 1999: 94–5). When the rituals associated with the liminal phase were complete, the image was installed in its temple and given its first meal.

Two aspects of these rituals to be highlighted are the materials used and the role of the artisan. Only certain materials were considered to have qualities that were appropriate for washing the image or that could facilitate the process of enlivenment (Hurowitz 2006; Benzel 2015). Even in their raw state, for instance, pure gold and silver do not oxidize, but maintain their colour and shine. This quality could very easily become associated with the brilliance and glory of deity and thus be conceptualized either as coming from divine realms or as a more pure or suitable habitation or conduit for divine agency/presence. This may account for the inclusion of gold and silver in the *buginnu* and the use of gold and silver plating over cultic images. While the core of the image was composed of wood, rather than precious metals, specific types of wood were still preferred. The tamarisk, called *eṣemti ilī*, 'bone of the gods', was probably most prominent (Hurowitz 2006: 5–6).⁸ If so, the use of a tamarisk *buginnu* and the inclusion of tamarisk in the mixture placed within it may have been intended to materially link the cultic image with the womb in which the precious materials gestated overnight.

While these materials could be considered divine in origin (scattered or hidden in the earth by the deities) or especially suited to transmitting or housing divinity, whether inherently or otherwise, certain acts were required (and demanded by the gods themselves) to commission them for divine inhabitation. The washing and opening of the mouth ceremonies transitioned the image from an earthly creation to a self-created divine entity, and some concomitant ritual was needed to signal the dissociation of the image from its natural/human origins.⁹ This would have amplified the perception of the image as inhabitable by divine agency and was accomplished most conspicuously through the

---

6 As Walker and Dick (1999: 71) observe, while the opening of the mouth seems more critical to the process of enlivenment, it 'was evidently subordinated in the first millennium to the concept of mouth-washing'.
7 While this may indicate the deity is compelled to inhabit the image, the Sumerogram GIŠ.ḪUR.ME could also be read as the Akkadian *gišḫuru*, which would be 'magic circle', reflecting the notion of the 'magic circles of the gods'; see Walker and Dick (1999: 81–2 n.81).
8 McDowell (2015: 75) summarizes: 'The tamarisk from which the buginnu was made ... may have been understood both as a component of the divine statue's formation, perhaps its skeletal system, and as a cleansing and purifying agent, possibly for the womb and the gestating divine embryo.'
9 Note the following comments from Pongratz-Leisten and Sonik (2015: 8):

> The Greek term *archeiropoieta* ... identifies miraculous portraits or representations that were 'not made by any [human] hand', encompassing in the Christian tradition such images as the Mandylion (Image of Edessa). The *archeiropoieta* are not limited to this context, however; ancient Greek sources include various accounts of divine images that had miraculously *appeared*, having fallen perhaps from the heavens or yielded by the seas, and that were understood as products of the divine rather than human agency.

symbolic amputation of the artisan's hands and declarations such as *anāku lā ēpu[šu …]*, '(I swear) I did not make (the statue)' (Walker and Dick 1999: 94–5).[10]

These rituals represent the most explicit reflective practices associated with the intuitive conceptualizations of divine agency as communicable and of certain inanimate objects and substances as animable by that agency. Variations in details, including the degree of independence of the image, the number of manifestations, the associations between the deities and the locations, and the types of materials used, are all products of diverse reflective considerations taking place within different socio-material ecologies.[11] What is consistent is the intuitive perception of agency as communicable and of personhood as partible and permeable. These intuitions need not be explicitly manifested in praxis or in reflective rationalizations of that praxis in order for them to be influential, of course. Related rituals and conceptualizations of enlivened statues from other societies around the world and down to the present time demonstrate the transcultural and transhistorical intuitiveness of this approach to unseen agency. These conceptualizations do not stand in contrast or contradiction to intuitive notions of human personhood and agency but rather represent more flexible and dynamic elaborations on both (*contra* Sommer 2009: 195 n.145). The general intuitiveness and broad consistency of these conceptualizations across ancient Southwest Asia, along with significant overlap in rituals and traditions associated with deity, support the preliminary application of the same conceptual frameworks to the interrogation of the way divine bodies were formed in Iron Age Israel and Judah.

Forming bodies in Iron Age Israel and Judah

Although we have no direct attestation of prescriptions for animating rituals in the material remains from the regions inhabited by Iron Age Israel and Judah, there is a rich tradition in the region of materially representing and presencing deity that reaches back into Neolithic periods. In the Bronze and Iron Ages, this tradition drew from the same conventions and intuitive concepts of personhood and deity which were circulating in the surrounding cultures.[12] Finds from Iron I–IIA that depict

---

10 A similar 'opening the mouth' ritual is attested in a range of Egyptian texts. Its full name was 'Performing the Opening of the Mouth in the Workshop for the Statue of PN', but it could also be referred to as the 'Opening of the Mouth and the Eyes' or just 'Opening of the Mouth' (*wpt-r* or *wn-r*). See further Roth (1992); McDowell (2015: 85–109). For a comparison of the Mesopotamian and Egyptian rituals, see McDowell (2015: 109–15). There is also a relevant Hittite text from the late fifteenth or early fourteenth century BCE that prescribes an eight- or nine-day regimen for commissioning a satellite cult installation for the 'Deity of the Night' (here the goddess Pirinkir); see further Beal (2002); Miller (2004: 259–311); Beckman (2010: 80–5). The process for installing the deity is long and complex, but on the fifth day, before leaving the old temple behind, the text in section 22 prescribes the following utterance: 'Honoured deity! Preserve your being, but divide your divinity! Come to that new house, too, and take yourself the honoured place!' (translation is from Miller 2004: 290). Niehr (1997: 78) notes related features of some Phoenician and Aramaic inscriptions: 'After a Phoenician temple had been built or restored, the divine statue had to be erected in the sanctuary. This is referred to with the phrase "I/we caused the deity to dwell in it" (*yšb yiphil*)'.
11 The question of whether or not the image is a 'full' or 'partial' deity would have emerged situationally and would have been addressed within the relevant rhetorical contexts. There is no need to impose a systematic ontology onto the discussion.
12 According to Keel and Uehlinger (1998: §§ IV–V), the material representation of deity in the highlands in the Late Bronze Age reflected heavy Egyptian influence, particularly in the prevalence of enthroned male Egyptian deities, and especially those who represented political domination and war. Bull imagery was particularly prominent, but while in earlier periods it could represent either fecundity or ferocity, by the Iron Age, it almost exclusively reflected the latter. The role of the goddess was diminished in Egypt, but southern Levantine artisans appear to have carried on a simplified version of a popular 'naked goddess' motif through the production of

deity include stelae, metal statuary (usually from earlier periods), objects in stone, terracotta cult stands, model shrines, shrine-plaques, anthropomorphic terracotta vessels and figurines, worship scenes depicted on seals and depictions of deity in or on clay (Uehlinger 1997: 102–12). Metal statuary depicting male deities does not appear to have been produced – or at least not widely – from the tenth century BCE onwards, which has been taken as a sign of programmatic aniconism, but is more likely a shift in preference governed by the markets and available resources. As Tryggve Mettinger (1995) convincingly argues, Israel and Judah were initially simply carrying on a '*de facto* aniconism' that had long been current throughout the broader West Semitic cultural milieu. This aniconism was not 'the result of theological reflection. Instead, it must be seen as an inherited convention of religious expression which only later formed the basis for theological reflection' (Mettinger 1995: 195). The more widespread use of symbols and substitute entities during this period suggests that a need for the cultic image to approximate the ostensible appearance of the deity itself was no longer especially salient (if it ever was). The priority was presencing the deity, not looking like it (cf. Ornan 2004).

While some of the depictions mentioned above may have had primarily commemoratory or dedicatory functions, many would have been widely understood to presence the deity or channel/transmit divine or otherwise supernatural agency, particularly if erected in a public setting and assigned a specific socio-material role in the functioning of the society. Such depictions no doubt represented a spectrum of deities running the gamut from deceased kin to socially concerned high deities. Among social elites, ancestral connections may have been asserted for those high deities. The archaeological bias towards the state and its elites has weighted our data overwhelmingly in favour of the few deities who predominated on a national or dynastic level, of course, so little may be said about the more private and personal end of that spectrum of deities. Naturally, there will be more variability in the depictions of deity utilized privately by individuals in family units, as they generally do not answer to broader prosocial forces.

Several considerations support interpreting stelae in Iron Age Israel and Judah as having functioned as divine 'bodies', presencing whichever deities they indexed.[13] The word מצבה, meaning 'stood up' or 'erected', reflects the upright orientation of the stones, which stand out within the environment, indicating intentionality and agency to viewers. Given its durability, stone was also likely perceived as one of the more suitable materials for hosting the agency of the deceased/divine. Unworked stone may have boasted the additional feature of a more natural state (perhaps the state in which a deity left it), rather than one forced on the stone by human industry. Flat stones placed horizontally before stelae to function as offering tables suggest rituals similar to those performed for the deceased were likely performed for the deities the stelae indexed (Garfinkel, Ganor

---

much more inexpensive terracotta plaques. The effacement of Egyptian influence meant the similar withdrawal of the wealth and markets it facilitated, so locally produced plaques, statuettes, stelae and cult stands became less expertly and more inexpensively produced. By Iron Age I, the fertility aspects of the divine were depicted primarily through symbols and 'substitute entities' like a tree, a scorpion or a suckling mother animal; see Keel and Uehlinger (1998: 128).

13 In addition to the well-known stelae at Arad, Iron Age stelae have been found in cult installations and other contexts in Tel Dan, Hazor, Bethsaida, Lachish, Tirzah, Tel Reḥov, Beth-Shemesh, Tel Qiri, Timna, Shechem, Khirbet Qeiyafa and in other locations. See further Mettinger (1995: 149–68); Bloch-Smith (2015: 100); Zukerman (2012: 41–3); Herring (2013: 53–63); Garfinkel, Ganor and Hasel (2018: 131–4).

and Hasel 2018: 131–2).¹⁴ For instance, two open air sanctuaries at Hazor dating to the eleventh century BCE prominently featured stelae and included cultic assemblages; the stele at Area A was surrounded by three offering tables (Ben-Ami 2006: 123–7). At Khirbet Qeiyafa, three tenth-century BCE cult rooms featuring stelae were discovered. Room J in Building D and Room G in Building C3 each featured large stelae with stone offering tables at their bases and benches adjacent to them (Garfinkel, Ganor and Hasel 2018: 134–46).¹⁵ The former appears to have been a public cult installation, while the latter was found among a row of houses and may have been private. Similar private installations dating to the end of the second millennium BCE have been found at Lachish and Tel-Qiri (Zukerman 2012; Garfinkel, Ganor and Hasel 2018: 144–5).¹⁶ A ninth century BCE open air sanctuary is known from Tel Reḥov that featured a raised platform with two stelae, an offering table, a pottery altar and a large number of animal bones (Mazar 2015: 27–8). The offering of food and the ritual sharing of meals before these stelae suggest the presence and participation of the entities they indexed.

Another consideration is the terminology used in comparative texts to refer to stelae. In addition to the upright and intentional posture of a מצבה, the Ugaritic and Akkadian words for 'stele' (*skn* and *si-ik-ka-num*) appear to derive from a verbal root meaning 'to inhabit' (Durand 1985; Dietrich, Loretz, and Mayer 1989; van der Toorn 1997a; Fleming 2000: 82–7; Hundley 2013: 356–8; Yasur-Landau 2016; Scheyhing 2018). This terminology resonates with Jacob's designation of a stele he sets up and anoints with oil as the בית־אלהים ('house of God') in Gen. 28.22. Anointing with oil likely represented a commissioning of sorts (cf. Gen. 35.14-15), although significantly (and perhaps deliberately)¹⁷ less elaborate than the complex rituals of Mesopotamia and Egypt.¹⁸ The shortened form, בית־אל, would later become a designation for 'stele' that would be adapted in Greek as βαίτυλος, 'betyl'. By the seventh century BCE, Assyrian sources identify a West Semitic deity named Bethel who also appears in later Aramaic and Greek texts (Sommer 2009: 28–9). In his first century CE *Phoenician History* (preserved in Eusebius' *Preparation for the Gospel*), Philo of Byblos describes betyls as λίθοι ἔμψυχοι, 'enlivened stones' (Baumgarten 1981: 16). The concept of the divine animation of stelae enjoyed wide circulation around ancient Southwest Asia.

The model shrine may have been another means of divine embodiment and presencing in ancient Southwest Asia. These shrines have been discovered at many ancient sites in Israel/Palestine, including Dan, Tel Rekhesh, Tel Reḥov, Tirzah, Megiddo, Jerusalem and Khirbet Qeiyafa (Zevit 2001: 328–43; Mazar and Panitz-Cohen 2008; Garfinkel and Mumcuoglu 2015; Mazar 2015: 36–8; Garfinkel, Ganor and Hasel 2018: 146–55). Temples were not as scarce in Iron Age Israel and Judah as previously thought, but the

---

14 According to Mettinger (1995: 191–2), stelae functioned primarily to facilitate sacrifices and shared communal meals. Note the communal meal mentioned in Exod. 24.11 after the elders of Israel 'saw the God of Israel' (יראו את אלהי ישראל). Smith (2008: 58–61) elaborates on the importance of the communal meal to covenant ritual.
15 A recently excavated Judahite temple from Tel Moza features a room near the entrance with five stelae at the base of a bench. See Kisilevitz (2015: 51).
16 In Zevit (2001: 123) and Hitchcock (2011), these installations are designated 'cult corners'.
17 Some already suspect certain idiosyncrasies were adopted as identity markers to distinguish Israel and Judah from the societies surrounding them, and this certainly may have been an additional way to distinguish themselves in their relationship to their deity/deities.
18 Sommer (2009: 49) rhetorically asks, 'Is it possible that, in these passages, anointing transforms the stele and thus functions in a manner comparable to the *mīs pî* ritual in Mesopotamia?' As he notes in a footnote (2009: 207 n.67), several midrashim insist the oil that anointed these stelae came down directly from heaven, which is reminiscent of the insistence at the end of the Mesopotamian ritual that the statue was not made by human hands.

discovery of model shrines in a variety of contexts suggests there was a desire to localize or perhaps mobilize the access to the divine that temples were thought to facilitate. Following patterns found in surrounding cultures, they were usually modelled from clay (sometimes stone), had large openings flanked by pillars, held doors at one time and included space likely intended for the placement of a figurine or some representation of a deity, whether anthropomorphic or otherwise, or iconic or not (Garfinkel, Ganor and Hasel 2018: 146–55). This interpretation is supported by the discovery of a Middle Bronze IIB clay model shrine in Ashkelon that housed a bronze calf figurine covered in silver plating, as well as by carved ivory representations of receding frames around a royal or divine woman's face (Stager 2008; Garfinkel, Ganor and Hasel 2018: 152). The reification of a temple's sacred space may have been a means of (1) facilitating fuller access to divine agency; (2) allowing the image to be carried in processions throughout the community; or (3) 'democratizing' access to temple worship. The use of clay and stone may reflect the perception that both 'natural' substances are efficient or effective means of channelling unseen agency.

The Taanach cult stand, dated to the tenth century BCE, likely overlapped in function with model shrines, although it is not prototypical of them (Hestrin 1987; Beck 1994; Keel and Uehlinger 1998: 169–79). The terracotta stand features four vertically arranged friezes that (beginning from the bottom) depict (1) a nude female with outstretched arms touching the ears of lions on either side of her; (2) cherubim-type figures on each side of a gap or empty space; (3) a stylized tree with feeding caprids flanked by lions; and (4) a horse below a sun disc, flanked by outward-facing volutes.[19] Above the top register is a row of clay circles likely representing roof beams. The four registers may vertically arrange the rooms of the shrine, rather than depict concentric entryways ('recessed doorframes') surrounding the image in the inner sanctuary, as in other model shrines (Garfinkel and Mumcuoglu 2015). If this is the case, the empty space between the cherubim may represent the entrance to the shrine (rather than aniconically signalling YHWH's presence between הכרבים, 'the cherubim', as in Exod. 25.22 and other biblical texts).

Brian Doak (2015: 129) contends that several observations support interpreting the stand as entirely devoted to a goddess. First, the clearest indications of the stand's referent are the bottom and third friezes, which depict a female deity anthropomorphically and as a tree. The other two friezes contain the empty space – likely representing the entryway – and the equid underneath the sun disc. Next, the equid is used predominantly to represent Anat and Astarte, as noted by Izak Cornelius (2008: 40–5) as well as Othmar Keel and Christoph Uehlinger (1998: 160), who also note that Early Iron Age terracotta figures predominantly represent female agents.[20] The multiple manifestations of the goddess may have been intended to represent the iconography of the different rooms of the temple and her manifestations within them, or to increase the accessibility or compound the potency of her agency. Model shrines were generally too elaborate for widespread private use, but

---

19 There has been some debate about these representations, and particularly regarding the animal in the upper register. Early interpreters understood it as a bull, perhaps as a result of the interpretation of the stand as Yahwistic in orientation. On the protective role of the naked female and her attendant animals on cult stands, see Darby (2014: 330–8).
20 Darby (2014: 333) also notes that 'almost every cult stand combines female figurines with zoomorphic images'. The fifty-seven clay figurines and zoomorphic vessels discovered at Tel Reḥov further support this observation. Almost half of the figures were anthropomorphic, and almost all were female, while nearly a third of the twenty-nine zoomorphic figurines and vessels depicted equids. See Mazar (2015: 38–9).

their use in local cult installations could increase access to the agency of the (primarily female) deities they indexed for those living nearby.

Forming divine bodies in the Hebrew Bible

The authors and editors of the Hebrew Bible usually downplayed the significance of presencing media, especially to the degree that the media in question overlapped with the practices of surrounding societies, and particularly those that socioculturally competed directly with Israel and Judah. That does not mean that the biblical writers unilaterally rejected the efficacy or appropriateness of presencing media; rather, it means they curated a very specific set of what were considered sanctioned means of forming divine bodies. In what follows, I will outline a trajectory towards the rhetorical compartmentalization of the deity from the loci of their agency. In other words, whereas Israel and Judah's earliest cultic objects functioned in many ways as divine 'bodies', as time progressed and cultic authority became more and more centralized, those authorities began to assert the deity's primary location elsewhere, even as they asserted the deity's ability to be presenced to some degree through accessible material media. We might frame this development as a process not only of subordinating and demoting presencing media but also of 'democratizing' access to that media.

Perhaps the most iconic of sanctioned icons in the Hebrew Bible is the ark of the covenant. In form and function, the ark closely parallels divine images from broader ancient Southwest Asia. Some biblical texts describe it as a container for the law, which resonates with the Mesopotamian convention of presenting treaties to divine images for their approval and enforcement. David Aaron (2001: 172–5) has highlighted a unique construction in Exod. 25.16, 21 related to the ark's relationship to the testimony (העדת). Rather than employing the conventional בארון, '*in* the ark' (Deut. 10.2, 5; 1 Kgs 8.9), these passages command Moses to 'give' (√נתן) the testimony אל הארן, '*to* the ark', which complements the practice of placing treaties *before* the divine image. The language is just fuzzy enough to be reinterpreted in harmony with the Deuteronom(ist)ic constructions, especially if much of the audience were unfamiliar with the technical sense of the phrase, and so it may have escaped excising editorial hands accustomed to removing other language that more explicitly framed the ark as a Yahwistic cult image.

As a container, the ark is also analogous to the portable model shrine. The storage of these shrines in cult rooms parallels the ark's storage in the cella of the tabernacle/temple, and their portability likely facilitated their use in processions, including before military forces, which would match the function of the ark in texts such as Josh. 6.4-11 and 1 Sam. 14.18. In ancient Egypt, model shrines often took the form of boats that carried the divine image within a canopied throne. Some were even flanked by winged entities reminiscent of cherubim (Noegel 2015). The more the divine image was embedded within material relationships that evoked divinity and the themes and imagery of ritual, the more strongly the image could be perceived to presence deity. These variations on the same theme were meant for the transportation of a small-scale divine image within an object that could reify sacred space. If the image was to permanently remain in the cella or cult room, the secondary reification of that sacred space would have been redundant. There is no need for a small-scale reproduction of sacred space that remains embedded within sacred space – the model shrine was intended to render the divine image portable.

The biblical texts nowhere explicitly mention an anthropomorphic image associated with the ark, although its conceptualizations as a throne and even as a footstool evoke concepts of an enthroned person and fits with Southwest Asian conventions regarding divine images. A wall relief from the Nimrud palace of Tiglath-pileser III (745–727 BCE) depicts a procession of deities taken from a conquered cult precinct (BM 118931). Three of the deities are unambiguously anthropomorphic (with two sitting upon thrones), but one depicts what appears to be a box sitting on a throne, with what may be a small hand, grasping a ring, protruding from the front of the box. This may depict a model shrine carrying a small divine image. An anthropomorphic image is not necessarily required, however, for a throne or footstool to function as presencing media. Offerings to thrones and other items of cultic furniture are known from Akkadian ritual instruction texts. One such text from the neo-Babylonian period includes the directive that twelve loaves of bread are to be prepared for the 'Throne of Anu' (Porter 2009: 155–6). The standard and the footstool of Shamash also had mouth-opening rituals performed for them at Mari (Walker and Dick 2001: 12).

At the same time, there is some biblical evidence that non-anthropomorphic statuary presenced the deity within the ark. It is not an enormous conceptual leap to link the tablets of the law with cultic stelae, particularly in the light of the command to write the words of the law upon cultic stelae in Deut. 27.1-10 and Josh. 8.32, 34-35 (Stavrakopoulou 2013). In Exodus 32 (P), the tablets of the law are also rhetorically cast as the authorized alternative to the golden calf – they are a divinely sanctioned medium for divine presencing. Both types of entity function as a cultic image in different ways. For instance, the golden calf and the stone tablets make use of materials traditionally associated with the divine. The divine production of the text of the tablets is emphasized in Exod. 32.16, while Aaron asserts in v. 24 that the golden calf just 'came out' of the fire, as if it were not the work of human production. A critical distinction is Aaron's assertion that the calf actually presences the locus of the deity's identity: 'These are your deities, O Israel!' (Exod. 32.4). This stands in contrast to the treatment of the tablets as a secondary divine agent.

If figurines such as the small bronze bull discovered near Dothan – likely associated with a model shrine – and the miniature anthropomorphic statue that may be jutting its hand out from the enthroned box in the Tiglath-pileser III relief are representative of the kind of media used in conjunction with model shrines, those media could have been miniature versions of full-scale divine images used in larger sites. The most explicit examples we have of full-scale divine icons used in an Israelite/Judahite cultic site are the stelae that were located in the cella of the Arad temple. We have already seen that such stelae were ubiquitous across the regions inhabited by ancient Israel and Judah, and the biblical texts are replete with references to cultic stelae, so they are very likely to have been broadly representative of the type of divine image employed in Israel and Judah. Tablets would very easily function as miniature stelae, and here the presencing function of cultic objects and of text converge (Watts 2016). The significance of this will be discussed further below, but given the ubiquity of stelae in and around Israel and Judah, and the general paucity of anthropomorphic statuary, the ark may have functioned at some point as a portable model shrine housing one or more stelae that presenced the deity or the deity and a consort. By the time of the work of the Deuteronomist, this function seems to have given way to other conceptualizations that still served to presence the deity without appealing to more conventional imagery associated with cultic objects.

Some of the clearest biblical indicators that the ark functioned to reify the presence of YHWH is the use of the phrase לפני יהוה, 'before YHWH', in connection with the location of the ark. In the Hebrew Bible, this is a technical construction that reflects appearance before a cultic object and/or within a cultic installation such as the Jerusalem temple. For example, in 2 Sam. 6.5, 14-16, David and all the house of Israel were משחקים לפני יהוה, 'dancing before YHWH', while they travelled with the ark towards Jerusalem. In a slight twist on that formula, Josh. 7.6 describes Joshua tearing his clothes and falling down on his face לפני ארון יהוה, 'before the ark of YHWH'. The Septuagint omits 'ark' (as it also does in Josh. 6.13). 2 Samuel 6.2 even states that the ark is נקרא שם שם יהוה צבאות, 'called by the name, the name of YHWH of hosts'. Deuteronomy 10.8 describes the tribe of Levi as being set apart to לשאת את־ארון ברית־יהוה לעמד לפני יהוה לשרתו ולברך בשמו עד היום הזה, 'carry the ark of the covenant of YHWH, to stand before YHWH to minister to him, and to bless in his name, until this day'. As Anne Knafl (2014: 131) explains, 'By carrying the ark, the Levites stand before YHWH and there minister to him.' Like the fire out of which YHWH spoke to Israel in Deut. 4. 12, 15, the ark does not necessarily reify the single and sole locus of the deity's very identity, but it does function as an extension of the deity's agency, thereby intuitively presencing the deity.

The ark likely functioned as a divine 'body' throughout its existence, even if its specific conceptualization as such was manipulated in the service of structuring power.[21] The ark narrative in 1 Samuel 4–6 makes use of the abandonment motif to assert the severability of the deity's agency from the ark and to account for the loss of the ark to the Philistines (pinning the blame on the wickedness of the sons of Eli), but (*pace* Sommer 2009: 101–7) this does not remotely approximate the outright rejection of any and all presencing facilities on the part of the ark. Instead, the data support a more nuanced renegotiation of the deity's relationship to the temple and its cultic accoutrements that compartmentalized the loci of both the deity's identity and the deity's agency. The ark remained a medium for, or extension of, YHWH's power and agency, even as it was decoupled or distanced from the main locus of the deity's identity. Deuteronomy 4 even more explicitly lays out this rhetorical agenda in explaining that although YHWH's voice was heard from the fire, there was no form seen because YHWH was located in the heavens. While still in some sense one of YHWH's 'bodies', the ark and the fire are subordinated and made secondary vehicles of YHWH's agency.

By the time these texts were written and in circulation, however, the ark was no longer extant. The weakening of the isometry of YHWH and the ark served several rhetorical functions vis-à-vis that absence. By presenting the (now absent) ark as a

---

21 In his 2009 monograph on divine bodies, Sommer argues that the presentation of the ark in 1 Samuel 4–6, and particularly its failure to secure victory for Israel at Ebenezer, demonstrates a rejection of the 'fluidity' model he constructs to account for the capacity for different material media to presence the deity (2009: 99–107). Rather than flatly deny the presencing power of the ark, however, it is more likely that the ark's apparent failure in battle is intended to highlight YHWH's abandonment of the ark in light of the wickedness of Eli's sons. Sommer acknowledges this rhetorical option in his discussion of divine fluidity in Mesopotamia, but it is not addressed discussing this narrative: 'The ṣalmu ... was itself a god, assimilated into the heavenly god yet physically a distinct thing that could lose its divine status at any moment, should the deity choose to abandon it' (2009: 23). Given the fact that communities in Mesopotamia could acknowledge the abandonment of the ṣalmu without rejecting the entire concept of divine fluidity (as Sommer himself discusses at 2009: 21–2), there is little reason to accept that the ark's failure to secure a victory indicates a rejection of the very ideology present in the latter half of the narrative (and for which Sommer is at pains to account). On the abandonment motif, see Cogan (1974: 9–21); Kutsko (2000: 104–23); Block (2000: 114–26); Holloway (2002: 54–5). The destruction of the temple at the hands of the Babylonians is also framed in terms of divine abandonment in Ezekiel.

uniquely situated medium for the deity's agency, the authors/editors of Deuteronomy and the Deuteronomistic literature limited the other available objects of potential worship, perhaps to mitigate the risk of other divine images replacing the ark. YHWH's abandonment of the ark was also a more favourable outcome than the deity's wilful self-exile to the sacred precinct of whichever empire absconded with it; it allowed for the assertion of YHWH's remaining with worshippers. The authoritative knowledge these rationalizations helped to codify not only served immediate rhetorical needs but also created new conceptual relationships that would have to be renegotiated as the corpus of Israel and Judah's authoritative texts began to take shape.[22]

One of the more significant of these conceptual relationships related to the presencing of the deity in the absence of the ark. Jeremiah 3.16-17 dismisses the significance of the ark and prophetically expands the purview of the Jerusalem temple beyond its physical existence to the point that the city itself is recast in the role of the ark as the throne of YHWH. Ezekiel 1 and 10 do not mention the ark, but similarly shatter the confines of the physical temple, envisioning a portable cherubim throne on which the deity travelled. Isaiah 66.1 further expands the rhetoric about the deity's purview, casting the heavens as the deity's throne and the earth as the footstool. While this rhetoric allowed authors to rationalize the loss of the Jerusalem temple while exalting the deity further, there remained a need to be able to focus the ritual/cultic attention of the people and still provide for the presencing of the deity among the people, particularly as the deity became increasingly transcendent. What better way to do this than to replace the ark as the loci of immanent divine presence with the very contents it was said to house: the Torah and the divine name that the Torah bore?

This role for the Torah (and more specifically the discrete lists of the deity's apodictic and casuistic laws) represents a significant innovation, within Judah, on the use of text to presence deity. This did not originate here, of course. According to Nathaniel Levtow (2012: 311), as far back as the third millennium BCE, 'text production was a ritualized activity that embodied divine and human subjects in textual form'. Deuteronomy 27.1-10 helpfully illustrates the way this innovation might have been implemented in ancient Israel/Judah. This text describes instructions given by Moses and the elders of Israel to erect (קוּם√) large stones, plaster them and write upon them the words of the Torah (likely an early law code later incorporated into Deuteronomy). They are then to construct an altar of unhewn stones, offer burnt offerings to YHWH and share a communal meal while rejoicing לפני יהוה אלהיך, 'before YHWH, your deity'. According to v. 9, this ritual process (which makes no mention of an oral recitation or a requirement to read the text)[23] facilitates their becoming the 'people of YHWH' (עם יהוה). The features of this ritual act combine wider cultural conventions of sealing treaties with traditional acts of communal worship before divine images. The use of the לפני יהוה formula indicates the stelae's presencing of the deity's agency, which was most likely reified through the divinely given words of the covenant that were written on the stones. These words would have included the deity's first-person speech and numerous iterations of the divine name. Writing the text on the stones may thus be thought of as sacralizing or commissioning the object,

---

22 For a fascinating discussion of how the ubiquity of abducted divine images may have undermined neo-Assyria's traditional conceptualization of the relationship of cult statues to their deities, see Richardson (2012).
23 It is not until Deut. 31.11 that the Sinai event is re-enacted with the reading of the entire law. See also Josh. 8.30-35, which has Joshua writing the law on the stones (apparently of the altar) and then reciting every last word before the Israelites. Cf. Schaper (2007).

endowing it with the divine agency previously facilitated by anointing, incantations and/or other ritual. As noted by Francesca Stavrakopoulou (2013: 228), 'The narrator appears less concerned with the specifics of the "message" of Torah than with the performance of writing and other rituals … it is the material manifestation of Torah that is of central concern in this passage'.

This biblical passage does not polemicize or prohibit the material presencing of deity so much as constrain the accessible and reproducible media for that presencing. By requiring the imposition of the text of the covenant upon the generic stelae, the Deuteronomist did not invalidate cultic objects but restricted the production of and access to sanctioned cultic objects to those who were literate and/or could access the text of the Torah.[24] The only such groups in this early phase of the Torah's existence were the elite scribal classes who produced that text under the purview of their cultic authorities.[25]

Also significant are the prescriptions outlined in Exod. 13.9, 16 and Deut. 6.6-9; 11.18-21, which are widely understood to be Achaemenid period compositions. These passages command the people to recite the words of the covenant to their children, to discuss them at home and abroad, to bind them as a sign upon their hands and as 'emblems' between their eyes[26] and to write them on their doorposts and gates. Here the text of the Torah is integrated into practices associated with inscribed amulets. The words of the law themselves have become salient, but still only insofar as they are both oralized and materially present (Schaper 2007: 14–16).[27] Stelae were marginalized within the scribal community by this time, but the words themselves, independent of their media, were not yet authoritative – the need for and the rhetorical utility of the material mediation of the law remained (cf. Polaski 2007).

There is a sense in which the promiscuous presencing of the words of the deity democratized access that had frequently been restricted in earlier periods, perhaps for some even privatizing the temple/cult site experience. By reframing that presence in terms of the Torah instead of the deity, however, the goal also (or rather) appears to have been to extend the centralized cult's reach out into the diaspora, transferring the people's socio-material focus away from YHWH and onto the scribal class' institutional

---

24 I use 'and/or' to reflect the reality that even those who could not read could recognize writing or even identify some words – especially those widely understood to be powerful. A person who could not read could conceivably reproduce a crude version of the Torah by copying the shapes, but they would still need some kind of access to it. Sanders (2019) finds that the inclusion of memorial inscriptions on mortuary stelae (and specifically inscriptions that presenced the dead and demanded their feeding) was an innovation of the early Iron Age in the West Semitic world.

25 Note Stavrakopoulou (2013: 234): 'In robust materialist perspective, socio-religious and economic power is thus held by those who literally and literarily hold Torah – to the exclusion of those who do not and cannot participate in the textuality of the covenant.' Another text, Josh. 24.25-27, reflects a similar renegotiation of the relationship of text and cult but employs the motifs differently (cf. Stavrakopoulou 2013: 229). There the words of the deity are materially manifested on a scroll rather than a stele, but that scroll is immediately backgrounded as a stele is erected to monitor the people's commitment to the covenant into which they have ritually entered. Again, pre-existing conventions of divine presencing are adopted to this textualization of the deity's words, even as those conventions are renegotiated to fit the new paradigm. The stone does not so much presence the deity as function as an independent agent, having heard the words of the deity and having witnessed the people's entry into the covenant. Functionally, the stone acts as a 'witness' by reminding viewers of the covenant, but its presence alone is enough to reify a sense of unseen monitoring, whether or not it was identified with a specific unseen agent.

26 I use 'emblems' here to gloss טוטפת. The word is unattested in the Hebrew Bible outside of these verses but may have indicated some kind of adornment for the head. See further Tigay (1982); Cohn (2008: 33–53).

27 The word traditionally translated 'meditate' in Josh. 1.8 (√הגה) means to read in an undertone or to mutter, not to silently ponder.

purview: the Torah. As with the passages discussed above, the words of the text itself were not the primary focus; rather, that focus was the material carrier of the text. At the beginning of this trajectory towards the textualization of divine presencing, the text either accompanied or was overlaid upon an existing means of materially presencing a deity, but the larger and more conspicuous of those means (such as stelae) were largely phased out by the Achaemenid period. This would leave smaller amulets and other adornments that had not fallen victim to priestly proscription, such as seals or the Ketef Hinnom amulets, to become the sacralized material bearers of the Torah and, just as significantly (if not more so), the divine name (cf. Schmid 2012).

The first-person voice of much of the Torah introduces an additional dynamic associated with divine presencing. Biblical traditions suggest the 'first' iterations of the Torah were written in the first person – even by YHWH's own finger – reflecting the deity's own voice and intuitively conjuring for the reader some concept of the speaker. This was likely in imitation of wider, developing conventions regarding monumental inscriptions (Hogue 2019c). Across multiple publications, Seth Sanders has promulgated the theory that monumental inscriptions not only served to mark property and memorialize socio-materially significant space, but also – by the time first-person narrative began to appear on alphabetic memorial inscriptions – to 'ventriloquize' the author (see especially Sanders 2008, 2010). While Sanders focuses on the Mesha Stele as one of the earliest examples,[28] a helpful example for the present discussion is the Katumuwa inscription, whose owner declares in the first line:

1 ʾnk.ktmw.ʿbd.pnmw.zy.qnt.ly.nṣb.b.
2 ḥyy ....
1 I am Katumuwa, servant of Panamuwa, who created[29] this stele for myself during
2 my life.

This first-person speech is intended to presence the agency of the deceased. According to Timothy Hogue (2019a: 200), 'It was the materialization of Katumuwa's presence and agency so that he might interact with future users of the monument.' In the absence of a son to erect a mortuary stele for him, Absalom is said in 2 Sam. 18.18 to have erected his own stele, which could well evoke an inscribed monument written in first-person speech. Seth Sanders (2012: 35) distinguishes first-person mortuary inscriptions from earlier iterations: 'The new inscriptions and monuments actually speak on behalf of the dead and make demands for themselves. They are designed to produce the presence of the dead and demand their feeding' (cf. Radner 2005: 114–55).

Compare such first-person speech to the opening line of the Decalogue: אנכי יהוה אלהיך אשר הוצאתיך מארץ מצרים מבית עבדים, 'I am YHWH, your deity, who brought you up from the land of Egypt, from the house of slavery' (Exod. 20.2). Whether read or heard, the agency of the deity is essentially made present by the first-person voice of the text. As Timothy Hogue explains,

---

28 See Sanders (2010: 114):

The stela of Mesha is the first known alphabetic inscription to address an audience in the first-person voice of the king. It presents a man who claims, in Moabite, to be the king of Moab. The shift in participants from earlier alphabetic royal inscriptions is decisive. The inscription now designates itself by the speaker, not the object. No longer '(this is) *the stela* which Mesha set up' but '*I am* Mesha, son of Kemoashyat, King of Moab, the Dibonite'. The inscription presents royal power by making the king present in language, ventriloquizing Mesha as if he were standing in front of us.

29 I have followed Hogue (2019a) in understanding the verb *qny* to reflect creation in certain contexts. Hogue bases his argument on the conventions of Luwian monumental inscriptions.

> The result is an imagined encounter with the projected speaker implied by the pronoun 'I'. This process of deictic projection thus conjures a speaker – reembodying them in the imagination of the audience. The opening line of the Decalogue – 'I am Yahweh' – is not a prosaic statement nor even a mere adaptation of royal monumental rhetoric. This statement actually produces the presence of Yahweh in the minds of the readers and hearers of the text. It is a theophany condensed into a formula. (Hogue 2019b: 11)

As the very first words of the law given by YHWH, these would have been the first words written, according to Exod. 31.18, on the tablets of stone given to Moses. This text also states the words were written with the deity's own finger, distinguishing the tablets from the golden calf, which in this particular version of the tradition is an unauthorized cult image produced by human hands rather than by a deity (cf. Exod. 32.15-16; Deut. 9.8-21).[30] In this way, the tablets of the Torah evince significant overlap with more traditional media for divine presencing. Humanity's role in the production of the tablets is also denied through the narrative which asserts their heavenly origins, in line with the authorized cult statues of surrounding cultures (cf. Parmenter 2009). As miniature stelae inscribed with the divine name and the words of the Torah, the tablets are functionally identical to the cultic stelae of Deuteronomy 27 and able to facilitate worship 'before YHWH'. The original objects (the narratives alternate between clay tablets or small stelae) were thus created by the deity, contained words written by the deity and spoke in the first person as the deity, combining multiple conventions of the production of divine images with those of monumental inscriptions to indicate the Torah's capacity to presence the deity. The later commandments to write the Torah (in whatever iteration) upon or before stelae reflect variations on this same theme: the agency of the deity is appropriately made present in the reading, hearing or even just the presence of the Torah.[31]

In later religious practice, the treatment of the divine name and texts bearing the divine name further attest to its conceptualization as a species of presencing media. The Jerusalem temple had been rebuilt in the late sixth century BCE, but the Torah was now presented as an equally powerful locus of divine presencing, and legal authorities were in no hurry to relinquish the access to, and influence over, divine agency their stewardship of the texts afforded them. Throughout the Second Temple period, Yahwistic theophoric elements were appearing less frequently in personal names, likely out of reverence for, and avoidance of saying aloud, the Tetragrammaton.[32] In a sense, avoiding writing or pronouncing the divine name in common circumstances evinced a desire not to invoke the deity's presence in 'profane' contexts.[33]

---

30 In Exod. 32.19, Moses goes on to shatter these tablets, but in 34.1, YHWH commands Moses to carve two new tablets, on which YHWH will again write the words of the Torah. According to 34.28, however, Moses writes on the tablets.

31 See Watts (2016: 21): 'the Pentateuch was shaped to lay the basis for Torah scrolls to replace the ark of the covenant as the iconic focus of Israel's worship'. Cf. Schniedewind (2009: 78–9).

32 See Schniedewind (2009: 75): 'By the end of the Second Temple period these names will have disappeared completely, corresponding to the increasing reverence for the Tetragrammaton that is evident in the late Second Temple period.'

33 This reverence for the texts bearing the divine name is demonstrated by practical observances associated with their transcription. For example, nearly thirty of the Dead Sea Scrolls manuscripts were written in the square Aramaic script, but represented the Tetragrammaton in a palaeo-Hebrew script. In many cases, scribes left gaps in the transcription where the divine name was to appear, and more senior scribes would come through later and

By the time of the destruction of the Second Temple in 70 CE, an authoritative corpus of literature was taking firmer shape, and Jewish authorities were once again wrestling with accessing divine agency through text and in the absence of temple literature. The form and function of the Torah and other authoritative texts became a focal point of early rabbinic literature, at which point standardized guidance began to come into clearer focus. The oft-quoted guiding principle from this period was the final clause from the opening passage of the Mishnaic tractate *Pirqe Avot*, which reflects the conceptualization of the Torah as reifying sacred space: 'make a fence around the Torah'. In the Mishnah's *Yadayim* 4.5, biblical texts are not said to 'defile the hands' unless and until 'they are written in the Assyrian script, on parchment, and in ink'.[34] The Talmud lays out further prescriptions regarding the preparation of the parchment from appropriate animal skins, the production of the scrolls themselves (codices were not adequate)[35] and their handling. Marianne Schleicher (2010: 14) describes these conventions as 'projecting a status of holy *axis mundi* onto the Torah scroll. ... In line with this conception, the Torah is even referred to as God's temple (*mikdashyah*) in medieval writings.' The sixteenth-century legal code *Shulkhan Arukh* even requires uttering the following statement out loud before beginning to write a Torah scroll: 'I have the intent to write the holy name' (*Shulkhan Arukh*, 'Yoreh Deah', 276). For Schleicher (2010: 15), this indicates that 'every Jew writing a scroll had to remind himself of its numinosity and thereby contribute to the maintenance of the status of the Torah as a holy artifact'. These practices have clear conceptual parallels to the preparation and installation of cultic statues (cf. van der Toorn 1997b).

Conclusion

In ancient Israel and Judah, divine bodies were conceptualized as partible and permeable. As a result, the loci of divine agency and identity were perceived as communicable via a variety of material media. The means of their production for immediate access by human agents do not represent significant departures from those of the larger empires that surrounded ancient Israel and Judah. Rather, they represent incremental innovations on shared conventions that likely came in reaction and response to rhetorical exigencies within specific social and cognitive ecologies. The much smaller and more limited markets of Israel and Judah did not require or particularly allow for elaborate rituals and expensive anthropomorphic statuary, but on a smaller and simpler scale, YHWH and other deities were still made accessible for authorities and devotees through stelae and other cultic objects that could be commissioned through sanctioned means in order to reify the presence of the deities and function as a localized 'body'.

A significantly more restricted and idiosyncratic view of divine embodiment remained after the projection of these socio-material conventions through the reflective filters of the authors and editors of the Hebrew Bible. Fewer instantiations of divine embodiment were permitted to be represented in a favourable light. The primary concerns, however,

---

insert the divine name in the palaeo-Hebrew script. That this was not just a stylistic consideration, but evidence of special treatment, is indicated by one manuscript, 11QPs[a], in which twenty-eight words were erased from the transcription, except for the Tetragrammaton. In another eight manuscripts, the divine name was substituted with four dots, sometimes called the 'Tetrapuncta'. See Tov (2004); Lichtenberger (2018); cf. Parry (1996).
34 For a brief discussion of the reception of translations of the Hebrew Bible as holy writings, see Smelik (1999). See also the contributions in Law and Salvesen (2012).
35 For the development of the codex as diagnostic of Christian literature, see Nongbri (2018: 21–46).

appear to have been related to the relationship of those socio-material conventions to surrounding social groups and to the vicissitudes of curating socio-material media, and not to the practice of divine embodiment in and of itself. As a result, some notable examples not only remained but became central to the changing conceptualization of YHWH's relationship with, and presence among, worshippers. The loss of the ark of the covenant necessitated a new means of divine presencing that could escape the risks inherent in a discrete cultic object that might be destroyed, captured or inappropriately worshipped. The text of the Torah, empowered by the material presence of the divine name, became YHWH's new 'body' and the medium for the deity's presence among people.

References

Aaron, D. H. (2001), *Biblical Ambiguities: Metaphor, Semantics and Divine Imagery*, Leiden: Brill.

Asher-Greve, J. M. (1997), 'The Essential Body: Mesopotamian Conceptions of the Gendered Body', *Gender & History* 9 (3): 432–61.

Barrett, J. L. (2011), *Cognitive Science, Religion, and Theology: From Human Minds to Divine Minds*, West Conshohocken, PA: Templeton Press.

Baumgarten, A. I. (1981), *The Phoenician History of Philo of Byblos*, Leiden: Brill.

Beal, R. H. (2002), 'Dividing A God', in P. Mirecki and M. Meyer (eds), *Magic and Ritual in the Ancient World*, 197–208, Leiden: Brill.

Beck, P. (1994), 'The Cult Stands from Taanach: Aspects of the Iconographic Tradition of Early Iron Age Cult Objects in Palestine', in I. Finkelstein and N. Na'aman (eds), *From Nomadism to Monarchy: Archaeological and Historical Aspects of Early Israel*, 352–81, Washington: Biblical Archaeology Society.

Beckman, G. (2010), 'Temple Building among the Hittites', in M. J. Boda and J. Novotny (eds), *From the Foundations to the Crenellations: Essays on Temple Building in the Ancient Near East and Hebrew Bible*, 71–89, Münster: Ugarit-Verlag.

Ben-Ami, D. (2006), 'Early Iron Age Cult Places – New Evidence from Tel Hazor', *Tel Aviv* 33 (2): 123–7.

Bennett, G., and K. M. Bennett (2000), 'The Presence of the Dead: An Empirical Study', *Mortality* 5 (2): 139–57.

Benzel, K. (2015), '"What Goes in Is What Comes Out" – But What Was Already There? Divine Materials and Materiality in Ancient Mesopotamia', in B. Pongratz-Leisten and K. Sonik (eds), *The Materiality of Divine Agency*, 89–118, Berlin: Walter de Gruyter.

Berendt, E. A., and K. Tanita (2011), 'The "Heart" of Things: A Conceptual Metaphoric Analysis of Heart and Related Body Parts in Thai, Japanese and English', *Intercultural Communication Studies* 20 (1): 65–78.

Bering, J. M. (2002), 'Intuitive Conceptions of Dead Agents' Minds: The Natural Foundations of Afterlife Beliefs as Phenomenological Boundary', *Journal of Cognition and Culture* 2 (4): 263–308.

Bering, J. M. (2006), 'The Folk Psychology of Souls', *Behavioral and Brain Sciences* 29: 453–98.

Bering, J. M., K. McLeod and T. K. Shackelford (2005), 'Reasoning about Dead Agents Reveals Possible Adaptive Trends', *Human Nature* 16 (4): 360–81.

Bloch-Smith, E. (1992), 'The Cult of the Dead in Judah: Interpreting the Material Remains', *Journal of Biblical Literature* 111 (2): 213–24.

Bloch-Smith, E. (2015), 'Massebot Standing for Yhwh: The Fall of a Yhwistic Cult Symbol', in J. J. Collins, T. M. Lemos and S. M. Olyan (eds), *Worship, Women, and War: Essays in Honor of Susan Niditch*, 106–10, Providence, RI: Brown Judaic Studies.

Block, D. I. (2000), *The Gods of the Nations: Studies in Ancient Near Eastern Theology*, 2nd edn, Grand Rapids, MI: Baker Academic.

Boden, P. J. (1998), 'The Mesopotamian Washing of the Mouth (*mis pî*) Ritual', PhD thesis, Johns Hopkins University.

Chudek, M., R. A. McNamara, S. Birch, P. Bloom and J. Henrich (2017), 'Do Minds Switch Bodies? Dualist Interpretations across Ages and Societies', *Religion, Brain & Behavior* 8 (4): 354–68.

Cogan, M. (1974), *Imperialism and Religion: Assyria, Judah and Israel in the Eighth and Seventh Centuries BCE*, Missoula, MT: Scholars Press.

Cohen, E. (2008), 'What Is Spirit Possession? Defining, Comparing, and Explaining Two Possession Forms', *Ethnos* 73 (1): 101–26.

Cohen, E., and J. L. Barrett (2008), 'When Minds Migrate: Conceptualizing Spirit Possession', *Journal of Cognition and Culture* 8 (1): 23–48.

Cohn, Y. E. (2008), *Tangled Up in Text:* Tefillin *and the Ancient World*, BJS 351, Providence, RI: Brown University.

Craffert, P. F. (2015), 'When Is an Out-of-Body Experience (Not) an Out-of-Body Experience? Reflections about Out-of-Body Phenomena in Neuroscientific Research', *Journal of Cognition and Culture* 15 (1–2): 13–31.

Darby, E. (2014), *Interpreting Judean Pillar Figurines: Gender and Empire in Judean Apotropaic Ritual*, Tübingen: Mohr Siebeck.

Dietrich, M., O. Loretz and W. Mayer (1989), 'Sikkanum "Betyle"', *Ugaritische Forschung* 2 (1): 133–9.

Doak, B. R. (2015), *Phoenician Aniconism in Its Mediterranean and Ancient Near Eastern Contexts*, Atlanta, GA: Society of Biblical Literature.

Donner, H., and W. Röllig, eds (2002), *Kanaanäische und aramäische Inschriften*, 5th edn, Weisbaden: Harrassowitz Verlag.

Durand, J. (1985), 'Le culte des bétyles en Syrie', in J. Durand and R. Kupper (eds), *Miscellenea Babylonica: Mélanges offerts à Maurice Birot*, 79–84, Paris: Éditions Recherche sur les civilisations.

Earl, J. (2015), 'Dad bikes 1,400 miles to hear deceased daughter's heartbeat on Father's Day', CBS News, 21 June. Available online https://www.cbsnews.com/news/dad-bikes-1400-miles-to-hear-deceased-daughters-heartbeat-on-fathers-day/ (accessed 8 May 2020).

Evans, J. St. B. T., and K. Frankish, eds (2009), *In Two Minds: Dual Processes and Beyond*, Oxford: Oxford University Press.

Fleming, D. E. (2000), *Time at Emar: The Cultic Calendar and the Rituals from the Diviner's Archive*, Winona Lake, IN: Eisenbrauns.

Garfinkel, Y., and M. Mumcuoglu (2015), 'A Shrine Model from Tel Rekhesh', *Strata: Bulletin of the Anglo-Israel Archaeological Society* 33: 77–87.

Garfinkel, Y., S. Ganor and M. G. Hasel (2018), *In the Footsteps of King David: Revelations from an Ancient Biblical City*, New York: Thames & Hudson.

Hallam, E., and J. Hockey (2001), *Death, Memory and Material Culture*, Oxford: Berg.

Hamori, E. J. (2008), *'When Gods Were Men': The Embodied God in Biblical and Near Eastern Literature*, Berlin: Walter de Gruyter.

Herring, S. L. (2013), *Divine Substitution: Humanity as the Manifestation of Deity in the Hebrew Bible and the Ancient Near East*, Göttingen: Vandenhoeck & Ruprecht.

Herrmann, V. R., and J. D. Schloen, eds (2014), *In Remembrance of Me: Feasting with the Dead in the Ancient Middle East*, Chicago, IL: University of Chicago Press.

Hestrin, R. (1987), 'The Cult Stand from Taʿanach and Its Religious Background', in E. Lipiński (ed.), *Studia Phoenicia V: Phoenicia and the East Mediterranean in the First Millennium BC*, 61–77, Leuven: Peeters.

Hitchcock, L. A. (2011), 'Cult Corners in the Aegean and the Levant', in A. Yasur-Landau, J. R. Ebeling and L. B. Mazow (eds), *Household Archaeology in Ancient Israel and Beyond*, 321–45, Leiden: Brill.

Hogue, T. (2019a), '*Abracadabra*, or "I Create as I Speak": A Reanalysis of the First Verb in the Katumuwa Inscription in Light of Northwest Semitic and Hieroglyphic Luwian Parallels', *Bulletin of the American Schools of Oriental Research* 381: 193–202.

Hogue, T. (2019b), 'Image, Text, and Ritual: The Decalogue and the Three Reembodiments of God'. Paper presented at the Annual Meeting of the Society of Biblical Literature. San Diego, CA, 26 November 2019.

Hogue, T. (2019c), 'The Monumentality of the Sinaitic Decalogue: Reading Exodus 20 in Light of Northwest Semitic Monument-Making Practices', *Journal of Biblical Literature* 138 (1): 79–99.

Holloway, S. W. (2002), *Aššur is King! Aššur is King! Religion in the Exercise of Power in the Neo-Assyrian Empire*, Leiden: Brill.

Hundley, M. B. (2013), *Gods in Dwellings: Temples and Divine Presence in the Ancient Near East*, Atlanta, GA: Society of Biblical Literature.

Hurowitz, V. A. (2006), 'What Goes in Is What Comes Out: Materials for Creating Cult Statues', in G. Beckman and T. J. Lewis (eds), *Text, Artifact, and Image: Revealing Ancient Israelite Religion*, 3–23, Providence, RI: Brown Judaic Studies.

Järnefelt, E., C. F. Canfield and D. Kelemen (2015), 'The Divided Mind of a Disbeliever: Intuitive Beliefs about Nature as Purposefully Created Among Different Groups of Non-Religious Adults', *Cognition* 140 (1): 72–88.

Keel, O., and C. Uehlinger (1998), *Gods, Goddesses, and Images of God in Ancient Israel*, trans. T. H. Trapp, Edinburgh: T&T Clark.

Keen, C., C. Murray and S. Payne (2013), 'Sensing the Presence of the Deceased: A Narrative Review', *Mental Health, Religion & Culture* 16 (4): 384–402.

Kisilevitz, S. (2015), 'The Iron IIA Judahite Temple at Tel Moẓa', *Tel Aviv* 42: 147–64.

Knafl, A. K. (2014), *Forming God: Divine Anthropomorphism in the Pentateuch*, Winona Lake, IN: Eisenbrauns.

Kutsko, J. F. (2000), *Between Heaven and Earth: Divine Presence and Absence in the Book of Ezekiel*, Winona Lake, IN: Eisenbrauns.

Law, T. M., and A. Salvesen, eds (2012), *Greek Scripture and the Rabbis*, Leuven: Peeters.

Levtow, N. B. (2012), 'Text Destruction and Iconoclasm in the Hebrew Bible and the Ancient Near East', in N. N. May (ed.), *Iconoclasm and Text Destruction in the Ancient Near East and Beyond*, 311–62, Chicago, IL: Oriental Institute of the University of Chicago.

Lichtenberger, H. (2018), 'The Divine Name in the Dead Sea Scrolls and in New Testament Writings', in R. A. Clements, M. Kister and M. Segal (eds), *The Religious Worldviews Reflected in the Dead Sea Scrolls: Proceedings of the Fourteenth International Symposium of the Orion Center for the Study of the Dead Sea Scrolls and Associated Literature, 28–30 May, 2013*, 140–55, Leiden: Brill.

MacDougal, R. (2014), 'Remembrance and the Dead in Second Millennium BC Mesopotamia', PhD thesis, University of Leicester.

Machinist, P. (2006), 'Kingship and Divinity in Imperial Assyria', in G. Beckman and T. J. Lewis (eds), *Text, Artifact, and Image: Revealing Ancient Israelite Religion*, 152–88, Providence, RI: Brown University.

Mandler, J. M. (1992), 'How to Build a Baby: II. Conceptual Primatives', *Psychological Review* 99 (4): 587–604.

Markschies, C. (2016), *Gottes Körper: Jüdische, christliche und pagane Gottesvorstellungen in der Antike*, Munich: C. H. Beck.

Mazar, A. (2015), 'Religious Practices and Cult Objects during the Iron Age IIA at Tel Reḥov and Their Implications Regarding Religion in Northern Israel', *Hebrew Bible and Ancient Israel* 4 (1): 25–55.

Mazar, A., and N. Panitz-Cohen (2008), 'To What God? Altars and a House Shine from Tel Reḥov Puzzle Archaeologists', *Biblical Archaeology Review* 34 (4): 40–76.

McDowell, C. L. (2015), *The Image of God in the Garden of Eden: The Creation of Humankind in Genesis 2:5–3:24 in Light of* mīs pî pīt pî *and* wpt-r *Rituals of Mesopotamia and Ancient Egypt*, Winona Lake, IN: Eisenbrauns.

Mettinger, T. N. D. (1995), *No Graven Image? Israelite Iconism in Its Ancient Near Eastern Context*, Stockholm: Almqvist & Wiksell.

Miller, J. L. (2004), *Studies in the Origins, Development and Interpretation of the Kizzuwatna Rituals*, Weisbaden: Harrassowitz Verlag.

Moore, S. D. (1996), *God's Gym: Divine Male Bodies of the Bible*, London: Routledge.

Morgan, J. (2016), 'Religion and Dual-process Cognition: A Continuum of Styles or Distinct Types?', *Religion, Brain & Behavior* 6 (2): 1–18.

Niehr, H. (1997), 'In Search of YHWH's Cult Statue in the First Temple', in K. van der Toorn (ed.), *The Image and the Book: Iconic Cults, Aniconism, and the Rise of Book Religion in Israel and the Ancient Near East*, 73–95, Leuven: Peeters.

Noegel, S. B. (2015), 'The Egyptian Origin of the Ark of the Covenant', in T. E. Levy, T. Schneider, and W. H. C. Propp (eds), *Israel's Exodus in Transdisciplinary Perspective: Text, Archaeology, Culture, and Geoscience*, 223–42, Basel: Springer.

Nongbri, B. (2018), *God's Library: The Archaeology of the Earliest Christian Manuscripts*, New Haven, CT: Yale University Press.

Ornan, T. (2004), 'Idols and Symbols: Divine Representation in First Millennium Mesopotamian Art and Its Bearing on the Second Commandment', *Tel Aviv* 31: 90–121.

Otto, R. (1917), *Das Heilige: Über das Irrationale in der Idee des Göttlichen und sein Verhältnis zum Rationalen*, Breslau: Trewendt und Granier.

Oviedo, L. (2015), 'Religious Cognition as a Dual-Process: Developing the Model', *Method and Theory in the Study of Religion* 27 (1): 31–58.

Parmenter, D. M. (2009), 'The Bible as Icon: Myths of the Divine Origins of Scripture', in C. A. Evans and H. D. Zacharias (eds), *Jewish and Christian Scripture as Artifact and Canon*, 298–309, London: T&T Clark.

Parry, D. W. (1996), '4QSam^a and the Tetragrammaton', in S. D. Ricks and D. W. Parry (eds), *Current Research and Technological Developments on the Dead Sea Scrolls*, 106–25, Leiden: Brill.

Pennycook, G., J. A. Fugelsang and D. J. Koehler (2015), 'What Makes Us Think? A Three-Stage Dual-Process Model of Analytic Engagement', *Cognitive Psychology* 80 (1): 34–72.

Polaski, D. C. (2007), 'What Mean These Stones? Inscriptions, Textuality and Power in Persia and Yehud', in J. L. Berquist (ed.), *Approaching Yehud: New Approaches to the Study of the Persian Period*, 37–48, Atlanta, GA: Society of Biblical Literature.

Pongratz-Leisten, B. (2011), 'Divine Agency and Astralization of the Gods in Ancient Mesopotamia', in B. Pongratz-Leisten (ed.), *Reconsidering the Concept of Revolutionary Monotheism*, 137–87, Winona Lake, IN: Eisenbrauns.

Pongratz-Leisten, B., and K. Sonik (2015), 'Between Cognition and Culture: Theorizing the Materiality of Divine Agency in Cross-Cultural Perspective', in B. Pongratz-Leisten and K. Sonik (eds), *The Materiality of Divine Agency*, 3–69, Berlin: Walter de Gruyter.

Porter, B. N. (2009), 'Blessings from a Crown, Offerings to a Drum: Were There Non-Anthropomorphic Deities in Ancient Mesopotamia?', in B. N. Porter (ed.), *What Is a God? Anthropomorphic and Non-Anthropomorphic Aspects of Deity in Ancient Mesopotamia*, 153–94, Winona Lake, IN: Eisenbrauns.

Pyysiäinen, I. (2009), *Supernatural Agents: Why We Believe in Souls, Gods, and Buddhas*, Oxford: Oxford University Press.

Radner, K. (2005), *Die Macht des Namens: Altorientalische Strategien zur Selbsterhaltung*, Wiesbaden: Harrassowitz Verlag.

Richardson, S. (2012), 'The Hypercoherent Icon: Knowledge, Rationalization, and Disenchantment at Nineveh', in N. N. May (ed.), *Iconoclasm and Text Destruction in the Ancient Near East and Beyond*, 231–58, Chicago, IL: Oriental Institute of the University of Chicago.

Roazzi, M., M. Nyhof and C. Johnson (2013), 'Mind, Soul and Spirit: Conceptions of Immaterial Identity in Different Cultures', *International Journal for the Psychology of Religion* 23 (1): 75–86.

Roth, A. M. (1992), 'The *Psš-kf* and the "Opening of the Mouth" Ceremony: A Ritual of Birth and Rebirth', *Journal of Egyptian Archaeology* 78 (1): 113–47.

Sanders, S. (2008), 'Writing and Early Iron Age Israel: Before National Scripts, Beyond Nations and States', in R. E. Tappy and P. Kyle McCarter (eds), *Literate Culture and Tenth-Century Canaan: The Tel Zayit Abecedary in Context*, 97–112, Winona Lake, IN: Eisenbrauns.

Sanders, S. (2010), *The Invention of Hebrew*, Urbana, IL: University of Illinois.

Sanders, S. (2012), 'Naming the Dead: Funerary Writing and Historical Change in the Iron Age Levant', *MAARAV* 19 (1–2): 11–36.

Sanders, S. (2013), 'The Appetites of the Dead: West Semitic Linguistic and Ritual Aspects of the Katumuwa Stele', *Bulletin of the American Schools of Oriental Research* 369: 35–41.

Sanders, S. (2019), 'Words, things, and death: The rise of Iron Age literary monuments'. in R. Yelle, C. Handman and C. Lehrich (eds), *Language and Religion*, 327–49, Berlin: Walter de Gruyter.

Schaper, J. (2007), 'The Living Word Engraved in Stone: The Interrelationship of the Oral and the Written and the Culture of Memory in the Books of Deuteronomy and Joshua', in S. C. Barton, L. T. Stuckenbruck and B. G. Wold (eds), *Memory in the Bible and Antiquity: The Fifth Durham-Tübingen Research Symposium (Durham, September 2004)*, 9–23, Tübingen: Mohr Siebeck.

Scheyhing, N. (2018), 'Fossilising the Holy: Aniconic Standing Stones of the Near East', in L. D. Nebelsick, J. Wawrzeniuk and K. Zeman-Wiśniewska (eds), *Sacred Space: Contributions to the Archaeology of Belief*, 95–112, Warsaw: University of Warsaw.

Schleicher, M. (2010), 'Accounts of a Dying Scroll: On Jewish Handling of Sacred Texts in Need of Restoration or Disposal', in K. Myrvold (ed.), *The Death of Sacred Texts: Ritual Disposal and Renovation of Texts in World Religions*, 11–29, London: Routledge.

Schmid, K. (2012), 'The Canon and the Cult: The Emergence of Book Religion in Ancient Israel and the Gradual Sublimation of the Temple Cult', *Journal of Biblical Literature* 131 (2): 289–305.

Schniedewind, W. M. (2009), 'Calling God Names: An Inner-Biblical Approach to the Tetragrammaton', in D. A. Green and L. S. Lieber (eds), *Scriptural Exegesis: The Shapes of Culture and the Religious Imagination. Essays in Honour of Michael Fishbane*, 74–86, Oxford: Oxford University Press.

Sharifian, F., R. Dirven, N. Yu and S. Niemeier, eds (2008), *Culture, Body, and Language: Conceptualizations of Internal Body Organs across Cultures and Languages*, Berlin: Walter de Gruyter.

Smelik, W. F. (1999), 'The Rabbinic Reception of Early Bible Translations as Holy Writings and Oral Torah', *Journal for the Aramaic Bible* 1: 249–72.

Smith, M. S. (2008), *God in Translation: Deities in Cross-Cultural Discourse in the Biblical World*, Tübingen: Mohr Siebeck.

Smith, M. S. (2015), 'The Three Bodies of God in the Hebrew Bible', *Journal of Biblical Literature* 134 (3): 471–88.

Sommer, B. D. (2009), *The Bodies of God and the World of Ancient Israel*, Cambridge: Cambridge University Press.

Stager, L. E. (2008), 'The Canaanite Silver Calf', in L. E. Stager, J. D. Schloen and D. M. Master (eds), *Ashkelon I*, 577–80, Winona Lake, IN: Eisenbrauns.

Stavrakopoulou, F. (2013), 'Materialism, Materiality, and Biblical Cults of Writing', in K. J. Dell and P. M. Joyce (eds), *Biblical Interpretation and Method: Essays in Honour of John Barton*, 223–42, Oxford: Oxford University Press.

Stavrakopoulou, F. (2016), 'Religion at Home: The Materiality of Practice', in S. Niditch (ed.), *The Wiley Blackwell Companion to Ancient Israel*, 347–65, Chichester: Wiley-Blackwell.

Steiner, R. C. (2015), *Disembodied Souls: The Nefesh in Israel and Kindred Spirits in the Ancient Near East, with an Appendix on the Katumuwa Inscription*, Atlanta, GA: Society of Biblical Literature.

Suriano, M. J. (2014), 'Breaking Bread with the Dead: Katumuwa's Stele, Hosea 9:4, and the Early History of the Soul', *Journal of the American Oriental Society* 134 (3): 385–405.

Taylor, J. H. (2001), *Death and the Afterlife in Ancient Egypt*, Chicago, IL: University of Chicago Press.

Tigay, J. H. (1982), 'On the Meaning of Ṭ(W)ṬPT', *Journal of Biblical Literature* 101 (3): 321–31.

Tilford, N. L. (2017), *Sensing World, Sensing Wisdom: The Cognitive Foundations of Biblical Metaphors*, Atlanta, GA: Society of Biblical Literature.

Toorn, K. van der (1997a), 'Worshipping Stones: On the Deification of Cult Symbols', *Journal of Northwest Semitic Languages* 23 (1): 1–14.

Toorn, K. van der (1997b), 'The Iconic Book: Analogies between the Babylonian Cult of Images and the Veneration of the Torah', in K. van der Toorn (ed.), *The Image and the Book: Iconic Cults, Aniconism, and the Rise of Book Religion in Israel and the Ancient Near East*, 229–48, Leuven: Peeters.

Tov, E. (2004), *Scribal Practices and Approaches Reflected in the Texts Found in the Judean Desert*, Leiden: Brill.

Uehlinger, C. (1997), 'Anthropomorphic Cult Statuary in Iron Age Palestine and the Search for Yahweh's Cult Image', in K. van der Toorn (ed.), *The Image and the Book: Iconic Cults, Aniconism, and the Rise of Book Religion in Israel and the Ancient Near East*, 97–155, Leuven: Peeters.

Wagner, A. (2010), *Gottes Körper: Zur alttestamentlichen Vorstellung der Menschengestaltigkeit Gottes*, Gütersloh: Gütersloh Verlagshaus.

Walker, C., and M. B. Dick (1999), 'The Induction of the Cult Image in Ancient Mesopotamia: The Mesopotamian *mīs pî* Ritual', in M. B. Dick (ed.), *Born in Heaven Made on Earth: The Making of the Cult Image in the Ancient Near East*, 55–121, Winona Lake, IN: Eisenbrauns.

Walker, C., and M. B. Dick (2001), *The Induction of the Cult Image in Ancient Mesopotamia: The Mesopotamian Mīs Pî Ritual*, Helsinki: Neo-Assyrian Text Corpus Project.

Watts, J. W. (2016), 'From Ark of the Covenant to Torah Scroll: Ritualizing Israel's Iconic Texts', in N. MacDonald (ed.), *Ritual Innovation in the Hebrew Bible and Early Judaism*, 21–34, Berlin: Walter de Gruyter.

Winter, I. J. (1992), '"Idols of the King": Royal Images as Recipients of Ritual Action in Ancient Mesopotamia', *Journal of Ritual Studies* 6 (1): 13–42.

Wyatt, N. (2012), 'After Death Has Us Parted: Encounters between the Living and the Dead in the Ancient Semitic World', in G. del Olmo Lete, J. Vidal and N. Wyatt (eds), *The Perfumes of Seven Tamarisks: Studies in Honour of Wilfred G. E. Watson*, 257–91, Münster: Ugarit-Verlag.

Yasur-Landau, A. (2016), 'The *Baetyl* and the Stele: Contact and Tradition in Levantine and Aegean Cult', in E. Alram-Stern, F. Blakolmer, S. Deger-Jalkotzy, R. Laffineur and J. Weilhartner (eds), *Metaphysis: Ritual, Myth and Symbolism in the Aegean Bronze Age*, 415–19, Leuven: Peeters.

Zevit, Z. (2001), *The Religions of Ancient Israel: A Synthesis of Parallactic Approaches*, London: Continuum.

Zukerman, A. (2012), 'A Re-Analysis of the Iron Age IIA Cult Place at Lachish', *Ancient Near Eastern Studies* 49: 24–60.

INDEX OF ANCIENT SOURCES

Hebrew Bible

Genesis
1	86, 150	32.22-32	28
2	154, 161	32.24-32	101
2–3	135	34	117
2.4	86	34.2	38
2.5-7	129	35.14-15	178
2.7	86, 87, 153	35.29	144
2.16-17	28	37.29	109
3.19	129	38.11	95
5.24	162	44.14	113
6.3	124	46.11	98
9.3-4	28	47.6	114
11.30	100	48.8-22	101
15.11	53, 54	48.10	100
15.15	128	49.29	144
16.2	100		
16.6	38	Exodus	
18.11	129	4	31
20.17-18	100	4.24-26	28, 31
22	82	6.16	98
24.3	114	9.33	112
24.4	114	12.21-27	28
24.7	114	13.9	184
24.37	114	13.16	184
24.38	95, 114	13.20	64
24.40	114	20.2	185
25.8	128, 144	20.10	95
25.21	100	20.22–23.33	100
25.21-34	34	21.23-25	100
26.8	35	22.22	95
27.1	130	23.6	96
27.1-40	101	24.7	100
28.21	95	24.8	28, 30
28.22	178	24.11	190
29.17	100	25.16	180
29.24	98	25.21	180
29.31	100	25.22	179
29.34	98	28.42	110
31.14	97	28.42-43	110
31.33-35	33	29.20-21	28
31.34	33	31.18	186
		32	181
		32.4	181
		32.15-16	186

32.16	181	11.25	127
32.19	186	16.31-34	161
32.24	181	18.2	98
32.26-29	98	18.20	159
34.1	186	19.16	55
34.15-16	106	25.1-2	106
34.28	186	26	97
		26.52-56	95
Leviticus		26.53	97
7.26-27	28, 29	30.3-16	37
8.24	28, 30	33.39	124
11.13	53	33.54	95
11.18	53		
12.1-8	28, 32	Deuteronomy	
12.5	32	4	182
14.14	30	4.12	182
14.25	28	4.15	182
15.19-24	32	6.6-9	184
15.19-30	28	7.3-4	106
17.3-4	68, 69	9.8-21	186
17.3-6	67	9.9	112
17.7	68	9.18	112
17.10	29	9.25	111
17.10-14	28	10.2	180
17.11	28	10.5	180
17.13	67, 68	10.8	182
18.23	65	10.8-9	98
19.2	35	10.18	96
19.10	96	10.19	97
19.14	93, 94, 101, 102, 103	11.18-21	184
19.27	110	12	68
19.27-28	36	12.12	29, 97
19.32	132	12.15	29
20.15-16	65	12.15-16	28
21.5	35	12.16	29
21.10	35	12.18	97, 99
21.11	35	12.20-24	68
21.14	114	12.23	28
21.18	100	12.23-25	28
21.18-23	100	14.1	35
22.13	95, 95	14.12	53
23.22	96	14.17	53
24.19-20	100	14.27	97, 98, 99
26.30	55	14.29	97, 98, 99
		16.11-12	96
Numbers		16.11-14	97
5	33	18.1	97
5.11-21	13	18.5	98
5.11-31	36, 37	18.6-8	97
5.18	37	18.9	112
6	36, 37	18.11	136
11	127	18.25	112

19.21	100	19.23	95
21	33	19.31	95
21.10-14	36, 37, 38	19.39	95
21.14	38	19.48	95
23.7	96	24.25-27	184
23.8	96		
24.14	96	Judges	
24.17-22	96	5.2	34
26.6	38	5.28	131
26.11-13	96	9.18	95
26.14	173	11.8	127
27	186	11.35	109
27.1-10	17, 181, 183	13–16	33
27.9	183	13.2-3	100
27.14-26	102	14.3	114
27.17	102	16	33, 34
27.18	93, 94, 101, 102, 103	16.16-21	110
27.18-19	102	16.21	100
27.19	96, 102	16.25	35
27.21	65	17.7-13	98, 99
28.26	54	19–21	117
28.48	111	21.21	99
28.49	53	21.21-23	114
31.2	124		
31.11	183	1 Samuel	
32.7	132	1	34
32.19-25	99	1.5-6	100
32.42	34	1.12-14	134
33.8-10	98	2.21-22	134
33.9	163	2.22	127, 133, 134
34.7	124, 129	2.23-25	134
		2.27-36	100
Joshua		2.31	100
1.8	184	2.33	134
2.12	95	3.1–4.18	100
6.4-11	180	3.2	100, 134
6.13	182	3.11-14	100
7.6	182	4–6	182
7.6-7	111	4.15	100, 134
7.16-26	153	4.15-18	134
8.30-35	183	4.18	134
8.32	181	9.19	28
8.34-35	181	14.18	180
13.23	95	14.32	28
13.28	95	14.32-36	29
14.3-4	98	17.44	54
14.7	98	17.46	54
15.20	95	21.13	111
16.8	95	22.15	95
18.7	98	28.6-7	116
18.20	95	28.13	146
18.28	95		
19.8	95	2 Samuel	

1.2	111	8.9	180
1.19	123	8.22	112, 161
3.6-11	117	8.38	112
4.4	101	11.1	106
6.2	182	11.8	106
6.5	182	13.2	54, 55
6.14-16	182	14.4	100
6.16	131	16.31	114
9.3	101	17.17-24	147
9.4	101	19	9
9.7	101	21.1-15	153
9.12	101	21.11	127
9.13	101	21.27	109, 111
10	33		
10.4	109	2 Kings	
10.4-5	35	1.8	34
10.12-19	109	2	9
12	14, 65	2.12	34
12.1-6	69	4.8-37	147
12.3	65	4.14	129
12.5	65	6.25	111
12.21	111	7.4	111
12.22-23	116	8.7-15	132
13.1-22	117	9.30	131
13.20	64	10.5	127
13.31	109	13.21	147
14.9	95	17.6	114
14.25-26	34	17.24	114
15.5-6	34	17.26	114
16.20-33	117	18.13-16	8
17.27-29	135	18.27	109
18.9-15	34	19.1	112
18.18	185	19.6-7	112
19	135	22.8	153
19.18	111	22.11	112, 113
19.23	134	22.18-19	113
19.26	101	22.19	112
19.27	101	23	113
19.31-40	135	23.14	55
19.32	127, 133, 135	23.16	55
19.33	135	23.16-18	54
19.35	135	23.20	55
21.10	54	25.3	111
		25.7	100
1 Kings			
1.1	128, 129	Isaiah	
1.4	129	1.15	112
1.13	134	3.5	132
1.15	127, 133	3.14	127
1.17	134	3.24	36, 110
2.5-9	134	3.26	111
2.9	134	7.17	95

7.20	110	Ezekiel	
8.19-20	136	1	183
9.15	127	6.4-5	55
14	158	7.18	35
14.1	98	8	127
14.9	158	9.6	55
14.9-10	158	9.8	111
14.9-20	16, 158	10	183
15.2	35, 110	14.12-23	153
18.6	53	16	117
20.4	110	16.36	32
21.9	111	16.39	110
22.14	141	17.24	129
26	147	18.2	153
26.14	153	20.3	127
26.19	145, 148, 149, 153	21.3	129
37.1	112	24	32
37.5-6	112	24.6	32
38.18	143	24.11	32
42.7	102	24.12	32
47.1	111	24.13	33
47.3	110	26.15-17	111
53.9-10	147	27.31	110
54.8	116	28	161
56.3	98	28.12-17	86
56.6	98	33.25	29
58.3	111, 116	37	56, 129, 145, 147, 148, 149, 153, 154
66.1	183		
		37.1-14	16, 52
Jeremiah		37.7-8	56
1	82	37.9	56
1.2-3	84	38	52
1.3-4	83, 84	39	13, 44, 52, 53, 54, 55, 56, 57
1.4	83		
1.4-5	14, 76, 82, 83, 84, 85, 87, 88	39.1-3	54
		39.1-21	52
1.5	83	39.1-29	52
3.16-17	183	39.4	53, 54, 55
4.31	112	39.4-5	52, 53, 55
7.29	110	39.4-10	52
7.32-33	53	39.4-20	56
7.33	54	39.9-10	55
12.9	53	39.11	55
13.22	110	39.11-15	55
14.12	111	39.11-16	53
16.6	35	39.12	55
31.29-30	153	39.12-13	55
32.37	114	39.12-16	55
41.5	109, 110	39.14	55
47.5	110	39.15	55
48.37	35, 110	39.16	55
50.5	98	39.17	53, 54
		39.17-20	54

39.17-21	52, 53	73	161, 162
39.18	54	73.24-25	161, 162
39.19	54	73.24-26	16
39.20	54	89.2-38	158
		90.10	124
Hosea		92.12-14	133
5.15–6.3	154	92.13-15	133
6.2	147	92.15	133
7.9	128	102	136
		106.28	173
Joel		108.9	9
2.12	111	108.10	9
		110	158
Amos		110.1	160
2.11	36	115.17	143
5.2	111	131.2	87
		137.1-4	8
Jonah		139	76, 86, 87
3.5	111	139.13	86
3.6	111	139.13-15	14, 85, 86, 87
		146	93
Micah		146.7-9	102, 103
1.16	53, 110	146.8	93, 94, 101, 103
Nahum		Proverbs	
3.5	110	7.6	131
		8.22-31	86
Psalms		23.31-32	161
2	158	24.12	142
6.6	143	27:23-27	14, 64
16	16, 159, 161, 162, 163	30.17	53
18	158	Job	
22	87	1.20	35, 109, 110, 111
23.6	133	1.21	153
24	158	10.8	86, 87
27.4-6	133	10.8-11	14, 76, 85, 87
27.10	133	10.11	87
31	136	10.20-22	143
32	136	12.12	127
38	136	15.10	127
44.21	112	29.8	127
44.24-25	116	29.12	102
44.25	111	29.12-15	93, 94, 101
45.11	95	29.12-16	101, 102
49	161	29.15-16	102
49.14-15	16, 161	32.6	127
49.15	161	42.16	124
49.15-16	161		
60.8	9	Song of Songs	
60.10	9	7.10	161

INDEX OF ANCIENT SOURCES

Ruth		7.14	107
1.11-13	99	7.16-19	106
1.12	130	7.21-23	106
2.2	99	7.25-26	107
2.8	99	7.27-28	112
2.10	111	8.21	111
2.22	99	9–10	15, 105, 106, 108,
3.1	99		113, 114, 115,
3.10-11	99		116, 117
3.16	99	9.1	114
3.18	99	9.1-2	105, 106
		9.2	106, 114
Lamentations		9.3	106, 107, 109,
2.10	111		111, 115
5.20	116	9.3–10.1	106
		9.3-4	105, 107, 110, 116
Qoheleth		9.3-5	107
1.1	130	9.4	107, 113, 114
2	135	9.5	105, 112, 113, 116
2.3	135	9.6	106
9.10	143	9.6-15	105
12	16, 130	9.8-9	117
12.1	130	9.9	112
12.3	130, 131	9.10-12	112, 113, 115, 117
12.4	131	9.11	106
12.5	131	9.12	114
12.6	131	9.14-15	116
12.7	131	10	114
12.14	147	10.1	105, 106, 111,
			112, 113
Esther		10.2	106, 114, 115
3.15	109	10.2-3	116
4.16	111	10.3	106, 113, 114,
9.27	98		115, 117
		10.5	106
Daniel		10.6	105, 106, 107, 111,
6.14	64		112, 113, 114
7	125	10.7	113
12.1	149	10.8	106
12.1-3	147	10.9	106, 113
12.2	149, 154	10.10	114
12.2-3	16, 148, 149, 150	10.12	106
		10.13-14	106
Ezra		10.14	113, 114, 116
1.1-2	112	10.15	106
4–6	117	10.15-17	106
5	127	10.17	114
6.22	112	10.17-19	114
7	106	10.18	114
7–10	112	10.19	106, 114
7.1-5	106	10.44	114
7.6	106		

Nehemiah

1.4	111
8	112
13.23	107, 114
13.25	110

1 Chronicles

8.34	101
9.40	101
19.4	109
23.1	128

2 Chronicles

6.2	161
6.12	112
6.13	112
6.29	112
8.2	114
11.21-22	114
13.19-21	114
21.13	95
24.3	114
24.15	124
34.19	112, 113
34.27	112

New Testament

Matthew

22.23	147
24.28	43

Mark

12.18	147

Luke

2.36-37	133
17.37	43
20.27	147

John

11.44	145
20	161
20.17	145
20.24-28	145

Acts

2.25-28	163
2.31	163
4.1-2	147
13.35	163
23.8	147

1 Corinthians

15.12	147
15.35-54	145
15.44	145

Revelation

2.11	141
20.6	141
20.14	141
21.18	141

Deuterocanonical Works

Wisdom of Solomon

4.16	137

Sirach/Ecclesiasticus

8.6	137
25.3	137

Susanna

1.50	127

1 Maccabees

4.36-40	111

2 Maccabees

7.9	149
7.11	149
7.14	149
7.23	149
7.29	149

2 Esdras/4 Ezra

5.49	130
5.53	129
7	147

4 Maccabees

16.13	149
17.12	149
18.23	149

Further Jewish Literature

2 Baruch	149
4 Baruch	149
1 Enoch	147, 148, 149
2 Enoch	149
3 Enoch	159
History of the Rechabites	149
Jubilees	149

Life of Adam and Eve	149	1.3 iii 28-31	160–1
Lives of the Prophets	149	1.4 viii 11-14	161
Psalms of Solomon	149	1.4 viii 15-20	161
Sibylline Oracles	149	1.5–1.6	157
Testaments of the Twelve Patriarchs	149	1.5 i 12-20	161
		1.5 ii 15-16	161
Testament of Abraham	149	1.5 vi 3-5	156
Testament of Job	149	1.5 vi 6-7	160
Testament of Judah	149	1.5 vi 26-28	156
Testament of Moses	149	1.6	158
		1.6 ii 15-17	156
Dead Sea Scrolls		1.6 iii	156
2QJer	82	1.10 iii 27-31	160
4Q385	149	1.15 i 4	161
4Q521	149	1.15 i 6	161
4QJer^{a-e}	82	1.16 iii 2-4	156
11QPs^a	187	1.12 i 38-39	159
		1.161	156, 157
Rabbinic Literature			
m. Sotah	37	Other Texts	
m. Yadayim	187	Atrahasis	78, 79
Targum Isaiah	141	Descent of Ishtar	141
Targum Jeremiah	141	Gilgamesh	43, 141
Pirqe Avot	187		
		Book of the Dead	141, 155
Other Ancient Sources		Coffin Texts	141, 155
		Pyramid Texts	141, 154, 155
Ugaritic Texts			
KTU		Iliad	141
1.2 i 43	161	Odyssey	160
1.2 iii 8	161		

INDEX OF AUTHORS

Aaron, D. H. 180
Abu-Rabia, A. 61, 62, 63
Aharoni, I. 53
Aker, J. 6
Albenda, P. 2, 4
Albertz, R. 84, 142
Alexander, P. S. 159
Allen, L. 87
Allen, J. P. 155
Allen, T. G. 155
Allentuck, A. 65
Altmann, P. 53
Ames, F. R. 7
Andersen, B. 77, 78, 84
Andrews, P. 45, 46
Antrosio, J. 4
Appell-Warren, L. 2
Ariès, P. 75
Asher-Greve, J. M. 4, 174
Assante, J. 9, 12, 108, 111
Astour, M. C. 142
Attala, L. 2
Avalos, H. 133
Ayayi, J. A. A. 125

Bagg, A. 9
Bahrani, Z. 6, 12, 47, 51, 52
Barcan, R. 4
Barmash, P. 30
Barnett, R. D. 1, 2, 3, 6, 8
Barr, J. 144, 150, 155
Barrett, J. L. 173, 174
Barron, A. E. 7
Barstad, H. 143, 144
Battini, L. 6
Baumgarten, A. I. 178
Bautch, R. J. 114
Bayliss, M. 141
Beadle, D. N. 158, 159
Beal, R. H. 176
Beck, P. 179
Becking, B. 105, 111, 116
Beckman, G. 176

Bell, C. M. 108, 113, 114
Bembry, J. 125, 127
Ben-Ami, D. 178
Ben-Dor, S. 94
Bennett, G. 173
Bennett, K. M. 173
Benz, B. C. 156
Benzel, K. 175
Berendt, E. A. 172
Bergmann, C. D. 75, 76, 78, 79, 84
Bering, J. M. 173
Betsworth, S. 75
Biggs, R. 76
Bleibtreu, E. 1, 6
Blenkinsopp, J. 75, 84, 107, 124, 153, 159
Bloch-Smith, E. 10, 145, 152, 153, 155, 158, 173, 177
Block, D. I. 182
Boden, P. J. 174
Boer, R. 65, 106, 115
Böklen, E. 152
Bonogofsky, M. 46
Borowski, O. 62
Bosworth, D. 75
Bourdieu, P. 38
Boutin, A. T. 10
Boyce, M. A. 152
Boz, B. 45, 46
Brichto, H. C. 53, 142, 143, 159
Brown, A. P. 105
Brown, B. A. 6
Buss, M. J. 162
Butler, J. 108
Bynum, D. E. 135

Camp, C. V. 105, 116
Canfield, C. F. 171
Casey, J. 63
Cauvin, J. 146
Chapman, C. R. 12, 35, 94, 108, 110, 112, 115, 130
Charlesworth, J. H. 145, 147, 148, 149
Chudek, M. 172

Cifarelli, M. 4, 6, 9, 12, 35, 108, 111, 112
Clauss, J. 114
Cline, E. H. 156
Clines, D. J. A. 126
Clough, D. 67
Cogan, M. 182
Cohen, E. 173
Cohen, M. E. 80
Cohn, Y. E. 184
Cokayne, K. 125, 126, 129
Collins, P. 6, 8
Collon, D. 6
Connell, R. W. 115
Cook, S. L. 147, 148, 156
Cooper, J. S. 47, 51
Cornelius, I. 179
Craffert, P. F. 173
Creanga, O. 106
Crenshaw, J. L. 130
Cuéllar, G. L. 6
Cullmann, O. 149, 150

Dahood, M. J. 155, 156, 158, 159, 161
Dalley, S. 6
Darby, E. 179
Dasen, V. 75
Davila, J. 159
Davis, S. 67
Day, J. 142, 143
Day, P. L. 32, 33
Dayagi-Mendels, M. 36
De Backer, F. 12
DeGrado, J. 6
Delitzsch, F. 128
DeMarris, E. 6
Dever, W. G. 2, 62
Dewrell, H. 75
Diamond, A. R. P. 116
Diaz, S. 77
Dick, M. B. 174, 175, 176, 181
Dietler, M. 111
Dietrich, M. 178
Di Vito, R. A. 152
Doak, B. R. 153, 179
Dolce, R. 45
Donner, H. 174
Douglas, M. 30, 32, 38
Driver, G. R. 53
Drori, A. 67
Durand, J. 178
Düring, B. S. 45

Earl, J. 172
Ebeling, J. 62
Eichrodt, W. 53
Eilberg-Schwartz, H. 31, 32
Elledge, C. D. 145, 146, 148, 149, 152
Emery, W. B. 154
Eng, M. 124, 127, 128
Eskenazi, T. C. 106, 114
Evans, J. St. B. T. 171

Faulkner, R. O. 155
Faust, A. 142
Feldman, M. H. 6
Fensham, F. C. 107
Fewell, D. 75
Finkelstein, I. 153
Fleming, D. E. 178
Flynn, S. W. 75, 99
Foster, B. 6, 79
Fowler, C. 2, 9
Fox, M. V. 130
Frankfort, H. 50
Frankish, K. 171
Franklin, N. 6
Frayne, D. 47
Freu, J. 157
Frevel, C. 152
Fried, L. 107, 112
Fuchs, E. 106
Fugelsang, J. A. 171
Fustel de Coulanges, N. D. 159

Galpaz-Feller, P. 37
Ganor, S. 177, 178, 179
Garcia-Ventura, A. 4
Garfinkel, Y. 177, 178, 179
Garroway, K. H. 2, 4, 75, 77, 99
Gawlinski, L. 4
Gedalof, I. 117
Geertz, C. 38, 39
Geller, S. A. 29, 31
Gennep, A. van 30
George, M. K. 115
Geyer, J. B. 30, 32
Gilders, W. 29, 30, 31, 68, 69
Goldstein, J. A. 149
Gorman, F. 108
Gottwald, N. K. 106
Goulder, M. 87
Grabbe, L. L. 107
Grappe, C. 150, 152
Green, J. D. M. 4

Greer, J. S. 66, 67
Griffiths, J. G. 142
Grol, H. van 116
Gruber, M. 4
Guenther, A. 114

Habel, N. 82
Haddow, S. D. 46
Hager, L. D. 45
Hallam, E. 173
Halpern, B. 153
Hamori, E. 77, 171, 174
Han, S. 4
Harris, J. G. 124
Harris, O. J. T. 2
Harris, R. 124
Hasel, M. G. 177, 178, 179
Hearn, J. 108
Helle, S. 4
Helmer, D. 61
Herring, S. L. 177
Herrmann, V. R. 155, 173
Hesse, B. 61, 66, 67
Hestrin, R. 179
Heuzey, L. 48, 49
Hiebert, P. S. 95
Hitchcock, L. A. 178
Hockey, J. 173
Hodder, I. 45, 46, 47, 57, 62, 67
Hogue, T. 185, 186
Holladay, J. S. 62
Holloway, S. W. 182
Holtzman, J. 62, 63
Hooker, A. 116
Horwitz, L. K. 67
Hübner, U. 76
Hultgård, A. 152
Hundley, M. B. 178
Hurowitz, V. A. 175

Ikram, S. 43

Jacoby, R. 2
Janzen, D. 66, 105, 109
Japhet, S. 114
Järnefelt, E. 171
Jassen, J. 75
Jassen, R. 75
Johnson, A. R. 144, 155
Johnson, C. 173
Johnson, W. M. 105
Johnston, P. S. 142, 143, 155

Jones, A. R. 9
Jones, L. 67
Joukowsky, M. 156
Joyce, R. R. 9

Kamionkowski, S. T. 110
Karrer-Grube, C. 106
Keel, O. 176, 177, 179
Keen, C. 173
Kelemen, D. 171
Kelso, J. 106, 117
King, P. J. 2, 6, 26
Kisilevitz, S. 178
Klawans, J. 32
Knafl, A. K. 171, 182
Knight, D. A. 124, 125, 127
Knüsel, C. J. 46
Koehler, D. J. 171
Koehler, L. 143
Koepf-Taylor, L. 75
Kogan, L. 53
Kohler-Rollefson, I. 67
König, F. 152
Korpel, M. C. A. 141, 142, 144, 154
Kramer, C. 62, 63
Krause, J. J. 9
Kunz-Lübcke, A. 75
Kutsko, J. F. 116, 182

Labat, R. 77
Lambert, H. 2
Lambert, W. 79
Lancy, D. F. 4
Laneri, N. 10
Lang, B. 156, 159, 161, 162, 163
Law, T. M. 187
Layard, A. H. 1, 6
Lemche, N. P. 94
Lemos, T. M. 10, 100, 108, 109
Leuchter, M. 98, 107
Levenson, J. D. 155
Levine, B. 107
Lévi-Strauss, C. 30, 38
Levtow, N. B. 51, 183
Lewis, T. J. 141, 144, 159
Lichtenberger, H. 187
Lipiński, E. 143
Lipka, H. 108, 109, 110, 115
Lippolis, C. 1, 8
Livingstone, A. 81
Llewellyn-Jones, L. 108, 110
London, G. 61, 62

Loretz, O. 178
Lust, J. 52
Lyons, D. 63

MacDougal, R. 174
Machinist, P. 174
Macqueen, J. G. 45
Maher, V. 4
Maier, C. M. 106
Malamat, A. 128
Mandler, J. M. 172
Marchegay, S. 156, 158
Markl, D. 75
Markschies, C. 171
Martin-Achard, R. 152
Mascia-Lees, F. E. 2
Mayer, W. 178
Mazar, A. 178, 179
McCormick, C. M. 6
McDannell, C. 38
McDonald, M. 2
McDowell, C. L. 174, 175, 176
McFerrin, N. 9
McGowan, K. J. 46
McGuire, M. B. 38
McIntosh, J. 2
McLeod, K. 173
McMahon, A. 6, 43
McNeilly, A. 77
McNutt, P. 94
Mellaart, J. 44, 45, 46
Meskell, L. M. 9, 12, 46, 47
Mettinger, T. N. D. 156, 177, 178
Meyers, C. 62, 95
Michel, A. 75
Milgrom. J. 32, 114
Millard, A. 79
Miller, J. L. 176
Moffat, D. P. 105
Molleson, T. 45, 46
Molloy, M. 117
Monroe, L. A. S. 55
Moore, S. D. 174
Moortgat, A. 47, 52
Morelli, F. 43
Morello, N. 6
Morgan, D. 108
Morgan, J. 171
Mowinckel, S. 87
Mumcuoglu, M. 178, 179
Mullen, E. 85
Murray, C. 173

Nadali, D. 7, 12, 51
Nelson, R. D. 68
Netzer, A. 152
Neusner, J. 32
Newsom, C. A. 102, 146, 152
Nickelsburg, G. W. E. 148, 149, 154
Niditch, S. 28, 30, 34, 35, 36, 109, 110
Niehr, H. 176
Nissinen, M. 107, 110, 115
Noegel, S. B. 180
Nongbri, B. 187
N'Shea, O. 9, 12
Nutkowicz, H. 155
Nyhof, M. 173
Nykolaishen, D. J. E. 115

Oesterley, W. O. E. 142
Økland, J. 106
Oldenberg, H. 151
Olyan, S. M. 10, 35, 93, 94, 101, 103, 107, 108, 109, 113, 116, 131, 144
Ornan, T. 6, 177
Orsi, R. 38
Otto, R. 171
Oviedo, L. 171

Palmer, C. 9
Panitz-Cohen, N. 178
Parker, J. F. 75, 76, 82, 99
Parkin, T. G. 125, 136
Parmenter, D. M. 186
Parrot, A. 50
Parry, D. W. 187
Payne, S. 173
Pedersen, J. 142
Peled, I. 4
Pennycook, G. 171
Pham, X. H. T. 107
Pilloud, M. A. 46
Polaski, D. C. 184
Pongratz-Leisten, B. 174, 175
Porter, A. 9
Porter, B. N. 181
Porter, B. W. 10
Portuese, L. 6
Postgate, J. N. 64
Potts, T. 61
Prinsloo, G. T. M. 6
Pyper, J. 123
Pyschny, K. 4
Pyysiäinen, I. 174

Rad, G. von 142
Radner, K. 12, 185
Raphael, R. 102
Reviv, H. 127
Richardson, S. 9, 12, 51, 52, 183
Riley, J. A. 2, 4
Roazzi, M. 173
Robb, J. 2, 6
Robinson, T. H. 142
Röllig, W. 174
Root, M. C. 108
Roth, A. M. 176
Rouillard, H. 153
Rowley, H. H. 142
Russell, J. M. 1, 2
Russell, N. 46

Sachs, A. 78
Salles, J.-F. 156, 158
Salvesen, A. 187
Sanders, S. 141, 144, 160, 173, 184, 185
Sasson, A. 61, 62, 63, 65, 66
Sawyer, D. F. 106, 116, 117
Schaper, J. 183, 184
Scheyhing, N. 178
Schipper, J. 94, 95, 101, 103
Schleicher, M. 187
Schloen, J. D. 94, 95, 155, 173
Schmid, K. 185
Schniedewind, W. M. 186
Schwyn, I. 4
Scurlock, J. 77, 78, 79, 84
Selz, G. 50, 51
Shackelford, T. K. 173
Shafer, A. 12
Shahack-Gross, R. 62
Shaked, S. 152
Sharifian, F. 172
Shilling, C. 2
Shipp, R. M. 158
Shonkwiler, R. 43
Sillar, B. 62
Sivan, D. 85
Smelik, W. F. 187
Smith, M. S. 155, 156, 157, 158, 171, 174, 178
Sommer, B. D. 171, 174, 176, 178, 182
Sonik, K. 175
Southwood, K. E. 114
Späth, T. 75
Spronk, K. 155, 156, 158, 161
Stager, L. E. 2, 6, 28, 179

Stallybrass, P. 9
Stavrakopoulou, F. 1, 2, 4, 9, 10, 12, 27, 38, 52, 53, 54, 55, 56, 66, 108, 109, 113, 153, 159, 161, 173, 181, 184
Steel, L. 2
Steinberg, N. 75, 76, 82, 95, 99
Steiner, R. C. 155, 173
Stiebert, J. 83
Stol, M. 4, 75, 80, 126, 133
Stone, K. 62, 116, 117
Suriano, M. J. 10, 43, 51, 54, 56, 133, 141, 143, 144, 145, 150, 152, 154, 156, 157, 158, 174
Sweeney, D. 4
Sykes, N. 62, 63, 66

Tamez, E. 131
Tanita, K. 172
Tappy, R. E. 145, 147
Taylor, J. 6
Taylor, J. H. 174
Tchernov, E. 67
Testart, A. 45
Theil, W. 84
Thomas, P. B. 9
Thomason, A. K. 7
Tigay, J. H. 184
Tilford, N. L. 172
Toorn, K. van der 94, 100, 178, 187
Tov, E. 187
Tromp, N. J. 142, 143, 144, 148
Tsukimoto, A. 141, 144
Turner, B. S. 2
Turner, G. 1, 6
Turner, V. 28, 30, 37, 38
Twiss, K. C. 46

Uehlinger, C. 2, 6, 8, 12, 176, 177, 179
Ussishkin, D. 1, 2

Van Dooren, T. 43
Vaux, R. de 142
Vawter, B. 155, 161
Veldhuis, N. 78, 79
Vidal, J. 7
Vigne, J. 61
Vleeming, S. P. 126, 133

Wäfler, M. 6, 8
Wagner, A. 171
Wagstaff, B. J. 6, 9
Walker, C. 174, 175, 176, 181

Wapnish, P. 66, 67
Ward, W. A. 156
Watson, P. J. 62
Watson, W. 161
Watts, J. W. 181, 186
Wehr, H. 161
Welton, R. 61
Westbrook, R. 132
Westenholz, A. 51
Williamson, H. G. M. 114
Wilson, S. M. 108, 110
Winston, D. 152
Winter, I. J. 35, 47, 48, 49, 50, 52, 53, 110, 174
Wintermute, O. S. 149

Wyatt, N. 141, 144, 145, 150, 153, 154, 155, 156, 158, 159, 160, 161, 174
Wynn, K. H. 101

Yasur-Landau, A. 178

Zaehner, R. C. 150, 152
Zenger, E. 87
Zevit, Z. 68, 142, 143, 178
Zimmerli, W. 52, 53, 54
Zinner, S. 149
Zsolnay, I. 115, 116, 117
Zukerman, A. 177, 178
Zwickel, W. 7

INDEX OF SUBJECTS

Aaron 98, 100, 124, 181
abdomen 172
Abishag 129
Abraham 54, 95, 117, 129
Absalom 13, 33, 34, 39, 185
abuse 9, 12, 52, 53, 54, 55, 56, 93, 95, 110, 132
acculturation. *See* culture
Achilles 141
Adam 86, 87, 153, 154
adulthood 2, 14, 31, 65, 66, 87, 88, 89, 101
afterlife 16, 128, 137, 141, 142, 147, 151, 152, 155, 156, 158, 159, 162, 163, 173; *see also* post-mortem existence
age 2, 4, 6, 15, 16, 37, 46, 66, 100, 101, 123–37; *see also* elderly
agency 6, 9–10, 12, 16, 51, 172–4, 175–7, 179, 180, 182–4, 185, 186, 187
Ahab 109, 127
Ahijah 100
altar 29, 54, 55, 67, 68, 98, 100, 178, 183
Ammonites 35, 107
amulet 6, 9, 184, 185
Anat. *See* deity
ancestors 16, 45, 46, 47, 56, 57, 66, 98, 132, 133, 144, 146, 151, 153, 159, 160, 162, 177
aniconism 177, 179
Ancient of Days. *See* deity
animal 1, 2, 9, 14, 28, 29, 31, 39, 43, 45, 46, 52, 53, 54, 55, 56, 57, 61–9, 177, 178, 179, 187
  bear 46
  bird 14, 43, 44, 46, 47, 49, 52, 53, 55, 56, 57, 67, 131, 142
  bull 176, 179, 181
  calf 14, 112, 161, 179, 181, 186
  caprid 179
  cattle 29, 61, 62, 63, 67
  cow 14, 61, 64
  goat 14, 61, 62, 63, 64, 67, 68
  horse 54, 179
  kid 14, 65
  lamb 14, 28, 64, 65, 68, 69
  leopard 46
  lion 179
  ox 1, 3, 6, 30, 61, 64, 67, 68
  raptor 44, 46, 48, 52, 53, 56, 57, 142
  sheep 14, 29, 61, 62, 63, 64, 67, 161
  vulture 13, 14, 43–57
ankle 2, 9, 12
Anna 133
anoint 17, 178, 184
Antiochus IV Epiphanes 147
Anu. *See* deity
Aqhat 157, 158
Aramaic 176, 178, 186
archaeology 2, 14, 62, 65, 66, 67, 69, 124, 125, 126, 142, 144, 145, 152, 156, 173, 177
ark (cult object) 17, 98, 134, 135, 171, 180–3, 186, 188
arm 1, 5, 6, 49, 79, 105, 112, 130, 179
Artaxerxes 107
Asalluḫu. *See* deity
ascension (to heaven) 141, 152, 154, 157, 158
Ashdod 107
Assyria 1–2, 4, 6, 7, 8, 9, 10, 12, 35, 36, 52, 76, 81, 83, 110, 111, 112, 115, 153, 178, 183, 187
Astarte. *See* deity
astralization 149
avatar 46

Baal. *See* deity
baby. *See* children
Babylonia 8, 64, 76, 78, 79, 80, 81, 83, 86, 110, 150, 182
Bach 131
baldness 35, 36, 39, 53; *see also* hair
barefoot 9, 12
bareness 6, 9, 37, 107, 109; *see also* nakedness; nudity
barley 80
Barzillai 127, 133, 135–6
Bathsheba 134

INDEX OF SUBJECTS

bear. *See* animal
beard 2, 6, 12, 15, 35, 36, 105, 107, 108, 109, 110, 126; *see also* hair
beauty 129
Bedouin 62–3
Belet-ili. *See* deity
belief 16, 39, 88, 108, 132, 135, 141, 142, 144, 145, 146, 147, 148, 149, 150, 151, 152, 154, 155, 156, 157, 158, 159, 162, 163
belt. *See* clothing
Ben-Hadad 132
Benjamin 113, 149
Bethel (place) 17, 54, 55; *see also* deity
bird. *See* animal
birth 13, 14, 28, 32, 33, 34, 35, 75–89, 95, 98, 99, 101, 114, 124, 153, 154, 175; *see also* pregnancy
black. *See* colour
blood 7, 9, 12, 13, 27–33, 35, 37, 38–9, 54, 66, 67–9, 80, 134, 159
blue. *See* colour
boat 81, 180
Boaz 111
body 2–13, 15, 17, 27–39, 43, 45, 48, 49, 69, 76, 77, 78, 80, 83, 88, 106, 107, 108–12, 116, 128–32, 145–8, 149, 172–4, 182, 187, 188; *see also* corpse
book. *See* writing
boundary 16, 30, 46, 51, 56, 102, 129, 163, 172
boy. *See* children
brain 172
bread 62, 111, 155, 181
breastfeeding 4, 77
breath 87, 154, 174
Brexit 147
bride. *See* marriage
bridegroom. *See* marriage
brother. *See* family
bull. *See* animal
burial. *See* mortuary practice
buttocks 109

calf. *See* animal
canon. *See* writing
cap. *See* clothing
caprid. *See* animal
captivity 6, 9, 12, 33, 36, 38, 39, 100, 102, 103, 106, 110
carnelian 80
Çatalhöyük 13, 44–7, 56, 57
cattle. *See* animal

centralization (cultic) 14, 17, 28, 68, 180, 184
cervix 77
chaos 14, 27, 30, 47, 54, 55, 56
charisma 33, 34, 35, 37
children 1, 2–4, 13, 14, 15, 32, 34, 64, 65, 75–89, 95, 98, 99–100, 113, 114, 115, 116, 117, 123, 124, 128, 129, 130, 132, 185; *see also* birth; family; pregnancy
  baby 15, 32, 77, 79, 80, 83, 84, 86, 87
  boy 2–4, 80, 110; *see also* gender
  foetus 14, 77
  girl 2–4, 32, 64, 80, 129, 131; *see also* gender
  infant 1, 4, 76, 124, 130, 172
  offspring 65, 95, 115, 116, 117
  preborn child 14, 76–89
  progeny 129, 135
chin 109, 110, 111
Christianity 67, 75, 142, 143, 145, 146, 147, 150, 151, 152, 175, 187
Cicero 136
circumcision 31, 109
clan 65, 95, 97, 98, 99, 101, 132, 152, 153, 159
class 75, 124, 133, 184; *see also* elite
clay 15, 62, 85, 129, 177, 186
cloak. *See* clothing
clothing 2–4, 6, 7, 9, 15, 30, 37, 38, 62, 64, 69, 87, 96, 99, 105, 107, 108, 109, 110, 111, 112, 113, 182
  belt 2, 7
  cap 2
  cloak 2, 110
  head covering 2, 9, 33, 36, 37
  hood 2
  mantle 9, 107, 109
  sackcloth 108, 109, 112
  sandal 9
  sash 2
  shoe 9
  skirt 1, 6, 110
  tunic 2, 6, 7, 9
colour
  black 143; *see also* darkness
  blue 80
  green 64, 129, 133
  grey 100, 128, 134, 151
  red 7, 34, 80
conception. *See* pregnancy
control 12, 13, 14, 29, 32, 35, 36, 37, 38, 43, 47, 51, 52, 54, 55, 56, 57, 77, 108, 115, 116, 131

corpse 1, 9–12, 13, 43–57, 155, 158; *see also* dead, the; mortuary practices
  ashes 10
  body parts 44, 45, 48, 49
  bones 10, 45, 46, 54, 55, 56, 129, 144, 149, 153, 154
  skull 45–6
cosmos 9, 14, 16, 39, 44, 86, 131, 150, 151
covenant 17, 28, 30, 31, 98, 100, 106, 115, 116, 171, 178, 180, 182, 183, 184, 186, 188; *see also* ark
cow. *See* animal
crying. *See* weeping
cult 13, 14, 15, 16, 17, 69, 76, 78–82, 83, 84, 85, 87, 88, 89, 100, 106, 107, 112, 113, 133, 146, 153, 159, 160, 163, 174, 175, 177, 178, 179, 180, 181, 182, 183, 184, 186, 187, 188
  icon 146, 180, 181
  image 16–17, 52, 160, 174–6, 177, 179–81, 183, 186
  figurine 36, 46, 177, 179, 181
  object 13, 16–17, 27, 46, 80, 173, 174, 176, 177, 180, 181–4, 186, 187–8
  pillar 46, 179
  standing stone 17, 177, 183
  statue 146, 173, 175, 176, 177, 178, 181, 183, 186, 187
  stele 13, 16, 17, 44, 47–52, 53, 56, 57, 155, 173, 174, 177, 178, 181, 183, 184, 185, 186, 187
culture 2–9, 17, 27, 30, 31, 43, 57, 62, 75, 79, 83, 89, 106, 108, 141, 148, 173
  acculturation 29, 35
  enculturation 4, 13, 15
cuneiform. *See* writing
curse 37, 54, 96, 102, 123, 126, 128, 134, 136, 159

Danel 156, 158
Daniel 127
darkness 82, 87, 102, 130, 142, 143
daughter. *See* family
David 29, 33, 34, 35, 65, 101, 109, 127, 128, 129, 133, 134, 135, 136, 182
dead, the 2, 9–12, 16, 35, 36, 37, 39, 43, 45, 46, 47, 50, 51, 52, 53, 54, 55, 56, 57, 111, 133, 136, 141, 142, 143, 144, 145, 146, 147, 148, 151, 152, 153, 154, 155, 156, 158, 159, 160, 163, 173, 174, 184, 185; *see also* corpse; mortuary practice

Deir ʿAlla 53
deity 13, 14, 15, 16, 17, 28, 30, 31, 34, 35, 39, 52, 53, 55, 57, 62, 66, 68, 76, 78, 79, 80, 81, 83, 84, 85, 86, 87, 88, 89, 96, 106, 112, 113, 115, 116, 141, 144, 145, 146, 154, 156, 159, 160, 171–88
  Anat 157, 158, 179
  Ancient of Days 124
  Anu 181
  Asalluḫu 78, 79
  Astarte 179
  Baal 125, 145, 156–7, 158, 161
  Belet-ili 79, 81
  Bethel 178
  divine being 1, 31, 67
  El 85, 125, 157, 159
  Enki 79
  God 29, 31, 33, 34, 35, 54, 56, 111, 134, 142, 143, 148, 162, 163, 178
  god 47, 52, 79, 83, 84, 112, 115, 116, 117, 145, 156, 160, 174, 175, 182
  goddess 15, 43, 45, 46, 76, 79, 81, 83, 86, 143, 158, 176, 179
  Hadad 173, 174
  Horon 144
  Isis 154
  Mami 79
  Marduk 150
  Mot 144, 161
  Mut 43
  Nekhbet 43
  Nephthys 154
  Ningirsu 47, 52
  Nintu 79
  Ninurta 80
  Osiris 141, 154, 155
  Reshef 144
  Seth 155
  Šuwala 143
  Yahweh 9, 14, 15, 16, 17, 29, 30, 31, 52, 53, 54, 55, 56, 57, 68, 69, 82–8, 89, 93, 95, 96, 97, 98, 99, 101, 102, 105, 106, 107, 110, 111, 112, 113, 114, 115–17, 125, 127, 128, 133, 143, 144, 154, 159, 160, 161, 162, 173, 179, 180–7, 188
Delilah 33, 34, 35
descendants 10, 98, 99, 114, 136; *see also* ancestors; lineage
diaspora 184; *see also* exile; golah
diet. *See* food
Dinah 38
disability 6, 15, 93–103; *see also* impairment

blindness 15, 93, 100, 101, 102, 130, 134
  deafness 15, 93, 102
  mobility impairment 101
disease 61, 66, 123, 132; *see also* illness
disempowerment 8, 9, 39
dismemberment 10, 155
divine being. *See* deity
divorce 38, 95
doctrine 143, 144, 150, 152
document. *See* writing
dream 48, 141, 146
dressing. *See* clothing
drinking 7, 36, 37, 54, 65, 105, 111, 112, 174, 175
drought 61, 111
dualism 47, 52, 150, 151
dung 14, 61, 62, 63, 68
dust 16, 35, 37, 51, 85, 129, 131, 148, 153, 157

E-annatum 48–52
ear 2, 30, 175
earth 9, 31, 67, 85, 86, 87, 129, 148, 153, 155, 161, 163, 175, 183; *see also* ground
eating 2, 28, 29, 30, 31, 39, 54, 56, 65, 68, 97, 111, 174, 175; *see also* food
economics 7, 15, 16, 63–4, 65, 65, 69, 75–6, 78, 80, 81, 89, 95, 111, 124, 126, 130, 184
Eden 161
Egypt 16, 31, 38, 43, 53, 75, 96, 97, 110, 112, 126, 132, 141, 142, 154–5, 157, 174, 176, 178, 180, 185
El. *See* deity
elder 16, 127, 132, 178, 183
elderly 6, 16, 100, 123–6, 127, 128, 130, 131, 132–6; *see also* age
Elephantine 155
Eli 100, 127, 133, 134, 135, 182
Elijah 9, 33, 34, 163
Elisha 129, 132
elite 6, 7, 9, 30, 61, 66, 107, 116, 151, 162, 174, 177, 184; *see also* class
embodiment 1, 13, 14, 15, 16, 17, 28, 30, 37, 68, 106, 108, 111, 112, 113, 114, 117, 146, 147, 171, 173, 178, 183, 187, 188
emotion 62–7, 68, 69, 78, 107, 108, 158, 172
empowerment 7, 8, 33, 37, 39, 56, 188
enculturation. *See* culture
Enki. *See* deity
enlivenment 174, 175, 176, 178
Enoch 162, 163

entanglement 9, 65, 69
epic 29, 43, 141
Esau 13, 34, 95, 101
eschatology 147, 149, 150, 151, 152, 155, 156, 162, 163
ethnicity 2, 6, 35, 105; *see also* race; whiteness
ethnography 14, 61, 62–3, 69
eunuch 4, 12; *see also* gender
evil 128, 135, 150
exile 1–9, 30, 36, 56, 105, 116, 117, 146, 147, 149, 152, 153–4, 155, 158, 183; *see also* diaspora; *golah*
exodus 1, 31, 112
eye 53, 79, 81, 100, 102, 130, 131, 134, 176, 184
Ezekiel 32–3, 52, 127, 154
Ezra 15, 105–17, 127

face 4, 12, 64, 81, 109, 110, 179, 182
family 1, 14, 33, 65, 132, 133, 136; *see also* household
  brother 95, 98, 111, 163, 175
  daughter 15, 33, 65, 95, 97, 99, 105, 114
  father 1, 15, 29, 33, 34, 37, 38, 81, 95, 98, 99, 102, 106, 125, 134, 157, 158, 163
  mother 1, 4, 14, 32, 33, 34, 36, 38, 77, 79, 80, 81, 83, 85, 86, 87, 88, 89, 95, 98, 105, 130, 153, 154, 163, 177
  parent 1, 88, 132, 136
  sister 33
  son 15, 31, 34, 36, 54, 77, 79, 85, 95, 97, 98, 99, 101, 106, 114, 115, 127, 129, 130, 134, 135, 156, 157, 163, 182, 185
famine 61, 111
farming 61, 62, 64, 67
fasting 15, 106, 108, 111, 112, 113, 133
father. *See* family
fatherless 93, 94, 95, 96, 97, 99, 100, 101, 102, 103; *see also* orphan
feast 53, 54, 55, 111, 157; *see also* festival
feet 6, 9, 12, 30, 31, 102, 110, 111
femininity. *See* gender
feminist criticism 105
festival 36, 97; *see also* feast
figurine. *See* cult
finger 77, 78, 145, 185, 186
fire 62, 150, 181, 182
flesh 10, 12, 13, 17, 28, 31, 39, 43, 44, 45, 46, 47, 54, 56, 69, 85, 87, 155, 162
flood 28, 29
foetus. *See* children

food 2, 28, 29, 31, 54, 61, 62, 63, 64, 67, 96, 105, 108, 111, 112, 132, 133, 135, 146, 173, 174, 175, 178, 179; see also eating
footstool 6, 181, 183
foreskin 31; see also circumcision
four-room house 62
fruit 1, 7, 28, 81, 133, 135
fuel 62
funerary rites. See mortuary practices

Galen 129
garden 28, 161
Gehazi 129
gender 2–4, 6, 12, 13, 15, 16, 27–39, 46, 62, 80, 99, 105–17, 124
  femininity 33, 105, 108, 109, 110, 111
  masculinity 7, 12, 13, 15, 33–5, 38–9, 105–17, 126
  non-binary 4
genitals 31, 32, 110
Gilead 127
Gilgamesh 43, 141
girl. See children
goat. See animal
god. See deity
goddess. See deity
Gog 13, 52–6, 57
golah 15, 105, 106, 107, 108, 111, 113, 114, 115, 116, 117; see also diaspora; exile
golden calf 112, 181, 186
gospels 57, 154
grain 37, 61, 62, 69, 77, 78
grave. See mortuary practice
Greek 125, 127, 142, 146
green. See colour
ground 9, 28, 29, 50, 68, 86, 105, 106, 1078, 110, 111, 112, 116, 149; see also earth
guilt 15, 29, 30, 37, 38, 39, 66, 68, 107, 110, 114, 115
gynaecology 76, 78

Hadad. See deity
Hagar 38
hair 2, 4, 6, 9, 13, 15, 27, 33–9, 105, 107, 108, 110, 128; see also beard
hand 30, 66, 81, 84, 85, 86, 87, 112, 143, 160, 175, 176, 178, 181, 184, 186, 187
Hannah 34, 134
harvest 96
Hazael 132
Hazor 156, 177, 178

head 2, 6, 9, 35, 36, 37, 38, 44, 45, 46, 47, 49, 51, 56, 100, 107, 108, 109, 110, 111, 134, 155, 157, 172, 184
head covering. See clothing
health 16, 30, 64, 65, 66, 77, 78, 123, 124
heart 64, 81, 113, 131, 134, 160, 162, 172
heavens 48, 130, 151, 158, 162, 163, 175, 178, 182, 183, 186
hell 150, 151
Hellenism 148, 152, 159
Hercules 34
hero 13, 29, 31, 33, 34, 35, 106, 127, 157
Hezekiah 8, 109, 112
hip 101
Hippocrates 129
Homer 43
Horon. See deity
horoscope 78
horse. See animal
household 1, 14, 15, 61, 62–9, 76, 78, 80, 81, 82, 88, 89, 94–103, 130, 131, 132, 153, 156, 159, 173
Huldah 113
humanity 12, 14, 17, 27, 29, 30, 35, 38, 39, 43, 47, 54,, 56, 57, 61, 62, 67, 78, 79, 85, 131, 141, 148, 158, 163, 171, 186
humiliation 9, 35, 36, 37, 38, 107, 108, 109, 111, 115, 116
humours 129
hunger 111
hunting 34, 45, 61, 67
husband 33, 37, 81, 98, 106, 115, 129; see also marriage

Ibn Ezra 31
icon. See cult
iconography 1, 4, 6, 12–13, 35, 46, 47, 110, 111, 112, 179
identity 2, 4, 9, 13, 27, 29, 30, 31, 33, 35, 36, 38, 39, 46, 51, 75, 105, 109, 110, 113, 141, 144, 145, 172, 173, 178, 181, 182, 187
ideology 2, 7, 8, 9, 14, 57, 66, 67, 68, 145, 153, 156, 158, 161, 182
illness 37, 62, 131; see also disease
image. See cult
immortality 16142, 148, 149, 151, 157
impairment 33, 37, 100, 101, 102, 103; see also disability
impurity 30, 32, 55, 56, 57, 105, 106

incantation 78, 79, 83, 86, 87, 88, 174, 175, 184
individual 9, 13, 15, 16, 27, 33, 37, 63–4, 66, 78, 87, 98, 113, 124, 130, 131, 141, 144, 145, 146, 148, 151, 152–3, 154, 156, 163, 177
infant. *See* children
infertility 33, 77, 100, 129, 133
inheritance 15, 64, 94, 95–9, 100, 101, 102, 126, 134, 159, 160, 161
injury 62, 101, 172
ink. *See* writing
inscription. *See* writing
Isaac 100, 101, 130
Isaiah 112, 127
Isis. *See* deity
Israel 54, 55, 56, 57, 61, 62, 63, 64, 65, 66, 67, 69, 75, 76, 81, 82, 83, 86, 88, 89, 94–103, 109, 110, 112, 113, 123, 124, 125, 126, 129, 133, 136, 142, 147, 152, 153, 154, 158, 162, 173, 176–80, 181, 182, 183, 187

Jaazaniah 127
Jacob 17, 31, 33, 34, 95, 98, 99, 100, 101, 178
Jehoiada 124
Jehu 127
Jephthah 109, 127
Jeremiah 82–4
Jerusalem 15, 28, 33, 55, 68, 84, 88, 106, 107, 110, 111, 112, 113, 117, 133, 135, 153, 156, 161, 178, 182, 183, 186
Jesus 145, 163
jewellery 9, 80; *see also* amulet
Jezebel 127
Joab 34
Job 87, 102, 109, 110, 124
Jonathan 29
Joseph 98, 111
Josephus 145
Joshua 182, 183
Josiah 54, 55, 84, 112, 113
Judah 1–2, 6, 8, 10, 12, 13, 14, 16, 29, 35, 36, 61, 62, 63, 64, 65, 66, 67, 68, 69, 98, 99, 112, 113, 142, 143, 147, 149, 152, 153, 156, 158, 159, 162, 163, 173, 176–8, 179, 181, 183, 187
Judaism 145, 147, 149, 150, 151, 152

Katumuwa stele 17, 155, 173, 185
Ketef Hinnom 185
kid. *See* animal

kingship 9, 80, 85, 110, 112, 113, 117, 133, 135, 154, 157, 158
kinship 10, 13, 38, 39, 63, 65, 68, 94, 96, 98, 99, 114, 130, 141, 174, 177
Kirta 85, 156, 158
kispum 141, 144, 146
knowledge 28, 34, 77, 78, 84, 135, 143, 174, 183

Laban 33
Lachish 1–2, 156, 177, 178
Lachish reliefs 1–13, 35, 36, 115
Lagash 47–52, 56
lamb. *See* animal
land 9, 15, 54, 55, 56, 57, 61, 87, 94, 95–9, 100, 101, 102, 103, 105, 113, 114, 116, 117, 133, 153, 159, 162, 163
lapis lazuli 80
law 32, 37, 53, 65, 69, 102, 115, 116, 126, 132, 136, 153, 180, 181, 183, 184, 186; *see also* Torah
Lazarus 145
Leah 33, 98, 100
leg 1, 101, 131
leopard. *See* animal
leprosy 28, 30, 31, 39
letter. *See* writing
Levi 98, 99, 182
Levite 15, 93, 94, 96, 97, 98, 99, 114, 159, 162, 163, 182
lex talionis 100
life expectancy 76, 77, 123, 124, 125
liminality 4, 30, 37, 144, 161, 175
lineage 107, 116, 153
lion. *See* animal

magic 14, 80, 175
Mami. *See* deity
mantle. *See* clothing
Marduk. *See* deity
marriage 14, 15, 31, 95, 99, 100, 101, 105–6, 107, 110, 113, 114, 116, 130
  bride 33, 37, 39; *see also* wife
  bridegroom 31; *see also* husband
martyrdom 150, 163
Mary 145
masculinity. *See* gender
materiality 1–13, 14, 16, 17, 27, 31, 32, 38–9, 62, 83, 84, 108–11, 171–7, 180, 184, 185, 187–8
meat 14, 28–30, 39, 43, 61, 63, 64, 65, 67–8

medicine 14, 76–8, 79, 81, 83, 84, 88, 125, 129
memorialization 12, 106, 173, 184, 185
memory 30, 37, 39, 45, 46, 51, 87, 106, 125, 130, 134, 135, 184, 187; *see also* remembering
men 1, 2, 4, 6, 7, 9, 12, 15, 29, 31, 32, 33, 34, 35, 36, 37, 38, 54, 62, 65, 78, 95, 96, 97, 100, 105–17, 124, 127, 129, 130, 131, 132, 135; *see also* boy
menopause 129; *see also* menstruation
menstruation 13, 28, 32–3, 39, 77, 130
Mephibosheth 101
Mesha 185
Mesopotamia 14, 16, 36, 43, 44, 51, 52, 75, 76–89, 126, 132, 142, 174, 176, 178, 180, 182
metaphor 35, 78, 80, 81, 87, 125, 129, 131, 133, 136, 145, 147, 148, 154, 158, 172
Michael 149
midwife 15, 78–9, 81, 83, 88; *see also* birth
migration 36, 38
milk 14, 32, 61, 63, 64, 65, 68, 85
mind 64, 78, 144, 172, 173
Moab 107, 185
monotheism 14, 83, 144
month 32, 38, 55, 77, 132, 157
morality 32, 65, 69, 128, 135, 142, 149, 172
Mordecai 109
mortality 16, 30, 46, 76, 77, 144
mortuary practice 10, 17, 36, 43, 45, 46, 54, 55, 56, 57, 66, 152, 154, 155, 156, 158, 159, 173, 184, 185; *see also* corpse; dead; mourning
  burial 13, 43, 45, 46, 47, 49, 50, 51, 52, 53, 54, 55, 56, 124, 144, 150, 152, 153, 154, 158, 159, 163, 173, 174
  grave 10, 52, 55, 56, 134, 136, 143, 154, 161, 163, 173
  tomb 54, 55, 142, 144, 145, 152, 154, 155, 156, 158, 161
Moses 31, 84, 95, 96, 98, 112, 124, 127, 129, 163, 180, 183, 186
Mot. *See* deity
mother. *See* family
mourning 15, 33, 35, 36, 38, 53, 105, 107, 108–15, 116, 117, 130, 131; *see also* mortuary practice
Mut. *See* deity

Naboth 153
nakedness 4, 9, 10, 11, 30, 32, 37, 49, 50, 56, 110, 176, 179; *see also* bareness; nudity

name 63, 64, 98, 144, 173, 174, 182, 183, 185, 186–8
Naomi 130
Nathan 65, 134
nature 12, 14, 30, 35, 37, 44, 50, 51, 54, 55, 56, 57, 132, 175, 177, 179
Nazirites 13, 33, 34, 35, 36, 37, 39
Nehemiah 107, 110
New Testament 43, 145, 147, 149, 161
Nimrud 181
Nineveh 1, 110, 175
Ningirsu. *See* deity
Ninurta. *See* deity
Noah 28
nudity 4, 100, 179; *see also* bareness; nakedness

ocean 79, 80, 83, 86
Odysseus 141, 159
offering 30, 36, 37, 54, 57, 66, 68, 80, 98, 107, 114, 159, 173, 174, 177, 178, 181, 183
offspring. *See* children
oil 7, 30, 37, 78, 178
ornamentation 6, 12, 80
orphan 15, 93, 95, 103, 133; *see also* fatherless
Osiris. *See* deity
ox. *See* animal

paradise 160, 161
parchment. *See* writing
parent. *See* family
partibility 9, 16, 17, 174, 176, 187
patriarch 29, 33, 99, 101, 102, 116, 124, 129, 133, 153
Paul 145
Persia 16, 52, 106, 107, 110, 112, 116, 117, 150–3, 184, 185
personhood 2, 4, 6, 9, 10, 12, 13, 17, 172, 176
Pharisees 147
Philistines 29, 34, 35, 142 155, 182
Phoenician 155, 176
pillar. *See* cult
pledge 67, 96, 106; *see also* vow
Plutarch 136
politics 6, 14, 35, 66, 94, 95, 101, 107, 108, 110, 112, 113, 114, 117, 123, 147, 150, 153, 163, 172, 176
polytheism 144
post-mortem existence 10, 12, 16, 141, 142, 144, 155, 162, 163, 173; *see also* afterlife; death

INDEX OF SUBJECTS

posture 6, 9, 12, 15, 27, 108, 109, 111, 112, 178
poverty 15, 65, 69, 93, 96, 100, 102, 103, 133
power 1, 4, 6, 9, 12, 13, 27, 28, 33, 34, 35, 37, 38, 39, 43, 46, 47, 51, 54, 55, 56, 57, 66, 79, 94, 101, 106, 107, 108, 109, 112, 113, 114, 115, 116, 117, 131, 132, 135, 136, 144, 154, 157, 171, 182, 184, 185, 186; *see also* empowerment; disempowerment
preborn child. *See* children
pregnancy 6, 36, 76–7, 79, 80–1, 84, 88, 124, 129; *see also* birth; children
conception 33, 76, 78, 79, 84
priest 28, 30, 31, 33, 34, 35, 36, 37, 38, 39, 54, 69, 78, 88, 95, 98, 99, 100, 106, 110, 111, 114, 133, 134, 151
professions 7, 76
progeny. *See* children
property 33, 64, 65, 69, 106, 126, 132, 144, 153, 159, 185
prophecy 13, 52, 54, 56, 85, 110, 145, 153, 154, 183
prophet 33, 34, 54, 82, 83, 84, 85, 87, 88, 100, 113, 154
psyche 152
psychology 144, 146, 152
puberty 14, 31
purification 28, 32, 35, 55, 174, 175

race 6; *see also* ethnicity; whiteness
Rachel 33, 34, 39
rain 113, 130
raptor. *See* animal
Rebekah 34, 101
red. *See* colour
Rehoboam 134
religion 13, 14, 16, 27, 29, 31, 33, 37, 38, 39, 45, 68–9, 76, 78–89, 105, 106, 108, 133, 141–63, 177–88; *see also* cult; ritual
remembering 16, 85, 87, 96, 97, 123, 130, 132, 136, 143; 160; *see also* memory
Reshef. *See* deity
Reuben 109
ritual 4, 10, 13, 14, 15, 27, 28, 29, 30, 31, 32, 33, 35, 36, 37, 38, 39, 47, 51, 55, 56, 57, 66–9, 76, 78, 79, 80, 81, 82, 83, 87, 88, 105, 106, 107–15, 116, 131, 141, 146, 154, 158, 160, 173, 174–6, 177, 178, 180, 181, 183–4, 187; *see also* cult; religion
Rizpah 54
Roman world 75, 126, 136

sackcloth. *See* clothing
sacred space 35, 179, 180, 187
sacrifice 14, 28, 29, 31, 36, 37, 39, 54–5, 57, 66–9, 107, 111, 114, 178
Sadducees 147
Samson 13, 33, 34, 35, 36, 39, 100, 110
Samuel 28, 33, 34, 36, 134
sandal. *See* clothing
Sarah 38, 129
Saul 28, 29, 54, 101, 135
scribalism. *See* writing
Scripture. *See* writing
scroll. *See* writing
seal 177, 185
secular 31, 173
semen 32
Sennacherib 1, 6, 7, 8, 9, 12, 112, 115
servant 95, 102, 112, 117, 131, 155
Seth. *See* deity
sex 2, 32, 33, 35, 65, 79, 83, 86, 87, 105, 106, 109, 110
Shecaniah 115
sheep. *See* animal
Sheol 134, 142–4, 159, 160, 161, 162; *see also* underworld
Shiloh 100
Shimei 134
shoe. *See* clothing
shrine 28, 44, 45, 177, 178–81
Shunammite woman 129
Simeon 133
sin 29, 30, 32, 66, 136, 141
sister. *See* family
skin 9, 12, 31, 85, 87, 109, 172, 187
skirt. *See* clothing
skull. *See* corpse
sky 43, 49, 50, 54, 56
slavery 38, 95, 96, 124, 131, 133, 185
Solomon 134, 137
son. *See* family
soul 142, 148, 149, 150, 151, 155, 156, 160, 162, 163, 173, 174
spirit 51, 56, 78, 127, 145, 146, 149, 151, 154, 156, 159, 163, 172, 173
standing stone. *See* cult
star 130, 148, 154
statue. *See* cult
stele. *See* cult
Stele of Vultures 13, 44–52, 53, 56, 57
storm 130, 156, 174
sun 79, 130, 154, 179
supernatural 66, 146, 177
Susannah 127

symbol 2, 9, 13, 14, 17, 27, 28, 30, 33, 35, 37, 38, 39, 43, 44, 45, 46, 52, 53, 54, 55, 56, 57, 80, 105, 108, 109, 145, 173, 175, 176, 177
synagogue 145, 171

Taanach 179–80
tabernacle 37, 68, 112, 180; see also tent
tablet. See writing
Tamar 34
teaching 98, 102, 107, 136, 149, 151, 160
Tel Reḥov 178
temple 14, 15, 80, 85, 87, 88, 89, 105, 106, 111, 112, 113, 115, 116, 127, 133, 153, 160, 161, 175, 176, 178–9, 180, 181, 182, 183, 184, 186, 187
tent 68, 98; see also tabernacle
territory 1, 9, 48, 51, 52, 55, 114, 116, 117
theology 16, 31, 67, 88, 101, 124, 125, 136, 142, 146, 147, 149, 150, 156, 171, 177
thirst 111
Thomas 145
throne 1, 6, 8, 12, 157, 158, 176, 180, 181, 183
Tiglath-pileser III 181
toe 30
tomb. See mortuary practice
Torah 15, 17, 107, 112, 115, 171, 183–7, 188; see also law
totem 46
transcendence 183
tree 1, 7, 28, 96, 129, 133, 135, 177, 179
tribe 97, 98, 99, 182
Trump, Donald 172
tunic. See clothing

Ugarit 16, 85, 125, 145, 147, 155–8, 160, 161, 178
Umma 48–52, 56
underworld 16, 141, 142, 143, 144, 155, 157, 158, 159, 160, 161, 162; see also Sheol
urbanism 12, 43, 62, 63, 67
urine 32

vagina 32, 76, 77
valley 55, 56, 154
violation 51, 55, 110
violence 29, 32, 69, 76, 82, 124, 132, 163
vision 48, 49, 52, 147, 148, 154, 156
vow 29, 34, 36, 37, 39, 134; see also pledge
vulture. See animal

war 1, 7, 12, 29, 36, 38, 39, 47, 49, 51, 52, 54, 55, 56, 57, 109, 111, 117, 176
warrior 7, 33, 34, 51, 117, 125, 151
water 35, 37, 51, 61, 62, 68, 78, 79, 80, 83, 86, 98, 111, 129, 131, 159, 175
wealth 16, 37, 39, 77, 80, 132, 133, 135, 177
weapon 6, 9, 12, 51, 55, 56, 67, 111
weeping 32, 38, 105, 106, 107, 108, 112, 113, 134
Western culture 6, 9, 34, 62, 63, 67, 146, 172, 173
whiteness 6
wife 13, 15, 31, 36, 38, 39, 81, 83, 95, 100, 105–6, 114–15, 116, 117; see also marriage
wind 129, 154
wine 7, 36, 97
womb 14, 77, 83, 84, 85, 86, 87, 88129, 175
women 1, 2, 3, 4, 6, 7, 13, 15, 28, 31, 32–9, 62, 64, 77, 78, 80, 81, 83, 94, 95, 96, 97, 99, 100, 102, 103, 105–6, 107, 108, 109, 110, 113, 114–15, 116, 117, 123, 124, 127, 129, 130, 131, 132, 135, 159, 179; see also girl
worship 16, 28, 69, 88, 106, 113, 132, 133, 160, 162, 177, 179, 183, 186, 188
wrist 12
writing 16, 47, 124, 130, 136, 183, 184, 186, 187
  book 82, 100, 153
  canon 137
  cuneiform 47, 48, 51, 77
  document 37, 64, 126
  ink 37, 187
  inscription 17, 43, 47, 48, 51, 52, 152, 173, 178, 184, 185, 186
  letter 76, 78, 81, 83, 125, 156
  parchment 187
  scribalism 6, 68, 77, 78, 82, 89, 106, 107, 110, 112, 117, 124, 184, 186
  Scripture 145, 147
  scroll 112, 184, 186, 187
  tablet 181, 186

Yahweh. See deity

Zebulun 149
Zedekiah 100
Zipporah 31
Zoroastrianism 43, 150, 151, 152

www.ingramcontent.com/pod-product-compliance
Lightning Source LLC
Chambersburg PA
CBHW080936300426
44115CB00017B/2843